THE GLOBAL IBM

THE GLOBAL IBM:

LEADERSHIP IN MULTINATIONAL MANAGEMENT

DAVID MERCER

DODD, MEAD & COMPANY
NEW YORK

First published in the United States in 1988

Published by Dodd, Mead & Company, Inc.
71 Fifth Avenue, New York, NY 10003
Manufactured in the United States of America.
First published in 1987 by Kogan Page Ltd., Great Britain
First Edition

1 2 3 4 5 6 7 8 9 10

Library of Congress Cataloging-in-Publication Data

Mercer, David (David Steuart)
The global IBM: leadership in multinational management/David Mercer.—1st ed.
p. cm.
Includes index.
1. International Business Machines Corporation—Management.
2. International business enterprises—Management—Case studies.
I. Title.
HD9696.C64I4853 1987
338.8'87—dc19 87-34041
ISBN 0-396-09259-4

CONTENTS

Section 3 The Lessons to be Learnt

CHAPTER 1

Introduction: A Unique Case?

The prime objective of this book is to give an insight into the management style that over a number of decades has made IBM the most successful company in the world. It attempts to draw out some lessons that might he more generally applicable in other companies, and in the process also throws some light on what has made the Japanese corporations so successful; for, as will be seen later, it is likely that IBM was also one of the first models for their all-conquering management style.

The importance of IBM's role in the creation of the "Japanese miracle" is not just its historical significance. It also has a particular importance even now, when so many companies are striving to match the Japanese performance. For, if nothing else, it shows that these apparently alien philosophies are *not* unique to a Zen-oriented culture, but are just as applicable to the less spiritual values of the Western hemisphere. Most important, it provides a usable model of the management style, and one which is couched in the culturally more understandable terms of the Western management idioms (and is not confused or camouflaged by the later irrelevant Japanese accretions).

The main part of the book is, indeed, intended as a model. It is a relatively detailed description of how IBM operates in the 1980s. In the main it is almost purely descriptive, and there is no overt attempt to deduce *detailed* lessons from what is a very rich set of data. My belief, implicit in the structure of the book, is that most managers probably learn best, in relation to their own specific needs, by reading about how other managers have handled various problems; and by occasionally recognizing that another manager's solution could also meet their own needs. I hope, therefore, that this book offers several hundred such solutions in search of a need. To help provide some perspective, at the beginning of each chapter

I have summarized what I believe may be the most important lessons, at least for me (though not necessarily for the reader), in that chapter.

The book is divided into three sections. The first section, however, does not describe this modern model, but is essentially historical. Its three chapters contain brief reviews of nearly three quarters of a century of developments that have led to the modern IBM. I believe that an understanding of how IBM developed to its modern form can contribute to an understanding of where IBM now finds itself: and can highlight some of the problems encountered *en route*. It may also indicate some of the methods that other organizations could consider employing.

The largest, middle section comprises a picture of IBM as it now is: the mature corporation of the 1980s. This is the model that I suggest should be investigated for the lessons that may be applied to other companies and organizations. It is in some respects a partial model, since its coverage is biased towards those aspects that I believe are unique to IBM, where the most important lessons may be learnt. This is not to say that the rest of the IBM model should be ignored. For example, somewhat to my own surprise, since my background is heavily biased towards marketing (and IBM is reportedly, at least according to the subtitle of Buck Rodgers' book, "The World's Most Successful Marketing Organization"), there is significantly less emphasis on classical marketing theory than on personnel policies. The lesson is not that marketing should be overlooked in other companies; far from it. It is simply to report that IBM's unique marketing position offers fewer lessons than does its rich panoply of personnel procedures. I have tried, however, as far as possible to extend the coverage into other areas to at least provide a context (and have also indicated other sources of information which offer a complementary coverage of these areas of the model).

The final chapter, which is perhaps the most important, reflects my main motivation in starting to write this book, which was to spread the gospel according to IBM to an outside audience, particularly to those managers, and businessmen in general, who might be able to benefit from its unique experiences. This still represents the final key set of lessons I offer. What I had forgotten, until I undertook the research for the book, was that Peter Drucker in *The Practice of Management,* had already conveyed a part of the gospel, not least to a very receptive audience in Japan, and even these limited lessons were probably a major contributor to the "Japanese miracle."

The lessons will probably be of most value to managers in the private sector (most likely in the larger companies) and are primarily concerned with management style, for it is as the pre-eminent multinational business corporation that IBM contributes most to management theory. At the same time it does, though, hold some of the keys to the information technology revolution; and some lessons in this field are also included in an Appendix B (so as not to confuse the main business management themes unduly). Appendix C incorporates a rather more specialized series of lessons that may be relevant to those specifically working in the field of government.

IBM: the myth

In essence, IBM *already* holds a unique position of importance in business dealings on a global scale. It is in its own right one of the largest companies in the world, ranking thirteenth overall in 1984; behind only the oil companies, car manufacturers and Japanese trading companies. Its performance in terms of profitability is even more impressive, its 1984 rank being third, behind only Shell and BP. Its 1985 and, in particular, its poor 1986 performances may have recently resulted in financial analysts reviewing their long-running love affair with the company; but, even though in 1986 it lost its laurels (to Exxon) as America's most profitable company, it still came in a commendable second. It still earned $1.4 billion in the quarter in that was described by analysts as a disaster. Most other large corporations would be ecstatic if they found they had such a "disaster"—even for their full year profits! Which is why IBM is still a legend. *Business Week* estimated that its 1986 market value was $91 billion, making it by far the most valuable company in the world.

Its even greater psychological impact comes, though, from two other factors. In the first place the specific business area it operates in and dominates—that of computers—has now become central to the efficient business operations of virtually all other companies; and in particular, central to their growth into the so-called information revolution. The second is that IBM has become a business myth in its own lifetime, setting business standards that not just its competitors aim to follow, but on an even wider canvas it has already become the model that sophisticated companies in almost all fields (and not just the Japanese) seek to emulate. At the same time it has become, in the popular daemonology, the archetypal multinational monster that even governments fear will overpower them.

More than the reality, the myth forms the picture the business world holds of IBM, and indeed on a large scale tries to copy. This book was originally intended quite simply to address that myth. In some ways it primarily set out to debunk it. This debunking did *not* however show IBM as any less important; it simply showed that its real importance was subtly different from that enshrined in the public image. Paradoxically, it was only the Japanese corporations, surely the most consummate plagiarists, who took IBM seriously enough to create a copy that encapsulated some of its real essence; arguably IBM's greatest influence to date has been in the Orient!

IBM: the model

In truth, as suggested at the beginning of this chapter, the book *now* sets out to go far beyond this limited objective. For what has emerged from the research is a coherent model, which is very different from the myths and which encapsulates many of the *true* strengths of IBM. Accordingly, I believe this model can be used to derive lessons which should be applicable in other Western companies and bureaucratic organizations.

In many respects it is complementary to the more general model derived from the McKinsey & Co. investigations of 20 multinationals, undertaken at the beginning of the 1980s; and most popularly reported in the book *In Search of Excellence* (1982. Harper & Row), by Peters and Waterman. That study covered a wider scope, but necessarily at a more superficial level (although not as superficial as their somewhat simplistic theory of "the seven S's of management" would imply). I believe that the reader may find that the greater depth of this present book, albeit based on the narrower front of just one corporation, reveals some new insights which go beyond the McKinsey material, to challenge further some of the more conventional assumptions of management theory, as well as offering a meaningful explanation of the Japanese successes.

In the book I have concentrated on those aspects, and in particular on those beliefs, or "philosophies," that I believe are the critical elements of IBM's success. I have, though, tried to provide a wider context; fleshing out this rather sparse framework by describing the range of its operations in most fields. In its totality IBM is a very complex and sophisticated model indeed, offering rich pickings for almost any political scientist, economist or business specialist; as well as for the working manager, to whom it is primarily addressed. I would hope that this book also tempts other researchers to explore the many facets of this apparently enigmatic, but ultimately fascinating, company. I would also hope that IBM allows such researchers in. I understand its right to protect its privacy (which it rigorously exercises), but I hope that IBM will recognize that as a model it has a unique place in the theory of business management (as well as that of economics and political science). As such it should be correspondingly willing, as a public service, to "open the kimono" (a particularly apt expression in view of the Japanese connections) to serious scholars, as well as managers in general.

Management style

The book concentrates on one aspect of management theory, that of management style (where IBM, the evidence shows, has most to contribute), but it does *not* set out to be a *general* guide to managing a business. There is, for example, no reference to payoff tables and decision trees, which are used by individuals within IBM, nor to such techniques as value analysis, which are inherent in much of its product design. It is taken for granted that IBM concentrates its resources on those activities that are key to its economic results, and exploits opportunities rather than solves problems; and indeed undertakes all its basic business activities in the most professional manner (would IBM ever be anything less than professional in any field!). The book's task is limited to deducing those specific lessons to be learnt from IBM's management style which enable a company to become an outstanding performer. For guidance on the more basic principles of business management I would suggest that the reader turn in the first instance to the considerable body of Peter Drucker's work. There is a myriad of other management texts, including for example the McKinsey-based work of Peters and Waterman, which may be helpful; but I have always found Drucker's work a particularly useful starting point for any enquiry.

Throughout this book I have frequently found myself using the word "unique"; for my investigations have shown that IBM really *is* unique, not just in a few minor ways, but in many major respects; though to a certain extent this uniqueness is confined to the Western world, as the large Japanese corporations did succeed in copying a number of its earlier, unique features. This comparison with the Japanese experience is perhaps best encapsulated in William G. Ouchi's *Theory Z,* and this comparison is explored as a sub-theme in a number of chapters. Even the Japanese, however, have not yet copied the later developments which are arguably just as revolutionary, and certainly are unique to IBM.

Perspectives

There has always been one major problem in trying to unravel the reality of IBM from the myths, which has to date obscured (at least to Western audiences) the significance of its management style, and that is the choice of perspective. It would seem that there have conventionally been two alternative perspectives. The first of these, which has to date been followed by the journalist-written textbooks, has been from the outside looking in. This view has tended to present IBM as the supreme example of a conventional, but very successful, company; only adding, anecdotally, some interesting but minor deviations. The two exceptions perhaps are that by Nancy Foy, *The IBM World* (1974, Eyre Methuen), which I would commend as providing historical material particularly complementary to this book, and most recently *Big Blue: IBM's Use and Abuse of Power* by Richard Thomas DeLamarter (1986, Dodd Mead), which contains much of the more interesting (if very biased) material that emerged from the last anti-trust suit. The other approach, that from the inside looking out, is usually limited by self-imposed IBM censorship to a small selection of public relations brochures, and such material is of correspondingly limited value. The two exceptions to this rule are Tom Watson Jr.'s 1963 book, *A Business and its Beliefs* (1963, McGraw Hill), which is largely definitive of IBM at that point in time, and the recent book, *The IBM Way* (1986, Harper & Row), by Buck Rodgers, which is directed more specifically at sales management.

In general the two perspectives are so different—in many respects almost diametrically opposed—that it simply is not possible to obtain a true picture even when they are combined. The resulting confusions are very understandable because on the one hand IBM is now almost paranoid in its pursuit of secrecy, so outsiders looking in have very little to see, and on the other it does not recruit senior management from outside, so the internal IBM view looking out is just as distorted, since it is heavily filtered by its own unique culture.

This book is, at its most basic level, an attempt to bridge the gap. It tries to marry the two perspectives to produce a picture that goes some way to being understandable to both audiences, to those inside IBM as well as those without. In the process I believe a more realistic picture emerges which shows that IBM truly does have unique features that set it apart.

Even in the purely descriptive material, this book is intended to be an *analysis* of the business methods (and more importantly of the styles and philosophies) that have formed the modern IBM, and have enabled it to be so successful; and it is this *analysis* that has led to the lessons I suggest. Previous books, and even IBM's own brochures, have tended to be anecdotal descriptions, typically written with great panache by journalists, of the *people* who made IBM. It is indeed impossible to ignore the influence of such people, especially of the Watson dynasty, but this book concentrates on their *policies* rather than their personalities. There are already a number of excellent books that flesh out the bare bones of the policies by descriptions of the individuals. These often include a deal of journalistic licence, but this does allow for greatly enhanced entertainment value; and I would recommend them as excellent light, but still very informative, bedtime reading. In particular, *THINK* (1969, Weidenfeld & Nicholson) by William Rodgers gives a somewhat scurrilous account of the Watson family and early IBM, and *IBM: Colossus in Transition* (1981, Truman Talley Books) by Robert Sobel describes the later IBM in a wider, if more academic, perspective.

It was tempting also to use the book as a vehicle for debunking a number of "classic" management texts. For example, as my main involvement over more than a quarter of a century has been in marketing, it might have been possible to claim that the IBM story undermined some of the lessons (in particular market segmentation) of Philip Kotler's classical *Marketing Management* (1976, Prentice Hall International). That would, I believe, have been a form of indulgence; because under the surface of IBM most of the "functional" theories contained in these classical texts can still be discerned (albeit often in rather bizarre forms). It would indeed be counterproductive in this context to question these theories, since they have a valuable place in the extensive armoury of devices any manager has at his disposal. More important, my observation, reinforcing that of the McKinsey work, is that the most valuable lessons to be learnt from IBM are not in detailed deviations from established functional theory, but in the real power that can be derived from the "simple" implementation of critical sets of philosophies and beliefs (summed up as IBM's management style), which in turn will usually generate many of the more detailed theories. Surprisingly these philosophies are still largely discounted in Western theory, which tends to be preoccupied (as is much of social science) with a search for a rigorous numeric, quasi-scientific context. Perhaps the underlying assumption is that they are self-evident (and as such not worthy of further exploration); but if that is the case then it is also worth noting that to date only IBM and the Japanese have made use of the evidence!

The book is also different from its predecessors in that it is not based on a limited number of well documented interviews. It is, instead, a synthesis of more than a decade of literally thousands of meetings, all undocumented, except in the archives of IBM! In general, the comments are deliberately unattributed; partly because the original authors of many of the ideas still hold positions in IBM, but mainly because most of the views are not those of individuals but are a synthesis of the views of a number of IBMers and non-IBMers. I believe that the resulting composite is more enlightening than any of the single views.

These individual views are, in any case, further complicated by being located within the context of a moving target. The nature of IBM is that *everything* changes at least every two years. Indeed, in the two years since the first draft of this book was commenced IBM has moved from peak to trough; where just that short time ago it was at the peak of its powers, it is now beset by all sorts of problems. Fortunately, since the acid test of any theory is to subject it to extreme environments, the model developed on the basis of the booming IBM works just as well for the depressed company; and, accordingly, the lessons are even more strongly validated by experience. In any case, only by abstracting the essence of the views can any sense be made of the constantly shifting kaleidoscope that is IBM. Otherwise by the time any specific view can be enshrined in print that function will most probably have been renamed, reorganized, relocated and (quite possibly) replaced; certainly to the extent that it will no longer be recognizable.

This experience, and the related "interviews," were obtained as part of a career with IBM, spanning a decade and a half, that took me from the sharp end of mainframe sales to the relative tranquillity of administrative staff. In the process I worked for extended periods in marketing staff, including product line (IBM's new product group), education, corporate affairs and the personal computer group. Most important of all, in terms of the content of this book and its perspective, for more than five years I ran the UK operations of IBM's first Independent Business Unit: IBM Biomedical Group. In this capacity I worked from time to time, along with my opposite numbers, in each of the other European "Majors" (Germany, France and Italy), as well as in the European headquarters and the USA.

In a decade and a half I was in contact with literally thousands of IBMers, from across all the continents, ranging from shopfloor workers to members of the corporate board. At the same time in relation to the outside world I was in touch, on behalf of IBM, with governments, occasionally at ministerial level but usually at senior civil servant level. Contacts also included board members of large corporations who were IBM customers. Perhaps the most interesting of all were those with the academic world, and particularly enlightening were those made during some three years working with the London Business School.

This breadth and depth of experience is rare in IBM, where individuals' careers are normally contained within fairly tight departmental and national boundaries. Thanks largely to the stimulation of the London Business School, who were as fascinated with IBM as I was, I was able to maintain an unusually detached appreciation of what was happening around me; a perhaps almost unique privilege within IBM, where total blind immersion in the culture is normally the rule.

In the past two years this perspective has been broadened by my experience of being an IBM customer, as a personal computer dealer, giving me direct personal experience of the third parties that are proving to be (at least at present) IBM's nemesis. It has also been broadened by the unique (in over half a century) picture of an IBM in retreat—from which the reader can also learn. These different perspectives have additionally allowed me to subject my "model" to the acid test of conflicting environments; and it has passed even these rigorous examinations.

Despite the wide (geographically as well as functionally) range of experience some of my more detailed analysis is inevitably based on the experiences of one country—the UK—where I was based. This might be taken to indicate that in some respects the view could be somewhat parochial. On the other hand the independent evidence that is available from the other countries (and, indeed, from Buck

Rodgers' book) shows that the "model" described is largely typical of IBM wherever it operates. At times, though, the narrower view does have the significant advantage that the picture is more containable. The equivalent in the USA would only be available to members of the central management committee, who (at least according to some of the critics of Buck Rodgers' book) are too immersed in the IBM culture to be able to adopt a sufficiently detached viewpoint.

In any case the true strength of the model, which is intended to be the prime contribution of this book, is at the operational level. It does not matter what are Armonks's (the overall IBM headquarters) intentions (though the evidence is that at least the Watsons, though perhaps not Buck Rodgers, were well aware of even the most sophisticated elements of the model I describe). What is important is the *de facto* implementation at the operational level. The UK experience is, therefore, no less valid than any other (and, as described above, is probably quite representative of the others). The details may sometimes be specific (though there is no evidence of this) but the philosophies are certainly general.

Learning from success

Most important, in the context of business journalism, the examples I have chosen are designed to illustrate the mode of IBM's "business as usual." Many of the examples in previous works have been interesting, in much the same way that the villain of a play is always reckoned to have the best part; but have been ultimately untypical. The pursuit of the sensational and salacious, albeit fascinating in terms of human moral frailty, would not have added anything to the theme of this book, which quite specifically aims to portray what is important and unique in business terms within IBM. Any company has managers who make errors of judgement, and IBM is no exception as the examples in DeLamarter's book testify. There are probably almost as many "bodies" buried in IBM as in any other large company; and I have in my time helped to bury a number of them. The difference is that in IBM the management ultimately do insist on adherence to IBM's avowed high ideals. As a customer or employee you may be at the mercy of any of the cowboys that prowl its corridors, as they do in any company, but if you yell loud enough for top management to hear then justice *will* always be very rapidly done. To document these lapses tells you nothing about why IBM has been quite so successful; and it is the unearthing of the roots of the *success* that reveals the most valuable and, at least in terms of business management theory, the most interesting information.

This book is, therefore, about the things that IBM does well. It will, incidentally, talk about some of the things that it has not done so well, including its recent set-backs; no company is perfect, and if I am proposing IBM as a model it is as well to know those parts *not* to copy. The book is not, though, intended as a eulogy. It is intended as a description of a working model, in which the main lessons are to be drawn from those elements that work superbly well.

Comparisons

The original insight that is at the heart of many of the ideas I put forward in this book came during my work putting together the business case, on behalf of the UK and then EHQ (IBM's European headquarters), to close down IBM's first Independent Business Unit. The justification for this difficult decision was surprisingly not the lack of IBM expertise in this very different area of business, for at least in the UK we had clearly demonstrated our ability to operate more effectively than any of our competitors; and indeed had achieved, in less than five years, a greater than 70 per cent share of business in the target markets. The reason was ultimately the impossibility of running such a small scale (around $30 million worldwide) conventional business operation within the culturally very different, and bureaucratically based, environment of IBM. The comparison between the two contrasting business structures threw into very sharp relief, for the first time as far as I was concerned, just how different were IBM's "normal" operations.

The most important differences in operation that this initially highlighted were mainly those generated by the very different, and very strong, corporate culture that exists in IBM. In some important respects it was apparent that it was comparable with aspects of the national culture that seem so sharply to differentiate Japanese companies from their Western counterparts. To a large extent the IBM culture emerges naturally from the existence of a uniquely high calibre workforce that in many respects has more in common with that of the higher levels of the civil service or the university common room than that of the conventional industrial company; again comparable with the larger Japanese corporations, in terms of its capture and use of the nation's brightest talents. A surprising outcome of this "skewed profile" is that the lessons of IBM, particularly those of undermining management authority and encouraging individualism, may be just as applicable to solving the apparently intractable problem of inflexibility within government bureaucracies as they are to commercial organizations (see Appendix C for further discussion of these ideas).

The second insight is hinted at above, the comparison not with IBM's Western contemporaries but with its Japanese counterparts. This insight developed during the final research for this book. The only references I came across during that time which matched the facts of IBM were to Japanese practices. Indeed it was only when the initial draft was complete that I eventually found William G. Ouchi's *Theory Z*; to discover that a number of comparable observations were already contained in this book (but in his case based on observations of Japanese practices). This stimulated further research which eventually unearthed the statement, chronicled in *MITI and the Japanese Miracle* (1982, Stanford University Press) by Chalmers Johnson, by Noda Nobuo (a former Mitsubishi executive and chairman of the management committee of MITI's crucial Industrial Rationalization Council during the 1950s) that the committee got its ideas for quality control and measurement of productivity from the USA. Later in the same chapter Chalmers Johnson reports that ". . . excited by the American concept of scientific management the Industrial Rationalization Council churned out publications and sponsored speakers, leading during the mid-1950s to what was called the 'business administration boom' (Keiei Bumu) and to making bestsellers of books such as Peter F. Drucker's 'The Practice of Management' (translated into Japanese in 1956)." Chapter 19 of this influential book is "The IBM Story," and Drucker refers to this extensively elsewhere in the text.

This chapter spelled out three lessons to be learnt from IBM which were, as far as can be ascertained, duly implemented in Japan: lifetime employment, job enrichment, and the precursors of quality circles!

This surprising conclusion will be developed in more detail in Chapter 13 of this book. Suffice it to say, at this stage, that there is (I believe) substantial circumstantial evidence to show that much of the Japanese management style (which many believe was at the heart of the "Japanese Miracle") was *not* a spontaneously national cultural phenomenon; but was at least in part a copy of IBM (imported, in the shape of Drucker's seminal book, with so many other "technologies" by MITI, the Japanese Ministry of International Trade and Industry).

Whether or not this was in fact the case, it *is* certain that IBM's management style (as of the 1950s under T. J. Watson) was a very close match for the now much vaunted Japanese style. As such it is still an excellent guide to Japanese practices, and (most importantly) is located in a cultural context that may be much more easily assimilated by Western management. Understand IBM and you—at least in key aspects—understand the Japanese corporations.

This is not necessarily the view of the Japanese themselves. They are typically rather vague about the process. But the consensus seems to be that, although these practices did not emerge until the 1950s, they were somehow a spontaneous development of the communal hardships experienced after the war. Suddenly in the 1950s the previous draconian (hire and fire) labour relations were abandoned. To quote a view which is typical of many, Kenichi Ohmae in his excellent book, *The Mind of the Strategist* (1982, McGraw Hill), says: ". . . the embryonic companies were more like communes than corporations. People shared their lives, hardships and toil."

It is an attractive explanation, and undoubtedly the release from the hardships, described by Ohmae, contributed to a climate where the policies could flourish. On the other hand, the very precise form of the policies, and their implementation by the large corporations most influenced by MITI (rather than by the small companies that the myth would predict) suggests to me that "The IBM Story" could well have been a seed planted in a very fertile soil; to ignore the possibility would be to undervalue the role of MITI in the "Japanese miracle."

In essence I believe that the stories told by the Japanese themselves are probably almost as mythical as the Western view that it was inherently cultural. This latter view, which emphasizes the impenetrability (to Western eyes) of the ideas that created the "miracle," has perhaps been most recently epitomized by the Pascale and Athos book, *The Art of Japanese Management* (1981, Simon & Schuster), which (paradoxically, since it was derived from the McKinsey work which has wider application) ascribes much of the Japanese success to the principles of Zen (and to "ambiguity" and "interdependence" in particular).

IBM: the lessons

As a company IBM is not perfect or infallible, and as with most things it will not last forever. Indeed it is currently (in 1987) in the middle of one of the great gambles that it is wont to indulge in every couple of decades or so. This time it has just sold off the "family silver" of its rental base to invest in manufacturing facilities that, it fervently hopes, will undercut the costs of even its cheapest Far Eastern competitors; indeed choosing to compete head-on with the Japanese precisely in those areas of their greatest strength. The next few years will show whether this was a wise decision; the short-term indications are that it probably was *not*. However, the record shows that even the unwise decisions can eventually be turned to IBM's ultimate advantage. Furthermore IBM alone has a number of unique advantages, particularly in terms of large numbers of very high calibre staff, which probably make it well nigh impossible for any other company exactly to emulate *all* its methods with any real degree of success.

Personnel policies

Despite these caveats it is my belief that there are a number of important business lessons which may still be learnt. At least some of the more sophisticated companies could profitably employ variants of the devices IBM regularly uses. As already noted, it is surprising for a company that is pre-eminently a marketing giant, that the main lessons relate to personnel policies, and indeed it was precisely these that the Japanese seized upon. A number of these, as well as being alluded to in the McKinsey work of Peters and Waterman, are more directly incorporated in William G. Ouchi's *Theory Z*; which is not surprising since this is based on his observations of Japanese corporations (and he too was involved in the earlier phases of the McKinsey work, and appears to have applied this more directly to the Japanese examples than did Pascale and Athos). He too credits his own ultimate insight to a meeting with IBM, but regretfully he does not follow this through to determine what further lessons IBM holds. This book hopefully will go some way to rectifying that omission.

Those philosophies that are incorporated in the Japanese model, and in Ouchi's theory, largely relate to the IBM of T. J. Watson; though they are, of course, still incorporated in the modern IBM. Of these perhaps the most important is that of lifetime employment; a concept that IBM will not legally commit to, but will state as an objective (which to date it has almost always met). Other features include the extensive use of implicit, rather than explicit, controls based on beliefs rather than on numeric targets; the combination of this with a strong common culture as a mediating factor; the provision of non-specialized career paths within the organization, backed up by extensive training programmes; consensual decision making (requiring formal approval by a large number of individuals); and holistic relations between employer and employed. All of these would have already been familiar to IBM employees of the T. J. Watson era, and were largely responsible for IBM's growth during this period (as they were to be for Japan later).

Ouchi's *Theory Z* (and to a lesser extent the McKinsey work) is, thus, a very reasonable first stage towards implementing some of the lessons to be learnt from IBM. His estimation that this stage might take 10 to 15 years is probably not unrealistic; since this is about the timescale that the Japanese, the consummate imitators, required. There are some lessons, though, not included in *Theory Z*.

One of the most important of these is that of attracting and holding the highest calibre personnel. It should be an obvious point, but in my experience very few companies indeed take the recruitment process seriously enough. IBM views each new recruit as a capital investment of up to a million pounds, and resources the recruitment process accordingly. The Japanese corporations, of course, also naturally attract the highest calibre recruits. The second is that of educating and re-educating staff to the highest standards. IBM has around five percent of its manpower permanently committed to internal education. Third, and probably the most difficult for many managements to commit themselves to wholeheartedly, is that of allowing the resulting well-educated, high calibre staff the very maximum amount of individual delegation so that all their talents are *fully* utilized. IBM achieves this difficult task positively by a range of personnel policies that encourage rampant individualism, whilst engendering a feeling of security; and negatively by a range of management policies which effectively undermine the authority of first line managers, and discourage them from interfering destructively in the naturally smooth-running operations that they head up. The end effect is an idiosyncratic form of highly organized anarchy!

This third aspect (although hinted at in parts of Peters' and Waterman's work for McKinsey) definitely has no Japanese counterpart. Indeed it is very largely in total opposition to the Japanese experience. This is understandable since this was Tom Watson Jr.'s personal contribution when he started to develop the individualistic anarchy to counter the bureaucratic tendencies then emerging in IBM; all of which came after MITI transferred the IBM lessons to

Japan. It will be interesting to see if Japan can make the same quantum leap (or even if, with its very different national culture, it will need to); particularly as Ouchi suggests that "no organizational structure" (surely anarchy) is the ideal (if normally unapproachable) precondition for Theory Z.

Finally, there is the establishment of an efficient *horizontal* communication process. In IBM this is an absolutely essential element of the company's very successful (self) control of its day-to-day operations in a very volatile marketplace. It is achieved largely because personnel of as high a calibre and as individualistic as those in IBM simply cannot be *stopped* from communicating with their peers. At the same time, the set of management undermining principles that ensure maximal delegation, also break down interdepartmental barriers; so there are no objections, let alone the taboos that aflict most companies, to cross-functional communication. Although not stressed in *Theory Z* the Japanese corporations are reported to have relatively good horizontal communications (not least because of the many contacts made during the building of non-specialized careers). They cannot, though, in any way match the great richness of IBM's implementation.

In more recent years these processes have been facilitated by institutionalized change, so that almost every IBM employee changes jobs, at least to some degree, every two years or so. This breaks down potential logjams, but it (comparably with Japanese experiences) also builds the individual contacts that are central to the development of the horizontal communication process.

IBM is currently in the process of reinforcing these processes with the introduction of a very sophisticated horizontal terminal network. The introduction of similar networks, always assuming they are very carefully designed to enhance horizontal communication and delegation, may be the best chance that other companies have of implementing at least some of IBM's "systems."

Although overall the end result is very similar to the processes that the Japanese have employed since the 1950s, the inherent "anarchy" of the modern IBM version does make it significantly different; and probably that much more relevant a means of introducing Theory Z to Western companies. More important, though, it will be essential to the development of the new business structures, which I describe (based on IBM experience) as "cellular organic," that are increasingly replacing the traditional functional (pyramidal, hierarchical) structures. These are described in more detail in Chapter 13.

Business controls

IBM is perhaps unlike any other company in the way that it deliberately manages its business. On the surface a business school professor would be able to find the signs of all the sophisticated financial management systems that theoreticians hold so dear. Underneath the surface, though, real control is exercised by a range of relatively crude, but very powerful, *non-financial* methods. Of these, direct control of headcount (the centrally approved numbers of permanent, "established" staff) is the most effective, and this is supplemented by a vice-like grip on capital projects. It is reasoned by IBM, based on considerable experience, that both of these areas have geometric "knock-on" effects, and if these alone can be controlled then most other expenses will also fall into line. Up to this point there may be some similarity with other companies, though their use of these "weapons" may be largely incidental, and certainly far less deliberate than IBM's.

The remaining control, that of "culture," is the one that actually determines the day-to-day running of IBM. It is, I believe, relatively unusual, at least in terms of Western companies and its *deliberate* long-term implementation; though Peters and Waterman stress the cultural aspect of all the successful companies they investigated. It is the corporate culture that ultimately makes IBM unlike any other company, and makes it so successful. In the case of IBM it is arguable that this culture is a product of more than half a century—from its inception by Thomas J. Watson—hence its great strength in depth. It is, unfortunately, a management tool that requires a great deal of foresight. It is also an unlikely tool, as the dismissal as "unbelievable" by professional IBM watchers (but not the Japanese; "beliefs" are a key element of Theory Z) of the repeated statements on the subject by the Watsons has shown. As suggested by Ouchi its use may have to span decades before the most dramatic benefits appear, and this must be seen as a luxury when many companies plan only months ahead. It is, though, a tool that should *not* be ignored; not least because in the cellular organic structure it is the only guaranteed control on the teams working within the individual cells. The timespan illustrates the remaining difference shown by IBM. It can, and does, look at timescales well in excess of a decade and its main detailed planning cycle genuinely is a full five years; as any theoretician would recommend but remarkably few companies even pay lip service to.

Philosophies I

IBM then is a company that looks, and really is, very different from most other Western companies, and indeed from the Japanese companies with which it might also be compared. It flies in the face of many of the conventional theories of sound management; yet it has been supremely successful far longer than most other companies have existed, and across a wide range of different environments. The moral would appear to be twofold. In the first place, the structure of "Western" management theory is not as firmly rooted as its practitioners would have us believe (even Ouchi's Theory Z is relatively unknown; though Peters and Waterman have achieved considerable popularity for their own criticisms of "rational" management); which leaves hope for those brave individuals who are the true innovators, the real entrepreneurs of our society. The second is that, along with some Japanese companies, IBM shows that it is possible to control, in a highly productive manner, even a very complex operation by using the simplest of means.

One line of management theory has moved from Theory X to Theory Y (as described by Douglas McGregor in *The Human Side of Enterprise,* 1960, McGraw Hill) and thence, at least for some, to Theory Z (and perhaps for many more to McKinsey's "Seven S's"). As you will appreciate, I believe that this moving finger has travelled even further in the past couple of decades. Based on the model of IBM in the 1980s I thus propose some additions to these previous theories. I do not believe, however, that there is necessarily just one definitive style of management which will be equally applicable to all companies, or to all personalities. I propose, therefore, to refer to this extension of theory as "Philosophies I." This is because at the heart of the matter are the various beliefs, or philosophies; and the I is an acknowledgment to IBM, which is the original model (where my contribution has been as interpreter).

"Philosophies I" has two more-or-less equally balanced components. The first of these approximates to Theory Z (and to a lesser extent to some of the work of Peters and Waterman). In essence this is the trust built up between management and employees, which stimulates the flexible working practices and worker motivation so typical of IBM and the Japanese corporations. The 10 major ingredients are described in more detail in Chapter 13 but are included briefly here to provide a perspective for the rest of the book.

Strong beliefs rooted in shared ethical values (leading to objectives set in terms of philosophies): the evidence is that, above all, it is the strength of the shared beliefs (shared by management and employees alike), and not just the resources at its disposal, that has made IBM so spectacularly successful over such a long period (and the "spiritual" nature of Japanese corporations—ascribed, I believe incorrectly in the context of their outstanding performance, to Zen—has long been marvelled at by the West).

Full employment policies ("lifetime employment"): this is perhaps the most difficult commitment for a typical Western firm, with short-term profit performance objectives to meet, but it probably is the *most* important foundation for success on the scale of IBM and the Japanese corporations.

Job enrichment: IBM was one of the first companies to put significant effort into offering its employees "enriched" jobs (a philosophy that was later also adopted very successfully by the Japanese). IBM employees can—at least to a degree—*choose* jobs that they feel are both interesting and fulfilling.

Personal incentives: this is a perhaps surprising element (in the context of the non-materialistic nature of the other elements), but the evidence does seem to suggest that (in both IBM and the Japanese corporations) a personal financial involvement adds to employee commitment (but not necessarily for conventional "capitalist" reasons).

Non-specialized career development: the concept of a career, perhaps spanning several quite different disciplines, developing within the one company (rather than in the traditional Western alternative of within one discipline across several companies), is typical of the Japanese corporations; but it is also (within the rather different confines of the Western culture) one that is adopted by IBM.

Personal (consensual) involvement in decision making: although IBM has no formal equivalent of the Japanese (ringi) system of widespread "sign-off," all personnel impacted by specific departmental activities are usually informally involved in the decision-making processes, and they have (in effect) some right of consensual veto (albeit very partial, and most obviously policed via indirect programmes such as the opinion survey) on the key policies affecting them.

Implicit control, rather than explicit (figure) control: IBM is as likely as any other Western company (but not Japanese companies) to indulge in numeric controls on all fronts (after all that is a large part of the service it is selling to its customers), but these are tempered with well-communicated explanations of the philosophies behind these "targets"; so that each individual knows exactly what he is expected to do (and why).

Cultivation of a strong culture: the ultimate implicit control is embodied in a strong culture which encapsulates all that the organization wishes to achieve (be it IBM or a Japanese corporation). All decisions, by all individuals, are thus taken in the (largely) correct context, even if no further brief is given.

Holistic approach to employees: IBM, especially in the T. J. Watson era, saw its role as addressing *all* the needs of its employees (a philosophy that is even now very evident in the Japanese corporations). The relationship was paternalistic (in the best sense of the "family"), rather than the more traditional capitalist exploitation of mere units of labour.

The second leg of this equation comprises the set of philosophies, most of which are unique to IBM (and described for the first time in this book), which now go *beyond* Theory Z. They are the anarchic, individualistic philosophies and horizontal communication devices which can contain the potential problems of a fully fledged Western bureaucracy and harness its energies to create a viable business machine; and are indeed probably a necessary prerequisite for the cellular organic structures emerging in the information technology revolution, since these are built around very small groups (with the individual as the ultimate building block) which are only very loosely linked into the overall company structure. Under these circumstances the *individual* has to be in a position to control his own destiny, otherwise there can be no really effective control (albeit even then exercised by new techniques) over the overall company. These 10 philosophies are, again, described in more detail in Chapter 13.

Strong (published) beliefs in individualism ("respect for the individual"): once again it is beliefs that are the driving force of this second leg of philosophies. In this case the key belief is that of individualism; one that is more normally seen to be *opposed* to the interests of any corporate body. Within IBM it is clearly and most publicly enshrined as its *first* belief: respect for the individual.

Personnel processes, to guarantee the working of these beliefs: to be most effective these beliefs need to be seen to have real teeth, and these teeth are best provided by effective personnel programmes; which indeed IBM runs under the collective description of "respect for the individual."

Single status, across the company (reinforced by status divorced from any management role): effective promotion of individualism implies a commitment to single status; where all employees (whether management or not) should clearly be subject to the same democratic conditions of employment. IBM has also shown that it is helpful (in terms of breaking down the remaining status barriers within the company) if status is formally divorced from its normally most obvious manifestation in terms of management position; hence an individual's status is not immediately obvious, and relations between individuals cannot be based on a "hen-pecking" order (where the nature of this is at best equivocal, and normally an unknown quantity).

Recruitment of the highest calibre individuals: it seems self-evident that a company is as good as its employees (a view, however, that is far removed from the conventional capitalist "units of labour"). But all too often companies willingly settle for second best by devoting too little effort (and expertise) to recruitment.

Extended training, particularly for top management: continuing the same theme, few companies make the best use of the talent they have. On the other hand IBM is committed (and resourced) to train and retrain all its staff to allow them to fulfill their true potential.

Maximal delegation, to the lowest possible levels: this is now almost a cliché of business management, but too few companies actually succeed in implementing the philosophy.

Planned constraints on first-line management: one of IBM's most successful innovations has been to force maximal delegation by, in effect, undermining the position of its first-line management. This forces them to become "team leaders," allowing their subordinates to fulfill their maximum potential and the managers to get on with the real job of management.

Encouragement of dissent: one key contribution to individualism, which has been heavily promoted within IBM, is the encouragement of dissent. When IBM management can rely on their subordinates to disagree, then they can rely on the information that is being fed upwards from the grass roots.

Encouragement of horizontal communications: in the newly emerging organizational forms (such as cellular organic) the vertical communications structure is being broken down, to be largely replaced by an extensive horizontal, peer-to-peer, communications network; and this process will be reinforced by developments in information technology.

Institutionalization of change: the final, and most recent, contribution of IBM has been to develop the concept of continuing change as a "lubricant" to free the organization from the potential stranglehold of bureaucracy. IBM now simply does not allow time between successive reorganizations for a fully fledged bureaucracy to become entrenched.

Overall one is still, to a certain extent, left with a fascinating enigma. IBM is arguably still the most successful manufacturing company in the world. It is the one relatively stable point in the fastest developing, and most volatile, market—at the very heart of the information revolution. Though its success is based on constant change (completely remodelling itself and its product line every five to seven years), it has constantly maintained the (product) leadership that Peter Drucker identifies as essential to achieving economic results. It has, however, found the secret to defying Drucker's accompanying prediction that any such leadership is likely to be transitory and short-lived; and this is a secret that has so far evaded the Japanese corporations (for although they appear all conquering to their Western competitors they are rarely dominant for more than two decades, then to be replaced by newer and more dynamic Japanese corporations—often in new markets—when the original corporation falls into liquidation). It is a company that *has* found the philosopher's stone: it can turn almost anything into gold. Yet even with the "Philosophies I," which report some of the major contributory factors, it is not totally clear, probably even to Armonk, just how it does this. It is ironic, for example, that one thing the Japanese probably learnt about from Drucker's book was IBM's precursors of "quality circles;" yet IBM had later to relearn this particular lesson from the Japanese! It is even more ironic that some of IBM's recent problems have resulted from copying inappropriate Japanese models!

Probably IBM's success is at least a function of the synergy derived from bringing together 400,000 of the most capable people in the world (including 42,000 managers and 1,500 executives), within the most stimulating culture founded on the pursuit of excellence. The calibre, and sheer innovative bravery, of Armonk management should not, however, be discounted by anyone. One thing is clear and that is that the workings of IBM are very different from those conventionally employed in most Western companies, and very different too from those recommended by many management theorists; and as such must pose a major question about such theories. "Philosophies I" (although central to IBM's success) is, I believe, probably just one of a range of options open to management; but (in the light of the outstanding successes of IBM and the Japanese corporations) it is clearly worth considering, and at least may provide a basis for a new discussion of such management theory.

The model that is progressively described in later chapters will, I trust, provide a particularly useful basis for this process of exploration.

SECTION 1
The History of IBM

CHAPTER 2

The Fathers

Introduction

The first half century of IBM's history belongs unequivocally to one man: Thomas J. Watson. As one of the last of the great turn-of-the-century corporate "entrepreneurs" he created, virtually in his own image, the IBM that has been so widely reported; and the part of IBM that was copied by the Japanese. It was he who, paternalistically, built IBM around an almost religious set of beliefs, and in the processs first developed its uniquely effective management style, despite his own earlier history of very questionable business ethics. It was certainly he who built IBM into just about the most effective selling machine yet seen; though the technology he championed never went much beyond the humble punched card. He took IBM from being a small scale producer of time clocks to a position in the front rank of multinationals; a feat of business management that has justifiably been recognized by all the commentators.

To provide a context for the "model" that is the modern mature IBM, the next three chapters review the various phases that IBM has historically moved through; most easily categorized by the leaders of IBM during each of them. This review is intended only to provide a perspective for the later chapters. It is not intended as rigorous history of everything of importance that happened to IBM over these decades. For a more complete history the reader should turn to books such as *IBM: Colossus in Transition* (by Robert Sobel) or *THINK* (by William Rodgers).

In particular, the historical reviews in this first section of the book do not attempt to record the events neutrally, or in the strict context of their own time. They are deliberately edited, with the benefit of the hindsight possible from the 1980s, to see what formative factors can be discerned which might account for the unique corporation that is the modern IBM. The importance attributed to these "facts," therefore, is coloured by the filter of how important they are to IBM *now*, not how important they were at the time. The approach is in some respects comparable with that of the committed "social historian," viewing history selectively through the perspective of the "theories" that emerge in later chapters. The intention is to use the history of IBM to illuminate its current position; and perhaps, at the same time, to gain some insight into how other companies might follow the same trail.

The formative years of IBM initially revolved around a series of paradoxes; at least in terms of its later development. IBM in the 1980s is very much a corporation of the twenty-first century, rooted in the ultrasophisticated technology of the information revolution; and it is a company uniquely inspired and controlled by a code of ethics of almost religious intensity.

Yet no-one observing its birth would have predicted such an outcome. Viewed at a superficial level it is almost as if Genghis Khan and Attila the Hun formed an alliance whose product was the Roman Catholic Church! For its origin was deeply rooted in the technology of the Industrial Revolution and in the entrepreneurial activities of the nineteenth century, whose ethics were those of capitalism at its reddest in tooth and claw.

Charles R. Flint: the founding father

The first "father" of IBM was Charles R. Flint. Born in 1850, he was a brilliant financier who built a business as a commission agent, doing most of his business with South America. His trade was mainly in raw materials, including nitrates and guano; the first paradox being that IBM's financial foundations were built on bird manure! He was best known as an arms merchant, as a supplier of munitions to warring factions, often to both sides at the same time; the second paradox being that a company so avowedly ethical as IBM, with the proud motto of "world peace through world trade," should have been founded on the profits of war.

This superficial reading is, however, to take Charles R. Flint out of his historical context, and to ascribe modern values to an age that had a very different view of the priorities of business. In that era selling armaments was a highly respected occupation, as indeed it still is for the management of the large aerospace corporations.

He was a workaholic who gloried in excitement—his only stimulant, for he never smoked or drank. He was constantly involved in a dozen or more ventures scattered around the world, of which IBM was just one; his record showed, apart from IBM, a tendency towards the numbers of ventures rather than their size.

The "father of trusts"

The one outstanding factor that was particularly important in the future growth of IBM was his ideologically based commitment to the creation of industrial combinations; an activity that earned him the title amongst his contemporaries of "father of trusts." He put a great deal of energy into promoting the virtues of big business, in speeches and articles, stressing the economies of mass production. In particular he set down a vision of monopoly (echoing Thorstein Veblen); and he believed that an irregulated marketplace would be highly wasteful, where competition forced lower quality goods.

To achieve the bigness he prescribed, he created "combinations"; bringing together companies with similar interests, to create a degree of synergy. The very large profits that he then took from those purchasing shares in these "combinations" were, though, created more by traditional tricks of "creative accounting" than by any immediate real benefit. This was achieved by capitalizing the new "combination" at a level far in excess of the capitalisation of the individual parts. The difference at the time was colloquially referred to as "water," and was claimed to be the goodwill and synergy resulting from the merger. The extremes of this were shown in American Chicle where individual assets totalling no more than $500,000 were recapitalized at $9 million. IBM was similarly founded on such a sham; a further paradox for this most financially secure and stable of companies.

The first, and ultimately irrelevant, components of IBM were created by Flint in 1900. One was International Time Recording, manuf acturing time clocks and with headquarters in Endicott, New York. The other was the Computing Scale Company of America, created from four companies making scales and food slicers. By 1910 International Time Recording had reached a successful level of $1 million a year revenue, but Computing Scale was not so successful.

At that time Flint considered combining them. The combination had a very questionable synergy as the components were in quite different businesses, and even their main facilities were separated by 1,000 miles. He argued, however, that there was a shared, if very tenuous, logic of measurement. He also argued that investors could earn more from the two combined. His final justification was that the two separate lines of business allowed investors twice the chance of meeting objectives and paying dividends!

The Tabulating Machine Company

In the event he engineered a *three*-way combination, the third leg of this was the real business basis for the future of IBM. It was a company, unusually in such circumstances, not already owned by Flint: the Tabulating Machine Company.

This company had been formed by Hermann Hollerith. Born in 1860, he graduated as an engineer (of mines) from Columbia University in 1879 and immediately obtained a job with the US Census Bureau. This was the inspiration for his one obsession as an inventor, and indeed for his one successful invention; his others were notably unsuccessful. Although he subsequently moved to MIT (Massachusetts Institute of Technology) as an instructor, he still continued to research a device for recording census statistics. He, of course, knew of the Jacquard loom which used holes in cards to program its complicated patterns of weaving, but it was reportedly the further inspiration of a punch photograph train ticket, on which passenger details (such as height and hair colour) were punched out around the edge by the conductor, that clinched his key invention. Hollerith decided that each census taker could do the same, with the resulting card being sorted by a variation of the Jacquard loom.

He left MIT to start his own company, being granted his first patent in 1884 and then successfully bidding for the Baltimore census in 1889. He filed three further patents in 1890 and finally, in 1890, obtained the contract for the US Census Bureau business, at a price of $750,000. It was, however, only in 1896 that he incorporated as the Tabulating Machine Company, and undertook his own manufacturing; previously he had subcontracted this. Thereafter his business success was more variable, as competitors offered similar solutions. Eventually his fortunes declined to a low ebb when he lost the contract for the 1910 census.

Thus in 1910 he was short on funds, as well as somewhat short on new inventions, so the approach from Flint came at an opportune time. The result, in 1911, was the corporation that was eventually to become IBM. As with all such ventures by Flint it contained a fair amount of "water"; it had a bonded indebtedness of $6.5 million, 25 times current assets, of which $4 million was borrowed from the Guaranty Trust Company. It had 1,200 employees and, with a deal of foresight, Flint called it the Computing Tabulating and Recording Company (CTR).

Thomas J. Watson: founder of beliefs

However, the most important "father" of the modern IBM had not yet appeared on the scene: Thomas J. Watson. Born on 17 February 1874 he was very much the country boy; again a paradox in view of the great sophistication he eventually built into IBM. His father owned a modest lumber business ultimately located in Painted Post, in the north of New York State. He himself as a child was something of a loner. An asthmatic, he was remembered as being shy at social gatherings; another paradox for someone who was to create one of the world's top sales forces.

Early lessons

Having given up his first job—teaching—after just one day, he took a year's course in accounting and business at the local Miller School of Commerce, finishing in May 1892. His second job as a $6 a week bookkeeper was almost as brief as his first, and he soon chose the excitement of "drumming." He joined a travelling salesman, George Cornwell, peddling organs and pianos around the farms, for the local hardware store (William Bronsons). When Cornwell left he continued alone, earning the sum of $10 per week. It was only after two years of this life that he realized he would be earning $70 per week if he were on a commission; a lesson that perhaps coloured much of his later approach in IBM. The impact of his indignation on making this discovery was such that he upped stakes and moved from his familiar surroundings to the relative metropolis of Buffalo.

After a very brief period selling sewing machines, from which job he was almost immediately fired, he once more set out on the road selling. In this case his partner was C. B. Barron, a showman renowned for his disreputable conduct; which Watson, as a lifelong Methodist, deplored. Jointly they peddled shares of the Buffalo Building and Loan. They were soon very successful and with his proceeds Watson set up a butcher's shop as an investment. Unfortunately, true to form, Barron absconded with the commission and the loan funds, leaving Watson with no money, no investment (he lost the shop as a result), and no job. Thus for the second, and not the last, time he was fired; and again these early experiences may have formed his own unique, for the time, attitude when (at IBM) he abandoned the contemporary practice of ruthlessly hiring and firing labour as a commodity.

Selling

Fate decreed that in his butcher's shop Watson had a newly acquired NCR cash register, for which he then had to arrange new repayments. On visiting NCR he determined to join the company; and after a number of abortive attempts he finally succeeded. NCR was then one of the leading selling organizations, and John J. Range, its Buffalo branch manager, became almost a father figure for Watson; and was a model for his sales and management style. Certainly in later years—in a 1952 interview—he claimed he learned more from Range than anyone else. But at first he was a poor salesman, until Range took him personally in hand; then he became the most successful salesman in the East, earning $100 per week.

In 1899, at the age of 25, he was rewarded with the NCR agency for Rochester. This was not exactly a desirable territory, it was bottom of the league table of NCR's 160 branches; but as agent he got 35 per cent commission (much as do the modern PC dealers!). In any case within months he had made it number six in the league.

The selling style of the time was, to put it mildly, rough and Watson later admitted that he felt ashamed of some of his sales techniques (and regretted using them). There is a widely reported tale of Watson being told by a competing salesman of a call he was to make the next morning, some 20 miles away. The salesman arrived to find Watson had already made the sale. The interest of the story is how it developed over the years. In the early days of IBM it was told by Watson as an essay in opportunism, as an example for eager salesmen to follow. Later, however, the story was turned around to illustrate regrettable conduct that should be avoided. Later still the story was expunged from the oral history.

As a result of these techniques, which largely revolved around knocking the main competitor (Hallwood), in four years Watson made Rochester effectively an NCR monopoly. As a reward he was called to the NCR head office in Dayton, Ohio.

Incentives

NCR had been built by John Patterson to be one of the most inspired selling organizations in the USA. His methods were ruthless; but no more so than his contemporaries, for the modern niceties had not yet emerged. He had a genius, though, for innovation in sales management. He gave his salesmen guaranteed territories, where the normal practice previously had been to have salesmen competing with each other for the same business. He gave them training, and motivated them with the reward of the Hundred Per Cent Club (an institution later to be so successfully transferred to IBM). He built a pleasant environment for his work-force; glass walled factories with swimming pools (facilities echoed more recently by Rolm, IBM's recent acquisition). Apart from the lavish buildings (which Watson couldn't initially afford, and made do with "theatrical" equivalents) all of these were eventually brought with Watson to IBM. Even the famous THINK slogan originated when he was at NCR; at least according to some reports.

Morality

Patterson was also, though, a tyrant who believed that as a capitalist he could set himself above the ordinary law; as also did many of his contemporaries, again reflecting the rather different standards of the time. His competitive methods were, by our modern standards, scandalous. He encouraged his salesmen to knock the competitors, by ever more dubious methods. He even set up a special "competition" department whose sole function was to conduct dirty tricks campaigns. They enmeshed their competitors in litigation and, reportedly, even produced carbon copy ("knock-out") registers to undermine their reputation. The department indulged in industrial espionage, even extending occasionally to sabotage.

Legality

Watson's role in the scheme of things was to knock out the competition in the used cash register market. As a process it was itself very questionable in terms of the anti-trust legislation. It was made even less legal by the chosen means. Using funds supplied by NCR he set up what was ostensibly a completely independent organization, Watson's Cash Register and Second Hand Exchange, in Manhattan. Undercutting the competition, for he had no need to make a profit (having effectively limitless funds from NCR), he gradually monopolized the business, until he was able to buy out the competitors, which he promptly did. He then moved on to Philadelphia and then progressively across the country, repeating the operation and covertly establishing another near monopoly for NCR in the second-hand business, to match that already established in the new machine market.

Watson later claimed that he didn't appreciate the implications of what he was doing, and indeed it is quite possible that he was so immersed in the work that he failed to understand the full depth of Patterson's machinations. Nevertheless it was a clear, indeed blatant, breach of the anti-trust legislation; though until that time such legislation had, in the spirit of the age, been more honoured in the breach rather than by adherence. Perhaps he was unlucky but, along with 30 other NCR managers (including Patterson), on 22 February 1912 he was indicted in an anti-trust suit instigated by managers previously dismissed by NCR.

In the six months before his trial he met his wife to be. Jeanette Kittredge. He married her on 13 February 1913 just two weeks after the trial finished, having been found guilty and sentenced to a $5,000 fine plus a year in Miami County jail! The jail sentence was unexpected, previously only fines had been imposed; and the sentence was appealed. Once again Watson's luck held out. On 26 March 1913 the Miami and Mad rivers inundated Dayton in the worst floods to hit the USA since 1889. The NCR plant, on high ground, became the town's sanctuary and Patterson there, and Watson in New York, organized the rescue operation; and in the process became national heroes.

He still had to wait for the appeal. In the meantime, in April 1914, he was fired by Patterson, a not uncommon fate for senior NCR executives; perhaps because he refused to consider signing a "consent decree" or perhaps simply because his new found reputation as a national hero was a challenge to Patterson, who insisted that he was the only king in his court.

So with a wife and small baby to support, and a one year jail sentence hanging over his head, he was unemployed (albeit with a $50,000 golden handshake). It was not an experience to be lightly forgotten, and the evidence is that it contributed significantly to the subsequent ethical foundations of IBM. Despite his ruthless sales techniques in NCR, he always had a reputation as a fair man, offering fair deals to the competitors he bought out. But the very dramatic change in ethical codes he underwent in moving to CTR (IBM), where other businessmen in those days never normally considered the wider effects of their actions, was somewhat akin to Paul's conversion on the road to Damascus.

I believe that the traumatic experiences of that time indelibly stamped his actions thereafter. He continued to deny his guilt, repeatedly saying "I do not consider myself a criminal" and "My conscience is clear." Yet the evidence suggests that underneath he had made a vow to himself that he would never again be put in that position. The philosophy, based as much on ethics as business management, that emerged from this "vow" was one of the main factors—if not the main factor—that shaped IBM.

The foundations

This was 1914 and Watson approached Flint, as a leading financier, for assistance in finding a similar job. Despite his apparently parlous situation he was still very clear as to the type of job he wanted. He had already turned down a number of offers. He wanted control of the business for himself, and a share of the profits. Flint offered him CTR. Flint was, as described earlier, a great promoter of trusts and was presumably less worried about Watson's impending jail sentence. The other members of the CTR board were less sanguine, asking who was to run the company while he was in prison! They only gave him the title of general manager, until his sentence was finally quashed by the Appeal Court.

So the die was cast and CTR was joined with Thomas J. Watson; the final paradox being that the true founder of the modern IBM, the most moralistic of companies, was at that time a felon convicted of business practices unacceptable even to a period that was notable for its lack of standards! Clearly, though, he had already decided that the future of CTR was to be very different.

Surprisingly, in view of his past record at NCR and his later colossal influence on IBM, he initially maintained a very low profile (tantamount to seeking obscurity) for the next decade; until 1924 when the chairman George W. Fairchild died, and he finally took over sole control. For the whole of that decade, in some ways uncharacteristically, he consistently deferred to Flint, Fairchild and Hollerith.

In the meantime he took personal charge of 400 demoralized and poorly supervised salesmen. His stated objective was to produce a sales force in the NCR mould, as well as advanced machines that would be superior to any of the competitors. In a series of small meetings he presented his "competitive proposition" to the sales force. Despite the aggressive sounding title, right from these beginnings there was as much emphasis on the ethics and philosophies of the business as there was on sales techniques. In particular he stressed sincerity, integrity and loyalty; saying that they should do nothing that could be construed as "unfair competition" and should conduct themselves in an "honest, fair and square way."

The other philosophies that still motivate IBM were also evident. The company motto was to be "We sell and deliver service"; CTR was to be in the business of genuinely assisting its customers. Watson strongly believed that when a sale was made both sides came out ahead.

Even the emphasis on the individual, later developed by his son, was present. His most memorable chalkboard presentation (even at that early stage the use of visual media, later to be the ubiquitous flipchart and now the overhead projected foil, was central to meetings!) showed:

The	Man ufacturer
General	Man ager
Sales	Man ager
Service	Man ager
Sales	Man
Factory	Man
Office	Man ager
Office	Man

Evangelizing the central nature of the individual in the operations of the company, Watson highlighted the central nature of "Man" in all these operations. In 1917 he said to a New York audience, "When practicing the art of selling use all your talents. Put everything you have into your efforts; above all put your personality into them. Never copy anybody, *Be yourself*."

So much for the IBM organization-man myth, promoted by IBM's detractors. It is possible that the origin of this myth was a function of appearance, for Watson brought from NCR the requirement for salesmen to be neatly dressed in dark suits and white shirts (a philosophy that has held to the present day); but as a mark of (business) respect for their customers rather than as a uniform. The usual dress for salesmen at that time was a loud check suit! In fact Watson definitely did not want any uniform; and when a uniform was suggested for his shopfloor workers he quite specifically rejected it: "I don't want any of our workers wearing uniforms." The dark business suit did, however, become a sort of uniform throughout IBM, and perhaps, however unofficially, it served the same function of promoting single status that actual uniform does in Japanese companies; but without the unacceptable, to Western eyes, loss of individualism.

There was, in addition, a uniform commitment to the ethics and philosophies of IBM; which effectively included, in the early years, a commitment to a personal lifestyle. IBMers were sober, almost puritanical, pillars of the community. They did not drink or indulge in licentious behaviour; and at that time even the house they lived in was of interest to IBM. But underneath these largely superficial similarities there was still a real commitment to individualism. The problem of image was simply that these similarities, however superficial, were so different from the much less restrained behaviour of other sales forces that theirs was the uniform image retained by outsiders.

The showbiz surrounding sales activities in IBM, of the Hundred Per Cent Club (HPC) for example, did nothing to dispel the myth. The "tent city" (with a circus tent, appropriately, for the main events and dormitory tents, but luxuriously appointed with every facility, for participants) that covered the ground of the Homestead and IBM Country Club (at Endicott) for the HPCs in the 1940s was a cultural wonder to be experienced. Even now, although based in modern convention halls, the US HPC retains the flavour with the main events still being held in the "main tent"! The IBM songs that were developed in the earlier times are also a cultural mystery to outsiders, and were later such an embarrassment that Tom Watson Jr. banned them for a while. Again they still linger on at US HPCs, an anachronism for Europeans, but hugely enjoyed (as are all the theatricals developed by Watson) by the participants.

In addition to the HPC Watson brought the idea of training schools from NCR. He didn't bring the more ruthless of the labour relations, though. For example even if a salesman constantly failed to make the HPC he was usually only moved to a less demanding position. Watson wanted to be a paternalistic employer, paying premium salaries with excellent fringe benefits; even paying for education, and providing country clubs (such as those at Endicott just mentioned). The policy of promotion from within—which was one of the key factors that shaped the present IBM—was also put into practice.

Many of these factors were later to be shared by the Japanese companies. Most important of all, though, was to be the policy of full employment which was the foundation of IBM's enduring strength; as it also was of the Japanese corporations, who were later so effectively to copy it, along with the other IBM practices.

Returning to the "history" of IBM, after Watson had been at CTR for 11 months the Appeal Court ordered a retrial. Although he refused to sign a consent decree a new trial never took place; and he was duly promoted by the board of CTR to the title of president.

CTR was a company with three separate elements. Computing Scale was always a problem; and the largest element of this (Dayton Scale) was eventually sold off in 1933 to Hobart Manufacturing. Time Recording was then still the main revenue earner, and was used by Watson as a vehicle for diversification; though none of these was a great success. Time Recording was retained by IBM—surprisingly in view of its irrelevance to the rest of the business—for half a century; it was only sold off in 1958.

The piece of the action that most interested Watson, perhaps because it was closest to his NCR experience, was the tabulating business and this was where he directed much of his attention; by the early 1930s this had indeed become the largest piece of CTR.

Returning to the 1920s, though, while still under Fairchild's domination Watson went for a significant degree of growth. This saw revenue grow from $4.2 million in 1914, when he took over, to the peak of $16 million in 1920. The price of this, however, was a precarious cash position and when in 1921 sales fell to $10.6 million he faced a cashflow crisis. Once again CTR was to be funded, indeed rescued, by Guaranty Trust. Watson was forced to cut costs across the board, including research and development (R & D). He never again allowed his cash position to fall so low. He subsequently maintained a policy of low dividends, high revenues and careful cost controls. He adopted the very conservative accounting principles that still hold true (no matter how many "gambles" IBM has undertaken since). He deliberately lagged on the introduction of new products (but not on research), even after competitors launched he still waited until the market was ripe for large scale development—again a feature that is still at the heart of IBM's new product policies.

International Business Machines

In 1924 Fairchild died and Watson at long last came out of the shadows to create the company in his own image. Almost the first prophetic move he made was to rename it International Business Machines, IBM. This was a name he had already given in 1917 to the Canadian subsidiary (and later to CTR's South American operations). It was prophetic because at that time CTR was only barely international, and was just on the fringes of "business machines"; a concept that didn't emerge fully until the 1960s.

He also celebrated his new status with the first Quarter Century Club. Even though CTR had only been going for 13 years, he based qualification on the earlier constituent companies. Personnel management was clearly the basis of the business.

The punched card

Over the next decade and a half, to the outbreak of World War II, IBM's business increasingly became that of tabulating. The essence of it was the punched card. The equipment in a typical customer installation comprised a number of punches to record the data (and some verifiers, similar to punches, to check the data by keying it a second time), a sorter to sort the cards into the chosen sequence, and an accounting machine; a printer with some basic arithmetical functions added. The essence though was the punched card, and it was from this humble commodity, ordered by the millions, that IBM's profits largely derived. The customers were typically large businesses, and IBM tailor-made each system to their specific requirements; a process that was to continue, for the largest part (in revenue terms) of IBM's business, until this day.

Throughout the Depression of the 1930s IBM was one of the few employers to maintain full employment; and it is still its proudest claim that it has not made anyone compulsorily redundant in half a century. This was partly because it was in an industry that was less affected by the Depression; the statistics of the unemployed required as much government processing, indeed rather more, than those for the employed. A commitment to full employment was, as described earlier, a central tenet of Watson's management; perhaps reflecting his own experiences. This was most dramatically evidenced by his building for stock for a period; to be dramatically rescued by unexpected government business that only IBM could supply. This was described in his son's book thus ". . . during the Great Depression . . . rather than resort to mass factory layoffs, IBM produced parts for inventory and stored them. It was a gamble that took nerve. . . . Happily the risk paid off in 1935. . . ." This has sometimes been ascribed by unkind critics to a simple error in forecasting, but that ignores the basic philosophies of IBM; and it would have required a quite deliberate decision to override IBM's very carefully controlled, and conservative, accounting practices.

He never lost his respect for even the humblest members of his work force, and in turn this earned him their trust. Even half a century later the veterans at the Poughkeepsie plant fondly remembered his tours of inspection. As the "royal" entourage swept through the factory Watson would almost invariably sneak away unnoticed, to be discovered, as the alarm spread some time later, sitting with one of the older workers. As likely as not he would be sharing his sandwiches, and certainly listening to his views; which kept Watson abreast of what was truly happening in IBM! Certainly as a lifelong Democrat he was an ardent supporter of Roosevelt (as his sons were later of Kennedy). This support did not, however, stop the US Supreme Court, in 1936, from upholding the judgement that IBM, together with Remington, should cease its practice of requiring its customers to buy their cards from it alone. In the event it made little difference because IBM was the only effective supplier to the market; and profits continued undiminished. His membership of the Democratic party did not, incidentally, stop him from later playing a large part in Eisenhower's presidential progress. In particular Watson arranged for him to be granted the presidency of Columbia University, which became his powerbase in the run up to the presidency.

During World War II mobile IBM punched card units followed the front-line controlling the logistics of supply; in the process exposing a new generation of users to the benefits of data processing. In any case IBM's business, in common with that of many other manufacturers, grew substantially on the back of the increased economic activity generated by the war effort. From a revenue of $34.8 million in 1939, sales climbed to a high of $143.3 million in 1944, before falling off slightly at the end of the war.

Early design

Towards the end of the war the research arms of the services started to develop requirements for the first true computers; the nuclear weapons industry perhaps being the most significant potential customer (the Bletchley Park code-breaking work in England was very much a side event; though it did produce Alan Turing as one of the great theoreticians of computing). IBM's contribution was the Mark I, an electro-mechanical monster 51 feet long by eight feet high! It cost $1 million and was installed at Harvard.

The real action was, however, elsewhere at the University of Pennsylvania where the ENIAC team were developing the first electronic computer.

Even with this example IBM did not really get into computing in its modern forrn. It built a further electro-mechanical marvel, the Mark II, which it grandly installed in its headquarters. Even in 1949, despite Watson's alarm at the progress shown by the UNIVAC (which had emerged from the ENIAC project), IBM was only just starting to design its first family of true electronic computers, the 701. At that stage it was probably at least two years behind UNIVAC.

Conclusion

Thus ended a decade and an era, for control of the future of IBM then moved to Watson's sons. With sales of $214.9 million in 1950, IBM was already one of the giants to watch.

It was an era spanning three and a half decades, in which IBM had aggressively pursued the technology of the punched card, and largely ignored the computer. It was an era, though, in which the sales organization which is the real source of IBM's muscle-power was built. It was also a period in which the ethics and philosophies which ultimately distinguish IBM from most other companies, were established and developed. Indeed an article in *Fortune*, during 1940, retrospectively described the young T. J. Watson as having the appearance and behaviour of a ". . . somewhat puzzled divinity student"! It went on to quote almost religious fervour by IBM senior executives, including one who said: "Mr. Watson gave me something I lacked—the vision and foresight to carry on in the business, which from that day forward I have never had any thought of leaving." The reporter also singled out for comment the widespread display of the THINK slogan; comparing it with the roadside crucifixes in some Catholic countries! The products may not have been there, but the structure of the modern IBM was already in place.

Perhaps surprisingly, in view of the miracles of growth now routinely expected of IBM, apart from the war years the rate of growth was relatively slow. Revenue only increased by a quarter in the 11 years from 1920 ($16 million) to 1931 ($20.3 million); admittedly after a very fast start (which showed in the 1921 fall back to $10.6 million). Similarly in the six years from 1931 to 1937 ($31.7 million), when the company was relatively successful despite the Depression, sales only increased by a half. Even in the six years immediately post war, 1944 ($143.3 million) to 1950 ($214.9 million), when IBM built its solid reputation, sales also only increased by a half. One should not, however, underrate the very solid achievements of these periods, typically averaging around seven percent growth per annum, which although apparently unimpressive against those of the modern IBM were still significantly ahead of most other companies (indeed for any company to have even held its sales levels through the 1930s was seen to be near miraculous).

The biggest sales increase, by more than four times, came in the war years from 1939 ($34.8 million) to 1944 ($143.3 million); a better than thirty percent per annum compound growth rate. Once more the fortunes of IBM were paradoxically built on the profits of war; though not literally since the wartime excess profits tax ensured that profits did not grow apace, and indeed at $9.7 million in 1944 they were virtually unchanged from the $9.1 million in 1939 (and thereafter never regained their previous high percentage levels).

If you want to read more deeply into the detailed personal histories of the Watsons during this, and later, periods I would suggest you find a copy of the entertaining, if slightly scurrilous, THINK. For a rather less anecdotal approach I would recommend *IBM: A Colossus in Transition*.

CHAPTER 3

The Sons

Introduction

The second phase of IBM belongs to Thomas J. Watson's sons, Arthur K. and, in particular, Tom Jr. Such "nepotism" is not unique, for many owners of businesses pass on their mantle to the next generation. T. J. Watson was, however, not the owner in the true sense. He was a manager, an employee, with only a very small personal stockholding. Yet such was his personal domination over the company that the succession was seen as a foregone conclusion.

What was particularly surprising was the degree of success that was achieved by the sons, and by Tom Jr. in particular. Conventional business theory, perhaps rather dogmatically, would dismiss nepotism as a means of providing sound management. Indeed it may be that the refusal of the various commentators to recognize the true greatness of Tom Jr.'s contributions (and to dismiss him merely as an inheritor of his father's achievements, and his ideas as impractical nonsense) may owe something to an unwillingness to countenance the idea that (morally repugnant) nepotism can still produce successful managers. Yet the sons, in the case of IBM, showed more vision and courage than any of their more conventionally recruited contemporaries. Under their guidance IBM grew to be a true computer giant; achieving the dominance that it still retains, and looks set to retain for some time to come.

Thomas Watson Jr. was born on 14 January 1914 just before his father was summarily, and so traumatically, dismissed from NCR. Then came two daughters, Jane and Helen, before the younger son, Arthur Kittredge (and rather oddly thereafter known as "Dick"), was born.

Both sons were immersed in IBM from a very early age; Tom Watson Jr. was later to say that IBM was always in his unconscious. He was taken on plant inspections, business tours to Europe and made appearances at the Hundred Per Cent Club, even before he was old enough to attend school. In the home Thomas Sr.'s discipline was erratic, and often harsh and irrational. It is accordingly always possible that a rebellion against these "impositions" in their formative years was one of the factors that influenced both their management styles later at IBM.

Tom Watson Jr.: Domestic

Talking to a reporter in 1974 Tom Watson Jr. described his relationship with his father; "My father and I had terrible fights. . . . He seemed like a blanket that covered everything. I really wanted to beat him but also make him proud of me." But this relationship was not all negative as Tom himself admitted in the same interview; "I really enjoyed the ten years (working) with him." (Katherine Davis Fishman, *The Computer Establishment*, 1981, Harper & Row.) Certainly Tom Jr. was a determinedly mediocre student, despite the fact that in later years he was clearly one of the most intelligent businessmen of his generation. He only scraped into Brown University, clearly showing he was not interested in most of the courses while there. He was instead the young playboy (though that was the traditional employment for his equally wealthy contemporaries). Inevitably he joined IBM, and just as inevitably he was an outstanding success. He immediately became class president at IBM trainee school; though I cannot conceive of any trainee, in the climate of that period, even considering voting for anyone else! He achieved this position despite the fact that he drank openly (a fault that would have resulted in a severe admonition, if not even instant dismissal, for others). Indeed he reportedly had a drink "problem" which was not fully resolved until the end of his wartime service. His younger brother, Dick, had such a problem throughout his life. No doubt amateur psychologists would read into these problems a reflection of their strict upbringing; but any such problems as did exist were not of importance in the context of their enormous contributions to IBM.

Both sons served in the forces during World War II, Dick (dropping out of Yale) as a major in Ordnance and Tom Jr. as a pilot, a lieutenant colonel chauffering top brass around the USSR. Tom Jr. later admitted to journalists that the one career he really would have liked to follow was that of an airline pilot; running IBM, which was then already a future mapped out for him, came a poor second best! After the war, Dick (at the insistence of his father) returned to Yale to study languages, recording a better academic performance than his brother. Tom Jr. in the meantime began his training, his grooming for stardom, in IBM.

This training programme was to take him, over the next five years, through many of IBM's operating groups. Tom Jr. himself believed that of all the influences on him during this period the most important was Al Williams, a chartered accountant (CPA) who became president of IBM in 1961; it was Al Williams who said of IBM: "It is not bigness we seek, it is greatness. Bigness is imposing. Greatness is enduring." (Fishman op. cit.)

Institutionalized nepotism

It is an unrecorded benefit of nepotism at its most productive, that training can be given in far greater depth and for a much longer period (even sometimes at the expense of the job the individual is supposedly currently undertaking) than is usually possible for the less privileged manager, fighting his way up the management pyramid. It is, perhaps surprisingly, a feature retained by IBM *since* the Watsons. Their successors in the process (as the potential crown princes), now young managers chosen for their ability not for their family connections, are identified very early (typically when they reach the level of branch manager) and then spend perhaps a decade or more being subjected to the same extended training for royal succession that was accorded to the young Watsons. This has the immense benefit that no matter how poor the initial choice (and it is difficult in IBM to find *anyone* who is less than very capable), the subsequent training is almost bound to create a top level executive who is head and shoulders above his contemporaries in other companies. Perhaps only IBM has, in this way, managed to institutionalize nepotism successfully, finding strengths in the most unlikely of situations.

New initiatives

Tom Watson Jr.'s influence was first felt in IBM's move to computing. Although his father fully recognized the importance of the emerging computers and had already started the experimental 701 programme, it was Tom Jr. who initiated the crash programme to develop this into the 702 version as a true commercial computer. This was a courageous decision, requiring a substantial investment (the first of a number of such investments that have been needed as IBM computer generation succeeded generation). For the first time in three decades retained profits would not suffice. IBM would have to sell bonds, placing the company deeper in debt than ever before. This was at a time when the market for computers was anything but obvious; and some observers thought it would be limited to a handful for use by government (no-one else would surely be able to afford them or to find a suitable use for them!).

Behind this decision was another one, that of spending more on R & D. Al Williams had pointed out to Tom Jr. that IBM was only spending three percent on R & D when other high technology companies were spending between six and nine percent. Tom Jr. learnt the lesson, and ever since IBM has consistently spent nine percent. This is, in fact, still a relatively high level of R & D. It compares with the typical average for the top 20 US companies of around four percent (3.7 percent in 1983—the equivalent figure for Japan being 5.1 percent, though its high technology companies exceed even the IBM level—with the 1983 spending for Canon being 14.6 percent and that for NEC being 13 percent).

Although the initiative—and as such much of the credit for the birth of the information revolution—must go to Tom Jr., a considerable courage was also displayed by his then ageing father who, despite his long commitment to internal funding, backed his son to the hilt, reportedly with the words: "It is harder to keep a business great than it is to build it." (Robert Sobel, *IBM: Colossus in Transition*, 1981, Truman Talley Books.) Tom Jr.'s position was regularized when he was made president in 1952, but the justification for his earlier decision did not come until 1954 when the first orders for the 702 were canvassed; and ultimately in 1956 when after the launch of the more powerful 705 (which, again on Tom Jr.'s initiative, was developed in parallel with the 701/702) IBM regained the technological imperative from UNIVAC, and also regained its position as market leader in sales. His decision was justified: in the longer term it redirected IBM to its present day position dominating the computer market. Even in the short term it paid off, for revenues more than tripled in six years, from $214.9 million in 1950 to $734.3 million in 1956. This dramatic rate of growth almost matched the wartime years; a better than 30 per cent compound growth rate that Tom Jr. more or less maintained for the full 20 years of his leadership of IBM. It was a record that few business leaders can have matched, and outshone even that of his illustrious father.

Right through to 1955, despite the presence of his son, Thomas Sr. still kept a firm grip on the reins. Then Tom Jr. took over control in a moment that, according to some reports, might have been worthy of a Hollywood epic. The occasion was the decision to sign the consent decree which was offered by the government after its latest investigation. Thomas Sr. resisted, for as a matter of principle he had never signed a consent decree; even when the alternative, in 1914, was possibly a jail sentence. His son was more of a pragmatist and saw that the consent decree, which sought to strip IBM of half its card making capacity, was largely irrelevant where the future of the company was already in computers not cards. There was another condition, that IBM had to sell machines outright as well as lease, that was to have repercussions in the late 1960s when leasing companies recognized the financing loophole that it created.

According to the more dramatic version of the story, Tom Jr. having had a row with his father called a cab and left to sign the decree. The other story simply has Thomas Sr. eventually, without the histrionics, agreeing to support his son's recommendations; a story less worthy of newspaper copy, but probably more believable. Both versions, however, agree on the one touch that was worthy of the direction of Orson Welles. While actually in court to sign the decree Tom Jr. received a note, delivered by messenger, from his father. It simply said:

> 100%
> Confidence
> Appreciation
> Admiration
> Love
> Dad

The father had finally handed over to the son in one of the most elegant ways that business has recorded!

Dick Watson: World Trade

In 1949, six years earlier, Thomas Sr. had resolved the dynastic problem of succession by his two sons in a truly imperial style. While the US corporation, even now in the 1980s the backbone of

IBM's business, was to become the personal fiefdom of the elder, the rest of the world, the newly formed World Trade, was to be the property of the younger son, Dick; thus protecting both their positions from sibling rivalry.

It is less easy to see the full impact of Dick's career than it is of his brother's; the person at the centre of the IBM web in Armonk always receives the credit for most of the gains. What is clear, however, is that World Trade grew immensely in stature under Dick Watson, and IBM became a true multinational.

International Time Recording had established an office in Paris as early as 1914. Over the next decades up to World War II, CTR established further offices in a number of countries around the world, though the operations were still typically small in comparison with the US business. The war obviously destroyed this international side of IBM; though some companies proved immensely resistant to destruction. The Hungarian company, for example, survived the Nazi occupation, and indeed the subsequent Communist takeover; still as an independent company which was firmly part of IBM. There is a, probably apocryphal, story of the Watson sons doing the rounds of the Communist bloc in the late 1960s and asking the relevant ministry in Hungary how IBM should do business; only to be told, to their surprise (at least according to the tale), that they should use the local company as normal! Whatever the truth of the story it is certainly true that IBM Hungary is still in existence as one of the handful of capitalist subsidiaries officially operating behind the Iron Curtain.

When I visited it in 1982 it was perhaps not the typical IBM country operation, with offices above a shop and a charming female general manager (definitely a rarity in IBM), but it was according to its staff a fully functioning part of IBM; and certainly the staff were just as enthusiastically full of the IBM culture as any other IBMers. Apparently the IBM culture is so strong that it is even able to assimilate Communist society! It has to be recorded, though, that a general manager in another Communist country had to be bought out of prison by IBM following that country's Communist takeover; their secret police reportedly could not believe that the summary customer engineering records (returned to the USA on punched cards, ready for processing) could be anything other than coded espionage reports!

In the late 1940s the one obvious exception to IBM's worldwide coverage was the UK, together with its Commonwealth. In these areas the British Tabulating Company had an exclusive right to make and sell IBM products. With the arrival of Dick Watson at World Trade in 1949 negotiations were commenced to ensure that the whole (non US) world was its oyster; and IBM eventually started to market for itself in the UK in 1951. The British Tabulating Company went on to become ICL, one of IBM's lesser but not inconsiderable rivals. It too can claim to have been in effect founded by the Watsons, father and son!

Dick Watson's achievement was to weld the disparate companies into a global whole, which was World Trade; to become a genuinely equal partner with US Domestic (IBM's name for its US corporation). That philosophy later came of age with the development of the 360 range of computers, where World Trade shared as an equal; including, for the first time, the R & D. The modern World Trade, which is equal in size to IBM Domestic and just as profitable, is now a fully equal partner. Although subject to Armonk's directions it is to a degree autonomous and has its own manufacturing facilities for each of IBM's products; for the main products it has them in each of its regions.

The potential problem of "insularity" of Armonk management is best illustrated by the story told by a senior (IBM) European executive during the late 1970s. When he and his wife were attending a very impressive and congenial meeting hosted by a number of IBM main board members and their wives, he attempted to return the compliment by inviting one couple to a similar event in Europe. He was astonished to receive the reply from the wife that neither of them even possessed passports! I know that the particular executive involved has since that time travelled the world extensively and is now anything but insular, but the incident highlights the very real achievement of Dick Watson in establishing World Trade as an equal partner within IBM.

The intention, since Dick's arrival, has been that there should be no export of products from US Domestic to the rest of the world. My own experience, confirmed by that of other observers, is that the transfer price for products sourced in the USA, but delivered outside, incorporates a remarkably high mark-up. The other observers see this as the classic capitalist ploy of returning hidden, locally untaxed, profits to the USA. This is not *my* view, because the figures show that such trade is in IBM's terms negligible. My view is that it is precisely the opposite; it is a penalty clause built in to *force* World Trade to build locally.

Although Dick Watson was able to build World Trade in volume terms, he was not able dramatically to increase its true geographical spread; though that was never his stated intention. IBM would boast that it operates in most countries, but its volume business is still really confined to Europe (and even then to the four "major" countries—Germany, France, Italy and the UK) and Japan. Such concentration is inevitable in an industry whose customers have to be highly developed, both in a technical and financial sense. The Third World is not, yet, a significant market for large computers.

The new broom

Research and development

Of the two brothers, however, it was Tom Watson Jr. who, possibly unfairly, was seen to make the most obvious impact on IBM as a whole. One of the greatest of these was his impact on the technology. Prior to his time IBM had been just about the best selling organization in the world, with a reasonable range of products; for Thomas Sr. had always insisted on sound products. Tom Jr., however, created and funded the R & D structure that is essential to modern high technology industry. It was under his supervision that the laboratories were built up, to a point where they now contain a respectable number of Nobel Prize winners; and to the point where the R & D function can now stand on an equal footing with marketing, true to his original objective.

When Tom Jr. started this process in 1949, IBM was reportedly two years behind its main competitor, UNIVAC. Now, in the 1980s, it is arguably up to a decade ahead of anyone else. This is not so obvious to the outside world, because the new products still follow the conservative release pattern started in the 1920s (and pursued very profitably ever since). Only when the market is sufficiently developed, and a launch is financially justifiable, does IBM commit its marketing resources. In the laboratories though, thanks to Tom Jr., they are able to dream the dreams of decades hence; independent and untroubled by the commercial winds blowing elsewhere. It is an ideal environment for an industrial researcher, and highly productive for IBM.

The first sour fruit of this was the STRETCH programme to develop a "supercomputer" a hundred times more powerful than the 704, but still based on the vacuum tube. It failed, at a reported cost of $20 million. Although embarrassing in terms of the rumours that drifted to the outside world (it would not however be the last IBM computer series to be killed), the cost was small in

IBM's terms, and the experience gained was invaluable. One of IBM's strengths is that it really does learn from experience. Most other companies are only too anxious to bury deep their embarrassing mistakes; and never use the invaluable information they have gained. IBM on the other hand makes very good use of these particularly hard earned lessons. I cannot think of a single fiasco—and there have been quite a few in the history of IBM—that has not been used to learn lessons that have later returned a dividend many times over when incorporated in more successful plans and activities. So it was with STRETCH.

The three actual computer ranges that eventually emerged from 1958 onwards comprised the 7070 and 7090 (for large government business), the 1620 (for the scientific community) and the 1401 (for commercial use). Despite the fact that many observers believed that Tom Jr. was frittering away the resources his father had built up, these new ranges were remarkably successful, doubling IBM's sales once more over the six years from 1958 ($1.17 billion) to 1964 ($2.31 billion), maintaining IBM's dramatic growth rate virtually undiminished at approaching 30 per cent compound. The effect was that IBM became independent of outside funding.

Only 18 months after work had started on the 1401, Tom Watson Jr. set the labs to work on what was to become the 360 range of computers. This was perhaps IBM's biggest gamble, and one on a scale that has rarely been equalled by governments, let alone by companies. It was a decision on the part of Tom Watson Jr. that can only be described as truly courageous.

The initial R & D reportedly cost $500 million, but this was merely the tip of the iceberg. The total investment, including six new plants built around the world (with IBM switching from being the world's largest purchaser of electronic components to being the world's largest producer of them!), was estimated to have cost $5 billion over four years. It was indeed the most costly privately financed programme in history; according to Tom Wise it cost more than the Manhattan (atomic bomb) project up to the time of Hiroshima. It eventually absorbed 2,000 programmers, when problems with the "leading edge" software caused the delivery schedule to slip near disastrously. It also added 50,000 to IBM's total work force worldwide.

Most adventurously of all it was incompatible with the preceding ranges of machines; at a time when the Honeywell 200 had been announced as the first plug compatible (that is a machine that simulated, or copied, the 1401), to which the customers' existing programs could be easily transferred. It was the last time IBM could afford the luxury, for by the time of the 370 the customer base was too valuable, and too tightly locked into the technology, for any such risk to be commercially viable.

It is understandable that Bob O. Evans, then head of IBM Federal Systems Division, described it at the time to reporter Tom Wise as: "You bet your company. . . ." He did though add the much less publicized rider ". . . but it was a damn good risk and a lot less risk than it would have been to do anything else, or do nothing at all." (William Rodgers op. cit.) The gamble was of course a success, and made IBM virtually unassailable. The 360 range was announced on 7 April 1964 and the first 360/40 installed (albeit late, but with the production problems resolved) a year later in April 1965.

Although the project was Tom Watson Jr.'s greatest business achievement, as reported outside IBM it was masterminded by his heir apparent, T. V. Learson, with Gene Amdahl (covering technical matters and later to found one of IBM's least welcome rivals), Albert Williams (who had the critical, and unenviable task of keeping Wall Street happy with the massive investment programme), and Dick Watson (handling the production plan). It was later claimed that TVR (as Learson was known) used the predictably impossible task of bringing in the production on schedule to destroy Dick as his competitor (though Dick probably wasn't helped by his reputation for hard drinking and occasionally literally falling down on the job; as he reportedly did at one family dinner at the Hursley Labs).

Organizational structure

Perhaps Tom Watson Jr.'s truly greatest (but largely unrecorded) contribution to IBM was in terms of organizational structure, as had been his father's; for one new range of products, no matter how successful, carries a company for a few years only. This achievement was, however, less widely reported, and even less widely appreciated.

In 1956, in a move that has since become a biannual event, he reorganized IBM on divisional lines, to give a decentralized organization, with five major divisions (in the USA). The new structure comprised:

Field Engineering Division: the most important group selling to (and servicing) commercial customers.

Federal Systems Division: selling to (and servicing) the special requirements of the US government (including, later, major involvement as subcontractors to the NASA space programme).

Systems Manufacturing Division.

Components Manufacturing Division.

Research Division.

In the wings, almost as also-rans, were Electric Typewriter, IBM World Trade, Service Bureau Corporation and Supplies Division; as well as Time Division (which was sold off two years later in 1958).

Tom Jr.'s own comment on the situation was: "We had a superb sales organization but lacked expert management organization in almost everything else." (Sobel op. cit.) He set out to rectify the lack and redirected IBM into an organized bureaucracy capable of absorbing the shocks of change; and indeed eventually designed even to create its own shock waves of change.

The final element of formal organizational change was the isolation of headquarters staff in Armonk, in up-state New York. This was said by him to be in order to be near his family. He lived close by in Connecticut, where taxes were lower; but kept his staff across the border in New York State so, it has been suggested, that IBM would not be seen as similarly evading taxes! Cynics have indeed said it was his fear of nuclear warfare (he was the owner of a fall-out shelter). I suspect that such cynical views miss the point, for (whatever the reason) the physical separation of Armonk has, I believe, contributed to subsequent senior management's ability to survey the world IBM scene more dispassionately; a degree of detachment that it has used to particularly good effect in its strategic planning.

Principles and beliefs

Perhaps his most important organizational contribution was, however, in the area of ideology. He had a very clear moral and ethical sense, just as strong as his father's but more in line with the twentieth century. He extended the IBM practice of protecting its employees. They were already protected and preserved under the philosophy that people were IBM's finest asset. The open door policy originally started by his father was continued, but he introduced a whole series of new programmes that added up to IBM's respect for the individual, which is still at the core of its present day personnel policies; described at some length later in this book. For the first time he directed managers to hire negroes and members of minority groups to every extent possible. He was a liberal, in a liberal era; following the tradition set by his father he promoted the careers of the Kennedys (and as with his father's experience, this still did not protect IBM from the inevitable anti-trust suit).

He was also a disciple of individualism, and this led to the controlled anarchy which is, I believe, at the heart of IBM's continuing success (though I doubt he would have subscribed to the description of anarchy!).

He deliberately set out to destroy the patriarchal worship and evangelizing that was a feature of his father's reign. He had all the IBM song books banned, and indeed destroyed; so that those illicit copies that survived had a rarity value when allowed back in again a decade later! He was even seen wearing a striped shirt; the foundations of the old IBM really were being rocked!

The "Wild Duck"

At the heart of this philosophy was the wild duck. In the 1950s he (or perhaps one of his speech writers) had read a fable in one of Kierkegaard's books (not Ibsen, as reported by a number of writers, but still surely the most unlikely of models for a modern multinational!). In the fable, which is also featured in Tom Watson Jr.'s own book, some villagers took pity on wild ducks flying south and fed them with corn. Unfortunately those that became tame and depended on the corn didn't continue south and died in the winter; only those which remained wild were able to continue their flight south. The moral was that it is easy to tame a wild duck, but impossible to return a tame duck to the wild. Tom Jr. genuinely believed in a cult of individualism, and could express real contempt for what he saw as conformity.

Promoting the message of the wild duck at every opportunity he said: "As you stand up and are counted you will first run into the group who equate newness with wrongness. . . . Second you're sure to meet cynics, people who believe anyone who sticks his neck out is a fool. . . . Follow the path of the unsafe independent thinker. . . . Speak your mind and fear less the label of crackpot than the stigma of conformity." (William Rodgers op. cit.) It was heady stuff for any large corporation; and particularly for one of the calibre of IBM.

He took the beliefs sufficiently seriously to incorporate them in 1962 in "Principles and Beliefs" in the McKinsey Foundation Lecture Series, published in 1963 by McGraw Hill under the title *A Business and its Beliefs: the Ideas that Helped Build IBM.*

In it he said that he believed a corporation like IBM ". . . owes its resiliency not to its form of organization or administrative skills, but to the power of what we call beliefs and the appeal these beliefs have for its people. . . . In other words the basic philosophy, spirit and drive of an organization have far more to do with its relative achievements than do technological or economic resources, organizational structure, innovation and timing. . . . IBM is still very much the company it has always been and what we intend it always shall be. For while everything else has altered, our beliefs remain unchanged."

Such philosophical, indeed near religious, thoughts were seen by most IBM watchers as hypocritical nonsense. William Rodgers in THINK, for example, dismisses them as "While Tom railed against conformity IBM enforced, it was a clear example of an intellectual, or perhaps emotional, disposition to honour what corporate policy stifled." An old colleague of Tom Jr. was found who said: "Tom doesn't believe it; he probably just wishes it was true. Life would be simpler and better that way. And who wouldn't like that?"

Undoubtedly there was an element of hope outstripping experience in his pronouncements. Equally, I imagine, a number of the more die-hard managers merely paid lipservice to the new climate, but otherwise continued to enforce conformity in their ranks.

But ultimately, I believe, the cynics were wrong to dismiss all the evidence offered by Tom Jr.'s many pronouncements across more than a decade and a half. It was no temporary fad and a prolonged "climate" promoted (and indeed enforced) by as strong a manager as undoubtedly was Tom Watson Jr., over such a long period has to have some significant impact. The evidence in the modern IBM indicates that Tom Jr.'s efforts were not wasted and he succeeded in his ambition. I had already come to the conclusion that near rampant individualism was close to the heart of IBM's recent success long before I rediscovered Tom Jr.'s views in my researches for this book.

Mind you, he was lucky in that the ethical nature of IBM that he promoted, paradoxically, was strongly reinforced by the threats of the US Justice Department!

Anti-trust suits

At the time of the launch of the 360 range IBM was under considerable competitive pressure from the large 6600 computers offered by Control Data. To counter this IBM announced, in August 1964, the 360/91, followed over succeeding months by a number of replacement machines. Only a few of these were ever produced (reportedly only 25 machines; and at a loss of $110 million) and in 1967 IBM stopped selling them.

Control Data, understandably, was less than happy with this spoiling strategy (as they saw it) and claimed these were only "fighting machines" (such as had been used by Watson Sr. at NCR) purely designed to keep Control Data out. It is possible, as I for one believe, that IBM simply outstripped its own capabilities and just couldn't meet its promises; even IBM does not usually contemplate a $110 million loss to fund a fighting machine. The jury is still out, however, for although CDC instituted an anti-trust suit in December 1968 a settlement was reached in 1973.

The history of the CDC anti-trust suit, and the host of copycat suits by other companies that it spawned, is worthy of a book in itself (and indeed there is at least one such book). Ultimately, though, it adds little to one's knowledge of IBM as a whole. Of the literally millions of pages (to be precise 66 million pages and more than 2,500 depositions) that have been archived in the case, those that have been abstracted—apparently almost exclusively by the prosecution in the case—were designed to show IBM in a bad light. More important from the point of view of this book, they were not representative of how IBM normally does business; no matter how reprehensible, or even illegal, each individual item so reported might be considered to be.

The most important impact, though, was that it possibly prompted the US Justice Department in January 1969 (at the very end of Johnson's presidency) to mount its own anti-trust suit. This one was not so easily settled. It consumed the efforts of hundreds of lawyers and probably hundreds of millions of dollars over a decade and a half; until it was eventually withdrawn in January 1982.

Richard Thomas DeLamarter's book (*Big Blue*) provides the best review of material abstracted from that case; though its "prosecution" bias means that it offers a very one-sided picture—in particular, its examples are very carefully selected to support his main thesis (that IBM indulged in "predatory" pricing).

The key effect of this suit, though, was that for a critical decade and a half IBM was under the constant scrutiny of the US government; which was ready to pounce on the slightest transgression, and almost continuously threatened break-up on the lines of Standard Oil earlier in the century. The ethical standards promoted by Tom Jr. might possibly have faded into obscurity under the demands of normal business pressures. Under the scrutiny of the US Justice Department, on the other hand, they became the very backbone of IBM.

Thus, I believe the anti-trust suit, which has usually been portrayed as a threat to IBM, was in perverse reality a critical element in its success; and indeed was essential to the development of the modern company, founded more on philosophies than profits. The paradoxes did not cease with the departure of Thomas J. Watson Sr. It is perhaps not coincidental that IBM's recent results, now that the pressures of "anti-trust" have been removed (and there is no longer a member of the Watson dynasty to oversee its moral values), are worse than in more than half a century. DeLamarter and his colleagues had forecast that, released from the chains of anti-trust, IBM would be unstoppable (even to the extent, such is their thesis, that it would rapidly become a danger to the community at large!). The evidence, so far, is exactly the reverse; and tends to support my own, contrary, views.

One element of philosophy that applies only to Armonk, but is I believe a critical factor of IBM's longevity as a dominant feature in the most volatile of markets, is an acute awareness of its own fallibility. This was derived from the Watsons. Tom Jr., for example, in 1974 revealed to a reporter that: "The secret I learned early on from my father was to run scared and never think I had it made. . . . I never felt I was completely adequate to the job and always ran scared. . . . The fundamental for our (IBM) success was running scared. I've seen us go by companies whose chief executives used to make me shake in awe." (Fishman op. cit.)

Succession

The final act of Tom Jr. was to plan his own succession. After Dick fell from the race, stumbling or pushed, the one contender was T. V. Learson. It appears from contemporary descriptions that, although he was an outstandingly capable man, he was a consummate politician and in his time the upper echelons of Armonk occasionally saw a number of casualties. He did however, like Tom

Jr., recognize the need for a sound team; and Buck Rodgers, for one, believed: ". . . he was tough and demanding, but fair." Thus in 1974, after retirement, he said: "Success is having good men around you," though, perhaps typically, he added: ". . . all these fellows had guts, plain guts. They were willing to risk their job on any decisions." (Fishman op. cit.) It is rumoured that Tom Jr. planned to keep him from the succession by the simple ploy of instituting a compulsory retirement age of 60, whereby TVR would have to retire before him, since TVR was the older.

In the event fate intervened when Tom Jr. suffered a heart attack in 1970. Thus, after all, T. V. Learson assumed the chairmanship in 1971, at the age of 58.

It is clearly not possible for anyone, not even TVR, to create a unique impact on a company like IBM in only one and a half years. He did, however, preside over the introduction of the 370 range. Unlike the 360, though, this could not be revolutionary but, constrained by the investment in the customer base, was merely evolutionary. TVR has been seen by some as a follower rather than a leader, but this is to underestimate his dynamism. As he himself said soon after his retirement, his philosophy was: "We've never stuck with anything—its the excitement, the gamble, move, move, move." (Fishman op. cit.)

His truly revolutionary machine, the Future Series—which would have been initiated in his period of office—unfortunately never saw the light of day. His "epitaph" therefore was the 360 which he masterminded, and which is still at the heart of the "architecture" of modern computers.

For further reading I would suggest *The IBM World* (by Nancy Foy). This contains a detailed account of IBM in the early 1970s, and still gives a reasonable feel for the modern IBM (which has remained relatively unchanged in many of the areas she describes). If you want to balance these more optimistic (the critics would say "sanitised") views, then *Big Blue* by DeLamarter is the best source; but, even though it is the most recent book, much of its material (coming from the anti-trust case) relates to the 1960s and 1970s and it is almost exclusively concerned with IBM's relations with government (and, as such, it is referred to in more depth in Appendix C of this book). Best of all, though, I would recommend that you track down a copy of Tom Watson Jr.'s own book, *A Business and its Beliefs*. This is a definitive statement of his philosophies, and conveys in relatively few pages an excellent feel of the culture that has made IBM great.

CHAPTER 4

The Bureaucrats

Introduction

The most recent phase of IBM's history belongs to the bureaucrats, assuming power from the dynasty. Their first achievement was quite simply to manage that difficult transition successfully, and indeed to make IBM even more successful; though that proud record has recently been dented by the poor results of John Akers' reign. Their second achievement was that of maintaining product leadership by moving IBM and its customers into the era of distributed data processing. Finally, and most critically, the campaign against bureaucracy was successfully extended, and in particular the very successful (if hazardous for most companies) device of continuous change (to deny the bureaucrats a firm foothold) was introduced.

For most of the time this continuing "revolution" was surprisingly guided by two archetypal bureaucrats working together; Frank Cary and John Opel. Frank Cary, especially, was (once more) significantly underrated by the commentators. His style was certainly that of the self-effacing bureaucrat, but the changes he instigated both in terms of product strategies and in terms of the continuing development of management style, were as far-reaching as any of those initiated by his more ostentatious contemporaries. The modern IBM is almost as much his legacy as that of the Watsons.

The new management

The third phase of the IBM story should by rights have been that of bureaucratic consolidation. After more than half a century of idiosyncratic and paternalistic rule the dynasty had been handed over to the bureaucrats.

The chosen inheritors, Frank Cary and John Opel, were both long serving IBMers. They could not match Tom Watson Jr.'s claim to have been immersed in IBM since infancy but both entered IBM via the sales training programme (Cary in 1948 and Opel a year later; both after obtaining MBA degrees). They had spent virtually the whole of their careers in IBM; a large part of which was spent being groomed for stardom. John Opel in particular had an even more rigorous apprenticeship than Tom Jr., having visited almost every area of IBM during his decades long training.

It was Cary who first inherited the mantle of the Watsons. He was seen by the media as very much the IBM bureaucrat. He was for example described by Katherine Davis Fishman in *The Computer Establishment* (1981, Harper and Row) as ". . . a man who would neither squander the inheritance by rash decisions nor let it diminish through excessive caution." His, and John Opel's, image was rather different within IBM. T. V. Learson said of them: "We have a bureaucracy, no question about it, but the fellows who were winning would cut right across it. John Opel goes where the action is, Frank Cary the same. They're tops intellectually" (Fishman op. cit.); and Buck Rodgers described him as: ". . . a master strategist, who at the same time encouraged creative thinking." Certainly Cary did not have the charisma of the Watsons; and indeed deliberately chose to keep a low profile throughout his term of office. His second in command and successor (in 1981), John Opel, had a rather different reputation, that of being a very shrewd operator. A former colleague said of him "John is the most brilliant guy in the business, but with the brilliance comes a little autocracy" (Fishman op. cit.). But he too maintained a remarkably low profile through the Cary era and his own. The most interesting feature, though, was that as far as can be ascertained it was, during the Cary era, a genuine partnership. Indeed a colleague was reported as saying "Learson and Cary both wanted him [Opel] to be president, but John wasn't ready at the time. Cary took over" (Fishman op. cit). Cary ensured that Opel was involved in all the important decisions; a far cry from the strident political battles that reportedly enlivened TVR's days.

The low profile (much as it fooled the media) hid a continuing revolution, rather than a decline into reactionary middle age. Even the absence of personal charisma was part of the new IBM. In much the same way that IBM salesmen are exhorted to sell IBM rather than themselves (the theory being that they will, in any case, soon be moved from the account by one of the frequent changes that afflict IBM, so the customer had better be prepared for this), its very leaders themselves concentrated attention on the corporation rather than their own personalities, and IBM itself became the character in the spotlight.

It is difficult to write about this latest period of IBM. There is, of course, the perennial problem of writing about recent events; that of deciding what trends will still be seen as critical in twenty years' time. This is particularly difficult where this decade's make or break gamble for IBM appears to be only just now at the decision point. I am aware, however, that almost all the previous books have reported a similar situation. It would appear that, despite its unparalleled stability, the story of IBM is a continuing cliffhanger on the lines of the "Perils of Pauline." It is fair to report that IBM has always escaped from whatever predicament it has appeared to be trapped in; and most probably will continue to do so for some time to come. Even its recent woes may well pale in significance, seen from its perspective of two decades hence.

Consolidation

The low profile adopted by the new management has meant that they have been less inclined than the Watsons to go on the public record as to their philosophies. It is true that in any case the media dismissed the Watsons' claims as bogus, but their philosophies were at least overt. In the case of Frank Cary and John Opel, I have been forced much more to read hidden messages into the events, and this is always fraught with hazard. The justification has to be that, whatever their true intent, the philosophies I report are the ones perceived on the ground within IBM, and are the ones that now drive it.

There was clearly, however, a commitment to continue the philosophies of the earlier years. Thus Cary stated to a reporter: "If I were to select one single business procedure that was most important to our success in the early days it would be that we only leased equipment. This put a discipline on the business that was excellent. It motivated IBM people and it built a great relationship of trust between the customer and the company. The customer knew he had leverage." (Fishman op. cit.)

But it certainly was still a period of consolidation. The new IBM had to be run in very different ways; it could no longer be the personal property of one individual. Such consolidation, moving from a dynasty to more normal management, has been the downfall of innumerable other companies. IBM at least started with the advantage that Tom Watson Jr. had felt personally secure enough to develop a *very* strong management team with a clear succession; where other dynasties often can tolerate no potential competition from below and their only succession is thus to poor, unprepared management. Certainly there was a considerable degree of financial security. By the end of 1976, for example, IBM already held around $6 billion in very liquid assets (usually cash), and this made it in its own right (and with its own money!) one of the largest "banks" in the world; and it made, in the process, vast sums playing the newly volatile currency markets (this was soon after the breakdown of the Bretton Woods accords).

IBM was now a mature corporation. Its structure was such that Armonk could distance itself from the rest of the IBM world, confident that the business as usual would be well run, to spend its time planning the future.

There are few senior managements confident or brave enough to take this step.

Expansion

At the start of the era the extended process of unwrapping the various evolutionary developments hidden under the covers of the 370 range was well under way. At the same time the development programme for the Future Series (FS) had just started. This was intended to be just as revolutionary as the 360 had been. It was to be the most open-ended system ever, with flexibility built in that would be able to handle virtually any future developments. It was a brave dream, but it was unfortunately not to be fulfilled. Thanks to Tom Watson Jr.'s investment in R & D talent, the technical capabilities were there but the computing overhead needed to drive such a complex system was just too great for the hardware available then, and in 1975 the project was quietly abandoned.

It was a dream that has haunted IBM ever since. It reappeared, at least in part, in 1977 in the S/38. The architecture under the covers of the S/38 was a dream for the computer buff; almost every aspect of it was totally flexible, "device independent" in the jargon, to the extent that it appeared as if it would even support networked CPUs (something almost unheard of at that time, especially for a relatively small system). But even on the (relatively small) S/38 the problems were still to prove far from simple. The overhead was even more massive than expected, with the main operating system reportedly growing from 12 million to 20 million lines of code during the last few months; and absorbing ever greater numbers of development personnel, until it eventually matched the 2,000 used on the 360. Largely as a result it did not become the range that it was originally planned to be. I still believe, however, that the S/38 is IBM's most advanced machine; particularly now that it is being given the power necessary to run its more advanced features.

On other fronts the machine ranges evolved. The 4300 and 303X/308X series allowed users to move ever deeper into the use of widespread data communications, and the 3090 range looks set to be even more revolutionary when (if ever) all its features have finally been activated. One senses, perhaps mistakenly, that the dream of FS still lives on.

The real machine revolution of the period was outside the CPU, though driven by it. This was the explosive growth of teleprocessing (TP), as it was called at the beginning of the 1970s. Over the period this grew into distributed data processing (DDP) and is now moving on to true networking. It is strange to recall that only a decade and a half ago, at the beginning of the Cary era, most computing still originated with, and revolved around, the humble punched card and its attendant time-consuming processes and heavy costs.

The revolutionary approach which appeared at the beginning of the 1970s was simply based on the concept of allowing users to talk directly with the computer. The user (wherever he was in the world) sat down at his own visual display unit, the now ubiquitous VDU, and entered his own data. This was instantaneously transmitted by wire to the CPU, where the answer was just as quickly transmitted back to appear on his screen, in "real time." This did not merely cut out unnecessary processes and the related costs, but business information was available in minutes, not days as previously; and a whole new industry—the provision of instantaneous management information systems—was born. The punched card had disappeared; I haven't seen one in more than half a decade (where once they were the basis of all important communications in IBM; almost every message was written on the back of a used card!). The large central CPU still, however, did all the processing.

Distributed data processing

The move in the later 1970s was to distributed data processing (DDP), where part of the processing power itself was put closer to the users, often in mini-computers based in their own departments, with the large central computers still running the main databases. In this scenario the user departments did not just communicate with the computer, they actually controlled their own part of it and could determine how it was to be used. In the 1980s this has moved towards its logical conclusion, with processing distributed to the individual who now has his own personal computer sitting on his desk. The near future will see all these elements linked by local area networks (LANs) where the processing will be automatically handled, locally or centrally (without the users needing to worry about this), by the most suitable processor.

It is widely believed that IBM has fought the move to DDP tooth and nail; as a reactionary company rooted in centralized processing this is where it saw its interest lying. It is certainly true that a large part of its revenue, and an even larger proportion of its profits, still come from the big centralized CPUs; and IBM would be foolish in the extreme to ignore these. It is also true that it was possible to perceive a much warmer feeling towards the "PC revolution," at least within "Big Blue" (as outsiders and, alone within IBM, PC Group call the large mainframe part of IBM), when the calculations of management showed that for every one mip (million instructions per second; a measure of processing power) installed as distributed PCs in an organization, a further two mips were needed on the mainframe at the centre (to support the extra demands of communications and databases). It was no longer a zero-sum game; the two sides of IBM were no longer in competition, but were complementary (and indeed showed considerable synergy).

General Systems Division

In terms of Armonk strategy, though, it was Frank Cary's stated prime objective, from the end of the 1960s, to move IBM into DDP and beyond. The first obvious element of this was the creation of the infant General Systems Division (GSD) in 1969, to market smaller (S/3) computers. It has been argued that this division was formed to compete against the then emerging DEC mini-computers.

Indeed this probably was part of its function. It did not in practice keep DEC out of the scientific area, but it did stop it penetrating the commercial area; and in the process GSD in its own right became the second largest computer company in the world (with perhaps a quarter of IBM business, it eventually generated around $10 billion in revenue annually). It has also been argued, perhaps more cynically, that it was a possible sacrificial spin-off, if needed, for the antitrust suit; and the dates of its creation, and indeed dissolution, do parallel those of the suit. Indeed, though it is specifically denied by Buck Rodgers in his book, DeLamarter documents (in *Big Blue*) that IBM *did* offer to sacrifice the group as part of a deal with the US government (which, though, refused the deal).

But the most reliable evidence shows that it was the first step in Armonk's, and Frank Cary's, drive to DDP. Thus in 1971, when many discussions elsewhere revolved around whether it was preferable to use 80 or 96 column cards, Frank Cary stated: "The market will move to remote computing and non-central processing unit equipment will be a continually increasing portion of the business." (Sobel op. cit.)

The policy was consolidated in 1974, after Cary came to power, with an enhanced GSD adding responsibilities for creating new small computers and attempting different approaches to DDP. It was given the quite specific mission to compete with DPD (Data Processing Division—the large mainframe division); healthy rivalry was to be the order of the day.

DDP was not a policy limited to the General Systems Division. DPD was also given the same strategy. In terms of hardware this eventually resulted in the 8100 series of distributed minis (after DPD's first attempt with the rather poorly received 3790 series). Most important of all was that it resulted in SNA (systems network architecture); now increasingly the basis for all IBM data communications, only a decade later is it really coming into its own. This was the concept, the architecture, behind the software which was to allow DDP to become a reality for the larger systems and within which framework all IBM systems, with very few exceptions, now operate. As with most such IBM architectures, it has now become the industry standard.

The new division, GSD, deliberately based on headquarters in Atlanta (away from the mainstream), was however also used as a vehicle for things other than DDP technology. In particular it was used by Cary to stimulate innovation within IBM, and to provide some real competition for DPD; where at that time the outside competition was relatively weak. Its role as gadfly was reinforced by its initial staffing, with a number of leading dissidents from other divisions being deliberately included.

The effect was somewhat diluted a year after the formation of the enlarged division, when in 1975 GSD was included in the larger grouping GBG (General Business Group). This had the best of intentions, increasing its competitive size and muscle power so that it could compete internally with DPD. The dilution, in practice, was because the other piece of GBG was OPD (Office Systems Division): the ailing typewriter division which had been declining for more than a decade, with corresponding problems to divert management. The result of this forced marriage was at best lacking in synergy; but despite this GSD was still successful in its own right.

Change

Cary was clearly aware that a developing bulge of bureaucratic middle age, with a resultant loss of drive in all departments, was probably the major danger facing IBM. Throughout business history it has always been too easy for a successful company, as IBM undoubtedly was, to rest on its laurels; until its market is inevitably taken away from it.

GSD was just one of the gadflies created by Cary and Opel to stimulate a sedentary IBM back into life. The Independent Business Units and similar strategies, also used as stimulants, are the subject of the next chapter. The main weapon, in any case, was change itself. Armonk deliberately set out to institutionalize change. It was under Frank Cary that the process of biannual structural changes started.

"I've been moved"

Thus was another essential ingredient in the success of the modern IBM forged. It already had the strongest of cultural bases, derived from ethics and individualism, of any company. Now to this mix was added the ferment of continuous change, which would stop IBM lapsing into a self-righteous and self-congratulatory arrogance (where it already has a reputation for this, incorrectly as it so happens, with the outside world). The successful introduction of change as a central element of the culture (to the extent that

IBMers, cynically but also in a perverse way proudly, claim that IBM stands for "I've been moved") was perhaps the greatest organizational success of the Cary era. It is difficult to think of any other company that not only accepts change but actively seeks it (so that it is almost addicted to it) for its own sake. In most companies employees dread change (usually feared as a "night of the long knives"). In IBM, as far as I could ascertain, with very few exceptions everyone positively looks forward to it. It is a time for "fun," new experiences, not pain. It has the great defensive virtue for IBM that almost any unexpected development can now be handled, often in a matter of weeks.

This institutionalization of change was perhaps Cary's own greatest legacy. He described it himself, to a reporter in the mid-1970s, as: "Some aspects of bureaucracy are terrible, but some are essential. We have changed the organization every couple of years—changed the approval procedures and so forth. If you leave the structure in place you endanger it. We don't change the organization just to be doing it—we change because our problems change and we need different leverage." (Fishman op. cit.).

At the same time Armonk developed the panoply of non-financial controls that are generally ignored by the management textbooks (since they are normally very blunt instruments) but which, used in a very sophisticated manner, allowed Armonk to steer its newly created bureaucracy.

Competition

Some of the changes during the period were, however, not of IBM's own design. They were forced upon it by outside developments.

The first of these was a thorn in its flesh during the early 1970s; but ultimately did not pose any major threat to its future, and accordingly did not result in any enduring changes within IBM. This was the boom period of the leasing companies. These companies built their business on the principle of purchasing IBM equipment and then leasing it over a longer period, typically seven years, than that used by IBM to calculate its own rental charges (it typically used a four-year pay-back period; though this has now dropped to three years—to persuade customers to purchase outright). The difference allowed the leasing companies to undercut IBM and obtain the business, and at the same time make a substantial profit. The main problem for IBM was the loss of control over its customer base. The leasing companies clearly owed no loyalty to

IBM and would just as happily sell anyone else's equipment; and some of them even started to market their own lines of hardware. The embarrassment for IBM was relatively short-lived (at least in IBM terms), since the leasing companies pursuing the most aggressive pricing policies contained the seeds of their own destruction; for when IBM announced its new range earlier than expected, the financial equation that was the foundation of their business disappeared and their empires crumbled. The moral for them (and also for Lloyds which foolishly underwrote much of their business) was that "borrowing" long and "lending" short can also be a gamble.

The second problem was that of the plug compatible manufacturers. In the 1960s Honeywell had shown the way, but in the 1970s it became IBM's most direct form of competition; on the principle if you can't beat IBM then look just like it (and charge a lower price). The "seven dwarfs" (including UNIVAC, Honeywell, Burroughs, and NCR) of the the 1960s, and the later "mini" vendors such as DEC and Hewlett-Packard, had by then found their own special niches where they were not in direct competition with IBM, but instead offered expertise and products that IBM could not offer profitably; as such they were tolerated, and in some cases even welcomed, by IBM. The plug compatible suppliers, however, took sales directly from where it hurt IBM most. Imitation may be the sincerest form of flattery, but where it cut into sales and profits IBM could not afford to be sanguine about it.

At first the competition was in the area of "peripherals." In particular, companies such as Memorex and Telex challenged IBM's hold on storage (disk, tape and memory). IBM's reaction to shake off these gnats, was simply to let loose its most advanced technology and suck its competitors into a crushing race to produce ever more advanced equipment. It was a race that only IBM could win; which it well knew.

The remaining problem, of plug compatible CPUs, has been found to be much less susceptible to easy solution, and still remains a major threat to IBM's dominance. Paradoxically, the individual who was the catalyst for this was one of those most responsible for the success of the 360. After managing the technical side of the 360, Gene Amdahl eventually left IBM because he was unhappy with the hybrid technology it was using; he wanted to move on immediately to LSI (large scale integration). He then set out to beat IBM at its own game of leading edge CPU technology, and succeeded brilliantly. He chose, however, not to produce a new architecture; but instead to duplicate the 360 architecture he knew so well (having designed large parts of it). The resulting plug compatible CPUs operated just like IBM's except that the hardware inside was more advanced, and cheaper.

Worst of all, from IBM's point of view, was that Amdahl took Fujitsu as his collaborators. In the mid-1970s Japan, under the prodding of its government agency MITI, announced that having destroyed all competition in shipbuilding, automobiles and consumer electronics it had now set its sights on computers. The shock waves ran through IBM. Japan appeared unbeatable, for it had overwhelmed and destroyed the native industries in all the previous markets it had attacked. It was particularly adept at taking existing technology and developing it (and in the process producing it to a higher quality standard and at a lower cost). In association with Amdahl it already had access to technology which was demonstrably in advance of IBM.

The word went out from Armonk in the late 1970s that Japan was its most feared competitor. The message was clear and unambiguous. The other competitors could be tolerated but no mercy should be shown to any Japanese entries. The countries set up organizations under the somewhat confusing initials SSSO (confusing because there was already an SSO organization supporting third parties—but perhaps the confusion was not unwelcome) whose sole function was to provide the muscle for competitive situations where plug compatible (i.e., Japanese) vendors were involved. As always with the modern IBM such activities were spotlessly ethical. The grapevine much appreciated the story of one middle manager (jokingly) suggesting at a key meeting that all competitors and prospects should be given a free copy of the "Camp on Blood Island"; but it knew, as was indeed the case, that the campaigns had to be irreproachable. Nevertheless it was a mark of IBM's seriousness, and thus of its fear, that such campaigns *were* mounted at all.

In the event I believe that IBM probably overreacted. Japan did not succeed, or at least has not yet succeeded; for it is still trying desperately. The computing market was ultimately very different to those where its heavyweight tactics had previously been so successful. In particular it required software support that was largely beyond the capabilities of a Japanese industry cut off behind a bamboo curtain of its own marvellous, but non-Western, calligraphy.

Challenges

It does however show that IBM is anything but complacent. It still runs scared. In some respects IBM welcomed the challenge. The IBM vocabulary no longer contains the word problem. Instead there are challenges; and (in the cynical atmosphere of the grapevine) those problems that are seen as being impossible are relabelled as "insuperable challenges" (or even more cynically as "insuperable opportunities"!). In the case of Japan, though, it was almost as if IBM was looking for a fight, for a challenge, simply to tone up its flabby muscles. Armonk uses many different devices to keep IBM on its toes.

In any case the ultimate outcome is indicated by the terminology. "Plug compatible" indicates that there has in the first place to be a model, a standard, set by a dominant force in the industry; thus the very concept presumes the continuing dominance of IBM.

Even though the Japanese challenge has not been outstandingly successful, the impact on IBM was, and still is, massive. The 3030x was announced at a price that stunned competition; but was *still* matched by Amdahl. Thereafter IBM was to set out its new, and very different, objective of becoming the lowest cost producer; quite simply so that it could not be undercut by Japan. Over the past half decade, therefore,the investments in new plants has put those of the 360 in the shade. Something like $5 to $10 billion per annum (an annual figure equal to the total investment in the S/360) has been invested in this way. Speaking to investment analysts in November 1985, John Akers said: ". . . our investments in research, development and engineering, plant property and equipment—$32 billion over the past five years, an amount we expect to exceed in the next five years" (*Computing,* November 1985). The fruits of this investment have largely still to emerge. The jury is still out on this latest gamble, though even IBM itself already appears to have decided it was a wrong decision. Admitting such, John Akers in 1987 announced a reversal of the policy. However, the strategic momentum, where plants take a number of years to commission, will mean that its effects remain with IBM for several years to come. So will the biggest problem it caused, that of relative inflexibility. In the best part of a decade that has elapsed since the original decision, the market has grown much more volatile—with "product life cycles" reduced to as little as three years (and well below two years in the case of some personal computer products). IBM's massive investment in plants was designed to serve the old, longer, life cycles; and, even with IBM's high calibre of management, it had considerable difficulty matching the speed with which the new "fashions" have emerged.

The biggest casualty, perhaps, was one of IBM's beliefs. "Lowest Cost Producer" was in conflict with "Customer Service"; and this conflict has weakened IBM's responses, particularly in its crucial dealings with its "third parties." The strength of "beliefs" has been, at least for me, as much demonstrated by IBM's problems when it diluted them.

This new found aggression was in part fuelled by the ending, in 1982, of the anti-trust suit (with the US government discreetly throwing in its towel), to be followed in 1984 by the ending of the related suit brought by the EEC. The apparent result was that IBM's actions became more overtly aggressive. It started to talk rather more in the language—then popular in Western political circles—of overt capitalism; competition, and indeed confrontation, were in this language admirable qualities, where for decades they had been carefully avoided.

I believe, though, that this overt flexing of its muscles is an essentially superficial phenomenon. It has, however, gone on for rather longer than I would have expected; and I have a suspicion it could reflect another of the inappropriate "lessons" IBM has tried to take from the Japanese corporations. But it may be one of the devices that Armonk has used, sometimes opportunistically, to maintain its continuing philosophy of change. Underneath the surface the strength of IBM is still its ethics and philosophies. It has always been competitive; competition is a way of life in the IBM sales force which is at the heart of a great deal of IBM's philosophical foundations. The IBM salesman or manager who loses the order is not expected to commit *hara-kiri,* but the loss of face is just as great, just as painful, as it is for his Japanese counterparts. The recent years have simply made this more public. The real IBM is essentially the same (as Tom Watson Jr. claimed) as it always was, and always will be. I hope John Akers believes this too.

Strength

At the beginning of 1985 when John Opel handed over the guardianship to his successor, another bureaucrat in the same mould (John Akers), it began to look as if IBM was a rather sickly child. For the first time in a number of years IBM was facing a drop in earnings. This was all the more unfortunate because the year had started with some very bullish speeches by John Akers. The legacy of these was all the more embarrassing when in the second half of the year, with commendable honesty (which perhaps only a company with the strength and security of IBM could afford), he admitted the unforeseen downturn.

This must be put in the perspective of a product cycle of between five and seven years, on which such low ebbs feature quite regularly. Thus there was a similar low ebb in 1979, and previously in 1969. At each of these the watchers have forecast doom and gloom for IBM only to be confounded by the boom at the beginning of the next cycle.

It has to be recognised, on the other hand, that IBM *is* currently still in the middle of a crisis (at least by its own standards), and this crisis is the worst since the 1920s; there is now no member of the Watson dynasty to lead the company to calmer waters. John Akers' term of office has not so far been a happy one (to the extent that there have been rumours circulating that he might be forced to resign—an unheard of prospect in IBM, and probably an unfair one since so many of his problems were largely inherited). Amazingly, IBM has lost its confidence; IBM salespeople are now at times almost humble, when compared with their previous arrogance. Worse still, its customers have lost confidence in it; in one year (1986) it plummeted from being top of the Fortune list of most admired companies, to languish in seventh place.

As mentioned earlier, I believe many of these problems are the direct result of John Opel's decision in the late 1970s to turn IBM into the lowest cost producer. "Customer Service," which had been IBM's dominant external policy for more than half a century, was the main casualty. IBM had always, at least in later years, talked of "price performance," where "Customer Service" contributed a large element of the "performance." Talking about "price" alone, as the new aggressive IBM of the 1980s was wont to do (where in 1987 even its largest mainframes were being offered at a discount) allowed little or no room for IBM's traditional values.

At the same time it had consigned large parts of its business to third parties, dealers and agents, whose levels of competence and values were almost exactly opposed to those of IBM. They rapidly developed a reputation for high pressure sales techniques and this rubbed off on IBM. Unfortunately, as you will see later, IBM has few of the mass marketing skills that other companies using "third parties" (for example fast moving consumer goods, FMCG, companies selling through supermarkets) use to counter such problems. With such poor quality dealers being the most visible aspect of IBM (where IBM, its "Customer Service" beliefs undermined by considerations of "Lowest Cost Producer," is forced to publicly defend them; despite the fundamentally indefensible, in IBM terms, nature of most of their philosophies!), and IBM itself talking mainly about price, it is not surprising that IBM's image has slipped; both with its customers and with its own staff.

However, I would still argue that, if IBM can retrieve at least some of its old values, its long-term future has never been more secure. It is still in perhaps the most volatile of high-tech industries, and its history does show its performance cycling from boom to recession (though the latter in IBM usually means *only* 10 per cent increase per annum, a rate of growth lesser companies would look forward to as a boom). As suggested above, in large part these cycles follow IBM's own product cycle; IBM is an admirable example, from the business theorists point of view, of a company that really does milk the very last drop of profit from the declining life of a product cycle.

The real strength of IBM, though, lies in the structural factors lying unobserved beneath the surface, and in particular in the culture. The true success of Frank Cary and John Opel was to consolidate an idiosyncratically, "revolutionary" *family* company into a *bureaucracy.* From dynastic domination IBM has now developed into a true bureaucracy, with many of the most positive features predicted by Max Weber. The IBM staff were the ideal analytic and rational actors Weber sought, and the first characteristic he identified (that of a well ordered system of stable and exhaustive rules) was certainly present. On the other hand the other two characteristics (of hierarchical organization and management based on written documentation) were largely missing in practice (even though present in theory). IBM doesn't obey the rules of bureaucracy either, and is still, perversely, successful.

Its particular success, which guarantees its long-term future, is that in becoming a bureaucracy it has lost none of its previous benefits, it is just as efficient and just as flexible as it ever was; and in the process has picked up a few extra strengths. It shows that a bureaucracy can, given the right conditions, actually be an efficient, and indeed innovative (to the point of being near revolutionary) device for management.

Apart from Buck Rodgers' book, *The IBM Way* (which concentrates on the sales management aspects), I can recommend no books about the modern IBM. It is for this reason that the next section describes key aspects of the IBM model in some detail, before I try, in the last section, to draw out some lessons from all these facts.

SECTION 2

The Modern IBM: the "Model"

CHAPTER 5

Independent Business Units

Introduction

In some respects this chapter should be viewed as a continuation of IBM's history, rather than as an important element of the model of the modern IBM. The Independent Business Units are the legacy of John Opel, who used them as an attempt to introduce the "intrapreneurship" (most popularly promoted by Peters and Waterman). In the event they have been largely unsuccessful in this role; though they have contributed to the overall environmemt of "change" within IBM (and have provided the personal computer [PC] which by itself justified the whole programme). Their value, in the context of the model of IBM, is (apart from showing IBM's failings as well as its strengths) to highlight how different is IBM in its management style. In particular, the Biomedical Independent Business Unit (the first, but arguably the least important, of the IBU's) is described in some detail precisely because, being so far removed from IBM's normal business, it best illustrates those unique aspects of IBM's style.

The main reason that I eventually persuaded IBM to close down this IBU was that there appeared to be no simple way that IBM (and probably other companies operating on a similar scale) can avoid the impact of its bureaucracy, no matter how hard it tries to isolate and shield key developing businesses. The problem of the bureaucracy has to be faced squarely, and in the case of developing businesses this means (at least in the case of IBM) they are unlikely to be profitable (when saddled with all the overheads of the bureaucracy) on a gross revenue of less than $100 million per annum; and IBM's organizational and investment strategies now have to take this into account.

This next section of the book describes how IBM is operating in the mid-1980s. It contains many references to earlier, historical, events but the essence is intended to be a description of the model that is the modern mature IBM. Inevitably this represents a snapshot of one period of time, the mid-1980s, and largely of one country, the UK. As such, though, it is (as far as I can ascertain) quite typical of the larger whole (across geographical divisions and through recent time).

Why IBUs?

Through its earlier years IBM was not averse to acquiring other companies; after all it was itself a conglomeration of several companies. For example, in the 1930s it bought Automatic Scale as well as National Scale (despite T. J. Watson's vision of a punched-card future). In the tabulating field it bought the Ticketograph Company and Peirce Accounting Machine. It also bought Ellis, with its Electromatic typewriter to become the basis of its Office Products Division.

This activity ceased, however, before World War II. Nearly four decades later, in the 1970s, all these takeovers had long since been forgotten. IBM had by then concentrated on its main business. In a time of merger mania in the business world as a whole, it (almost alone) had emphasized to outsiders, and in particular to its own staff, that its remarkable growth record was all internally generated. Unlike other organizations showing dramatic growth by acquiring other companies, IBM had achieved its position by virtue of hard work; acquisitions were definitely not in the IBM style. A single-minded concentration on the business in hand was the watchword.

Thus the antics of Frank Cary, and particularly of John Opel, during the late 1970s, were quite shocking to some IBMers; exactly as they were intended to be! After the success of GSD as a gadfly, there was a twofold need: to create further such stimulants, and to explore the new branches of high-tech business that lay outside the main highways that IBM was following.

The vehicle for this new adventuring was (eventually) to be the creation of Independent Business Units (IBUs) away from IBM's normal bureaucracy; to flower as completely new and independent businesses, unadulterated by the rest of IBM. With the one notable exception of the PC, which is the subject of the next chapter, none of these IBUs has yet had any real impact on IBM's overall business, or to any great extent on its organizational structure. Some, such as Biomedical, never will. Their importance in the context of this book is the light they throw on the *normal* workings of IBM.

This chapter then is mainly a diversion into areas that are not of substantial import for IBM in general. All of the IBUs (again with the one notable exception), recent acquisitions and joint ventures could be shut down immediately without making a significant blip on the overall profits curve, and with Wall Street hardly noticing. The justification for this excursion into these little known backwaters is not, therefore, what it reveals about these minnows, but what is revealed (by comparison) about IBM as a whole. For the way that the IBUs, in particular, operate reveals a great deal about how the bureaucratic structure works.

Biomedical Group

I will concentrate on the story of Biomedical Group, partly because this was furthest from IBM's business as usual and hence most clearly illustrates the differences inherent in IBM's normal mode of operation, and partly because its life cycle is already complete. There is one further, personal reason; and that is that this is the part of IBM that I "researched" in most depth. The reason for this was simply that as part of my IBM mission to review the future options for the group, and in the event to recommend its demise, I had to look at its operations more critically than most such IBM operations have ever been examined.

The earliest roots of Biomedical lay in the personal tragedy of one of IBM's development engineers, George Judson. One of his children contracted leukaemia shortly before Judson was due for a sabbatical, funded by IBM, working on a research project of his own choice. The research project he chose was to develop a device (the IBM 2990) which could harvest white cells from donors, to support leukaemia patients—to keep them alive.

IBM is not the first company to run development laboratories where the programmes encompass activities well outside the normal scope. What this illustrates in the case of IBM is the degree to which such a freedom to stray from the main path of IBM's research is not merely tolerated, but actively encouraged. From the time of Tom Watson Jr., IBM has put considerable effort into creating a research environment where even the most idiosyncratic academic could feel comfortable. The price is the many culs-de-sac explored, but the benefit is the enviable record of innovation.

What it also illuminates is the role of particularly strongly motivated individuals in directing IBM into new paths. The route that George Judson chose was perhaps uniquely idiosyncratic; there was simply no justification for IBM following it. Yet even here IBM was swayed by the force of argument, and personality, of an individual (agreeing against all logic to manufacture the resulting blood processing equipment). IBM is not always bureaucratic. Similar examples, in areas of more relevance to the mainstream of IBM's business, can be seen in the decisions stretching from the S/360 through to the PC. It is IBM's achievement that it manages its bureaucracy in such a way that these individuals can still make their contributions. Perhaps the greatest contributor to this is the willingness by senior management to make themselves available to listen to such individuals; in the extreme in the form of the open door programme.

At the same time that the work on the blood products was taking place, in the early 1970s, in another part of IBM yet another scientist was also working outside the normal scope of research; though in this case closer to conventional computing. Ray Bonner was developing one of the first artificial intelligence programs, designed to analyse ECGs (electrocardiographs) to the same standards as a consultant cardiologist.

Thus the origins of Biomedical Group, as with so many more conventional IBM products, lay with individual enthusiasts independently developing products outside IBM's mainstream product plan.

Systems Supplies Division

One of the plants considering the competitive tenders for some of these products was that of Systems Supplies Division (SSD) in Dayton, New Jersey. Not long before, SSD had been at the heart of IBM, for it produced the millions of punched cards that had been IBM's cash cow for more than four decades. In the 1970s business was declining, as IBM's concentration increasingly turned to computing. In Europe the simple response was to shut down the whole business and absorb the personnel elsewhere (though EHQ was to resuscitate it in the 1980s when it realised the business while marginal was still highly profitable). In the US the vice president in charge of SSD, "Van" Hoesen, had a much larger problem (with far more workers to place) and chose an alternative solution. For most of the 1970s he avidly searched for any new business that could be slotted into SSD. So SSD, an otherwise dying division, became a hotbed of innovation.

Searching for these new products Van started a campaign to win the first (2991) product "mission," though SSD did not have any significant history of machine production. One key factor, though, was that the products being tendered for also comprised a substantial element of on-going income from the related supplies. In the case of the blood products the annual supplies income could easily run at a rate approaching the capital value of the machine! It was a situation that was familiar to SSD, brought up on the similar philosophy inherent in the punched card business. Van won the mission, probably due to his enthusiasm; and assisted by the fact that the business was much less attractive to other plants.

It would appear that chance—being in the right place with the right proposition at the right time—aided by the inevitable enthusiasm of Van, eventually (after a number of years of small scale operation) swayed the Central Management Committee (CMC) into expanding this "pilot" operation into the Biomedical Group; though it was not to become the first IBU until later.

Marketing mistakes

One of the first problems that IBM faced (and still faces) in diversifying, was encapsulated in the bundle of Biomedical products. IBM's inventive genius has resulted in the laboratories holding a veritable cornucopia of new product ideas to meet almost any possible requirements; the problem is the dearth of profitable marketing concepts to unite them. In the case of Biomedical Group IBM persuaded itself that there was synergy to be obtained. All three products were, after all, in the medical market.

Unfortunately the (5880) ECG products were marketed to totally different users (cardiologists) from the blood products (whose users were haematologists). There was no synergy at all. Even within the blood products the 2991 and 2997 were, again, bought by different groups of purchasers. In this case the synergy was marginal (even the technology, though employing similar concepts, was not truly shared). Why, you may ask, was this lack of synergy not obvious? The answer is that, as in most companies, the developers (particularly those with abundant enthusiasm) are ultimately the worst people to advise on future prospects for their cherished offspring; the Concorde airliner project in the UK amply demonstrated that.

Elsewhere in IBM the product launch programme is firmly in the hands of marketing staff; who are carefully divorced from the developers, and can consequently have a more dispassionate view of the product prospects. This separation of powers may look an arbitrary aspect of the bureaucracy, but the Biomedical example shows how essential this is.

Product policy

The subsequent development also illustrated the rather unusual processes at work within IBM. There was surprisingly little screening of markets, product concepts or products themselves: one ECG product was tailored, in one critical aspect, to the rather special needs of the one hospital most involved in helping the developers. The process consisted largely of designing and building only one option at a time; no alternatives were apparently investigated in any great depth. This is a variation on the standard IBM development process. The diversity that is normally built into a sophisticated development process is provided in the IBM system by a very different procedure; by having individual products fully developed in separate laboratories in competition with each other. It is not uncommon that only when up to three fully developed contenders are available does the selection process begin. In some cases this process even extends to marketing the competing products; there were no less than three separate products launched as contenders for the PC market. This may appear very wasteful, but if it can be afforded it provides a number of advantages. It allows the developers to concentrate on building the best product, rather than on meeting a compromise specification (such as was the downfall of Ford's Edsel car in the 1950s). It also allows the decision-makers, the marketing men, to choose a working product not just a nice concept; which makes the decision making process much easier. Unfortunately very few companies can afford such an overhead; though the rewards for IBM, in the tens of billions for the PC, make it well worthwhile.

The only danger in such a development process lies in the lower volume, lower value, products, where IBM may not consider it worthwhile funding competing development teams. Then it may experience the worst of both worlds, committing itself to the only product available without the ability to see whether this best meets the market needs. Biomedical was lucky in that the "single" products designed by its engineers were excellent in most of the key respects. The ultimate demise of the group was on other grounds. IBM was even more fortunate that its later PC IBU also developed "single" products that were remarkably successful; since the other runners in the race would have probably been handicapped by their marketing approaches. But the PC as a "single product" surely would have been difficult to better! The price was paid later when the PC Junior failed, and the AT had its widely reported disk problems. IBM PC Group, and Armonk, only then realized the difficulties inherent in single product development and sourcing; where the overall IBM system expected otherwise.

It might seem that, as a result, there is a lack of control in IBM's product policy. This is not the case, as IBM very clearly tracks its products and concentrates its resources on those products which will show economic returns. Drucker specifically identifies a product life cycle that drives IBM. According to him (in *Innovation and Entrepreneurship*, 1985, Heinemann) the development period is five years (though IBM itself has recently suggested that it may now be closer to three years). Thereafter there is a "matching" five year "exploitation" phase (again this may now be somewhat shorter). According to Drucker the product is expected to reach market leadership and profitability within a year. By early in its third year it should have achieved a payback (that is, it should have recovered all the costs incurred in the development phase). The remaining three years are pure profit; and it is IBM's genius for stretching the end of this period, for squeezing out the last ounce of profit, that is reflected in its financial results.

In the same book Drucker rather surprisingly reports that he believes that: "IBM [is] the world's foremost creative imitator" and draws the conclusion that, ". . . it is thus still doubtful that IBM can maintain leadership in the automated office"! I suspect that this is a misreading of IBM's policy (since the time of T. J. Watson) of deliberately lagging its product launches behind the more leading edge technological trailblazers; waiting until the market is ripe for development. In the labs there is generally little evidence of direct imitation, indeed the main problem is the NIH (not invented here) syndrome, which positively discourages them from following such a route (even when it might be the most sensible approach).

Insularity: plus or problem?

The Biomedical engineers, breaking new ground for even IBM, produced products that were innovative and worked well. In keeping with IBM's rather introspective, not to say incestuous, approach they incorporated very little from outside ideas. This was best illustrated by the first ECG machine. When the DHSS experts first opened the covers in the UK they nearly fell over laughing. It simply did not follow any of the design rules that previous ECG manufacturers had learnt over the years. It worked remarkably well as it happened—but it did reinvent the wheel in another shape. It may be due to intellectual arrogance that IBM developers adopt this insular approach, but I suspect it is more a search for intellectual "elegance." This "not invented here" syndrome is predicted, as a form of xenophobia, to be one of the negative properties of Theory Z companies; and IBM, with its very strong (but inward looking) culture and pursuit of excellence, is a very good example.

The balance between the benefits of not being constrained by the precedents of (probably poor) traditional design (based on incremental development), and disadvantages of not learning the possibly valuable lessons of past experience, is probably a fine one. Overall IBM's developments while insular are sound.

This insularity also illustrates another problem which can beset some of the key developments within IBM. In much the same way that developers are isolated from, and indeed not particularly interested in, the outside world, they are uninvolved in developments *within* IBM. As a result development architectures diverge, and products developed in different parts of IBM can be inherently incompatible. This is perhaps most evident in the software products, where it is much more difficult to define common standards, particularly for a product such as VM which is developed outside the mainstream, and then grows (by force of popular demand) to become a strategic product.

Another feature of the search for ultimate intellectual elegance in Biomedical was that the product development cycle was extended far beyond the planned dates. The follow-on products, including the key ECG range, were too late for a group that desperately needed volume selling products. The search for the perfect machine meant that, in at least one case, a whole two years of development was abandoned, to start again on a better concept. Such "wastefulness" was debilitating to a small development team, but is a way of life in the mainstream laboratories. It is an essential element of the ruthlessness that is necessary to allow resources ultimately to be concentrated on the winners; the Josephson junction work in IBM was finally cancelled after more than a decade's work and many million dollars' investment. Few other companies would have the courage, or the resource, to make such a decommitment, and so would pay the higher price (perhaps even of bankruptcy in certain cases) of launching the wrong product simply because it was on the books as a major investment. In the smaller IBM groups, however, resources are simply too scarce to be squandered in this way.

The resulting IBM products were superb, though most of them were never to be appreciated by anyone outside IBM, because they were still in the pipeline and were never launched. This over-engineering is a problem typical of IBM: it is a problem for IBM but not for its customers, who get just about the best engineered products in the world. Sometimes, though not often, it does mean the product really is more expensive (if unnecessarily better). Very occasionally the over-engineering results in the product failing to meet the customer needs; it puts engineering elegance before market requirements. In the early days of GSD the applications (software) packages were in general designed to be so flexible as to be able to be all things to all men; a tremendous feat of software engineering. Unfortunately the subsequent research I undertook showed that the main requirement of the (targeted) unsophisticated customers was in reality no choice. They simply didn't know what to choose, and were looking for someone to tell them what they should have. The competitive (and technically very inferior) software, which could not allow any choices, was thus far preferable!

Manufacturing

In the beginning the Biomedical manufacturing unit was part of the SSD plant in Dayton, New Jersey. There, among the punched cards and diskettes, the first IBM high-tech medical equipment was built! Rather to the surprise of those concerned, production went relatively well throughout the life of Biomedical Group. Despite the lack of experience there were no insurmountable manufacturing problems.

As is usual with a significant proportion of the IBM business, production in practice meant a limited amount of assembly and rather more testing and quality control. The machines were built as far as possible from standard (tried and tested) components. The remainder, which could not be bought off-the-shelf, although designed by IBM, was generally sub-contracted. IBM has a commendable, and highly profitable, philosophy that it should only manufacture something itself when all other possible sources are exhausted. If it can find another company which has the manufacturing capability to at least match the quality and price that it could achieve, then IBM will not manufacture itself (unless its position might be exposed by single sourcing). It should be noted, however, that despite this philosophy it does still manufacture a large amount of its output; an indication as much as anything of just how leading edge is the technology it sells.

Supplier monitoring

The machine manufacturing function, then, is mainly concerned with finding the right suppliers; sometimes internally in the component divisions but often from outside IBM. It then monitors their deliveries, and in particular the quality, to ensure that these meet the production plan. From the supplier's viewpoint there is one major advantage. Being an IBM supplier is the best possible reference of quality and technical expertise for quoting to other customers. The disadvantages are rather more numerous. The main one, apart from having to learn the rather peculiar intricacies of the IBM bureaucracy, is that IBM's quality standards are incredibly tight even for the humblest of components. Its zero-defects philosophy means, in effect, that every component has to be perfect! This can be a nightmare for suppliers, particularly when this special quality has to be provided at normal prices. The fact that IBM has no difficulty in selecting suitable suppliers from the long queues at its door indicates, however, that they must consider the deal worthwhile.

There is one, sometimes unforeseen, problem caused by the enthusiasm to become an IBM supplier. That is the tendency of such new suppliers to quote lower prices, and underestimate the quality problems, in order to obtain the business. This is apparently to IBM's advantage; but only in the short term. In the longer term the suppliers must realize the error of their ways and raise their prices to compensate for the quality problems. IBM then usually has no alternative but to live with these new prices, since they are realistic. Where IBM has experienced buyers and designers these realistic prices are built into the product cost. Where there is less experience, as there was in Biomedical, the initial (falsely) low prices are used for all planning. The result is that the final product is costed, and priced, too low. When the inevitable cost rises feed through these are too large to be passed on in their entirety to customers, so the margins are cut! In the case of Biomedical the effect was most marked in the case of supplies, which should have been the main profit earners (as the punched cards had always been); in practice, after the cost rises, at best they only barely broke even and some even made a loss!

Paradoxically the elements that seemed to cause the most soul searching were those concerned with the simplest "metal bashing." In particular, the frames and covers caused endless design refinements, to cut costs. This always struck me as rather illogical where the essence of high technology lies in what is under the covers. The customers, though, demand high quality even in the covers; they may be unimportant technically but if they are shoddy in any way, that reflects on the quality of the whole machine. The problem is, of course, the relatively short production runs usually involved (the PC and other workstations apart). At the quality standards demanded, even this, "metal bashing" therefore had to be hand craftsmanship of the highest calibre, comparable with that going into a Rolls Royce. As a result it actually represented a significant part of the cost of the machine. So while it is the leading edge electronic engineering that provides the major part of the function, it is the crude mechanical engineering that (together with the basic power supplies) accounts for an unexpectedly large part of the cost! It is an aspect of IBM's product cost, at least on relatively low volume boxes, that is not appreciated even within IBM. It may also explain why IBM eventually chose the "copyright" of its external physical designs as a major element of its attacks on the cheap PC clones flooding in from the Far East; the costs involved in changing the covers are not necessarily negligible.

Space planning

The constant change syndrome, which is so effective elsewhere in IBM, exacted a price in the case of Biomedical manufacturing. In its seven year life the plant was moved no less than three times, admittedly all within a radius of five miles (with the same work force), but still with considerable disruption and associated cost. But the biggest cost was that this ultimately resulted in the decision being taken to move to a building which could cater for all foreseeable future expansion, so that future moves would be unnecessary. This building was of the order of 100,000 sq ft. The cost of leasing and servicing it, was in itself not negligible. The biggest overhead, though, was a variant of that identified by C. Northcote Parkinson, in his observation that work tends to expand to fill the time available; in this case it expanded to fill the space available. It was evident on walking into the building soon after it was occupied that it was already being relatively fully utilized. This was presumably to avoid the perennial IBM problem of being saddled with temporary squatters who turn out to be permanent! The result, though, was something of a bonanza of hiring people and buying equipment; with predictable results. It is at times like this that one appreciates how effective is IBM's normal rule of rationing out space very frugally; Biomedical was very much the exception that proves the rule. IBM staff are always complaining of being cramped (though with little justification because the space standards are very generous and can be reduced significantly before they match the standards of other companies); in general the space plan seems to lag up to two years behind the reality of the numbers of employees. The effect of this rigorous space control is that the tendency for other costs to rise proportionately *has* to be controlled if there is simply nowhere to put the extra people or equipment.

One space planning oddity, which surely only IBM could commit, was to separate its head office (and also ECG development lab) from the plant. This has an admirable pedigree in IBM, and normally generates a number of advantages; it allows a better, less biased perspective and improves security on new products. But for what was, in effect, a small company, this was an unjustifiable overhead and resulted in some loss of top management control (where even the sales operation was based at the plant). The two locations were only some 60 miles apart, but were on opposite sides of New York city (the head office was at Mount Kisco in upstate New York), and the travelling time between the two was of the order of three hours. The head office was, though, conveniently close to Armonk, which may have entered into the original political calculations of the group's general management (there is no evidence that Armonk itself wanted this!).

The sensible decision *was* eventually taken, and the head office was consolidated with all the other functions at Dayton. It was clear, however, that the ECG development staff would *not* relocate, and they were accordingly moved to Poughkeepsie; even further from Dayton! The assumption as to their unwillingness to relocate was correct—when this lab too was eventually moved to Dayton almost all the key personnel transferred to other divisions.

Sales inertia

The marketing side of the operation in the USA looked very much like an SSD branch, with a few elements of marketing staff thrown in. This was not surprising where all its founders originated in SSD sales. In true, and generally commendable, IBM style the management of the new 50 strong sales force was given to the original half-dozen salesmen. This had one major drawback. Their own experience had been exclusively on the 2991. For this product there was, at least in the USA, a defined market with a very closely defined set of selling requirements (which were, surprisingly for a medical market, relatively non-technical). The new management had been locked into this rather rigid environment for half a decade (a very long time indeed in IBM terms). The new markets for the 2997 and ECG machines were very different. They required a great deal of in-depth technical knowledge combined with considerable flexibility in the sales story. In practice this change of style proved very difficult for the new management to handle; particularly at a time when they were also learning how to manage their new sales force. As a result the US organization continued to sell the 2991 in the main; where the rest of the world sold mainly the other products (since these were proved to be the bigger sellers). Thus the traditional base of all IBM operations, its US domestic business, was undermined by a relative failure to develop the newer markets.

This innate conservatism reached extremes in the US Biomedical sales team, although it is also present elsewhere in IBM but is simply not quite so obvious. There is a considerable degree of inertia behind the best sellers; for this is where the sales effort will go, even when different winners start to emerge. This is not unique to IBM, but it is a hidden element of inflexibility where IBM elsewhere justifiably prides itself on its great flexibility.

This build up of new expertise is a problem throughout IBM. In the main business areas, problems are easily overcome since IBM operates a system of in-depth support; with specialists located at each level from branch back to corporate (usually in the plant or laboratory, but sometimes in a special support centre). It has such expertise in vast quantities. The problems come when it moves into new areas, typically with relatively small numbers of personnel. The small units simply cannot afford the overhead of support in great depth by dedicated specialists. At the same time the distributed expertise is not yet there; and retraining to acquire it depends, critically, on the quality of the in-depth support! This was a problem seen, for example, when the S/7 was developed for sensor based systems (typically for in-plant "production engineering" related uses); but was one of IBM's more notable failures. This was not because of the product (which was excellent) but because of IBM's inability to develop the requisite application and user expertise in its marketing force.

This then is part of the explanation of why IBM has been relatively unsuccessful in addressing the smaller markets; and why there are still so many niches where other companies can make a nice living without having to constantly look over their shoulders to see what Big Blue is up to. In any case the Pareto 80:20 rule says that IBM, no matter how greedy it is, shouldn't diffuse its resources by even investigating these smaller markets.

Where IBM *is* sometimes successful in these marginal areas it is usually due to the impact of a small group of enthusiasts, or even one individual. Arguably the PC emerged from such a process. Certainly in the 1970s, IBM UK's very vigorous penetration of the manufacturing marketplace by GSD could be largely laid at the door of one individual (who actually had no personal experience of manufacturing but believed in its potential for IBM with an amazing intensity). He evangelized, promoting and training a whole sales force.

In Biomedical this factor was evidenced by the UK, which became the world leader in the 2997 market, eventually achieving a 90 per cent market share within the UK and perhaps as much as half of IBM's worldwide sales, by becoming the internationally recognized centre of leading edge competence in the new medical science of apheresis; sponsoring its own learned medical journal, international symposia, and medical research which led to major breakthroughs. At the same time a rather differently motivated group of individuals in Germany made that the centre of IBM's ECG expertise. One of the failures of Biomedical Group was its inability to capitalize on these developments and transfer these expertises and enthusiasms between countries (and in particular to the expertise starved USA); something that even Big Blue rarely excels in. IBM is superb at sharing expertise within countries, but this breaks down at the national boundaries; it is the price of maintaining the country identities.

Little America

This leads naturally on to how Biomedical Group handled the problem of organizing the World Trade countries. As the formation of Biomedical Group, and of most of the other IBUs, was US based, the international drive largely bypassed the traditional World Trade organization—and showed a surprising lack of sophistication in the process. Indeed it showed many of the naive failings that accompany the first moves overseas by any new venture. At its crudest it betrayed signs of being based on a remarkably insular "little America" approach; that looked at the map of Europe, saw that it was about the size of Texas and accordingly set up a sales operation based on a single "branch" located in the main town (Paris in this case) with "salesmen" in the local territories (i.e., countries). The relevance of the red lines (showing the national boundaries) was lost in the translation! This insular view eventually reached its most ludicrous extreme when a US despatcher shipped a machine for Germany into Lisbon (where IBM Portugal didn't even market the products) because that was the part of Europe closest to the USA; and the country was expected to send a van to pick it up!

There was, on paper, a perverse logic to the decision. The logistics said that, at least in the initial stages, the individual countries could not profitably provide their own support to the level needed. The chosen solution was to centralize this support on the "branch" in Paris. The structure of this "branch" was, however, in this case set by a World Trade precedent, which was alien to the US concept (which was in any case clearly unworkable). The nearest previous European international equivalent was seen to be the Support Centre; designed in theory to provide very high level technical back-up for all, but in reality supporting the minor countries (with the majors providing their own support, but carrying most of the costs). This precedent was compounded by the appointment as the general manager for Europe (with a reporting line straight back to Biomedical in the USA) of a (very capable) manager who had previously headed up such a Support Centre; albeit the apparently very relevant Medical Industry Centre. The eventual outcome of this was that the European "head office" had as many staff in Paris as there were on the ground in the countries. This is not an abnormal ratio for support staff to salesmen in a branch. Unfortunately, because of country independence (and travel problems), these personnel were not in a position to provide the correct "branch" support. In the absence of this conventional workload they justified their presence, in best Parkinson tradition, by reinforcing the (supposedly minimal) bureaucratic element of the Support Centre role. As a result they actually required bureaucratic support *from* the country personnel; and considerably lengthened the communication processes with the USA. This illustrated a more general problem of IBM regional (international) staffs, be they in EHQ or a Support Centre. Due to their distance, and resulting isolation, from the sharp end in the countries there is a tendency to emphasize the bureaucratic aspects of their role. It may be for this reason that Armonk has recently run down the operations of such centres;

pushing the work back to the countries, where it is more directly accountable.

The only countries that managed to avoid this trap were the UK and Germany where, once more, strong individuals backed by strong (and involved) country management, established their own nationally based operations with (illicit) communications direct with the USA. Their secret, in both cases, was simply tapping into the existing national organizations, and redirecting their resources (a sure recipe for success within IBM). The important role of the informal structures and communication processes that permeate IBM (even between countries), was thus most practically validated. Even so the UK was probably the only country to achieve overall profitability, since profitability was impacted by the costs of supporting the staff in Paris. For example nearly *tuo-thirds* of the UK's marketing costs were accounted for by the Paris group (for although their numbers were equal to the countries, the Paris personnel, on assignment from the countries, were twice as expensive per head). Against this direct cost there was no significant direct contribution to the country's activities. In IBM it is clear that international support cannot be said obviously to benefit the majors (the larger countries) no matter how attractive the theory. Indeed the remaining role for the international centres now recognizes this, since it is clearly directed to support of the smaller, minor countries; which *can* still benefit from this central expertise. Biomedical EHQ staff eventually spent most of their time with the minors, even though their potential levels of sales were questionable.

To a degree this same sort of structural mismatch has bedevilled other such "small" groups. Even the highly successful PC Group was subject to the same bureaucratic overhead. The difference in that case was that the business volumes were so much higher that the overhead was, relative to the revenue generated, easily affordable by the individual countries, which could still afford to dedicate their own resources to cover all their needs. As mentioned above, over the course of time the role of Europe (EHQ) has rapidly declined; IBM is adept at learning the lessons that really matter. This mismatch did, though, highlight just how independent are the national structures within IBM. It is too easy to see IBM as a multinational ruled in all things by Armonk; with the countries merely being its servants. Biomedical showed that the true picture is much more complex. It was very definitely the countries that laid down the law to their national groups, not the centre, even where the operation was so relatively unimportant to them. I was faced, at one international meeting, by a disbelieving general manager of Biomedical (who reported direct to a sub-committee of the CMC at Armonk) when I had to answer one of his "instructions" with the statement that I would do my best to persuade my country management to support his "request"; I knew very well from experience (even if he, attending one of his first such meetings, didn't) that the decision was theirs, not his! This also highlights just how effective and sophisticated is the World Trade organization set up by Dick Watson. It effortlessly coordinates the various national organizations, without ruffling national feelings of independence, but nevertheless keeping the overall integrated transnational structure running like clockwork. It illustrates just how underrated is the bureaucracy in IBM.

Biomedical: what went wrong?

The anomaly of Biomedical's overall structure was brought home to me eventually, during my review of the future options for the group, as a result of a comparison with my previous company, BTR. Shortly before its demise Biomedical had a worldwide turnover of around $30 million, and a work force approaching 500. Prior to joining IBM I myself had run a part of BTR—its Burton on Trent (Polymeric) Group—which coincidentally had been of very much the same size. Although BTR was even then a very sophisticated company, the comparison with IBM could not have shown a greater difference. The structure at BTR was still that which would be recognizable to a manager in almost any other medium-size company or division. It was a structure that was relatively autonomous (indeed the "hands-off" management style developed by BTR head office at that time is believed to have been largely responsible for its subsequent success), with its own separate identity. The structure of communications typically ran back from its periphery to its own centre. Communication with the rest of BTR was, in the main, hierarchically via senior management; and typically through myself. For most of its employees the focus was the narrow confines of the group itself, not BTR overall. The pyramidal organization of the group would be instantly recognizable to most other businesses (manufacturing, engineering, accounts, sales, etc.).

Biomedical Group on the other hand looked most like an IBM branch—or staff department, since the environment is much the same throughout the whole IBM marketing operation. It did *not* have a unique identity, with a clearly definable periphery. It was instead most obviously a part of a larger, relatively uniform organization. Communications did not lead from the periphery to the centre, but covered the group in a matrix, which led outside, at all levels, to connect with company wide systems.

At the end of the 1970s Armonk took the further decision to create Independent Business Units (IBUs) quite specifically to remove the bureaucratic load from the smaller venture operations; the type of approach which was later to be, rather trendily, referred to as the "intrapreneur" approach. In many respects what was asked for was the type of operation that I had already seen BTR successfully implement; though by then I had been steeped in the IBM culture for so long that it took me nearly six years to recognize this! Biomedical Group was chosen as the first of these new IBU experiments in minimal bureaucracy. Despite all the brave intents the IBM culture rapidly reasserted itself at the Armonk "cabinet" office. The result was soon almost exactly the opposite of what was intended. The communications, in a bureaucracy (whatever it was called), inevitably required suitable formalized paperwork. To meet the stipulated new non-bureaucratic procedures a whole raft of new procedures had to be created, and to play safe (because no-one really trusted these new untried procedures) the original procedures were still retained! Thus at a stroke the bureaucratic load had been doubled (not halved, as intended). Previously, key decisions had been approved at the relevant monthly meetings of the CMC. With the change they had to be held for the three-monthly meeting of the special CMC sub-committee; thus trebling the timescales!

Even within the supposedly "untainted" Biomedical Group the bureaucracy in fact predominated. The highly distinctive IBM functions such as Business Practices/Legal and Pricing, prominent in the rest of IBM to keep the various operations in line with Armonk policy (but generally non-existent as separate functions in most other organizations), had their exact counterparts in Biomedical Group. Unfortunately the group was simply not big enough to carry this overhead, either in terms of its direct costs or its indirect time and resource penalties.

This was highlighted for me by two examples. In one case, as the focal point for Biomedical in the UK, I had (at length) followed the many rules for a new product launch, by obtaining the necessary formal sign-offs (very similar to the Japanese ringi process) from all the relevant departments in the UK bureaucracy. I was surprised, therefore, when most of these functions then passed on to me a number of elaborate questionnaires (which they asked me to complete; as they themselves did not have the relevant specialized biomedical expertise). These had been sent to them quite independently by the US Biomedical head office, who wanted to make doubly certain the procedures were followed!

The second example was observed shortly before the group's demise. I counted 13 workers on the production lines (which, in view of the commitment to an assembly-only philosophy, was not unreasonable). At the same time, however, there were up to six people working on pricing decisions that in other companies of similar size would have taken a small part of the time of one senior manager—which clearly *was* abnormal, and financially unjustifiable for an operation of that size.

My interpretation of the comparison with BTR and other companies, was quite simply that the modern IBM cannot easily, if at all, avoid its bureaucratic structure. No matter how hard it wishes otherwise, the structure and the culture are far too strong. The bureaucracy will strike back. The series of IBM senior managers drafted into Biomedical to resolve the problems (and there was a new general manager every two years or so) certainly could not handle it; for they were not in a position even to recognize that the structure should be otherwise (it was, after all, exactly the same structure they had been immersed in previously). Even an outsider (the standard answer in many other companies, but an unthinkable option in view of IBM's internal promotion philosophy), who might perhaps have recognized the anomalies, would have been ineffective because he would still have been unable to cope with IBM's unique communications with the rest of the bureaucracy outside Biomedical Group.

Bureaucratic overheads

I calculated that, as a very approximate rule of thumb, a revenue of $100 million per annum was the minimum required for an IBM group to be able to carry the overheads of the bureaucracy. In the case of PC Group, which quickly followed Biomedical in being formed as an IBU, it was indeed fortunate that within the honeymoon period it easily surpassed the $100 million barrier and became the tremendous success it now is, despite the overheads. This was, in all probability, largely possible because the Armonk bureaucracy fortunately *did* lose control—as John Opel wanted—for a matter of a few crucial months, when it could not initially cope with the new policy directives of no bureaucracy!

It was clear to me that Biomedical Group would not reach this $100 million level before the weight of the bureaucracy pulled it under; so 1 accordingly recommended, for this reason alone, that the group be discontinued. It is to the credit of EHQ (European Headquarters) that, after some initial reservations, senior management there backed this recommendation. But most of all my admiration goes to John Opel who, presented with this recommendation in competition with one from the USA for further investment, took the decision to close down the IBU. This was a brave decision. Biomedical was, after all, the first of his IBUs; launched in a fanfare of publicity. To kill it could be seen as an admission of defeat, just before he was due to retire. It is a measure of his, and Armonk's, maturity that there was no hesitation. It is my observation that the quality and courage (or security) of senior management, is best shown by how it handles its failures. How it handles the closure of such a venture says more than how it copes with success. Armonk passed with flying colours; though such decisions take longer than necessary, as even within the security of IBM there are few management teams willing to present Armonk with such a brutally clear decision as did Biomedical.

The conclusion that can be drawn from this experience is that IBM is locked into its existing business, except where new ventures can rapidly grow past the $100 million limit; not necessarily that onerous a condition for a company with IBM's financial muscle. Survival is, in any case, helped by a recognizable link to the existing business; which makes the mismatch with the bureaucracy that much less severe. Even then the success of the new venture is very dependent upon having a critical mass of enthusiasts who can "manage" the traditional IBM bureaucracy to the new group's advantage. Small inexperienced groups, such as Biomedical Group, might be very successful in relation to other companies in their chosen marketplaces (as indeed Biomedical Group was—it achieved technological and marketing leadership in its field), but within the IBM framework they simply could not be profitable.

Some of the possible difficulties were illustrated by the formation of the Business Development Division, which was the home of the IBUs in the UK. It was also the home for something of a rag-bag of IBM's other ventures, including typewriters and bureau services, which were declining businesses rather than growth potential. For me it was most graphically illustrated at the management "kickoff" meeting. As a succesion of speakers extolled the glowing future for the growth business (the PC in particular), I looked around and noted that less than five per cent of the management present belonged to these new growth groups; 95 per cent were concerned instead with halting the decline in the other, dying, businesses! Since those heady days IBM has, inevitably, reorganized, and the new structure does have rather more direct relevance. The real value of the IBUs, in the context of this book, is the light they shed on how IBM works; they are the exceptions that prove the rule.

Lessons learnt

It is my belief that Armonk did learn a great deal from Biomedical Group and the other IBUs. However, Buck Rodgers, in his book, still reports that: ". . . [IBUs] are not subject to the company's strategic planning and review processes. No five-year plans for them. No rigid rules or inflexible policies. A freewheeling management style is encouraged, and their autonomous boards are free to make decisions beyond what is typically permitted by the company. In short all organizational roadblocks have been eliminated." It is still an attractive theory (as indeed it was in 1980 when it was first spelled out to the staffs of the IBUs), but the reality has turned out to be rather different for IBM. In any case Armonk has not, since the plethora of new IBUs half a decade ago, created any totally new IBUs. It subsequently switched to acquisition of outside ventures, which were not staffed by IBMers and were kept well away from any contamination by the bureaucracy. Rolm, in particular, only has contact at the level of Armonk.

Its drive in the main business has indeed been to return to consolidation, bringing together its previous DPD and GSD components, but splitting them to a more manageable size by "regionalization." Indeed, even PC Group is being to a large extent consolidated within the business as usual organization; recognizing that the bureaucracy cannot be avoided (and hence had best be controlled by IBM's other techniques).

It may possibly have learnt one further lesson. Some months after we promoted the need for a clear product-based organization in Biomedical (prompted by the considerable differences between the separate product lines) Armonk introduced such business area marketing as a key organizational structure in the main Big Blue business. It is tempting to think that it derived some part of this particular lesson from the Biomedical documents that had so recently been through its offices.

The limit on IBM, constraining it to its main markets, is not as problematic as it may appear. It may be a one-product company, but that product (information processing) accounts for nearly two thirds of all business activity! Though the remainder of the IBUs (with 11 operating in the USA at the end of 1983) are apparently not significantly more successful in IBM terms than Biomedical, with of course the exception of PC, there still remains some synergy with IBM's normal business; and there is accordingly no justification for discontinuing them (even if their managements were as brave, or some would say suicidal, as Biomedical's). Indeed a number of them, such as Academic Information Systems, are merely spin-offs from business as usual repackaged in a more convenient and controllable form.

The most similar to Biomedical in many respects is Robotics. It has, however, the virtue, from Armonk's point of view, of completing the CAD/CAM package which covers all aspects of production from initial design (CAD) to shopfloor manufacturing (CAM). In its most sophisticated form the output from the shopfloor computer systems is sent direct to robots. Once more, for very much the same reasons, one of the prime movers was "Van" Hoesen.

Buying insurance

The various communications oriented groups are probably those with significant potential yet to be tapped. They are, in effect, at least part of IBM's answer to AT&T (IBMs major rival). By the late 1970s it had become obvious that the future of information processing lay in two increasingly interlinked and interwoven disciplines: computing and communication. In the USA the latter was dominated by AT&T; though it did not have the advantage of a worldwide strength as does IBM (and this may be AT&T's insuperable weakness). It was forecast then that there would be a battle of the giants, as IBM moved into AT&T territory and vice versa. Certainly a battle of sorts has been joined. AT&T has tried to move into computing, buying into Olivetti for example. Despite the fact that it was the owner of the key operating system—UNIX—which unfortunately was in the public domain, it has as yet been rather unsuccessful.

IBM for its part bought into Satellite Business Systems (SBS). As the fortunes of this have varied, so has the exact form of IBM's holding; and it is currently (in 1986) held as a stake in MCI, still available as a potential vehicle for future developments. The original, and as yet unrealized, intention apparently was that larger customers would install their own dish aerials at their main locations, to pump vast quantities of networked data via IBM's satellites. This break has yet to occur; the main customer for the service remains IBM itself. To reinforce this service IBM has attempted, outside the USA, to go into partnership with the local PTTs (the local telephone operators; mainly government owned). It has had some success, but one notable, apparently politically influenced, failure in the UK. In this context the latest in jargon is VAN (value added network). The idea is that suppliers of these, such as IBM and its partners, do not just supply the "wires" to connect the various pieces of a customer's data network but they go further to "add value"; in the form, for example, of programs for manipulating data or, in particular, information held on databases. To add some weight to these claims IBM's bureau service has now been rolled into this group.

I must admit to being a great supporter of the concept of VANs. I believe that information provision (and not just data processing) will be a boom industry over the next few decades. Unfortunately, this is a view that I, along with other forecasters, have held for half a decade; and the predicted take-off simply has not happened yet (except in the specialist area of financial information services). When, if ever, it does happen, VANs, and IBM's in particular, will at long last fulfill their potential.

In the late 1970s and early 1980s, after its abstinence of nearly half a century, IBM went on a discreet buying spree. Apart from Satellite Business Systems it bought, and sold again, a stake in Discovision, the laser disk system for the home market. It bought instrument companies which it grouped into III (IBM Instruments Inc.); that this was a truly independent operation was evidenced by the fact that it produced its own PC, based on the 68000 chip (which is incompatible with the PC!). At more or less the same time IBM was buying a minority stake in Intel, the supplier of the 8088 chip (and subsequently the 80186, 80286 and 80386) which are the basis for IBM's PC ranges.

Perhaps most significantly of all, after a brief affair with Mitel, it bought Rolm, one of the main suppliers of switchboard equipment to the US market. IBM itself had dallied with such equipment in Europe (in the form of the 2750, 3750 and 1750 computerized exchanges) but never in the USA. Rolm was one of the archetypal successes of the Silicon Valley culture. Its technology in voice communications was already very sophisticated, and it was starting to link this to data transmission as well. In the USA it supplied a terminal device that linked both voice and data into the switchboard; offering a much cheaper form of local area network (LAN). It was apparently the answer to IBM's need for a vehicle to take on AT&T, as well as possibly posing a future threat as a serious contender for the LAN market.

The culture at Rolm is reportedly as strong as that of IBM itself, but markedly different. It apparently subscribes to the Silicon Valley tattered jeans and unkempt beards image; which does not sit easily with that of IBM. Its Silicon Valley headquarters are one of the marvels of the valley, beautifully landscaped with a swimming pool and patios for its fortunate employees to relax on. Perhaps as a result of the mismatch of cultures, or perhaps of lessons learnt from the earlier IBUs, Rolm has been deliberately kept at arm's length, if not even in quarantine. Its contact with IBM is only at the level of the management committee. There is no contact at lower levels; at least not yet. It will be interesting to see how this approach works; certainly it avoids some of the bureaucratic pitfalls of the earlier experiments.

IBM has also set up various joint ventures with groups ranging from Sears Roebuck (to investigate home shopping by terminal), through Merrill Lynch (for financial services in competition with Reuters), to the UK Clearing Banks (to produce an EFPOS, a point of sale and electronic funds transfer system). These are not minnows; the latter for example will employ a team of around 100 developers during its two-year development phase.

It has to be assumed that although none of these many ventures is a minnow (Biomedical with its $30 million revenue was probably the smallest; and was still one of the biggest companies in its sector), their profits (and more likely losses) are petty cash in IBM terms. Where the original motive for creating the IBUs seemed to be to create a new structural dynamism in IBM as a whole, this objective now seems to have been displaced, learning from experience, by the more mundane need to keep a presence in each of the more innovative areas, in case one of these turns out to have significant business potential (and in any case the cost of this insurance is minuscule in IBM terms).

Retail shops

There remains to chronicle just one of IBM's brave new ventures; recognizing the need to find new channels, to market the new higher-volume but lower-price products, IBM's initial attempt was to enter retailing itself. In 1981 it set up the first retail shops. Initially these sold typewriters and supplies, to be followed by the PC. Unfortunately they were never a great success, for reasons discussed in Chapter 10. By the end of 1985 they were in effect discontinued. At least IBM did not make the mistake of some of its competitors and promote these stores heavily, against the interests of its other (third party) channels. As these competitors have found out, just as much as IBM, running your own retail chain is not a guarantee for success; what is guaranteed is that it will alienate your third parties, who may in protest cease stocking your product.

As always, though, IBM learnt a great deal from the lesson. The requirements it later laid on its PC dealers, for example, are clearly derived from its own experiences. It also meant that in negotiating with such prospective dealers it was talking from strength, knowing as much about their business as they did.

In summary, there has been evidence of a great deal of activity in all of these ventures; but generally to little effect, at least as yet, apart from the invaluable lessons learnt; but Rolm, and probably the communications groups, should take off very rapidly in the near future. In any case IBM has already paid for the whole programme many times over, with the stunning success of its PC Group; which is the subject of the next chapter.

CHAPTER 6

The Personal Computer Revolution

Introduction

The personal computer (PC) has been hailed as a triumphal vindication of IBM's management style. Indeed this was true, at least in the short term, but *not* for the reasons normally put forward. For the emergence of the PC was almost pure serendipity, a succession of happy accidents. The genius of IBM management was that it was able to *let* this happen, and build on these fortunate occurrences. IBM has consolidated its position in a new market; and in one that is particularly important, as it will account for up to one-third of IBM's business in 1990 (and after IBM had previously lost the mini market to DEC). The business micro will be the building-block of networking over the next decade, and IBM has established an especially strong product position (already setting the standards that others must follow).

At the same time, the initial unplanned growth of the PC created at least two hostages to fortune. The first of these was the open architecture, which was forced by the urgent timescales, but was also a great contributor to its success (allowing other suppliers to provide the hardware and software IBM could not deliver). It does mean, though, that IBM does not have its usual firm grip on the market. Its competitors can easily create "clones," which are functionally identical; and IBM is even now losing volume sales to such cheaper copies produced in the Far East. This means that IBM must produce new, and more difficult to implement, policies and products, such as the PS/2 range, to counter (and block out) these "parasites."

The second potential problem is that of losing control of its end customers. A key to the success of the PC was the introduction of dealers (third parties) to sell it. IBM enthusiastically embraced these, but in the process failed to recognize that it still needed to control the end-users; but by using the techniques of the mass marketer. It still has finally to learn all these lessons; and is currently suffering the consequences.

In the process IBM built a new group of personnel (largely recruited from outside IBM) with a very different culture, which in addition to the successes made a number of atypical (for IBM) blunders; including that of producing follow-on products that did not as fully live up to their technical promise and, most importantly, that of stimulating a price war that was ultimately to be very damaging to IBM itself. The predictable (and probably correct) Armonk response was to return the group to the fold of the mainline computer organization, where damage control measures are now under way, though with as yet little apparent success.

As has often been the case in the past, IBM probably did not invent the PC (depending upon how you define the process and the product); but in the same way as Japanese companies have developed and expanded other markets, IBM has so far made the PC its own.

Silicon valley

Legend has it that the PC revolution started humbly in a garage in Silicon Valley—are there perhaps biblical undertones in such reverence for the new technology? As with most legends there is a grain of truth, but there is also a great deal of hype. The Santa Clara valley—the Silicon Valley of the myth—had long been the home of leading edge electronics developments; ever since the 1930s when Fred Terman, as Professor of Radio Engineering at Stanford University, started to sponsor high-tech companies in the area. Indeed one of his biggest successes, William Hewlett and David Packard, also started their own company (Hewlett-Packard; HP to the industry) in a garage there, but while Fellows at Stanford (so even theirs was not quite a rags to riches story).

After 1945 a number of other high-tech electronics firms were started in the area, often as breakaways from earlier start-ups. At the same time a number of larger companies brought plants, and in particular development laboratories, to the area. Foremost amongst these was IBM, with no less than four development labs in the area (Menloe Park, Santa Teresa and two in San Jose). The area, as a result, is an ideal nursery for new electronic developments (with the complete infra-structure of suppliers within a few miles" radius), and a significant number of new computer companies have indeed been founded there, including Rolm, IBM's recent acquisition.

It was in this environment, then, that Steve Jobs and Steve Wozniak made the first Apple computer; indeed once more in their own garage, using the proceeds of thc sale of Jobs' car, a humble Volkswagen, for their capital. The original Byte shop ordered the first 50 units, and they were on their way to becoming billionaires.

The key facts that are omitted from the legend are that Apple was still a very small-scale operation until Arras C. Mirrkula, already a millionaire, put in $91,000 himself, persuaded the Bank of America to chip in $250,000 and relieved other venture capitalists of a further $600,000. Thus Apple was bankrolled to the tune of a further $1 million beyond the cash from the sale of the Volkswagen before the main take-off occurred. The message for the budding inventor is, first find your tame venture capitalist, and then start in your garage! The Apple II computer then produced was, as the PC too was later to be, largely assembled from off-the-shelf components. Wozniak's brilliant design used these in new ways, however, and the floppy disk controller, in particular, only required eight ICs (integrated circuits) instead of the 30+ used previously; and allowed disk storage of data, a basic requirement of business computers, to be a practical addition to PC. By the end of the 1970s, Apple had emerged as the leading force in personal computing. It was in the right place at the right time with the right product, just when program developers wanted such a vehicle. Indeed its main strength by then was the literally thousands of programs which had been developed to run on it.

Early PC markets

At the beginning of this chapter I said that IBM *probably* didn't discover the PC. This is not to say that IBM didn't investigate the market; just that initially it was relatively unsuccessful. Ever since the formation of GSD there had been a drive to produce ever smaller machines, to tap ever wider markets, which was then the mission of GSD (a mission that has only recently been passed on to third parties). The first PC launched by IBM was the 5100. Announced in 1975, after the first Altair 8800 but *before* this stimulated Apple and other developers to produce their own machines, it did not have disks (it was based on a tape cartridge for data storage), but it did have almost all the other features of the latest PCs. It had only 64K of RAM (random access memory)—the same as Apple—but it had up to 400K of ROM (read only memory) with a very sophisticated operating system and the ability to run programs in APL language as well as Basic. It was even portable, though at a weight of around 70 lbs this did stretch the imagination (and arms) somewhat.

It was primarily intended for the scientific market, hence the provision of APL (a mathematically based language particularly used by scientists). It was a dramatic flop, since the marketing force in GSD did not give it the resourcing needed (and in any case it no longer had a customer base in the scientific area).

The development team at Rochester rethought, and came out with the 5110; aimed fairly and squarely at GSD's traditional commercial market. It was a 5100 with diskette drives capable of storing up to four megabytes of data on floppy disks. At around $8,000 it was more expensive than modern PCs; but only just so (where the average PC, with its peripherals and software, probably costs around $5,000). Once more though it was a relative failure; but not because of the technology. As the announcement manager (new product manager in non-IBM parlance) I, together with my colleagues, was well aware that the 5110 was unlikely to be a dramatic success, since the marketing resource would be limited to what could be obtained riding on the back of the mainline GSD products, such as the very successful S/34. We recognized that no salesman worth his salt would, or should, consider selling a 5110 when he could spend the same time (in a resource constrained GSD) selling up to 10 times the value of larger computer.

It is arguable therefore that the greatest breakthrough the PC eventually achieved was that of opening up the third parties distribution channel. Until this was available IBM simply could not release the resource necessary to reach the PC market.

The earlier developments contributed nothing to PC Group; though the research and awareness that they promoted certainly did (as early as 1976, the UK, at my prompting, was putting pressure on the US labs for a genuine micro to compete with Commodore and Apple, then just starting out). As explained above it did not use conventional IBM sales channels. It did not even borrow any of the technology. Indeed the Rochester development group were still struggling with their own separate line of development to produce the follow-on to 5110, the S/23 Datamaster, to be sold as before through GSD. In fact this was launched at the same time as the PC, as IBM inevitably hedged its bets! Needless to say, although it was an excellent product technically it disappeared into obscurity.

The birth of the IBM PC

IBM was, therefore, definitely in the business of trying to enter the PC market. Apart from the GSD S/23 entrant there was already another entrant from IBM Instruments Inc. It was inevitable, therefore, that an IBU would also be set up to explore the opportunity; this was after all the heyday of IBUs!

Some time in 1980, therefore, Philip (Don) Estridge was given the "mission" to set up an IBU at Boca Raton; initially supported by just 10 engineers (albeit with proven track records). According to Buck Rodgers they were given the brief: "We want an IBM Personal Computer. We're already late, so you'll have to hurry. Do whatever you feel is necessary to get it done." In a matter of only a few months he and his small team then put together the whole PC operation. Somewhat mysteriously, Peter Drucker claims that four task forces were set up as early as 1977, but there is no evidence that any action was taken before 1980 that directly led to the PC itself.

The birth of the PC has sometimes been presented as a triumphal vindication of the IBM system, a careful implementation of Armonk strategy. The timescale, however, precluded such niceties. To achieve what they did, in months rather than years, they had to bypass almost all of the traditional IBM systems. As explained earlier, the factor that allowed this was probably the temporary hiatus in the Armonk bureaucracy. In this "window" the PC slipped out in a form that otherwise might have been difficult to obtain approval for.

The form of the PC itself, and of its marketing operation, was in part determined by the short timescales and limited resources available, and in part by the trends in technology and in the marketplace, that were already clearly evident. This still left some critical decisions to the team, and to their great credit it is these decisions that made the PC so successful.

The existing trends meant that the PC would almost inevitably use Basic as its main language, and it would at least offer the existing main operating system, CP/M. Its physical layout would follow the individual box approach so successfully adopted by Apple; with a processing unit, a separate monitor and a separate printer. It would in its most minimal form take input from a cassette recorder, but would offer five-and-a-quarter inch floppy disks as an option. The processor (or "system" unit) would be based on a "bus" or "motherboard" approach so that extra cards could be easily added to offer additional facilities (and to allow for unpredictable future developments); and indeed this was the most revolutionary departure, in hardware terms, for IBM. All of these technical requirements were firmly in place in competitive equipment and in established market demand when the PC was designed, and it would have been difficult for IBM to avoid them.

Some of them would, however, not have been so inevitable if the "window" through the bureaucracy had not been open. Thus, the open architecture in particular, would probably have been anathema to more conventional IBM thinking. The use of existing, commercially available, operating systems together with a motherboard, that almost begged to be filled with competitive cards, would surely have rung alarm bells in an IBM busy fighting off plug-compatible suppliers on other fronts.

The timescales and lack of resource also forced a number of decisions on to the team. It had to buy as many components as possible off-the-shelf; from its main processor chip (the Intel 6088) to the printer (a standard Epson, rebadged, which proved somewhat of an embarrassment when Epson later started to sell their next generation, improved printer for less!). It was a period when there was considerable emphasis in the IBUs on subcontracting as much as possible. This was an ideal philosophy for the PC: indeed, without such subcontracting the team would probably still be trying to develop the product. This was particularly true of the decision to subcontract the main operating system software.

The basic product that, according to all the odds, should have emerged from this process is still discernible in some redundant appendages. Thus there is still a socket to plug in a cassette recorder for data storage, and even more obviously the machine "boots up" (i.e., initially loads) the Basic for cassette tape support (the advanced version, Basica, which is now normal, has to be loaded from disk!). At least the "paddle" *games* controllers were on an additional board!

Decision-making

There remained some decisions still open to the management and these made the PC so dramatically successful; though arguably any PC with IBM's full blessing would have been unlikely to be an outright failure (though the PC Junior, of course, was). The first decision, and most obvious in the initial publicity, was the adoption of a 16 bit processor chip. Though not a full 16 bit chip in all respects (unlike the 8086 chip it only had an eight bit address bus), the Intel 8088 was markedly more powerful than its predecessors, such as that used in the Apple II. In particular it could address much larger amounts of main memory; the operating system allowing more than half a megabyte of main memory to be used, as against the previous limit of 64K (or 65,536 bytes of storage). With the benefit of hindsight this was clearly the correct decision, but it was not an obvious one at the time; since the chip was that much more expensive and all the existing programs were written to run within 64K. Indeed the Basic language offered with the machine was still limited to addressing only 64K; and in fact still is! In the event the extra memory was used to great effect by the program developers.

The next main decision was to commission a new operating system, PC DOS. This again was a brave decision when it would initially have no applications software to run on it, and was incompatible with IBM's other offerings. In practice there was a degree of luck in that the expected developers, Digital Research who had developed the industry standard CP/ M, unexpectedly (according to reports in the press) played hard to get and the contract went to Microsoft (and thus made their fortunes). The new operating system offered program developers a better tool; and they accordingly seized on it.

The final decision, of selling through third parties and in particular through PC dealers, was perhaps the most important. Again, though, there probably was no real alternative. It was not an inevitable decision though: PC Group could have been forced into the normal IBM channels, as the S/ 23 team were. It could have been by the route of agents, as IBM is currently attempting, not with outstanding success, on its smaller mainframes.

The decision to use dealers was helped by the fact that even at announcement there was immediate distribution by Sears Roebuck (who would set up a handful of centres) and, most important, by the more than 190 stores of Computerland (whose owner in the process became yet another billionaire!).

Success. . .

As almost everyone knows, the US launch of the basic PC in August 1981, was an outstanding success. On the day of announcement there were already orders for 30,000 PCs from IBM's US employees alone! This meant that around 20 per cent of its own work force took the machine, and in the process began to develop programs and act as trend setters in their local communities. Not that much leading was necessary, for sales far exceeded target and were limited by production capacity for the first 18 months of the product's life; and this was the main reason for the delay in announcing the PC in World Trade, where it was not until 1983 that it finally reached users.

Despite the cassette bias of the basic machine, it is clear that the team also took another (hidden) key decision. This was that the main product would be primarily diskette based and for business use. Prior to that time many PCs were in reality used as home computers, and indeed many IBM PCs in the USA were bought for home use. I have pleasant memories of visiting the home of an IBMer in the Santa Clara valley, and proudly being shown the family's PC which was almost exclusively used to control the "inventory" in their cellar—they were wine buffs as well as PC enthusiasts and saw nothing odd in combining their two hobbies. Despite these idiosyncrasies the PC was placed firmly in the mainstream of business use.

The early days of PC Group were, therefore, spent in dealing with the problems of success. The resulting business process, which was eventually extended to World Trade, was essentially a screening process. At one end the "manufacturers," the technical experts in the software and hardware groups, screened suppliers of products. At the other the "sales management," DAMs (dealer account managers), screened the applicants for dealerships. At both these extremes there was a queue of excellent applicants waiting at the door, and as the volume of business was more or less directly proportional to the number of suppliers and dealers accredited, the most necessary IBM skills were those involved in rapid processing of large quantities of application forms. For a while it was a marketing operation totally unlike anything found elsewhere in IBM. The simultaneous glut of supply and demand was a bonanza for IBM, but it also hid some possible problems which were to emerge in less hectic times.

The hard disk version, the PC XT, was announced in 1983, and was as great a success as the basic PC. Indeed the PC XT has become the workhorse of the business world; normally configured with the maximum 512K of memory, it could hardly be further from a home computer!

. . . and failure

So, for the first two years IBM apparently could not put a foot wrong. Of course, infallibility always begs retribution and the image of the group began to slip with the announcement of the PC Junior. This was conceived as a home computer, which could also be used for work brought home from the (compatible) office PC. This was targeted to be a high volume seller, in Europe as well as the USA. It never met this objective and due to this sales shortfall it was never actually announced in Europe and was eventually, in 1985, withdrawn from the US market; an unusually humiliating experience for IBM. It was not clear why it failed almost as spectacularly as the ordinary PC succeeded, for the specification was not too dissimilar. It did have a relatively poor keyboard (which was eventually replaced), and it was more limited than the PC G. It seems that the marketplace demands *only* the best (the general tendency to configure the PC with 512K of memory, my own included, when this is not used by most programs probably illustrates the drive to have the very "best"). The PC Junior also fell into the black hole that seems to lie between home and business use. IBM failed in its move *down* into this void, and almost everyone else has failed in trying to *upgrade* their home computers into this area.

1983 also saw the US launch of the PC 3270, which is the Big Blue development of the PC. This is the machine inspired by the research showing that for every one mip (million instructions per second, a measure of computing power) purchased by end-users a further two mips would be needed centrally (usually on Big Blue's large mainframes) to support the additional communications and database requirements. The concept is clear in the design of the PC 3270, particularly as it can maintain communications simultaneously with *four* separate mainframes; in the process absorbing mips at a rate that Big Blue salesmen dream about! A further Big Blue development in 1983 was the XT/370. In this case the ubiquitous PC was enhanced with a complete S/360, with most of a mainframe VM operating system, all on one card! It was a technological *tour de force,* but was probably not an indication of things to come. It was instead intended to be a development tool for programmers in mainframe installations, and targets were accordingly modest.

By 1984, PC Group was reaching maturity. Its first announcement of that year, the Portable PC, was however also a failure. It had been beaten to the draw by a start-up company, Compaq, which announced its own portable earlier and better; IBM's later offering had a poorer built-in screen and no hard disk available. The Compaq was sold at virtually the same price as the IBM (and finally at significantly more, as IBM cut price to sell its stocks). It should be noted though that IBM's portable was still a good product, which I can vouch for as this book was written on one (for *aficionados,* I used Displaywrite 2 and a Proprinter). It was only marginally less attractive than the Compaq, yet the market voted firmly for the slightly better machine. Again the market's embarrassing habit of choosing the best product, even if it is so only by a relatively narrow margin, and giving it by far the greatest share of sales was evidenced; as was its willingness to adopt an unwelcome *lèse-majesté* approach to IBM!

IBM recovered its nerve, and its market leadership, in August 1984 (just three years after the launch of the PC G) with the launch of the PC AT. This was the next generation replacement for the XT. It was immediately received to rave reviews as the new advanced standard for PCs. It had a much more powerful 80286 processor chip, which could be used to address in excess of two megabytes of memory and to run up to three terminals. In practice neither of these facilities was extensively used in its first two years of life; it became instead the up-market replacement for the standalone XT (which however still managed to keep most of the business rather than falling away as planned).

Unfortunately, IBM immediately ran into significant production problems with the hard disks. For whatever reasons, and there have been many rumours, the quality was not up to spec and IBM could only ship small quantities for a year; and it is perhaps significant that IBM is now making its own disks. This meant that there was a whole year for the competition, in particular Compaq, to step in with compatible "ATs." IBM thus for the first time lost the overwhelming psychological lead that it had previously had (though it should be noted that it still maintained, and indeed increased, its market share). In addition, the AT has still not fully realized its expected potential, probably due to the hidden snags in its Intel 80286 chip architecture. Thus it is near impossible to switch between "protected" mode where the real power of the 80286 is available (particularly in terms of addressing large amounts of memory and multiple workstations) and the "emulate" mode where the AT looks like its predecessor (the XT with an 8088 chip) and can utilize the vast library of software available on that machine. The result was that the AT effectively became a faster XT;

which was a particularly inviting target for the "clone" suppliers to attack.

At the beginning of 1986 the eagerly awaited PC Convertible (the "lap top" designed simultaneously to replace both the Portable and the PC Junior) was announced, as were upgrades to the XT and AT (both designed to make it more difficult for dealers to pack the boxes with non-IBM cards; and, perhaps more important, the latter promising to start to fulfill its multi-user potential). But it still did not meet the expectations of the market for the much trailed arrival of the PC 2, the next generation expected, and demanded, less than two years after the last!

Another of IBM's failures, which signally failed to sell in volumes (though IBM, possibly hedging its bets, never claimed it was other than a specialist product), is a workstation (ostensibly for CAD, but seen by many IBM watchers as potentially much more ambitious). Despite its low sales, I believe it may still hint of what IBM might be capable of doing in the future. It is the PC RT, or 6150, a full 32-bit RISC (Reduced Instruction Set Computer) processor which although supporting the same sort of open architecture as the ordinary PC is proprietary to IBM (so avoiding the worst problems of open architecture for IBM). It has a 40 bit addressing capability, running a relational database and virtual memory (and reportedly virtual machines); probably unnecessary for stand-alone use, but very powerful for driving networks! It is based on the UNIX operating system (developed by Bell Labs, part of AT&T), but heavily developed to be in effect proprietary again (and called AIX; Advanced Interactive Executive).

In 1987 IBM finally launched its much "trailed" PS/2 (Personal System/2), which is what the PC/2 (after a number of false starts) eventually became. Such was IBM's poor image that, after an initial fanfare of publicity, within a matter of weeks IBM was forced on the defensive over even this major new product range. The main problem (after IBM's almost total inability to understand mass marketing) seemed to be that IBM's development timescales just couldn't match the expectations of an increasingly volatile market (none of the key operating system, OS/2, would be delivered until a year later). In addition, for whatever reason, it couldn't seem to be able to sustain production of the most popular items—though it had started to learn some of its lessons, and was bringing back into its own plants production of most of the critical components, where these had previously been at the mercy of unreliable outside suppliers (who didn't have IBM's resources to throw at problem areas). Still, paradoxically, for a range that was supposed to have been in development for at least two years, the ramp up of PS/2 supplies was clearly below market requirements. Even worse, components for "Token Ring" networks (announced earlier than PS/2, but a critical, complementary element of IBM's network strategy) were out of stock for the best part of a year (even though the best informed commentators believed that sales were below target)!

Unfortunately, IBM chose to initially announce (with much publicity) those elements of the PS/2 range that were directly comparable with previous PC's (again perhaps betraying some unexpected signs of haste); which were overshadowed by existing compatible machines (notably the Compaq 386), which outperformed most of the PS/2 range. IBM did not unveil, at least not with any great fanfare or explanation, the communications aspects of the machines which will make them an integral part of IBM's next step into fully distributed processing. For the PS/2, under the covers, starts to look much more like a full blown mainframe. It can even support distributed processing *within* itself; something that has been an inherent element of Future Series since the 1970s. More important, it is clearly a key building block of IBM's network policies, which look towards the 1990s with all machines being able to talk on an equal basis ("peer to peer"). This will require software of potentially horrendous complexity (comparable with some of the most difficult aspects of SNA), particularly at the mainframe—but not of insignificant proportions at the PC end; and apparently (in an especially significant move) IBM is now undertaking this development itself, where previously it had relied on Microsoft. I believe that technically PS/2 is a major step towards genuinely distributed processing. The trouble was that IBM uncharacteristically fumbled the launch, so that the true importance was not understood by its customers.

Perhaps it was part of a subtle Machiavellian plan to persuade the "clone" manufacturers to go rushing off after the wrong target (and waste considerable effort producing clones of the wrong PS/2), where a few months later IBM would have announced the really new features and wrong-footed the clones (to the extent that many of them would have had to go into liquidation). It is the sort of technique that DeLamarter (in *Big Blue*) claims IBM used against earlier "plug compatible" competition. If so, it was too clever in this case; the gamble failed. The clone-makers mainly decided that the PS/2 was not going to be sufficiently different to be a major runner, and got on with the important business of the clone war.

Unfortunately, their (and IBM's) customers thought exactly the same; and the PS/2 turned into a sideshow to the main event. Everyone was still interested to see how it would turn out; but half the market remained undecided what their long-term policy should be and stopped buying anything (even the PS/2—which should have been, on the basis of previous launches, selling in vast quantities). Even worse, the other half of the market decided that its future lay with cheaper PC clones and redoubled its efforts (and purchases) in this direction! IBM *was* able to claim massive sales; but this was probably, at least in part, as a result of "pipeline filling," with IBM dealers stocking up with a product that they had to stock. This was undoubtedly complicated by the phenomenon of "multiple orders," which now bedevils launches in the PC arena. Dealers now know that they will have difficulty in obtaining early supplies (which will be in great demand), so they over-order spectacularly (so that the "rationed" level that they expect to receive will actually meet *all* their forecast needs). This is complicated even further by the fact that they may, in effect, place the same order with a number of suppliers (say, IBM itself and up to three of its distributors). In this way the booked value of orders may actually show anything between five and ten times what the reality is!

With these trials and tribulations PC Group has had to mature rapidly It could no longer rely on rationing out scarce PCs to the queue of buyers; it had to revert to the thing IBM knows best—selling.

PC Group and Big Blue

PC Group was initially staffed by true enthusiasts; they had to be, because as with all such small groups in IBM it was a Siberia in terms of career development (for traditional management progress is still very much via the large mainframe sales force). The numbers were swelled to a certain extent by a number of draftees, *sent* to Siberia! As soon as it started, though, it was almost entirely staffed at the lower levels by young, and very capable, recruits from outside IBM. Thus, PC Group came to have many of the dynamic characteristics of Big Blue in its earlier, very rapid growth days. It did, however, develop its own special culture. It was, after all, an IBU at a time when John Opel was calling for a new, more aggressive approach; a call essentially made to Big Blue, where its impact (as John Opel would have known) would have been moderated by the culture. PC Group though took it more literally and developed a pride in "shooting from the hip"; in fast decisive management. This was a highly welcome addition to counter the bureaucracy, which the newcomers did not in any case subscribe to, so its power was correspondingly diminished. Unfortunately the fast-draw resulted in a number of accidents where IBM shot itself in the foot; from PC Junior to the AT disk drives.

At the same time Big Blue was becoming more interested. The projections showed between a third and a half of IBM's long-term revenue deriving from third party (largely PC based) sales. But the PC was a single user system, with very limited mainframe communications facilities. Big Blue answered this in part by rushing into its own PC 3270, using an architecture that is unfortunately now out of step with the main PC line (and for once in its life Big Blue finds itself having to follow the line of one of its smaller brethren!). Almost all this business was, however, still outside the control of Big Blue. Although the target was for it to sell more than one-third of total PC volume, using large-volume sales to big customers, this never happened and Big Blue typically achieved only around 10 percent.

One outcome of the PC revolution was the drive for local area networks (LANs). Previously communications, encapsulated in IBM's SNA (systems network architecture) had been largely hierarchically driven, with communications controlled by the central mainframes; and even the move to DDP (distributed data processing on the minis) had not significantly changed this. Suddenly, though, there were many thousands of personal computers on the periphery with a need to talk to each other without the overhead of going through the mainframes. The result was a shift in emphasis to LANs, where local communications are on a peer to peer basis between PCs (using specialized communications controllers) with the mainframes only involved when a PC in one of these small networks wants to talk to another network.

In the rush to meet this latest market, once more PC Group and Big Blue were out of step (though in this case it was Big Blue that probably got it right for the long term). Thus the PC LAN was a limited capacity "collision detect" system, very much like its competitive predecessors, where the Big Blue version was a full high capacity "token ring," which offers the capacity needed in the longer term. To make matters even worse, at first the two LANs couldn't even talk to each other; though a solution to this was provided in 1986.

When it came to delivering the product, though, IBM once more ran into production difficulties—with outside suppliers; apparently not *all* the lessons of single sourcing had been learnt. For the best part of a year supply of the product was rationed. This put a significant dent in IBM's ambitions of establishing it as a defacto standard. Just when IBM's publicity started to persuade the market that networks were the thing of the future, the only products in supply were those of its competitors; and IBM had to watch as numbers of pilot sites were set up, just as it had planned, but with non-IBM equipment (which was definitely not what IBM had planned!). Why there was such a fiasco, on a product that was so strategic for IBM, is not easy to establish (unless it was another casualty of IBM's "least cost" objective).

IBM had found itself (in PC Group) with a new, and very rapidly growing, phenomenon on its hands; and one that showed every symptom of being out of control. The reaction was predictable. PC Group was integrated into the Big Blue business as usual, and its IBU "licence" was withdrawn. Over a couple of years, a large proportion of the management team (from Don Estridge downwards) was replaced by Big Blue appointees. By the end of 1985, at the time of the massive regionalization reorganization, PC Group was firmly entrenched as a division (albeit a disproportionately important one) of Big Blue. Its new management was gradually instilling the traditional IBM values and disciplines.

They were even starting to tighten up the quality of the dealer network. In the USA to enforce this they even used the equivalent of a headcount freeze, IBM's traditional internal answer; they froze the dealer network, not allowing any new additions.

Technical questions

The dramatically rapid growth of the PC has been an outstanding success, but it has left IBM with a number of problems; largely because the pressure of events demanded such fast responses that long-term planning was not always possible.

The first of these is the open architecture, with consequential vulnerability to, and reliance on, outside suppliers. This concept has a great many advantages, ranging from faster market growth (which must be IBM's goal) to competitive position (where IBM as the lowest-cost producer must be well placed). One suspects, though, that had IBM planned the strategy in its usual meticulous manner there would have been a significantly greater degree of IBM control written in. The evidence, from the recent RISC based PC

RT and in particular from the recently announced PS/2 range, is that IBM is gradually attempting to reassert some greater degree of control, and LANs (perhaps built around the new AIX operating system) may be the vehicle for this in the short and medium term; always assuming it can get its own act together! This leads on to the perennially vexed question of IBM operating systems. PC DOS was an excellent piece of software for its time, but was strictly limited in its scope. IBM has now had time to determine the long-term strategy (presumably LAN/communications based) it would wish to pursue, and the chances are that it is largely incompatible with PC DOS. Unfortunately, the success of the PC means that there is already a large base of existing PC DOS users (and in general IBM no longer ventures into the brave S/360 type gambles with totally incompatible machines). IBM must somehow or other bridge this gap. Perhaps the solution will be based on the somewhat shaky and controversial existing industry standard for multi-user micros: UNIX (and the more sophisticated level 5 of this, rather than the level 3 offered by the existing XENIX PC offering). On the other hand, although UNIX is in the public domain it was developed by Bell Labs, as part of AT&T, one of IBM's main competitors. Maybe the solution will be an IBM unique version of this.

Having written the above "specification" in the initial draft for this book, I was obviously very interested in the PC RT announcement. This had an IBM unique version of level 5 UNIX, with a considerable degree of sophistication (complementary to that of UNIX) built into it; and it can run PC DOS, as a virtual PC AT! The announcement was fairly low key, but IBM is never totally predictable.

It is still not yet clear, at the end of 1987, whether OS/2 (Operating System/2) will be capable of handling the "network concentrator" problems, together with all the other limitations posed by PC DOS, all by itself. Its screen handling, database and communications facilities are clearly designed to interface (via networks and on a "peer to peer" basis) with the mainframes. From the other direction, IBM's new commitment to SAA (Systems Application Architecture), which sets standards for applications in the same way that SNA did earlier for operating systems, will help to integrate all these various families of products. But it is interesting that IBM is *still* promising the UNIX based AIX on the upper end PS/2 systems (that is, on the ones powerful enough to run it). There *is* still a gap to be filled.

The price war

A bigger problem is that of the price war. As the market has become less buoyant (largely due to the end of product life cycle insecurity posed by the constant rumours, which started at the beginning of 1985, of imminent availability of PC2), the dealers, who are independent of direct IBM control, started a price war that has helped nobody, least of all IBM. In part this is due to the shake-out of those dealers who couldn't make the grade and who, with liquidity problems, started first to liquidate their stocks. Partly it was due to the more aggressive box shifting attitude of the earlier PC Group management; which did not recognize that end of life promotional discounts would destabilize the market even more. In the main though, it is probably due to IBM's discounting structure, which has price breaks that encourage dealers to sell the last few machines at a heavy discount, so that they can reach the next price break and obtain a better price on *all* their purchases.

It looked on paper as if this should maximize IBM business; loading in stock to create stock pressure on retailers is a standard consumer goods marketing technique. In fact this was true of the system units but not anything else. The end buyers wanted to see the IBM badge on the front; though increasingly retailers persuaded them that Compaq, which was not so heavily discounted in the price war (and hence more profitable to the retailer), was a better box! The retailers, on the other hand, wanted to see everyone else's cards in it, and peripherals attached, since these competitors offered better margins, and the customers were often unaware of the differences. The result was that IBM was shipping a number of relatively empty boxes; a fact which mightily offended it.

Typically, it most recently resolved this problem by giving the PS/2 a proprietary "micro-channel," which will make it difficult for other manufacturers to put their "add-ins" into the machines. In the process, however, this obvious tactical manoeuvre significantly diluted the technical impact of the micro-channel, which is a much more revolutionary device than much of the market yet realises. Its design looks to be a critical element of IBM's strategic networking policy in the 1990s.

IBM has, a number of times, tried to discipline its dealers. But its earnest attempts have generally been hijacked by its marketing people, who have just used them to sell more boxes! For example, "Business Centres" was an admirable idea, whereby dealers were in theory trained to be able to offer good advice to smaller business customers. But, in reality, the concept was used simply (and cynically) to sell IBM printers, which IBM's PC marketers felt were neglected! There have been a number of similar false starts; and IBM has yet to make any significant (or successful) attempts to really wean its dealers away from the suicidal (box shifting) philosophies that are undermining the whole marketplace; and with it IBM's long-term position.

Customer support

Perhaps the worst effect of the price war is that it has shifted the emphasis from quality of support to price. The market research shows that the buyers want high quality support above all else, and are less interested in marginal cost savings. This is an eminently sensible attitude, where a poorly designed and supported system can cost a company many thousands of pounds in extra costs, and the saving even on the highest discounts runs only into hundreds of pounds. This support is justifiably IBM's strength in the other markets it operates in; and the PC market, with its relatively unsophisticated users, is in greater not lesser need of it.

Unfortunately, after visiting a number of PC dealers who stress the importance of discounted prices, and can barely suppress a smile when support is mentioned, the user is, to say the least, confused. It is not surprising that PC dealer salesmen are rapidly ousting used car salesmen as the symbol of poor, blatantly dishonest, salesmanship. It could not be further from the traditional IBM style of salesmanship! This is bad for the image of the PC industry, and it costs customers millions of dollars in wasted assets. Worst, from IBM's point of view, it stunts the growth of the whole market, which is based largely on word of mouth recommendation; and if all the customer's grapevine has to report is a trail of disaster, who can blame buyers from holding back?

This is not necessary. It is a wound self inflicted by the dealers. Those "respectable" dealers that I have talked to have stressed that they are desperately aware that their customers need the support, and the lack of this is holding sales back. Despite this, they continue to discount on larger orders—they would claim by necessity—and the support cannot be offered. The less reputable box shifters stagger from discount to ever larger discount, and closer to bankruptcy; but they have nothing else to offer. It is definitely *not* the IBM style! Perhaps the greatest damage that has been done to IBM is that it has legitimized "cheap" machines. This in turn has let in large numbers of "PC clones," virtually identical copies of IBM hardware (though sometimes of questionable quality and copyright), to the major markets. IBM has recently lost a significant share of the PC business to these clones, typically produced in Taiwan and Korea (not Japan as IBM originally feared) by very low-priced labour, selling at perhaps half of IBM's price. If, as the price war has apparently demonstrated, price is all that matters, then such clones are just as legitimate as the IBM originals.

Low price is a simplistic story (for there are many more factors involved), but IBM will not find it easy to counter. On the other hand, there is some indication that IBM is trying to bring its unruly infants back into line with the more normal IBM philosophies. All those in the industry, and its customers, must hope it persists and succeeds.

At least, despite its outstanding problems with outside suppliers, PC Group has at long last got its production act together. It now has some of the most automated plants in the world supplying it with the highest (zero-defect) products, and the previous supply problems may eventually be a thing of the past.

Product cost

However, it does still have a potential profit (margin) problem, which was there even before the savage price cuts forced by the competition from the clones. It has had a great success in volume terms, but its own internal PC margins are undoubtedly less than the rest of the business. They may be as low as half those in the other groups (perhaps as low as 30 per cent gross); though the marketing and administration costs may also be much lower (perhaps below 10 per cent). It was for this reason that, in the first instance, the World Trade subsidiaries were set up as separate companies—largely to avoid the 10 per cent royalty on product cost that is normally paid back to the USA. The effect of this is around three per cent of overall revenue for the mainline business, where the product cost is below 40 per cent, but would have been in excess of five per cent of overall revenue for the PC, where product cost may approach perhaps 70 per cent.

It may be that these relatively very low (in IBM terms) margins may have caused IBM fundamentally to rethink its strategy. In mid-1986 even John Akers started to talk about the possibility of IBM abandoning parts of the business, "where it had become a commodity market" (i.e., very low priced), and IBM froze its advertising budgets as part of a drive to cut costs.

It would appear as if IBM may unsuccessfully have used the PC RT as a "Trojan Horse" to try and rectify, at least in part, this problem. Although introduced as a very low key announcement (indeed almost to the extent of being a covert operation; but with a specification that belies this), it contained one major change from previous precedents. All the dealers' margins were reduced by four percentage points (down from 36 to 32 per cent at the highest rate, for example). On the other hand the later PS/2 margins were actually marginally *better*; so IBM apparently now believes it cannot boost its margins in this way.

The PC may herald an era when IBM margins start to approach those of the real world; and perhaps some of the problems of the real world may also start to intrude. It is difficult to see anyone else approaching IBM's efficiency though, since this is already ahead of its Japanese rivals; and in any case IBM has already easily seen off one ill-conceived Japanese bid (in the form of the ill-fated MSX consortium). But, as in most of the other areas of IBM business, the rest of the 1980s seem once more set to be an interesting time for PC Group.

CHAPTER 7

Organization by Controlled Anarchy

Introduction

One part of IBM's strength is in its 400,000 employees, who are carefully recruited (essentially on the basis of their intelligence) to be the best in the world. They are then just as carefully trained and retrained to develop their full potential. IBM's greatest genius, though, lies in managing delegation so that this full potential is realized for the benefit of IBM.

This delegation would in any case be *demanded* by personnel of the calibre of those working within IBM, but IBM ensures the process happens, by creating a subtle form of anarchy which undermines the status of lower level management—forcing them to act as leaders (coordinating the cooperative efforts of their team members) rather than as hierarchical demagogues. These individual anarchic cells are supported by a powerful horizontal communications network; where such communications are more normally vertical. This revolves around a grapevine of great sophistication; but this is being increasingly supplemented by electronic data networks (with each employee soon to have his own terminal).

This horizontal communication is aided by the (encouraged) existence of large numbers of "fixers"; senior personnel (but not managers) who know their way around the very complex (and bureaucratic) IBM systems, and have built networks of contacts in other departments (in the same way as the Japanese managers, who perform the same function).

The other element of IBM's organizational strength lies at the opposite extreme, in the senior management at Armonk. Its normal worldwide planning horizons routinely cover five years, and its longer term planning (particularly in terms of new plants) regularly stretches beyond 10 years; yet its planners admit that their financial models (which are just about the most sophisticated in the world) are only accurate up to 13 months ahead! Possibly as a result, Armonk has a (relatively unusual) awareness of its own potential fallibility, and so plans for almost every eventuality—when the worst does happen there is usually a contingency plan to limit the damage, and when the best occurs IBM can make the most of it.

Below Armonk, the management structure is probably weakest at the most junior level (but this is contained by the team leadership approach). As the level of management rises so does its quality (where the reverse is true in many companies); for IBM chooses its senior management very carefully indeed (measuring their track record by their subordinates' comments in the opinion survey just as much as by their performance against revenue or profit targets), and it trains them by moving them around almost as much as their Japanese counterparts.

Unlike the Japanese, IBM implements strong financial controls, of which perhaps the most stringent is that each group and each country should not merely be profitable, but should also fund its own growth (not an easy task where high growth rates are endemic). But, like the Japanese corporations, it is the non-financial controls that are in reality the most important. Thus it is the sales plan (directed at the sales teams in the field), rather than the overall marketing plan, which most directly shapes how IBM's revenues will be generated; and it controls its expenses particularly effectively by strict controls on capital expenditure and numbers of personnel (headcount), as well as by more direct means. Ultimately the shape of the organization itself is used to exert control; and in the longer term, manipulation of the culture itself is perhaps the most powerful control of all.

Personnel policies

The strength of IBM's organization lies at two extremes. At the apex of the pyramid is a very small group of people, the Central Management Committee located at Armonk, whose strategic decisions have, up to the present, been consistently sound. At the other are the 400,000 or so workers at the sharp end, whose implementation of these policies has never been less than impeccable.

Recruitment

As with any company, and particularly with a Theory Z company, the greatest strength of IBM ultimately is the outstanding quality of the latter group. IBM is able to, and often does, employ as "workers" people who would qualify as directors in many other organizations; and can afford to pay them as such. The quality is evidenced by the number of graduates in the work force. In the UK for example in 1982 they accounted for 30 per cent of the total work force, where only 27 per cent had less than five O levels. This is just one indicator though; for IBM, as an avowedly single status company, holds no special brief for graduates, and the figure is merely a reflection of the quality of its recruits in general. It is reported that IBM receives in excess of 100 applications for *each* job it seeks to fill from outside the company! Naturally it can choose the cream, and it can even afford to indulge the most idiosyncratic choices of its managers without seriously diluting the overall quality. The Japanese corporations are in the same fortunate position.

All of its recruits come from the intellectual cream of the country; again comparable with the Japanese corporations. To reach even the stage of the first interview they will have had to show a sound track record. They will, of course, have had to demonstrate the degree of charm that is an essential prerequisite to passing through a number of such interviews, whatever the company doing the recruiting. Despite Buck Rodgers' claim that: "only first-line managers do the actual hiring in IBM," in practice a whole range of staff and management (usually including relatively senior management if it is sales force recruitment) interview potential recruits; IBM takes the process very seriously (and with justification). There is, however, one relatively uncommon requirement that, with very few exceptions, they will have had to meet: passing an aptitude test. In theory this merely ensures a minimal numerate ability in order that they may be able to understand the complexities of computing. In practice, it is really a rigorous intelligence test that ensures that all key personnel entering IBM have a high intellectual capability. IBM is just as prone as any other company to recruit its staff on the basis of the rationalized intuitive hunches of its managers. Despite this, the aptitude test ensures that in the end the odds are heavily weighted in IBM's favour, in terms of achieving a high calibre of personnel, even when afflicted by the worst vagaries of the recruitment process. The benefit of this one simple screening should not be underestimated as a contributor to the undoubted high quality of the key personnel within IBM.

Having recruited the highest calibre of personnel, IBM then

trains and retrains them. It is recognized that all personnel new to IBM must receive suitable induction training no matter what their job. This is no new fad, for one of the very first things T. J. Watson established on arriving at IBM (then still CTR) was training schools for its staff; and in particular for its salesmen. The one year plus that this training now takes for field personnel is just one extreme version of this. It is recognized, in addition, that staff training is an ongoing commitment and all staff are expected to attend regular courses, adding up to an average of five percent of overall staff time, and typically as much as a month a year in the case of the field force. Internal education cost IBM some $600 million in direct costs during 1984 alone.

Cult of individualism

IBM has in these ways, over its three quarters of a century of existence, developed a resource of some 400,000 very high calibre and especially well trained personnel. The final element in the structure that maximizes the effective use of this resource is a commitment to delegation, to the maximum degree possible, at *all levels*. This comes about mainly as a result of the calibre of personnel involved, since they are independent-minded enough not to settle for anything less. It is, though, also enshrined in IBM's business policies. Every employee has, as of right, the maximum delegated responsibility and authority for his own particular function. To a degree in theory, and to a large extent in practice, management is asked first to provide support for the individual rather than control him. IBM has largely managed to break down its operations into cells that can be autonomously run by one individual. This reaches its peak in the field force where the salesman is uniquely responsible for all IBM's activities affecting his customers. He is the single point of contact coordinating the many facets of IBM's activities, and he carries the prime responsibility for ensuring that the customers' needs are suitably met, and sales accordingly maximized; IBM's altruism usually has a secure basis in pragmatic self-interest. More important is that he is also given the comparable authority to guarantee that all this can happen. Perhaps uniquely among most industrial companies he is given the privilege of deciding the best policy for his customers, even if necessary over his management's views. He has the right to set such policy, and management must have *his* agreement to any changes; though it has to be admitted that it is a brave, or foolish, individual who risks his career by insisting on his rights in this way. Once again the field force is but an extreme example of the general degree of delegation that applies throughout IBM.

For many outsiders the typical IBMer is seen as the archetypal organization man, facelessly fitting into a rigid bureaucracy. The truth is almost exactly the reverse: IBM comprises some 400,000 individualists, each with his own defined territory which he jealously defends against all comers. In effect IBM consists of some 400,000 separate small businesses, and it is this anarchy that is at the centre of its success, for each business is superbly well run. Each is the personal responsibility of a uniquely well qualified "proprietor" whose expertise in his own special area is unchallengeable. The creation of a cult of individualism, under the promotional banner of the "wild duck," was Tom Watson Jr.'s greatest ideological legacy to the company.

Horizontal communications

The difficulties inherent in any attempt to manage such anarchy are obvious. IBM's formal response might be in the first instance to deny the merest possibility of any anarchy, and then to point out that it employs a very high ratio of management to staff; it aims to have no more than seven staff reporting to a manager, to guarantee effective personnel management. There is at least an intention to this effect and, albeit to a lesser extent than claimed by IBM, such a massive investment in management must have some practical impact. More important, even though unrecognized by many in IBM, are the very strong cultural factors that encourage cooperation between the many disparate fragments of the organization. For it is the horizontal communication, between individuals at the workface, that is IBM's particular strength.

This degree of cooperation is very high, and although the inevitable political games are played, these are less likely to be the most debilitating "zero-sum" confrontations. At the heart of this unusual willingness to cooperate is a degree of individual security and self-confidence. This reflects on the one hand the calibre of the individuals, and their secure grasp of their own speciality, and on the other the widely recognized rights of the individual to be responsible for his own special territory, unthreatened by incursions from others. From this strong position it is easy for individuals to build the communication links that are essential to make their part of the organization work.

This cross-boundary communication is made easier because interdepartmental taboos are largely absent, once more partly as a result of the culture. In addition it is, at least in part, a result of the single status policy, which tends to break down the barriers between management and the other ranks to a much greater degree than in other companies. An IBM manager may be seen in some respects as just another specialist. In the main though, it is a function of the personnel recruited, who tend to be good communicators with a natural desire to communicate with others.

The main communication within IBM, therefore, is horizontal, between peers. This is tacitly recognized and encouraged by IBM's plans for each individual to have his own terminal linked into a vast network; which was largely realized by the end of 1986. On this network the individual can communicate at electronic speed with any other individual in the organization. Interestingly, the IBM experience to date shows that it is this person to person communication that is the main currency of the network, rather than the use of the large centralized databases that is predicted by many information researchers. This horizontal communication, be it face to face or more frequently by telephone (or now increasingly by the data network), is another factor that differentiates IBM from many other companies. On paper the structure is the usual pyramid, but this hides the fact that the most important layer is horizontal, and at the bottom, with the upper layers in many respects remaining "transparent." Such one- or two-dimensional representation though does not do justice to the richness of peer group contacts of the average IBMer. The personnel policies that have led to this individual freedom are described later.

Much of the above description has its parallels in the organization of the larger Japanese companies, making up the third of that country's economy that is most visible to the West. In particular, the identical factors of maximal amounts of delegation, degree of job security and amount of horizontal communication are held (at least according to William G. Ouchi) to be mainly responsible for the dramatic success of such Japanese organizations. The importance of IBM's contribution is not just that (as we will see later) it was probably the original model, but that it is now a better, richer implementation of such philosophies, and certainly is one that is much better matched to Western cultures, particularly those facing the problems of the information revolution. Its implementation potentially has much greater depth because ultimately it is now based on the individual, rather than on the group, which is the basis of the Japanese version. It is better suited to Western values precisely because it respects the individual and does not require complete subordination to a group culture; IBM does not require its employees to meet each morning and sing company songs—at least not any more!

Armonk: central management

We now move from the profane to the sublime, to the rarefied heights of Armonk; to the small, very exclusive club that is IBM's Central Management Committee. From the Watsons onwards, this committee has had an enviable record of sound decision making. This has been partly a function of doing all those things that every professor of business management would recommend. IBM is so profitable that it, perhaps alone of companies, can afford the luxurious overheads of planning over an extended timescale. Where other companies plan for, perhaps, up to three years ahead, IBM looks at more than a decade ahead. Such very long-term plans are essential, for although IBM has now managed to reduce the average product development timescale to around three years, it has been unable to reduce the time needed to bring on stream new factories employing new technologies, much below ten years. The management committee, therefore, has to try and guess what will be happening, at least in broad terms, in a decade's time; in probably the fastest moving and most volatile market of all. Although this may, for example, lock IBM into water cooled technology for its large mainframes, it still allows the freedom to delay the determination of the exact product offering, such as the 3090 range, until just three years before its delivery to the market; and in an emergency, such as produced the PC, it can act in a matter of months.

Stratplan

If the very long timescales of plant technology are taken out of the equation then the most important cycle is that of the strategic plan—the Stratplan in IBM terminology—which forecasts five years ahead. The Stratplan is a very impressive process: its basis is a financial model that represents not merely a single country, as for example does that of the Treasury in the UK, but it encompasses the *whole world*; shades of world empire! Depending on the assumptions fed into it, out churn the sales forecasts by broad product group and by country over the next five years.

The problem is that inherent in all such financial models, the output is only as good as the input; GIGO, garbage in garbage out, with a vengeance. In practice, although the financial model(s) used take into account a large number of factors, over a number of years ahead, the IBM forecasters in the UK have to admit that the only really reliable trend indicators in their experience are the relatively crude, and short-term 13-month ahead indicators covering Financial Surplus/Deficit, FT 500 Share Index, Three Month Interest, GB House Building Starts and, in particular, CBI "Business Confidence." In many respects the latter is the most important indicator where IBM is selling capital goods which, as investments in the future, are highly sensitive to the business mood. The problem is quite simply that no matter how nice it is to predict accurately what your business volumes will be in a year's time, this will be no consolation if the plant commissioning plans ten years ago or even the product plans a mere three years ago were based on different, and in the event proved wrong, assumptions. IBM has contacts worldwide which it uses to input the best possible information, but if all the experts are caught off guard, so is IBM. It is certainly true that IBM was taken very much by surprise, albeit for the first time in a number of decades, by the downturn in the industry at the end of 1984. It was itself in the middle of a very ambitious exercise, involving large-scale investment in new plants, to treble turnover by 1990. The hiccup in the market, even if that is all it turns out to be, left IBM with unsold inventories and underutilized new plants coming on stream. Even then it took nearly a year for IBM to recognize the scale of the problem and take all the necessary steps, including starting to talk about reducing the total of its work force, for the first time in living memory.

So if one compares the very impressive, and indeed apparently infallible, Stratplan figures from year to year then one sometimes finds quite large changes—perhaps by as much as 30 per cent—which unfortunately invalidate many of the claimed benefits of long-term planning.

One of the main virtues of IBM executive management in Armonk is, however, that they are sophisticated enough to make the quantum leap of appreciating the limitations of their own figures and of their potentially high degree of fallibility. The key documents, therefore, are not the impressive computer modelled Stratplan forecasts, but the handwritten summaries that encapsulate the management committee's own expert interpretation; and it is these rough handwritten notes that are often the most secret of IBM's information treasures. It has to be admitted, however, that to the best of my knowledge *no-one* in IBM, or in the industry as a whole, foresaw the 1984 downturn with potentially, even for IBM, very embarrassing consequences; I suppose it is reassuring to discover that the gods are after all only human! An awareness of its own fallibility is indeed perhaps the greatest, and to me most endearing, virtue of IBM management. It was perhaps best summed up by the comment of Tom Watson Jr. that he always "ran scared." I have, perhaps almost sacrilegiously, a mental image of John Akers arriving each morning at his office desk and sitting down at it, that is if he doesn't follow the rather odd habit of his predecessors of working *standing* at a specially high desk, and head held in hands commencing to worry about the possibility of imminent bankruptcy; his task for the day being to rescue IBM from the brink of disaster. Clearly this is pure fantasy, because IBM must be more secure than almost any other organization including many governments; but a very real desire constantly to reappraise the future, and to contingency plan for all potential problems, is a virtue of the company—although perhaps a luxury afforded by IBM's wealth and actual security; its management can contemplate the unthinkable as a matter of course.

Junior management

The brunt of bridging the gap between Armonk and the "workers" is in theory borne by the thousands of IBM junior and middle managers. In practice, the problems that are endemic in management throughout all large organizations are just as prevalent in IBM. It would be claimed, for example, that there is a rigorous procedure behind the choice of management candidates. The reality is that at the junior level this choice is no more scientific than in most other companies. The first requirement of a putative junior manager is often no more than a burning ambition to be promoted, which needs to be clearly articulated to those of more senior management who can best influence this process; in fact at this junior level sheer persistent bloody-minded pursuit of promotion may well by itself succeed, regardless of merit. The second requirement is the will and ability to do exactly that which is needed (over the seven to ten years it now, on average, takes) to overcome the political hurdles *en route* to the higher level, regardless of the theoretical or practical exigencies of the current job. The popular culture of IBM deplores these practices and Personnel Department might want to deny their very existence, but, as in any larger company, the junior management system thrives on them.

Quality of recruits

Even at this junior level there are ameliorative factors, resulting mainly from the culture rather than IBM's earnest and praiseworthy attempts to train its management. Of these, perhaps the single most important is simply the very high quality of the pool of potential management recruits. No matter how poor the selection process, the minimum standard of qualifying employees is so high that any manager is likely to more than match the best found in other companies. This was brought home to me by the fate of a colleague who was not considered to be of very high calibre within IBM, and who recognizing the limits on his promotion prospects, despite his rather frenetic attempts to achieve this by any political means, chose to face the cold winds of the world outside IBM. When I met up with him only a year later he had already graduated from the junior management position he moved to on leaving IBM, to become, after a series of very rapid promotions, the vice president in charge of all non-US marketing activities; albeit in a medium-sized company rather than a giant the size of IBM. This illustrated to me just how scarce in most companies are managers of the calibre that IBM rates as merely average in its ordinary staff. For many years the rest of the industry in effect used IBM as a training ground for its senior management.

Equal status

The next factor that ameliorates the potential problems is that the junior manager's authority is often, by accident or design, "undermined"; so that delegation is almost forced on him. This is accomplished by a variety of policies ranging from that of single status—everyone from dishwasher to director eats in the same staff restaurant and is on first-name terms—to the inviolable (at least in the UK) requirement that management work at round tables not desks, so that there can be no inherent status evident in their meetings. Active dissent is even encouraged by the language. In IBM one does not have to disagree, one instead "non-concurs"—a much less loaded, if rather esoteric, term. Indeed, there is a formal right to such non-concurrence!

Vigorous discussion is also aided by the fact that there is less emphasis on a "hen-pecking" order based on management position. The status of an individual is, in fact, determined by his "level" (discussed in Chapter 12), which is unrelated to any position in management, and (particularly as it is supposed to be confidential) is also correspondingly less easy to determine. The junior manager may thus be dealing with non-managers who are actually of higher status than himself and, as a matter of safe political protocol, this is the basic assumption he has to make in any discussions. He thus often becomes only one (equal) member of a team, albeit usually *primus inter pares*. The result is a natural emphasis on teamwork between equals.

Meetings

The final factor is the workload (where IBM deliberately overloads all its staff) and in particular the meetings load. It is assumed, quite correctly, that management will spend the greatest proportion of its time in meetings; another justification for their mandatory round tables. This meeting time, it is argued, is an essential part of the communication and control processes. The truth is, though, that most such meetings are with their peers rather than their superiors or subordinates. The net effect is that, although it enhances the horizontal communications processes, it reduces the time that they might have available to interfere in the activities of the truly productive staff below them, who are anyway quite capable of delivering the goods IBM wants without *any* supervision.

The meeting is a special element of the IBM culture, for not infrequently an individual's overall performance is most importantly of all judged by his "theatrical" performance in front of his peers. As a dyed in the wool marketing company everyone, even the most unsuited, is judged by the standards of sales technique, of which the presentation is the most avidly followed. In the good old days the medium was the flip chart, but technology has moved forward and the focus of IBM meetings is now the foil, projected on an overhead projector. This has saved time in production, but the one-upmanship race has now moved to producing foils by the most impressive PC package; the first program chosen by an IBM manager for his newly acquired PC is likely to be that for producing foils. The form of the meeting is, therefore, something rather special to IBM. It is easy to make fun of it, but the end result generally is a well run meeting, with good communications; again, for whatever questionable reasons, a net gain for IBM!

However, it is probable that IBM does *not* deliberately set out to undermine the position of its junior managers. The reality, however, is that their workload coupled with the strong influence of the personnel policies does ensure that their position in relation to their staff is more equivocal than usual, and their role can best be described as team leaders, *primus inter pares* (very much in Theory Y mode), rather than hierarchical managers (in Theory X mode).

Middle management

IBM is able to control the quality of its middle management processes rather better than those of its junior management. It is indeed a remarkable feature of IBM that in general the quality of management improves as their level increases; the reverse of the experience in many other companies. This is a direct outcome of the increasing ability of IBM to measure performance the higher the level. The manager at the higher levels has a much greater degree of involvement in setting, or at least in accepting, the targets he is required to meet. In turn the targets themselves are generally more measurable and less subject to random variation. Against this better degree of control must be offset the lower awareness of the "real world" as management is increasingly insulated from the realities of the sharp end, only receiving signals that are heavily filtered by the management culture that passes them up the line.

Performance measures

Of course in many management positions, particularly within the staff functions, direct measurement of performance is difficult. Charged with introducing such a measurement system into IBM's marketing staff I eventually had to throw in the towel. There was no shortage of factors that could be measured and I was offered computer systems to measure these to the finest degree, but in the final analysis none of them were directly relevant to the most important components of the functions. A measurement and control system would simply have focused attention on the wrong factors, to the detriment of the genuinely important ones—paradoxically, the more efficient the control system, the worse would have been the negative impact. I have to report that my failure was not well received, for IBM despairs of controlling such marketing staff which represents one of its most important, and expensive, assets. Though its latest move, of regionalization to smaller operating units, may in practice prove successful in addressing the problem; using one of IBM's traditional blunt instruments, that of reorganization.

IBM has, as always, a range of devices to get round this problem, at least in part. Like the Japanese companies it moves managers from job to job, but even faster than the average (for a company that is anyway always on the move) with managers rarely staying in any, save the most senior positions, for more than two years. No doubt the main benefits of this are increased experience, wider awareness and reduced chances of management staleness. An incidental side benefit, however, is that they get exposure to a range of functions and to a number of contacts with both superiors and subordinates, and any major weaknesses are correspondingly likely to be detected; and this is reinforced by the fact that the IBM culture encourages detection. As far as possible, these moves pass key management through positions where performance can be most directly measured. In particular the most important positions require—as part of the company's myth of the supremacy of the salesman—some period of experience in the field; in the most measurable functions of all. This process of management career movement is taken to its logical extreme with those managers aimed for the most senior positions, whose careers are planned down to the last detail over a decade or more. Their own progress, in the most exotic school of management training of all, even takes precedence over the importance of the position they currently fill; and their "guardian angel" will rescue them from any potential fiasco before saving the function in question.

The most rigorous test of all applies to all members of middle and senior management. They are exposed, at least every two years, to the most searching scrutiny from their *subordinates,* in the opinion survey. This survey does not limit itself to the employee's views of IBM in general, it also examines in some detail their views of their management. This is indeed a *very* rigorous measurement since IBM employees are particularly sophisticated in their appreciation of management's roles, and of their shortcomings against these; and at least under the cover of the secrecy of the survey have no difficulty in registering their views. The results of the opinion survey are taken very seriously. Apart from obvious poor performance, nothing can damage or even destroy a management career more effectively than a poor survey result; it is a marvel to behold how assiduously managers look after their staff in the weeks running up to the survey.

Finally IBM ruthlessly removes managers who have, according to the Peter Principle, risen to their level of incompetence. This surgery is accepted by the culture, and by the managers themselves since, unlike other companies, the victims are not fired but are removed to positions (occasionally as professionals not managers) where their real talents can continue to be used. Just occasionally this can result in peripheral departments, to which poor managers are despatched, being less than effective. This price is, however, significantly less than that of having to accept poorer management of the key functions. Occasionally the more capable of these managers sent to the "sin-bin" are able to claw their way back, and even a few of IBM's most senior managers have survived such an experience and eventually continued their career progress.

Once again comparison with Japan is instructive. The same job security and cohesive culture is obtained, but it is, unlike Japan, not achieved at the price of an inflexible management structure based only on seniority; an inflexibility that even the Japanese are now attempting to rectify. Once more the gain to IBM is greater flexibility, but also better calibre managers at the higher levels.

Coordinating communication

However, this still leaves the problem posed by less well-controlled junior management and the resultant problem of coordinating activities across the company, where IBM's official theory that this is mainly the role of management is not necessarily borne out in practice. In the event it largely depends on peer group contact at the lowest levels. All IBMers are constantly in touch with a wide range of other IBMers; it is not just managers who are constantly in meetings. At the lowest level this contact may be more informal, and often is by telephone rather than face to face; aided by a worldwide internal telephone network that makes it just as easy to call Boston as Barcelona. This direct communication process covers those issues of immediate import to the individual. It is supplemented by a grapevine of great sophistication that keeps all personnel in touch with key developments; it is a matter of honour that no announcement, no matter how secret it is meant to be, should come as a surprise. As far as I could ascertain, during the relatively traumatic period for senior management in the UK at the end of 1985, when an embarrassing number of the UK board members resigned or threatened to resign (mostly for eminently sound personal reasons, such as lucrative offers from outside), at a particularly unfortunate time when they were needed to head up the new regions in the reorganization then under way, the grapevine was only a matter of hours (certainly less than a day) behind the board itself in learning of developments! At times it was probably *ahead* of the board, in terms of forecasting the likely reactions of the individuals involved! This grapevine is of considerable importance as it often provides the prime perspective—sometimes the only one—within which the individual plans his tasks. It is generally accepted that management briefing will usually be inadequate; with the gaps filled, very effectively, by reference to the grapevine.

Fixers

Seeded throughout the general medium of IBM personnel are what can best be described as "fixers." These are personnel who because of their length of service and consequent experience, together with a flexible and relaxed if not overtly cynical attitude to life within IBM (often backed by an almost bloody-minded delight in beating the system), have the wealth of contacts to solve almost any problem. They become, quite informally, the focus for much of the problem-solving that the system would claim is handled by management.

Although their functions are not formally recognized by the IBM structure they are informally recognized by a range of policies. Of these the most important is that of providing a career path for professionals, outside management, which enables them to reach levels and salaries which may well be in excess of that of many IBM managers. The other main element was the most direct implementation of the philosophy that was first propounded by Tom Watson Jr.; of the need for "wild ducks." In the philosophy's most directly applicable form it justified the people, usually the fixers, who management found uncomfortable to live with, but who were recognized (at least by Armonk) as essential to the well being of IBM. A weakening of their role may be one of the unintended problems induced by IBM trying to control an ageing population of bureaucrats who have achieved some seniority by length of service only. IBM's recent tightening up of the structures, to place greater emphasis on costs, may result in the fixers, who are in many ways indistinguishable to the outsider from the average bureaucrat, being forced out of business; with possible dire results for IBM.

In some areas these fixer functions are formalized as programme managers, responsible for resources and coordination but not for personnel; analogous in some respects to brand managers elsewhere. They may have no reporting personnel but they do have authority, and many chair committees with members who are themselves quite senior managers.

Task forces
Where change is required, the fixers role is also formalized by two devices. The first of these is the task force. This collects together a group of IBMers with as wide a range of experience as possible, to bring this experience to bear most fruitfully on the plans for the expected change. The use, and occasional abuse, of task forces is widespread. It has the virtue of combining the range of experience in the most positive manner, since normal rules are suspended and the thinking can consequently be that much more free ranging. The abuse comes about because the task force is only as effective, and its recommendations as innovative, as the participants. There is a natural tendency to use only personnel already involved in the problem, who may accordingly be the least able to develop the wider perspective needed. Biomedical Group, for example, welcomed a new general manager every two years, whose urgent brief was to sort out its profitability problems. The new incumbent in best IBM tradition immediately convened a task force, and subsequently acted on their recommendations. The ultimate problem this caused was that the task force, convened every two years in this way, was always composed of exactly the same members of senior management and came each time to identical conclusions; and the problems were once more perpetuated not resolved.

Where the task force is a short-term device limited to recommending the planned actions, rather more occasionally a complete project team is set up for an extended period, perhaps for many months. Again, though, this is usually multi-disciplinary with wide experience and again most importantly, the normal rules are suspended to ensure that their actions are as unencumbered as possible.

Routine rearrangement
One of the problems facing any organization, let alone one in a marketplace as volatile as that of computing, is that of failing to cope with change; of becoming locked into outdated ideas and systems. IBM (under Frank Cary) solved this problem in a particularly effective manner by institutionalizing change; as a matter of principle Armonk reorganizes IBM every two years—that at the end of 1985, for example, being regionalization, which changed the structure from a global split by division based on product to a consolidated structure split by local region. The impact is more usually lessened by reorganizing different functions at different times, for example, field and staff on alternate years; though the

latest most ambitious changes covered both. Despite this, even a routine biannual change may involve as many as 5,000 personnel in each country changing their reporting structures, managers and even locations. This is so ingrained in the IBM way of life, however, that the disruption lasts only a few days, rarely for more than a week, and then everything settles down to run as smoothly as usual; just as if nothing had happened. Due to the very open structure within IBM the price in terms of disruption is thus surprisingly minimal. It does mean, however, that the first question any IBMer immediately asks on meeting an old colleague is: "What is your job these days?" a question that is asked as a matter of fact, and with no sense of irony. This greeting is traditionally extended to *everyone* during the first weeks of January each year, when IBM almost invariably indulges in at least one significant reorganization!

The benefits are, on the other hand, quite dramatic. They allow IBM to reshuffle its organization, strengthening and pruning where necessary, whilst giving as many people as possible new experience. Most important, by throwing all the cards in the air it removes any blockages that are building up in the organization (including resolving the levels of incompetence resulting from the Peter Principle) and allows new initiatives to emerge. Armonk always is able to quote an eminently sound immediate reason for each of these changes, but one is bound to suspect that in this case the means is more important than the end: the process of change itself is the real objective, the end result is almost incidental—just one of many such alternative ends each of which would be just as effectively implemented by the ever patient IBM staff.

It is rumoured that the dependence on change has now become so addictive that Armonk has created a separate division to handle the process in the future. This is probably an apocryphal rumour; but it encapsulates the perceived reality. Perhaps the only equivalent exposition of such ongoing commitment to continuous structural change has been the various revolutions initiated by Mao Tse-Tung which have kept China in an almost permanent turmoil for four decades; strange bedfellows, the archetypal multinational capitalist and the most fervent revolutionary, both depending on exactly the same management technique! Change then is a means by which Armonk facilitates its overall control; with change in progress Armonk merely has to steer a course, it does not have to overcome the inertia opposed to movement.

Financial control

Even with the lubricant of almost continuous change, steering IBM in the direction Armonk wants is not an easy task, where the management structure is a relatively poor transmitter of vertical messages. At the top, country, level IBM can be controlled by those financial measures that one would expect of any large corporation; the key measures, of course, being revenue and profit. Control of the latter is, however, exercised in a somewhat idiosyncratic manner. In the first instance the absolute, and percentage, level of profit required as a matter of course would make most company treasurers reach for their tranquillizers. IBM really is immensely profitable, which is clearly an advantage to all concerned; except those in IBM trying to enter new fields, where projected profit margins may even be ambitious by the standards of the respective marketplaces but will usually be seen as alarmingly low by Armonk staff used to different standards.

Central reporting

In the second instance the direct relation to profit is brought home to a country by the fact that growth almost invariably has to be funded internally. This poses problems for the local management if, as is usually the case (where status is linked to growth rate), it is targeting rapid expansion, requiring equally rapid investment. This is compounded by the fact that there is normally a one- to two-year lag before this investment pays off in growth. The pressure is therefore on ambitious managements—and IBM does not want to know of any other sort—to declare very optimistic targets, since the formulae allow projected profits to be included in the cashflows that are being used to generate the investment. Against the odds their IBM "machines" work miracles to achieve these targets. Just occasionally the gap cannot be closed and the act comes apart at the seams, as it did with the UK General Systems Division in 1976 (and even more dramatically with IBM's home market in the US during 1986). Then the repercussions echo around the globe.

Obstructive funding

The control by the centre is, however, even more direct, for all expense budgets have to be approved down to a fairly fine level of detail, as do capital budgets, which are subject to even more rigorous scrutiny, since it is assumed, with some justification, that they will generate ongoing costs as well. Special projects which are suspected of having particularly heavy knock-on consequences come in for particular scrutiny, and have to be supported by separate "business cases." In return, approval is rarely given before March (even the plans and goals for IBM worldwide are only delivered by the chief executive officer to the company's assembled top officers, some 250 of them, at the end of January), and sometimes not until May, when the company's financial year starts in January; so a country has to commit a large proportion of its spend for any year without knowing what total will be finally authorized. Of course management will have had some indications, but there may still be changes before final approval, and sometimes after as well. As a planning process it represents considerably less than most business schools would advise, but as always in IBM the process is made to work.

In essence, the financial control system is that often employed to great effect by sophisticated bureaucracies which have no suitable financial controls. The backbone of this is control by degree of urgency. The bureaucrats charged with a duty to control expenditure have no way of knowing the real facts behind each request for funds; particularly where, as in IBM, the submissions are highly technical and in languages that are often unique to the function submitting the request. *Every* IBM manager can make a case, with great and most convincing eloquence, for more funds. The bureaucrats' response, and a very effective one at that, is simply to make the process of obtaining funds long, tortuous (often requiring sign-off by up to three totally different and non-communicating branches of the Finance Department; each with veto power) and painful. There is no direct logic to this, since a bloody-minded manager will still, eventually, be able to obtain funds for unjustifiable purposes; though the bureaucrats are unusually bright and tend to be able to filter out even these worst abuses. It does mean, however, that the process screens out the flippant applications. You must have a very strong need for funds to justify the time and sheer aggravation needed to beat the system. Finance assumes, usually correctly, that this will reduce their list to those items that really are essential; paring away all luxuries in the process and leaving a suitably lean and fit IBM.

Sales

These financial controls may irk country management and take a disproportionate amount of their time, but ultimately they are in fact not the *most* important controls; for these are essentially non-financial and never get near the Finance Department. The most immediate in their impact are the "quotas": the sales targets. These targets are split down by country, then by region, by branch and eventually to individual salesmen. At each stage these quotas are inflated by a few per cent to ensure that a reserve is built in, so management at that level may still meet their targets even if their subordinates fail. This poses no great problems in boom years, but in lean years it may result in a threshing around of quotas late in the year; since no IBM manager can afford to unfairly prevent any of their subordinates from making the HPC (Hundred Per Cent) Club.

Salesmen, who still drive the marketing efforts of IBM, are paid on commission, typically accounting for between a third and a half of their income, though there are usually guarantees that may take perhaps 70 per cent of the risk away, and the basic salary is in any case inflated by perhaps 15 per cent also to allow for the risk; so the real risk element may be as little as 15 per cent net. The commitment to such personal financial involvement is a deep-seated IBM principle and is implemented wherever possible, extending to many managers and even to some sections of staff; though IBM is very coy about telling its customers about just how their trusted IBM sales "consultants" earn their living. The character of IBMers is such that they would, in any case, put in just as much effort without any such incentives, for they are best typified as workaholic over-achievers. The commission system does, however, have a very real virtue in bringing home the "capitalist" message to a great many IBM bureaucrats who might otherwise set themselves different priorities even if they worked no less hard; and in the process it becomes a prime device for highlighting the objectives of the common culture (and helps very publicly to bind that culture together). The level of their targets, their quotas, is a very direct instruction to all involved; there is no confusion as to exactly what is, in the last resort, required of them. One has to question, however, whether the 30 per cent compound productivity improvement looked for almost every year in the UK, and actually delivered for most of the past half-decade, can continue forever. Indeed the 1985 shortfalls, initiated by the industry recession, may call what is essentially IBM's bluff in this escalation of productivity, for there would appear to be no technical basis for it.

If the sales figures for these recent years are examined more carefully, it can be determined that a large percentage of the increases from year to year have actually derived from switching IBM's customer base from rental to outright purchase of their machines. Without this bonus, which presumably required relatively less sales effort, the annual increases would have been much closer to 10 per cent per annum, in line with historical performances. This one-off windfall is now almost exhausted. It is not clear, however, exactly how Armonk expects the sales force to *increase* its real productivity to meet the 15+ per cent per annum compound growth inherent in the 1990 targets enunciated by John Akers to the world's press at the beginning of 1985. Perhaps one has to assume that IBM's new product plans, and even more the price competitiveness that its new plants can support, will prove *very* attractive to its customers over the rest of the decade; and indeed that, plus a significant degree of market buoyancy (which is most embarrassingly missing at present), was apparently the basis of Armonk's calculations. It would be unwise, particularly in view of the track record, to assume that Armonk will remain wrongfooted for very long.

The sales plan

Perhaps the most important strategic document, at least in terms of its effectiveness, is the sales plan. Its creation and maintenance is sufficiently important to justify as big a dedicated department within marketing staff as that for the marketing plan. Although an apparently simple document, it is uniquely important within IBM because it formally tells the sales force how it is expected to earn its living during the year. It spells out how the individual salesman can achieve his quotas, which are the only significant measures of performance imposed. Management can subsequently issue as many directives as it likes, but if they conflict with the sales plan they will be largely ignored.

The strength of the sales plan is the simple and very direct way the centre can control the overall direction of a country. This has been evidenced by the switch in emphasis from obtaining orders (albeit described as sales), which might be for equipment not due for delivery for up to two years, to closing business deliverable in the current year (in IBM-speak from NSRI, net *sales* revenue increase, to NIPII, net *installed* points increase, and now to *revenue* which is perhaps the first measure recognizable to the outside world); reflecting IBM's strategic movement over the past decade from an installed rental base to income now based mainly on outright sales.

The sales plan is not without its drawbacks, however. In the medium and long term, as opposed to the very short term, it has little impact on the overall pattern of sales because it now only stimulates "closing." This was still very effective in a number of recent years, living on the fat of closing existing business transferred from rental to purchase, with immediate gains in current year revenue. Unfortunately IBM has just come to the end of this windfall at the same time as a downturn in the market! It now has to face a rather different problem, that of creating *genuinely* additional increases in business, and this poses a new challenge for the sales plan.

A further complication is that the average "real" sale in IBM is still the result of a number of months work, typically stretching over more than a year; clearly not so susceptible to the sales plan, which covers only the current year and recently has emphasized revenue from business closed and installed, which exaggerates the problem even more. The result is that the sales plan tends only to energize business that is already in the pipeline. This may not be all negative however, since salesmen in general, and IBMers in particular, feel very comfortable with the initial stages of a sale but hate making the close; and any incentive at this stage, such as that imparted by the sales plan, can have significant benefits for the company. The great effectiveness of the stimulus can be observed from the pronounced banana shape of the sales curve during the year, with a very slow start leading to a rush at the December year end with perhaps up to two-thirds of business closed in the last four months. This is not the natural pattern of sales (PC dealers, for example, actually see December as a relatively poor month) and is observed regardless of whether the customer set has the same year end as IBM or, as with the government sector, runs from April; it is testimony to the single-minded efforts of the IBM sales force in meeting their year end targets.

Just occasionally, in 1976 for the UK GSD division (and apparently in the US at the end of 1986!), the banana effect rebounds (a drooping banana is a terrible fear for a company as macho as IBM!). If a significant proportion of the sales force have not beaten their (70 percent) guarantee level by November then they see no benefit in recording more sales that year. As a result they hold back sales still in the pipeline to be booked in January; giving them a flying start in the following year. The result for the country is that sales can, albeit very rarely, collapse spectacularly in December, just when maximum sales are normally expected. The fact that no sales are really lost, and a flying start to the following year is guaranteed, is no consolation to a management faced with a journey, cap in hand, to Armonk to explain their failure.

The resulting inventory problems, where this business now has to be delivered not just booked, have forced IBM for the first time to hold shelf stock. Again it is now somewhat embarrassed by the stocks left by the business downturn, where in previous years of only building to order it would have never produced these unwanted stocks!

The scale of the 1986 problem was reported in the computer press as being of the order of $8 billion, and growing rapidly. It is likely, however, that this was an exaggeration, and reflected *total* stocks, not just finished goods; for finished goods in 1984 only accounted for $1.6 billion of the $8.5 billion total. In any case, even the total represents only two months' inventory from raw materials on (and the 1986 year-end figures showed a reduction). One thing is for sure and that is that it will not bankrupt IBM. Those who expect otherwise should learn from the "fire sale" of excess stocks of the Portable PC just before it was discontinued. Those dealers who hung back expecting it to run and run lost out badly, because the stocks were exhausted in only a month; as might indeed have been expected from the above figures.

The biggest problem of the sales plan, and indeed of all IBM's most powerful control devices, is that it lacks subtlety. It can only recognize and motivate the broadest of strategic targets. It is impossible to use it to direct effort to more than a handful of targets. Traditionally, the only worthwhile target has been the overall quantity of business achieved, in terms of "points." Points are an artificial concept to allow IBM to give a correct weighting to the value of each piece of hardware or software, without resorting to a straight monetary value which would vary with exchange rates; a point originally represented a dollar a month of rental income. A salesman or a branch can do badly on a variety of fronts, just so long as the overall quota is achieved. Blessed is the salesman who "gets the branch into the club"—that is, who brings in the business to allow the branch manager to make his targets—particularly in a tough year; I was never so féted as the year I brought in the final order, on 31 December, to make the branch quota that everyone thought lost! This single-mindedness inevitably drives the salesmen into closing the easiest business, which is almost invariably made up of the largest boxes on the price list, sold to to the biggest existing customers—and the devil take the more esoteric equipment, and the small prospects, no matter how important they might be in future. If you subscribe to the Pareto 80:20 rule though, and I do (along with most business school theorists, but too few practising businessmen), this has to be the best use of the salesman's time, both in terms of his individual income and also IBM's overall income. It does, however, put significant difficulties in the way of many changes Armonk might want to promote.

One of Armonk's answers to this is to use organization as a means of control. The sales organization, in particular, has been fragmented into groups based on product lines, where the biggest box in each group has been the product Armonk wished to give attention to. The idea has been that in this way each such group should have a limited set of objectives, without the temptation to stray into other "easier" areas. Indeed at the branch level there is still a constant battle to prevent management from drafting all its resources into the largest end of the business available to them; to the benefit of their branch's overall performance but to the detriment of IBM's policies on the smaller boxes. IBM, at the end of 1985, reversed this policy and regionalized, breaking up the business into more manageable units, but breaking the divisions between products. Clearly, IBM hoped these smaller regional units with bottom line measurement (that is, measured by the NBT, net before tax profit; as recommended by all the pundits) would be more manageable, and profitable. At that time I noted "It will be interesting to see, however, what happens to IBM's fringe activities, such as the S/38 (still-one of IBM's most innovative boxes); will these go to the wall?"

In practice, as the results showed, that was exactly what happened. The IBM watchers enthused over how much more competitive the DEC product line must have become. But in reality IBM had foolishly abdicated this whole market to its main competitor; Frank Cary *had* fully appreciated the potential problems when he insisted on GSD being entirely separate.

The use of reorganisation as a device for lubricating the process of change *can* have its costs when the implications of such reorganisation are not fully thought through.

Headcount

Traditionally Armonk's response to the problems of misallocation of people resources has been very direct control of headcount. Thus the key resource budget is that of people, or at least of established, permanent personnel—the headcount. This is allocated down to the finest detail, since it is correctly assumed that most of IBM's costs, and in particular (in the light of IBM's full employment policies which do not allow any lay-offs) fixed costs, are *directly* related to headcount. If you control headcount you effectively control total costs; and this simple philosophy really does work in IBM.

At the macro level Armonk uses headcount, and in particular headcount freezes, to control its global costs. In a period when it sees business about to turn down it reduces its costs by freezing its headcounts. Initially this will be a *net* headcount freeze, holding the countries to their existing levels, a severe enough imposition where growth is normally endemic; though hiring from outside is still possible to meet the level of attrition. This net freeze is typically employed when IBM can see a downturn some time in advance, a possibility that was open to IBM forecasters over most of its life. In the next stage, the *gross* headcount freeze, no recruiting at all (at least not without approval of very senior Armonk management, and even then after a great deal of special pleading, only in numbers of dozens per country) is allowed even to meet attrition; so that there is a steady *reduction* in numbers. This latter state is only imposed in emergencies, such as existed in 1985, since it imposes a *very* rigorous discipline on the countries. As a result it is held in reserve as Armonk's ultimate sanction, to be used perhaps twice a decade.

Once more, though, it is not without its drawbacks. It was a more effective device, and hence needed to be applied for shorter periods, when IBM's attrition rate was higher. As recently as half a decade ago IBM still acted as the training camp for the whole industry, and during freezes those IBMers with less bright prospects often left for greener pastures. In more recent years, however, the industry-wide recession has made IBM seem a much more hospitable environment in a very cold world, and attrition has reduced to a mere trickle; currently only 2.5 per cent in IBM UK. In addition, when applied for an extended period, a gross headcount freeze has the distinct disadvantage of freezing the organization as well; the last thing IBM wants. Understandably, no group will release personnel, no matter how desperately they are needed elsewhere, when their own replacements will almost certainly not be forthcoming.

Temporaries

This rigorous control of headcount has also spawned a population of "temporaries," who are not subject to headcount. Although these do not figure anywhere as employees, and must leave within a year, the temporary posts they fill have in effect become permanent; and in the UK perhaps as much as a third of IBM's work force is now made up of such temporaries. In terms of costs this may indeed be advantageous, at least in the short term, since temporaries cost significantly less than IBM employees, even when their agency's fees are included. They are cheaper even on direct costs, since IBM refuses to acknowledge their existence, they cannot generate indirect costs (certainly not to the extent of the very elaborate infra-structure needed to support IBMers). Their hidden costs may, however, be high. They do not go through IBM's rigorous selection procedures, so dilute the overall quality; whether or not IBM considers them to be invisible the outside world does not know this, and sees it as very much an *IBM* problem when, for example, their enquiry is mishandled. Despite being "non-people" they still need some training, even though no formal resource can be allocated to this, which disrupts departmental activities; and this trained resource has to be, by definition, discarded within a year maximum. They stretch the fragile management system, particularly in the areas of high growth, where temporaries are most extensively used; in advance of the successful completion of very extended negotiations for new headcount. In these areas many managers control more temporaries than permanent staff, destroying IBM's carefully worked out ratios.

It should be noted that it is a basic feature of Japanese business that relatively large numbers of temporary staff are employed, in order to iron out fluctuations in workload. There is no evidence that IBM is applying the same principle, but the effect is much the same whether it is due to strategic decisions or oversight.

Corporate culture

The final control available to Armonk, and the most powerful of all, is that of control of the culture. Over a three-year period, during the late 1970s, I undertook a study with the London Business School to try and establish the best means of controlling the activities of the then General Systems Division (field) marketing activities; as part of an overall programme of business training for that division in the UK. The surprising conclusion was that, as compared with other sophisticated companies, the key factor controlling the activities of the individual was not any of the usual management activities, but instead was an immensely strong culture. Again in many respects this parallels the Japanese experience; though IBM's culture is a corporate, not nationalistic, affair.

Pursuit of excellence

It is difficult to describe the culture briefly. From the outside it is often mistaken for arrogance; from the inside it is seen as pursuit of excellence. It is a cocktail of elements, usually dismissed by IBM watchers as hypocritical nonsense, which was carefully nurtured by the Watsons during the formative years of the company, and was, I believe, the key difference that made IBM so successful. Even after more than half a century it is still relatively uncorrupted; though it is now facing its greatest challenge, of which more later.

So, IBM's third belief can be summarized as pursuit of excellence. The apparent arrogance comes from the assumption, sometimes unjustified but usually correct, that IBM is or at least should be best in all that it does; an assumption that all IBMers are required to live up to in their own performance. It also incorporates an idiosyncratic commitment to a form of integrity where, for example, the customer's needs really do come first (as spelled out by IBM's second belief) and any questionable practices are the only grounds for instant dismissal. It goes beyond just producing the highest quality output; it embodies a demand that *every* option is considered, to ensure that the optimal route is not overlooked due to slavishly following the book. The essence of this was encapsulated in the famous THINK campaign brought by Thomas J. Watson from NCR. The result is a unique degree of flexibility, coupled with intellectual application, which can be overpowering to the outside world.

Surprisingly, the corporate culture remains as strong, and very much the same, across national boundaries. Of course there are recognizable national characteristics overlaid on it. The French and Italians for example *insist* on serving wine in their staff restaurants, against IBM's otherwise puritanical rule of absolutely no alcohol on company premises; in the UK it requires the signature of a main board director to allow wine even to be served to customers or dignatories attending functions on IBM premises. One suspects, though, that the French and Italians are really asserting their independence rather than any unbreakable dependency on alcohol; though alcoholism caused by stress is documented as possibly the major industrial illness afflicting IBM managers. Underneath the apparent, but essentially trivial differences, the common culture predominates. Walk into any office or plant worldwide and you will immediately be at home. It helps that the business language in all offices is English (the US version thereof), expertly spoken by almost everyone. The main link, though, is simply the cultural "feel." This is not a centrally imposed hierarchical uniformity, for that *would* be opposed by the various nationalities involved. It is instead a natural expression of a remarkably strong shared culture; in much the same way that Roman Catholic churches are instantly recognizable regardless of where they are. The commitment to quality, to excellence, was unchallenged until recent times. Cost was never an issue, though price/ performance was exalted; and IBMers did not of course ignore cost issues. The only *critical* parameter, however, was the quality of the final output. This, coupled with the marginally more direct (and largely opposed) target controls, gave IBM its unique strength. The quotas gave the immediacy of action but the culture directed this.

The 1980s have, however, produced a need for a new culture. The new objective, established at the end of the 1970s in the face of the perceived Japanese challenge, was to be the lowest-cost producer. This may well be diametrically opposed, at least in terms of the culture, to the pursuit of excellence. Paradoxically, the main vehicle for this new message has been the use of "quality" as a synonym for lower cost. Quality coordinators and quality circles have been implemented throughout IBM, with as yet little effect but (as with all perceived gimmicks in a company that is cynically resistant to overt manipulation) causing much derision; apart from the plants where IBM had pioneered this approach (long before the Japanese, who in any case copied it in the 1950s, from the then most successful US companies, probably from IBM itself).

Sub-cultures

Within IBM there are many sub-cultures. There has always been a degree of competition between groups, and this has been encouraged. Each group developed its own special rituals and beliefs, but ultimately they all recognized the supremacy of the shared culture and loyalty to IBM above all. The joker that has recently appeared in the pack is the emergence of PC Group. This has grown up entirely since the change in direction, and has been largely populated at the lower levels with recruits from outside IBM. As a particularly distant outsider its reaction, in order to defend itself against the rest of IBM, has been to develop not a variation on the main culture but instead a completely new counter-culture—which is paradoxically in line with the new direction, where the rest of IBM is out of step with it.

Whilst the two groups held each other at arm's length there was a degree of creative tension, which probably worked to IBM's benefit. Now, however, the decision has been taken to reintegrate PC Group into Big Blue. There may as a result be a clash of cultures, between the larger sitting tenant of Big Blue and the smaller but much more dynamic PC Group (with the support of the new directions). If IBM is lucky, this merger may once more result in a productive synergy. If it is unlucky, what may emerge may be the lowest common denominators of both cultures and IBM may begin to look increasingly like any other company. The odds against a successful outcome are not helped by the unfortunate timing, since it is being implemented at the time of a major unexpected recession in the industry, which is hitting even IBM hard. The indications are, however, that IBM has grasped this particular nettle, by reintegrating it back into the mainstream of Big Blue; though this has yet to be reflected in any degree of tighter control over its third parties.

Marketing philosophy

I am aware that throughout this whole description of IBM's organizational controls at work I have so far excluded almost all the conventional measures of management by objectives, that so many management textbooks argue are essential to the efficient control of a sophisticated company. This is not an oversight. It is quite simply that even in those few situations where IBM feels it necessary to appear to follow convention, the results are largely ignored.

For example, the classic document for any marketing-oriented company—which IBM most certainly is—should be the marketing plan. IBM does in fact produce, at the end of some considerable effort, a marketing plan. This is an apparently very impressive document, as is also the preceding EHQ document that spells out the guidelines. Both documents appear to be admirable essays in business sophistication. The detailed, group by group sections encapsulate dozens, perhaps hundreds, of activities. Indeed, the overall count may show in excess of a thousand separate programmes and activities. The questions only start when the management summary section is compared with the detailed sections, and this comparison starts to show some significant discrepancies. In some areas it does not just summarize; it may actually present a *different* set of plans, often complementary but sometimes contradictory. It should be self-evident that even a company of IBM's sophistication cannot do justice to more than a thousand different directions, especially when they are to be implemented by just two sales forces. It is the classic situation where the 80:20 rule should be applied, and indeed it is; by the field force. Perhaps less than 10 per cent of the programmes ever reach the customers they are aimed at, and maybe only one per cent are widely used; in any case the field force prefer to extemporize. The actual plan on the ground is managed *ad hoc* by the IBM field staff in the branch and not by the staff functions at head office.

On the surface the management summary appears more realistic in its scope. But upon closer examination even this may reiterate the phrases of the moment; much of IBM management is as susceptible as any of its contemporaries in other companies to the latest jargon, and unfortunately often falls victim to a belief (at least in formal planning documents) that suitable reference to the current jargon is an acceptable substitute for a workable set of action plans. The reality is that IBM's sales branches are effectively autonomous, setting their own marketing directions and providing their own support largely unadulterated by head office ideas; but strongly guided by the factors listed earlier. Where the branch's views and those of the marketing plan coincide there may be some synergy. Where, as is more usual, they do not then the branch's ideas are implemented.

To marketing theorists, such as Philip Kotler (*Marketing Management*) there would be some *very* surprising omissions, particularly for a company that is renowned as one of the pre-eminent marketing organizations of the world. Indeed, many of the normal precepts are missing: the most enlightening aspect of Buck Rodgers' book (particularly in view of its subtitle Insights into the World's Most Successful Marketing Organization) is the virtual *absence* of all normal marketing theory; despite Buck having been IBM's vice-president of marketing. There is very careful coordination of the product portfolio; albeit with one eye always on the competition. Preemption rather than balance may well be the main objective. The concepts of market segmentation and product positioning are, though, largely missing in their truest sense. This is not as naive as it seems, since such techniques are largely unnecessary for IBM. Its domination of the marketplace is such that it determines segmentation and prime product positioning simply by its own actions; *whatever* they may be. Its competitors, however, do have a much bigger problem since the targets they are trying to hit are constantly moved by IBM!

The importance of such domination is also evidenced by the Japanese example. Thus, Abbeglen and Stalk (*Kaisha, The Japanese Corporation,* 1985, Basic Books) state that: "In the high-growth Japanese economy a 'winner's competitive cycle' has become apparent. Those companies who establish and maintain this cycle have consistently emerged as strong, profitable and respected companies in both the Japanese and, within the last decade, the world business community. For a company to establish a 'winner's competitive cycle' it must grow faster than its competitors." It is a process that produces more losers than winners in the Japanese economy, where liquidations of very large corporations are perhaps a more common phenomenon than in the Western economies (which in the process undermines some of the supposed benefits of lifetime employment). The West generally only sees the winners; and even some of these are on the verge of insolvency as their markets move on. Many of the winners of the earlier stages of Japanese development are no longer to be seen; and many of the others are no longer the dynamic leaders that they were—unlike IBM the Japanese have not yet found the secret to prolonged market leadership. In many ways Japan Inc. looks somewhat like those speculative conglomerates that hide their losses by ever-increasing numbers of new acquisitions, until their time eventually runs out.

In some respects IBM's marketing philosophy (or apparent lack of it) mirrors that of the Japanese, who also pay remarkably little attention to marketing in the purest Western sense. To quote Kenichi Ohmae's typically Japanese views (*The Mind of the Strategist,* 1982, McGraw Hill): "What business strategy is all about—what distinguishes it from all other business planning—is, in a word, *competitive* advantage . . . the sole purpose of strategic planning is to enable the company to gain, as efficiently as possible, a suitable edge over its competitors." In support of this, Abbeglen and Stalk report that: ". . . the kaisha [Japanese corporations] share four key perceptions:

1) Market share is the key index of performance in a high growth market;
2) Investment in facilities must at least keep pace with—and preferably exceed—the growth of the market regardless of short term impact on profits;
3) Price is the principal competitive weapon to gain and hold market share; therefore, prices must decline steadily as costs decline; and
4) New products must be constantly introduced to continue the cycle of investment, cost reduction, price reduction, and market share gain."

All of these are now visible in IBM's strategies, though 2 and 3 above only achieved prominence in the late 1970s when IBM recognized the Japanese challenge on these fronts.

Forecast assumptions

Indeed, unlike the Japanese example, the other item that often features in a conventional marketing plan, that of pricing policy, has (perhaps until very recently) usually been notable in the IBM plans by its absence. It is, in fact, the responsibility of a totally separate department. In highly competitive situations, IBM *does* carefully price its products to maximize profitability. On the other hand its control of prices is not as sophisticated (or as Machiavellian) as DeLamarter suggests in *Big Blue*. Indeed the key, and most informative, document in the new product process, "Forecast Assumptions," is ostensibly primarily concerned with determining prices (or at least obtaining country sales forecasts at different projected price levels). But much of the time, despite the forecast assumptions input, pricing still appears to be on a "cost plus" basis; albeit once again with markups which would shock most other companies. Once more the process is successful simply because IBM *is* the price setter! In this respect I have to admit that DeLamarter's claims that IBM is monopolistic do have some grounding in reality. This is not to say that IBM does not put effort into pricing decisions; the reverse is very much the case. It ponders at very great length, and pours in significant resource to the process; to the rather ludicrous extent in Biomedical Group that at one stage there were up to six professionals working on pricing decisions when there were only 13 workers on the production line!

In appearing critical of the value of the IBM marketing plan I am, in effect, telling a joke against myself; for I coordinated the 1985/1986 UK plan. As always with IBM, though, there is a benefit derived from the process, from the informal activities surrounding it if not from the words that eventually appear on paper. The series of meetings, in particular the three-day residential think-tank/brainstorming session by the most senior managers involved, which are an integral part of the process, allow the management the time—and excuse—to discuss their individual departmental plans in the most positive environment. As always within IBM it is the informal discussions, not formally documented in the marketing plan, that really form the basis of the finally implemented "grass roots" plans. If nothing else, these meetings, as with many meetings in IBM, provide the common perspective for the individual managers to optimize their own individual, and largely informal, plans.

The risk factor

Another, albeit much more esoteric, illustration is that of risk analysis. In the mid-1970s, when risk analysis was much in vogue in management circles, the London Business School asked IBM, along with a number of similarly sophisticated companies, how it managed risk; only to be greeted by a blank response. IBM did not even recognize the concept, despite the volatile nature of its market place. A bemused London Business School probed further, only to be informed that to meet any unseen problems it simply poured in resource until the problem was beaten; and this had never failed! The London Business School eventually rationalized this as being IBM in effect carrying its own insurance, albeit unconsciously. IBM's scale was such that it did not have to evaluate risk; it simply poured in the resource necessary to get where it wanted to go, regardless of conventional business theories. The cost to IBM of changing overall direction to cope with any risk was just too expensive.

It is arguable, though, that at least in this respect recent history may prove IBM wrong. The lowest-cost producer policy has involved IBM in massive investments in automated plants, which are relatively inflexible, both in terms of operation and of costs. The result may be that IBM can no longer use its unique flexibility to divert resources, and the recent downturn in business has left it with investments in factories that simply *cannot* be redeployed; the classic case where risk analysis should be used.

In retrospect, though, this too may be a problem of mismatch between IBM actions and outside theory. IBM *does* take the risk factor very seriously; as evidenced by Tom Watson Jr. "always running scared." It is shown even more clearly by IBM's planning (Stratplan) process. Having put together the long-term strategic plan and short-term operating plan that are realistic and attainable, then according to Buck Rodgers, IBM says: "Look, we made our commitment. Now let's see if we can stretch beyond that." This is the goal level (though resources and commitment are made to the original base plan). Then IBM prepares a risk plan in order to, again quoting Buck Rodgers: "have something to fall back on. Thus you can avoid making dangerous, hip-shooting decisions, because you already thought through the problems during calm times, before they occurred."

IBM thus has not one, but *three,* plans, all of which are just as rigorously planned: the base plan, the goal plan and the risk plan. Once more IBM can indulge in the luxury of planning for almost every contingency.

An MBA, of whom there are very few in IBM UK, would feel almost totally disoriented; except that by the time—after a number of years of obtaining relevant IBM experience—he was let anywhere near the plans, he would have long since been completely brainwashed by the culture. IBM effectively insulates itself from the outside world by almost exclusively promoting from within. This is admirable from a personnel viewpoint but potentially incestuous. As shown particularly by the Independent Business Units, nowhere does IBM, upon close examination, look much like other business operations. As a result it does not, and probably cannot, profit greatly from the experiences of others.

This is not to criticize IBM for its surprisingly naive rejection of apparently sophisticated management techniques. The reality is that it is *IBM* that is successful, not the majority of companies earnestly implementing sophisticated management theory. It is for this very reason that it is the model for the "Philosophies I" described in Chapter 13.

In summary then, the reality, as opposed to any theory, is that IBM works well at the top level in terms of very long-timescale strategic management, and particularly well at the bottom level of virtually autonomous individual operations. Its ability to recruit extremely capable individuals and then delegate to them the very maximum amount of responsibility unhindered by management intervention, means that it has achieved a creative degree of controlled anarchy not seen elsewhere. The nearest equivalent is that of Japan; but anarchy would be the last description to be applied to that rigidly organized society. The equivalence is only in the freedom, given by job security and maximal delegation, available to the lower levels of staff. At this lowest level, again reflecting the high calibre of the individuals, the extent of the horizontal communication network, which allows effective coordination of activities, is again unmatched; once more the only relevant comparison being with Japan. On the other hand, its use of unconventional—but ultimately with very sophisticated impact—constraints on middle management minimizes the risks of their jeopardizing the performance of the lower levels, and maximizes their own contributions. Control is then implemented by a few very crude and unconventional, but powerful devices. These cannot be fine-tuned by any of the usual management tools, but are integrated by the uniquely strong culture; which culture is ultimately the invisible hand that guides IBM.

CHAPTER 8

The Countries and Their Divisions

Introduction

IBM's major organizational structures are regionally based; though for many years—until the end of 1985—the picture was complicated by a marketing split between customer or product groupings (with large multinationals or large mainframes handled by one division and smaller companies or small mainframes handled by another division; with yet another handling the "also-ran" products). Now regional organization (and autonomy) is the essence. At the highest level this is represented (as it has been for a quarter of century) by the rigid split between the two equals (certainly in size and to a large extent also in authority) of Domestic (the USA) and World Trade (the rest of the world; though in practice this mainly comprises the five major countries—Japan, Germany, France, Italy and the UK).

IBM's handling of its various individual country organizations offers many lessons for other multinationals. For although IBM manages to, and indeed is forced to, manufacture and develop on a worldwide (integrated) basis, it still manages to offer each country a remarkable degree of autonomy; and in the process avoids many of the worst criticisms levelled at other multinationals (and still makes a handsome profit). Although each country's management (typically headed up by a board comprising almost exclusively nationals of that country, with perhaps one token foreign director) must ultimately defer to Armonk (and because of the integrated nature of the worldwide manufacturing, has little say in product or pricing strategy) in most respects it runs its own country's operation without any great outside interference. Despite this autonomy, the IBM culture is so strong that IBM offices and plants across the world look (and indeed are) remarkably similar.

On the other hand IBM suffers, almost as much as any other

multinational, from the bureaucracies entrenched in its regional offices; but at least Armonk is well aware of the problem and is trying significantly to reduce the scale of their operations, by increasingly devolving their functions to the lowest possible (usually country) level.

IBM's development laboratories *are* organized on a worldwide basis, though even then they still have to fund their operations from their royalties on previous products, and report, for pay and rations, to their "host" country management. IBM cossets them far more than other groups, giving them resources and locations (even extending to suitable settings on the Côte d'Azure or in similar sought-after areas) for which any university professor would sell his soul (and sometimes does); and then it gives them at least as much freedom as any university. The result is a plethora of invention, and IBM has the great advantage of then *choosing* which of a number of possible products best suits the market needs (and often allows the market itself to choose—by launching competing products); thus does IBM maintain its product leadership and market domination (where even the individual Japanese corporations eventually slip from their dominant position). The description "laboratory," though, conveys the wrong image, for the essence of IBM development is large software teams working at desks in conventional office buildings. IBM does, however, still allow for the input of the talented individual; and many of IBM's most successful products (particularly in the all important software area) have come from such individualistic work—and again it is IBM's genius to be able to absorb these unsolicited efforts and then build on them.

The choice of the location of new plants is where, or rather when, IBM is usually most involved in negotiation with the host governments. These governments look for an investment in new jobs; not very fruitfully because IBM is spending vast sums on building plants that are almost completely automated. The typical factory worker is, once more, an office worker! IBM, as a matter of principle (like the Japanese), buys in all those components that it believes can be produced at least as well by outside suppliers (but then exacts draconian quality standards on these suppliers); despite this philosophy IBM still makes many of its components—which is an indication of just how far ahead its technology normally is. The other main difference from other companies (including the Japanese) is that caused by the integration of its manufacturing worldwide. A computer on the assembly line may contain parts from

IBM plants in half a dozen countries, as well as from hundreds of suppliers. Tracking and coordinating these items is a major activity (particularly where IBM now works to the Japanese—Toyota—"just in time" system). The factory floor is, thus, dominated by quality control and administrative staff, with very few "conventional" workers indeed (an early portent of the true impact of the information technology revolution).

The general administrative staff are as much of a problem for IBM as for any other company; particularly where they are spread uncontrollably around the organization, staffing many hundreds of sophisticated functions which other companies have never even heard of. IBM's only successful solution has been to hold the numbers down by making physical office space available to them late; and growing the rest of the company faster than the natural (almost cancerous) growth of these potential bureaucrats. When, as in 1985 and (particularly) 1986, sales do not grow as fast as it would like, it faces a major problem with its growing administrative costs threatening its profitability. In 1987 it attempted to counter this by a major redeployment of personnel out of administration into more productive areas. It remains to be seen if this will be any more successful than earlier policies; I personally doubt that it will be.

World Trade and Domestic

With the advent of the young Watsons the world had to be split into two; the USA as the jewel in the crown was given to the eldest, Tom Jr., while the rest of the world went as a consolation prize to the younger son, Dick. The two brothers thus ruled separately their own more or less equally balanced empires; even now the two halves are approximately equal, though the strength of the dollar has recently pushed Domestic slightly ahead again. The principle has been maintained to this day. The two halves of the company are largely independent; only development is now on a global scale. Each has its own complete set of manufacturing facilities, and there is remarkably little export, or import, between Domestic and World Trade. This provides an insurance that IBM is never exposed to insurmountable problems with a single source of supply on any product; there is always the fall-back of the sister plant(s) in the other half of the corporation. PC Group's problems with the hard disk for the PC AT were compounded by the fact that, unusually for IBM, it was single sourced on one supplier; PC group will not repeat that mistake, as subsequent management moves indicated; the Token Ring supply problems involved a number of suppliers.

Within World Trade there is now a further split between two, once more autonomous, halves: EMEA (Europe, Middle East, Africa) which in volume terms mainly comprises Europe, and AFE (Americas, Far East) which is dominated by Japan. This split is, however, not balanced; for EMEA is twice the size of AFE in volume and profit terms.

General Business Group

Despite the regional splits, in organizational terms the most important layer below Armonk, outside of the USA, is the country. The positions of the World Trade headquarters at White Plains (discretely close to, but not too close to, Armonk) and the regional headquarters, EHQ (European Headquarters) Paris in the case of EMEA, has always been somewhat anomalous. For a number of decades EHQ, at least in theory, provided a major focus for planning. A large, and high powered, staff was supposed to bring a significant degree of "local" European expertise to strategic planning. In practice EHQ, as seen from the larger countries (in IBM parlance the majors; Germany, France, Italy, UK), was rarely more than a further layer of bureaucracy; simply transmitting messages between Armonk and its colonies. Its success, such as it was, lay in its good sense, in its minimal real interference in the country operations. The undermining of even the formal role of EHQ started in the 1970s with the formation of GBG (General Business Group), which in essence reported direct to White Plains, and often had its closest links with the US divisional headquarters in Atlanta. The official recognition of the demise of EHQ as the prime focus for regional planning had however to wait nearly a decade, until 1984.

As indicated above there was for more than a decade, up until the end of 1982, another organizational split layered over that inspired by geography. This was the divisional organization, GBG. It is arguable that this had its genesis, at least in part, in response to the threat posed by the emergence of DEC to dominate the "mini-computer" market. The very successful commercial computer the S/360 had unfortunately overshadowed the earlier 1130, which was in its time IBM's equally successful scientific computer. As this progressively became long in the tooth, and IBM preoccupied with greater things neglected it, DEC took the opportunity effectively to steal this whole marketplace from IBM; a mistake IBM does not often make! In the process DEC produced a range of innovative small computers, in particular the PDP 11, which also threatened the lower end of IBM's main business computing market; and IBM was not about to repeat the earlier mistake. The response was the System/3 range of small commercial computers. To ensure dedication of resources to meet the challenge IBM located marketing of these machines in a new division, GSD (General Systems Division). This market oriented view would also justify the subsequent merger with OPD (Office Products Division; in other words typewriters), to obtain economies of scale (though in the event this expected synergy never appeared).

It is clear that whatever the reasons for its creation Armonk subsequently used GSD as a balance, if not even as a gadfly, to the much larger DPD (Data Processing Division) and as a stimulus to new business. In practice GSD did not halt the growth of DEC, but it ensured that this growth was largely limited to the scientific market, and GSD did outstrip DEC in overall sales, albeit in the business market, to become, in its own right, the second largest computer "business" in the world.

A more cynical interpretation, which was prevalent within IBM, held that GSD/GBG was a creation designed to produce a sacrificial lamb, should the US government anti-trust suits appear to be approaching any degree of success. This view held that IBM was thus restructured so that the logical, and indeed only, split possible was between DPD and GBG; and this would have still resulted in two viable companies, though GBG would have been significantly less viable than DPD. In the event the sacrifice was never needed. Circumstantial support comes from the fact, possibly coincidental, that the period of existence of GSD paralleled fairly closely that of the judicial processes of the anti-trust suit. It was created in the US when the suits started, was expanded worldwide as they reached a critical stage and was formally dispensed with when it became clear that a suitably inoffensive outcome was in the offing! It should be noted that Buck Rodgers in his book claims that there was no contingency plan associated with the anti-trust suit. Interestingly, though, DeLamarter in his book (*Big Blue*) claims that IBM *did* make just such an offer:

> "During the course of the 1969 U.S. antitrust case, IBM even volunteered to divest itself of an entire division (the small systems business, which today is a sizeable part of the com-

pany) as a means of settling the case (The government rejected this offer as not significantly increasing overall competition)."

Perhaps, at times, IBM *is* as devious as DeLamarter would have us believe!

Majors and minors

Before discussing the role of the countries in more detail, it is important to recognize that not all the countries are handled in the same way. The main split is between the majors and minors. The majors are the largest markets, which represent the biggest part of IBM's business, and in turn they are the countries with clout at Armonk. They used to be known as the "product-line" countries, because only they were allowed to maintain product-line departments interfacing with the USA (and the development labs) to input national requirements; such input for all the others being provided by EHQ. Indeed EHQ's most important real function has long been to provide central support for the minors on a wide range of specialized activities (though, paradoxically, funded in the main, by "taxes" on revenue, by the majors).

Although the minors in EMEA are self-supporting in terms of their main business, they do require extensive technical support for the more specialized products, as well as for the more obscure markets. The result is a rash of specialist centres, ranging from Milan giving technical support for the smaller mainframes to Munich for production industry. In theory these support *all* the centres, and are funded by a revenue based (not usage based) charge on the countries; which results in them being predominantly funded by the majors. In practice, as stated above, they mainly support the minors, typically by providing the range of expertise they cannot individually afford. At times the logic of this does produce some anomalies, where for example the Nordic Centre (supporting Scandinavia) is located in Basingstoke, England, next to the UK marketing expertise they wish to tap. This is I suppose no more illogical than South Africa being grouped with the "Northern Europe" countries, presumably to avoid any unfortunate conflicts with the other African countries in EMEA.

In the case of the majors, and to a lesser extent the minors, IBM aims not just to market in each country but also to manufacture;

and where possible also to locate a suitable research or international support facility. In the case of all the other smaller countries this is not the case. These countries, mainly in the Third World, are only a target for marketing activities. IBM's market place is disproportionately sensitive to the level of development, so that like many other multinationals the business generated by the Third World is, at least in its terms, virtually negligible; and accordingly *is* neglected. The only presence therefore is often at best a small local office selling a limited range of equipment; IBM for commendable reasons will not market individual products where the low volume of sales will not justify adequate support. This may limit choice somewhat, but it does maintain high standards. In a number of countries, though, it has more recently appointed local agents; particularly where local conditions require business customs or payments that IBM itself could not ethically support. To a certain extent this is a change in posture from the less flexible days of the 1970s when India was "abandoned" because of unacceptable government restrictions; though the loss in terms of business to IBM was probably minimal and India was probably the worst loser. Now, for example, Saudi Business Machines in which IBM has only a share, handles almost all of the lucrative Saudi Arabian business.

IBM will, however, go where the business is. Thus it has periodic love affairs with the Communist bloc, their temperature depending mainly on the current state of US foreign policy rather than on the lowlier commercial considerations. Based, perhaps with good reason, in Paris rather than Moscow, the cyclical nature of "IBM Trade Development" business made life very interesting for its often bemused employees.

Country autonomy?

As was stated earlier the kingpin of the World Trade (non-US) system is the individual country. To state that it is effectively autonomous, as IBM may claim, is to ignore many of the facts of life. Although a country is involved, at least in theory, in negotiations with Armonk leading to a mutually agreed plan, in practice the country is very much the junior partner and ultimately may have Armonk's wishes imposed. Thus a country has no autonomy in the key areas of the products it will sell and their prices, the headcount it can employ, its sales targets, its capital and expense budgets, and funding for any significant individual projects. In fairness to IBM it needs to be recognized that much of this is not simply due to "centralization" run amok, as Marxist/Structuralists might claim. IBM, and all the major computer manufacturers, are forced to run globally integrated business operations. It has to manage a *vast* range of products, all of which need to be to some extent compatible with each other, and with earlier products. It would be quite impossible, and indeed irresponsible from the customers viewpoint, even to attempt to control this complexity on a decentralized basis.

Within these somewhat draconian constraints, which are usually accepted without comment, the countries are autonomous. Each is typically run by a board of its own nationals and chooses its own officers. It usually has no more than one foreign board member; traditionally the head of World Trade or EMEA (who is, in any case, conventionally the token European on the central management committee at Armonk). It is staffed and manned virtually exclusively by its own nationals; as compared with the Japanese who have a penchant for introducing a significant number of their own key managers. There are indeed very few US citizens anywhere in World Trade to intrude on national aspirations. To the majority of its employees, therefore, IBM can justifiably claim to be effectively as "national" as any of its local competitors; particularly so when many national computer companies now only survive by rebadging equipment made in Japan!

In most respects IBM behaves, in terms of its relations with its employees and the outside world, exactly as if it was a national company. Many of the remaining rules that apparently limit its autonomy are also imposed by a wish to avoid any chance of being accused of laundering profits through the most tax advantageous countries, or tax havens, by rigging "inter-company billing prices" (ICBPs in IBM jargon; that is the transfer prices between countries); which is the greatest criticism levelled by Marxist/Structuralists. As in many things, IBM really is whiter than white; which cannot necessarily be said to be true of all multinationals in this respect. Many more of the rules, though, are there to ensure maximal achievement of targets (in its simplest form this can be viewed as capitalist maximization of profit).

There is, within a country, a belief in a form of continuum, whereby everyone is of a single status and all functions are accordingly interchangeable, as the business changes. So that the example is often given, in the UK, of the chef whose position was displaced but who was then retrained to become a buyer. There are undoubtedly many equally commendable examples, but in the main the reality is that the company is divided in a fairly rigid manner into a number of functional groupings.

Of these the most important, in myth and practice, is that of marketing, and this being a law unto itself is the subject of a separate chapter.

Development systems

In any case, there is inevitably a degree of separation between the purely national activities and those groups which are internationally controlled, such as the laboratories and plants; both of which are integrated on a global scale. For the former, the country largely acts as a "host" (an often used IBM term) providing little more than pay and rations for the troops, not deeply involved in policy or management. The UK is not untypical in hosting a major development laboratory at Hursley near Winchester. This is the largest in World Trade with some 1,500 staff, representing nearly 10 percent of the UK total, but essentially under non-UK control. Interestingly, even the laboratories are, though integrated as part of a worldwide development function, in effect also run as autonomous businesses. They bid for new development work, and fund their activities from the royalties Armonk passes back from their previous successful work; Hursley in the UK is reportedly still living, very well, on the royalties from its very successful developments in the area of disk technology. In addition the UK also hosts a number of international centres including that for ESE (Entry Systems Europe; the latest reincarnation of EHQ's personal computer group head office), as well as the Nordic Centre, the Finance Industry Centre, the Installation Support Centre, the International Airlines Support Centre, the UK Scientific Centre and IBM Information Services Ltd; which runs the data network covering the whole of EMEA.

As the laboratories, in particular, are not integrated into the national structure, they are in the enviable position of choosing their location purely with a view to the attractiveness to their employees. Thus Winchester is one of the most pleasant UK locations, though not as pleasant as that of La Gaude on the Riviera (surely the most sought after European posting). The brave attempt at support for the UK development areas which initially placed the UK Scientific Centre in the northern wastes of Peterlee (near Newcastle) had to be reversed, and that too is now cosily settled in Winchester.

The term "laboratory" gives a misleading impression of how the inmates work. The buildings they occupy are essentially standard office buildings, whose inhabitants have mainly desk jobs. There are very few additions which would be recognizable as conventional laboratories to a visiting scientist or engineer; though the Zurich laboratory, which does more basic research, has more exotic facilities, which was, at least in part, justified by scientists working there winning the 1986 Nobel Prize for Physics. Indeed their only real concession to any difference from the office work that dominates the rest of IBM is the availability of much greater raw computing power. Even the hardware is now largely developed by software generated simulations. In any case the major development work, even that relating to so-called hardware, lies in software. It is accordingly teams of software specialists, programmers, and in particular testers, that sit at the desks.

These teams may range from as few as 100 people spending five years developing a specialized industry terminal system, such as that for the licensed trade in the UK (or for the EFPOS, the electronic funds point of sale system due in the late 1980s), to the 2,000 people that were reportedly eventually set to work to rescue the S/38 when its coding became almost impossibly complex; the operating system requiring some 20 million lines of code rather than the 12 million originally planned. You will gather from the above figures that the average IBM development team is relatively large. It needs to be so because the real problem is ensuring the resulting programs are bug free; IBM justifiably prides itself on the quality of its work.

The innovative efficiency of such teams, though, probably decreases exponentially with size. They accordingly show many of the worst problems of design by committee. On the other hand, brilliant individuals can still often make quantum leaps that are impossible for such teams. In my time I have watched amazed as one particularly "way out," but brilliant, researcher at the UK Scientific Centre supplied me with the key elements of a totally new design for a 200 mips processor literally on the back of a piece of scrap paper, in less than half an hour. Over a somewhat longer timescale I have had a systems engineer write a complete, workable bill of material processor for a mini-computer in only three days. Scale of resource may not be all in research; though it certainly helps in the absence of genius! It is also essential where it is reported that IBM announces an average of 10 new products every week (albeit these are often relatively minor variations on existing ranges).

Product choice

As described in Chapter 5 it is the richness of these competing products that is a great source of IBM's strength—for each of these 10 new products perhaps two others were offered by competing teams and IBM is in the enviable position of being able to choose the best product. Further amongst the 10 products launched each week there will (over a period of time) probably be some duplicates; and IBM lets the market (and its sales force) directly decide which is the best runner. As a result of this multiplicity of potential products (as well as its tight grip on control of the *de facto* industry standards) IBM maintains its product leadership, and related market domination. This is against the odds as described by Peter Drucker, and is in spite of even the Japanese experience—where over time (admittedly decades) the individual corporations do (as Drucker predicted) lose their grip on the product leadership and their market domination slips; though this is not obvious to the West as their psychologically dominant role in the economy as a whole has by then been assumed by yet another Japanese corporation.

At the other end of the scale, as mentioned earlier, the myth of the Silicon Valley start-up should not be swallowed in its entirety. It is true that Steve Wozniak, of Apple, did design some very innovative touches—it was certainly the right product in the right place at the right time; but was hardly a garage start-up in the true sense. Even earlier David Packard and William Hewlett also started HP in a Silicon Valley garage, but after two years they were still only a 200 employee company with a $2 million revenue; their large scale expansion took decades. So much for the myths of instant stardom!

Such individual contributions are not barred from the IBM development systems, even though the main effort and resources are reserved for the larger teams. In part these smaller scale inputs may be the result of a small informal development, possibly from an individual and possibly even from outside IBM, that is seen to have some promise; and IBM is willing to "fly a kite" by adding it to its product list. The most obvious example of this is the VM software that has now become one of IBM's two large mainframe operating systems, and reportedly key to many of the developments into the 1990s, more than a decade after it was first offered as an effectively unsupported alternative from IBM's Cambridge, Massachusetts, laboratory.

The other likely stimulus is the panic of dire necessity. The need to get a product to market in a very short timescale, because of a sudden realization of a potential exposure or because the flagship product will not be available on time or to spec, is traditionally a great-spur. At one extreme the whole PC range was developed in this way to meet the newly recognized market needs and at the other IBM's mainline operating system, DOS, was a "temporary" response to the planned implementation of OS simply being far too large to fit on the smaller machines. IBM is nothing if not flexible, even if it does take a decade to recognize formally the virtues of an interloper.

Production: politics and policies

Manufacturing is also integrated on an international scale; and it too follows the same broad reporting line as the laboratories. In a similar manner to the laboratories the theory is that as each new production requirement, or "mission" in the jargon, enters the plan it is put out to competitive tender to all qualifying IBM plants, and the most attractive (that is the lowest price) tender wins. As always with IBM the reality is far more complex. The balancing act involved in assigning new production requirements often revolves around political factors that are little related to economics.

In particular this has become the time when IBM conducts its most important negotiations with host governments. This wheeling and dealing is, not unexpectedly, never made public. Although it is a function of sound government as much as of good corporate management, to negotiate the best terms, there is within IBM—and many multinationals—a distaste for the process and in a particular for making it public. It is, however, a matter of public record that immediately prior to taking the decision to locate the European PC manufacturing plant at Greenock near Glasgow, the whole IBM board met in London, and met Margaret Thatcher in Downing Street. It is not unreasonable to assume that *some* discreet negotiations took place, which both sides presumably at some stage considered fruitful. Certainly it was my experience on a more limited scale that the UK Department of Trade was very willing to talk terms (revolving around financial incentives, in line with government policy) to obtain any commitment to further IBM production in the UK. In the case of the PC perhaps both parties obtained less from the deal than they expected.

IBM has undoubtedly seen a very large increase in the proportion of business it receives from government sources, but this might have been expected where the otherwise preferred government suppliers, notably ICL, could no longer meet the technical requirements imposed by the very large networks needed. Despite the new "partnership" IBM has still been subjected to some notable political losses; at the DHSS and Inland Revenue, as well as the much publicized decision against its joint VAN (value added network) with British Telecom. On the negative side for the government, although the prestigious PC plant *has* been located in the UK it probably has resulted in remarkably few jobs—a few hundred at most. The PC is, due to its history and nature, mainly an assembly of bought-in components. These components are bought worldwide, from the most suitable (cheapest) sources; typically from low-cost suppliers in the Far East. Local purchases of components are, therefore, probably not dramatically greater than if the plant was elsewhere; though there must remain some convenience factors and emotional/language reasons for choosing local suppliers. IBM would claim that these still represent a significant amount of business. As with most IBM plants, even assembly is heavily automated, with extensive use of IBM's own robots; so even within the plant the numbers of additional personnel were limited. The gross export figures for PCs, to help the UK balance of trade, look impressive, probably already in the billions of pounds sterling. The net figures, balanced off against the import of the various components, are probably less than half the gross. Overall then although there is undoubtedly a net benefit to the UK, the size of this may be rather less than many would imagine.

Investment in automation

However when all the political debates have been resolved, IBM builds a plant which is as automated as is humanly—or at least robotically—possible, in the belief that this will ensure it maintains its position as the lowest cost supplier. Since the late 1970s, when this policy was first enunciated, tens of billions of dollars have been expended on creating the most technologically advanced factories in the world. In addition, the product itself represents leading edge technology of the very highest degree; so the combined result is a level of manufacturing sophistication that is several orders of magnitude in advance of virtually all other manufacturers. IBM once more hopes that this investment will make its future position unassailable, since no other company can afford even to contemplate the vast sums needed; it is the one classic example of IBM attempting to use its massive size to guarantee its future.

The evidence is that, for a change, this is a philosophy that IBM *has* perhaps learned from the Japanese (though economies of scale were already at the heart of the trusts that Charles R. Flint created; of which IBM was his masterpiece). Indeed, as a relatively recent development, at least in terms of the *unusually* high degree of commitment (for IBM has always invested heavily in plant), it closely follows the key perception shared by Kaisha (one of four identified in Japanese corporations by Abbeglen and Stalk) that: "investment in facilities must at least keep pace with—and preferably exceed [which IBM recently has to a quite extraordinary extent]—the growth of the market regardless of short term impact on profits."

The potential payoff is shown by the IBM Lexington, Kentucky, plant where some $350 million was spent on automating a 25-year-old plant. Before automation labour accounted for one-third of manufacturing costs. The target for the automation was to cut this to only 5 per cent (needless to say IBM spent some $5 million retraining the displaced workers rather than making them redundant).

The cost has, however, not been negligible. A strong rumour circulated in IBM to the effect that the first fully automatic factory never worked to spec, and as a result IBM lost a billion dollars. But as always with IBM this was affordable from "petty cash," without even showing as a blip on the profits curve in the final accounts. The invaluable lessons learnt have been incorporated in the later plants; and as a free spin-off the technology for IBM's Robotics Group emerged. IBM always emerges smelling of roses no matter what mire it falls into!

Level scheduling

At the same time IBM has also learned and implemented the lessons of the "just in time" methods of scheduling, first developed by Taiichi Ohno of Toyota in the 1950s, and a natural extension of IBM's own computerized systems. The evidence for this was most graphically demonstrated when the UK's Havant plant proudly opened its newest (and largest) clean room in what had previously been the warehouse holding the stocks of components (and which was clearly no longer needed for this function). There is, though, one potentially major limitation with "just on time" scheduling, and that is the relative lack of flexibility; since it demands level scheduling, and this requires that the production schedule is frozen for perhaps a month at a time. There may also be a further hidden cost in that (despite strenuous assertions to the contrary by the theory's supporters) one effect may simply be to push the stocks of components back from the assembly lines to the supplier (where they still have to be financed, but as an element of the component price).

As indicated above, one cost which may yet emerge, especially from the massive investments in fully automated plants, is that of reduced flexibility. IBM has a history of creative improvisation on a massive scale whenever a quick solution to a major problem is needed; the launch of the PC was just the most obvious of a number of such sagas. With increasing *fixed* investment in plant, which is *not* flexible, IBM's options are increasingly narrowed. This shows most obviously in its continued commitment to some technologies that have been largely superseded elsewhere. Once it has committed its investment to the 10 year timescales of the automation of a given technology even IBM cannot easily afford to divert to newer technologies, no matter how attractive they may appear. The problem is, once more, illustrated by the example of the Lexington plant. The projected product costs might well, in theory, have been significantly reduced; but only when the plant was running at optimum capacity. In reality, the demand for its products (in the main typewriters and small printers) has apparently been rather *less* than forecast; and this would indicate that the low costs anticipated may not actually have been achieved. On the other hand, the $20 billion IBM has built up in current assets, of which the $10 billion net current assets can be switched almost at a moment's notice, do indicate a readiness for even the most disastrous emergencies.

Quality control

The philosophy works the same whether it is implemented on the automated lines producing the chips and substrates for the largest 3090 water cooled mainframes or a robot testing keyboards for the PC. This large-scale automation means that there are very few conventional shopfloor workers, and those that remain are largely devoted to quality control. Learning once more from the Japanese, IBM has set itself the target of zero-defects. It was always the tenet of the traditional quality control department that there had to be a trade-off between the percentage of defects and the cost of removing these, and this was an exponential relationship; there was no possibility of achieving 100 per cent defect free product, and even achieving 99 per cent was usually prohibitively expensive. The key to success was thus traditionally seen to be in achieving the correct balance via the AQL (acceptable quality level). The Japanese revolutionized this by refusing to accept that 100 per cent was impossible, and IBM followed suit; the solution was simply in designing to *achieve* 100 per cent. IBM now rationalizes this by a rule of thumb that says that the cost of removing defects rises by an order of magnitude at each stage as work progresses from design through production to installation and then use (a ratio of 1000:1 overall).

There is a degree of irony in IBM learning from the Japanese. It is true that the Japanese originally took their quality control practices from the USA; and at the beginning of the 1950s recognized this by creating the Deming Prize, named after the American professor. Their breakthrough came with their development of quality circles, which ultimately led to the zero-defects philosophy. The irony is that it is very possible that the original model for these circles was IBM itself. The description of IBM in Peter Drucker's very influential book *The Practice of Management* (1955, Heinemann)—a bestseller in Japan—included admiring reference to its job enrichment programmes, and in particular to its very productive involvement of the plant staff in the design of new products; both concepts that the Japanese seized on and (as usual) developed to their logical conclusion. There is no indication that IBM, in later imitating the Japanese, realized that it was itself probably the original source.

The concentration of quality control functions is exaggerated by IBM's policy of not producing any item itself that another supplier could produce to the same quality and price. The quality demands are not, however, relaxed. Even the metal-bashers who produce cabinets are not excused the demanding quality standards that should make any supplier think twice. In my previous company, BTR, we struggled for five years in the late 1950s to produce the most basic handmade rubber tube that simply held a wiring loom in place. We never actually succeeded in meeting IBM's quality standards; but as with many IBM suppliers the totally disproportionate costs were justified on the basis of the cachet, and reference potential possible if we succeeded. Paradoxically, about the first thing I realized on reaching IBM was that the part had long since become obsolete in terms of current production!

The other major difference in IBM manufacturing is its *global* scale. Apart from the PC plants, which largely contain assembly lines, IBM factories only produce *parts* of a complete computer system. Thus, for a given system as ordered by a European customer, the water-cooled CPU might come from France (but with ceramic multi-layer substrates and memory modules from Germany, and power supplies from Spain), the disk drives might come from Germany and the tape drives from Spain, the printers from Sweden, and the display units (VDUs) from the UK but with network mini-computers as controllers coming from Italy! The result is that IBM in effect has to run a "single factory" with a number of separate departments producing a large range of components that are eventually bolted together to produce the final product. The fact that these individual departments are separated by thousand of miles is easily ignored. Physical transport, even by air, is relatively cheap compared with the very high cost (and now miniaturized) components; and is rapid. Electronic communication, which is essential for integrating control is, of course for IBM, second nature. In essence the logical factory, the "electronic shop floor," is held on computers at ISL (IBM Information Systems Limited), which is, amongst other things, IBM's own computerized production control centre, located at Portsmouth, England. Scheduling of all EMEA plants is accomplished there; even if the final destination is in South Africa and the plant is in Italy.

This problem is compounded by the fact that the development laboratory may be on the other side of the world (for example Rochester, Minnesota, for much of the Italian production), with customers spread over three continents. As a result, a major difference in IBM Manufacturing is the number of personnel specifically dedicated to communicating with other remote groups, from departments whose sole function is to maintain contact with the development lab to the centres of customer engineering expertise ("competence" in IBM's somewhat understated jargon), to support the maintenance (CE) engineers in the field.

So, in many respects, the majority of even the production personnel in IBM largely operate in an office environment.

Administration and General

This naturally leads on to the area in IBM which, in the manner that now afflicts all large companies, is threatening to consume all, particularly the profits: Administration and General (A&G). In IBM the sharp end, be it sales at one extreme or manufacturing at the other, is rigorously measured, and as such is containable and indeed is contained. A&G though is, as with any bureaucracy, essentially unmeasurable and IBM has as much difficulty as any other company in finding out just what this bureaucracy thinks it is doing, let alone in exerting control.

A&G is a global description for a wide range of functions. At its most obvious it contains the administrators who process all the paperwork, the many thousands of different forms that make any large organization tick. At least in IBM such material is now largely held in electronic form, which reduces the paper mountains to somewhat more manageable proportions; though anyone who has waited for a computer system to recover from a "crash" will be able to extol the virtues of the pencil and paper! IBM's stated intention is that almost *all* its desk workers in the UK will have their *own* dedicated terminal, with approximately 10,000 terminals in use in the UK, and nearly 200,000 worldwide, within IBM. The main problem this causes is that IBM has now become its own most complex customer, with the most advanced leading edge requirements. This may be very welcome to the other large customers who are normally used as "guinea-pigs," but problematic for the IBM administration system which as a result depends on a very fragile computer network.

At its most basic, the complexity of the IBM administrative system reflects the real complexities of that which it seeks to administer. There is no way that the activities necessary to bring together all the components (hardware, software and support) involved in a new 3090 water-cooled computer suite can be anything other than complex. At the same time much of the complexity is a function of incremental growth of systems to handle steadily growing complexity of operation; with no chance to start from scratch and design the ideal systems to meet even current needs, let alone future needs. As one particularly graphic example of this, in the 1970s when the main IBM World Trade Administrative System (WTAAS) was being developed, a particularly forward-looking decision was taken to provide this from the start as a terminal based system, which each administrator would access through his own terminal; a concept that has only been matched by reality in recent years. As this was not possible in the short term a temporary "batch processing front-end" was written to handle the paperwork which was then still the backbone of the system. This temporary front-end was incrementally improved over several years to handle new requirements. When, however, the fateful day came to switch to the full terminal based implementation it was found that these incremental changes had taken over the system and the front-end could not be discarded. Instead a new terminal handling front-end had to be written to feed the "temporary" batch front-end which in turn fed the original terminal oriented front-end!

A&G covers a multitude of functions, which is in itself one of the problems of control; how do you control a function which only its members understand? As an example of its diversity A&G even includes a range of departments handling property development. IBM is, in its own right, one of the world's major property developers, typically developing up to half a million square feet of new office space every year in the UK alone; not a bad achievement for a company dedicated to making the office building obsolete! To illustrate further the extremes of ephemera which IBM can support, and indeed needs to keep its bureaucratic functions alive, surely only IBM could afford to have a department headed by a manager with the title "Facilities Requirements Planning Manager"; whose sole function is rigorously to establish what new office buildings are needed every year in the UK!

A growing problem?

A&G may well be a black hole in absorbing ever increasing resource from IBM, but it is probably better controlled than most bureaucracies, simply because the calibre of the individual personnel and their motivation are once more significantly higher than in other companies. In the main the workers do exactly what is necessary, often by minor miracles, to ensure that their function fulfils its role effectively. The classic image of the bureaucrat as a work avoider is certainly *not* true of IBMers; they are indeed very close to the rational actor ideal behind Max Weber's optimistic theories of bureaucracy. The problem is simply the classic management dilemma of ensuring that the goals of the bureaucracy, and of each separate part of the bureaucracy, and those of IBM are in step. It is only too easy in an organization as culturally oriented as IBM for the departments to develop their own (superordinate) sub-goals; linked to survival of the group (as described by the cybernetic models of bureaucratic behaviour). The result may often be a more rigid bureaucracy implementing the formal rules of IBM to the very letter, and indeed adding further very professionally produced rules to protect the best interests of IBM as the group (somewhat parochially) sees it; unfortunately though without the wider perspectives of what constitute IBM's operations outside of the department in question. A&G is, even more than most organizations, prone to some of the symptoms identified by C. Northcote Parkinson. Being highly motivated self-starters, the members of any such IBM department will, in the absence of wider guidelines, very rapidly produce their own version, which makes the best possible sense but is based exclusively on the view from *within* the department, and probably in conflict with the wider unseen requirements.

The problem of geometric growth of the administrative bureaucracy may be even greater than IBM is willing to admit to itself, because all of its headcount figures are based on permanent employees. For whatever reasons, IBM in the UK for example, now employs temporary and contract staff on a regular basis in excess of one-third of its total work force; perhaps as many as 8,000. If most of these are allocated to A&G, for the functions they can handle fall into this area, then the scale of the true problem emerges.

This problem is perhaps highlighted by comparing the 3,000 permanent employees employed in administration in the UK at the end of 1983, with the total of only around 200 (permanent and temporary) supporting the new PC business at its current level of around 20 per cent of overall revenue; perhaps rising to 400 persons when PC business accounts for nearer half of IBM's total business in the 1990s. IBM's only answer, and it is a very effective one if it is available, is to grow the overall business so fast that the natural growth of A&G lags behind!

Apart from these largest groups in IBM there are a number of smaller departments which have an oddly disproportionate influence. One of these, Personnel (which also includes the rather lasciviously titled "Corporate Affairs"; handling relations with government), is so pivotal, both in myth and practice, that it is the subject of a separate chapter.

Finance

Finance is a key department in any company but its previously underrated position in IBM has possibly been strengthened by the new strategy of being the lowest cost producer. The role of Finance may well be the joker in the pack, for if it really develops the authority that it believes it ought to have then it will inevitably come into conflict with the culture and the less financial of IBM's controls.

On the other hand, the Japanese corporations, from whom IBM has learned its lowest cost producer approach, do not employ sophisticated financial techniques. Thus, Abbeglen and Stalk report: "Few Japanese companies employ the elaborate capital budgeting processes widely practised in the West. Indeed, few Japanese companies have the massive organizational apparatus called 'Finance' which is characteristic of Western companies." Once more IBM (though it does follow, at least in principle, the conventions of Western financial procedures) has some of the characteristics of a Japanese corporation, in that its key controls are non-financial and are the responsibility of a variety of departments far removed from finance.

Legal

One department that is uniquely powerful in IBM, where it probably barely exists in most other companies, is Legal. IBM has a long history of almost continuous legal battles with the US government, typified by the decades long anti-trust suits. As a result it is pathologically nervous of the legal implications of almost any decisions or activities; details that other companies would not even consider contentious. This is reflected in a unique, and important, offshoot; the Business Practices department. Its sole function is to act as a reference point, and in the process as a vetting agent, on any activity where there is not already a well-documented precedent. IBM, and in particular the field force, is ruled by a document entitled "Business Conduct Guidelines" which is a set of commandments by which every IBMer is required to live his business life. For the field force, who bear the brunt of implementing this code of ethics in a heathen outside world, this is extended to the tune of several hundred pages of the innocuously titled "General Information Section" of the sales manual.

This may seem very constricting, but in reality what is spelled out are the ethics of IBM's business behaviour. In essence it exhorts the individual to meet the highest standards in all his business dealings. This actually makes life easier for the individual who does not have to divert his efforts into bending the system to achieve his targets; for he knows the system is unbendable. He can accordingly concentrate all his efforts on doing the necessary job of providing the customer with the highest quality of support. This reached its peak in the fixed price list. For decades IBM salesmen did not have *any* flexibility in pricing. This was often extremely frustrating for those salesmen up against competitors buying business at low prices. It did, however, remove a very difficult problem for the salesmen (and for IBM); fraught negotiations over discount have crippled many customer relationships (and will the customer later find someone else who has negotiated an even better deal?). IBM's increasing domination of the marketplace over this period does not seem to indicate that this was really a weakness; rather the reverse, and IBM was never sucked into the self-destructive price-cutting spiral that has harmed many companies.

IBM is, however, in a state of flux. As you will see from other chapters, IBM is starting to think the previously unthinkable. It has for example, introduced discounts and is already being inexorably drawn into the whirlpool of ever more savage promotional pricing. For many years there has been a desire by some of the field force (often at junior management level) to be allowed to sail closer to the wind, to indulge in the more aggressive (if not questionable) sales tactics employed by its competitors; and to be rather less ethical with its customers. Such unworthy notions have traditionally been weeded out by Business Practices, backed by Legal, and IBM's purity has been maintained. Now, however, the question of how much IBM can get away with is being asked more frequently and more strongly; and occasionally it is now also being asked *by* Business Practices rather than *of it*! Its role has changed subtly from that of gamekeeper to poacher. IBM no longer has the threat of anti-trust action hanging over it, and a decade and a half of repressed aggression against its competitors is threatening to surface. IBM will not allow this to get out of control. The new role of Business Practices, though, may well be to channel this into the most acceptable forms of action; competitively productive but without discarding its basic ethics.

CHAPTER 9

Sales Supermen?

Introduction

Since the days of Thomas J. Watson the sales force has been at the focus of IBM's successful formula; and as such IBM's salesmen are rated higher than almost any other. But the factors responsible for their outstanding success are far removed from what most spectators might expect. They are the subject of Buck Rodgers' book, *The IBM Story,* which is an excellent, extended description of just how IBM makes its sales. It has been criticized as being simplistic (and to a degree there is indeed a lack of awareness of exactly how much IBM differs), but in fact it is merely an accurate description of IBM's *simple* formula for sales success.

For, once more, IBM is motivated by its beliefs; and in particular its second belief, "customer service," is the powerhouse of its sales activities. Its special strength is that this philosophy is implemented not just by a few salesmen, but by *all* IBMers in all departments. There is a genuine commitment by all employees to ensure that the customer's needs really do come first. Even the IBM salesmen work to the same philosophy; and it proves to be a uniquely strong guideline for developing the most powerful sales messages.

The salesmen and support staff are selected to be, above all, highly intelligent; with sound experience in the real world of business. They are then trained for more than a year, giving them the best possible technical and business appreciation; and they are given the best possible sales training, and which allows each to develop his own special talents.

Yet they are often poor performers in terms of conventional sales techniques. But they are superb at establishing rapport with their customers, understanding their businesses and solving their problems; and as a result their customers, justifiably, believe that they are just about the best sales force in the world.

They are motivated, and directed, by a particularly sophisticated sales plan, around which their (and their managers') commission system revolves; but above all they are inspired by the theatricality of the Hundred Per Cent Club, which around 80 per cent of the sales force attend each year (for most IBMers have to be winners, even if by design).

Sales training

Perhaps the best flavour of the IBM sales machine is contained in Buck Rodgers' book, *The IBM Way*. A great deal of its content may seem self-evident (indeed to the extent of being dismissed by critics as "motherhood"), but careful reading will show the philosophies that make the IBM sales team truly great. Not the least of these is his statement: "IBM is a sales-oriented company. That's because at IBM *everybody sells* . . . every employee has been trained to think that the customer comes first."

Sales School

For a number of years I was a manager of the UK "sales school." In that time I saw literally hundreds of IBM sales trainees and salesmen pass through the various programmes. Most of these were from the larger mainframes area, then DPD (Data Processing Division), but they also included a substantial number from GSD (General Systems Division). Though the latter group included a few salesmen recruited from other computer companies, the great majority had no previous sales experience; or indeed any data processing experience. IBM for many years had the philosophy of taking its sales trainees from industry.

The requirement is first that such recruits are highly intelligent; they must above all pass the Data Processing Aptitude Test (DPAT), which is in essence an intelligence test. The success of this simple filter is evident in the very high intellectual capacity of its sales force. The second requirement is that they should have had extensive experience of industry. This will enable them to communicate with their customers on the basis of their own experience rather than theory; or worse, as most non-IBM sales theory would emphasize, by sales techniques. Preference is given to those who have obtained such industry experience at a senior level, and best of all in management positions; I, for example, had been a general manager before entering IBM.

Sales ability, or even potential ability, is not therefore the prime measure of the recruits; though it must obviously play some part in the decision. As a result, the stream of recruits entering the sales school had more in common with that entering most companies boardrooms than their showrooms; and that was exactly as IBM wanted it. My personal observation was that, even at the end of their extensive sales training, they were just about as far removed from the conventional picture of the smooth sales operator as they could be; very few of them indeed would have lasted more than a few minutes selling from a stall in a town market.

How then have they achieved their enviable reputation? The answer was evident in the final product of the sales school. If observed carefully their sales styles could be faulted, on almost every front, by theorists of sales technique. But the sales trainees themselves were even more aware of their shortcomings; and they accordingly overcompensated massively in other areas. The style may not have been of the best but the content was superb! They had researched the customer needs in great depth and understood his problems as well as, and maybe even better than, he did. Their proposed solutions were, therefore, rooted in that customer's own experiences. They talked the customer's language, rather than that of sales technique. The customer was, quite justifiably, dazzled by the content; and missed the accompanying flawed technique. In any case the rapport they achieved is surely the epitome of a successful sales technique. The reputation is, therefore, based on content rather than on style.

IBM develops the sales skills over a very long training period. All those going into the sharp end of the field force, both salesmen and systems engineers, face a minimum of a year, and perhaps up to 18 months or two years of formal training. The length, content and level of this training is directly comparable with that of many post graduate courses; and indeed at one stage I used a large segment of the London Business School MBA course as an integral part of the training. IBM in its own right runs the largest private educational establishments in Europe.

The great part of this training concentrates on the content rather than the style of the sales pitch. The trainee spends perhaps as much as six months of the time sitting in the classroom learning about data processing. He learns in depth about languages and architectures, about software and hardware. He also learns about the wider business impacts of DP.

As one example of the sophistication of this process, for three years I myself ran the GSD Business School, through which passed nearly 200 of its trainees and field force. In two weeks of classroom teaching they learnt the fundamental theories of business management, based on material from the London Business School MBA course, as mentioned earlier. For a further two weeks they attended a residential course actually at the London Business School. This was taught by the lecturers and professors of that school, and took them through 20 of the case studies that are the heart of the MBA programme.

I describe this course in some detail not just because it was at that time recognized to be the most successful *sales* training course, but because it epitomizes the strengths of the training. It obviously did not teach a single sales technique. It did however teach an immense amount about business management; knowledge that would enable the salesmen to develop the necessary rapport with their customers.

It is possible that not all senior management at Armonk fully appreciated the subtleties of the programme (though John Opel certainly did). For example Buck Rodgers describes the very similar but later US developed Presidents Class as run by Harvard: ". . . requiring the marketing rep to role-play an IBM customer." The professors of the Harvard Business School may feel that this is somewhat of an understatement of their world famous case study technique which they used on the course (as we also did in London)!

"Calls"

There is, of course, specific sales training as well. Partly this takes place in the branch, by on the ground experience assisting salesmen and in-branch training programmes. Its heart, though, is typically two or three dedicated "communications" courses (often run as modules within the technical courses) leading up to the final sales school. There is a limited amount of classroom teaching of techniques. But, unlike much of the conventional sales training in other companies, these are taught not as the "correct ways of selling," but simply as components that trainees may wish to incorporate into their own selling style. The real meat of all these courses is a series of "calls," with an instructor playing the role of the customer or prospect. Typically run with a group of five or six trainees, each takes a turn to make a "call" on the instructor. The trainee has a written brief describing the outline of the call circumstances; and the instructor has a more detailed brief to allow him to play the role of the specific customer or prospect. These "calls" are very realistic and last much the same length of time (30 minutes), and follow much the same course, as a real life call; the situations are in fact derived from real life experiences in the field.

Over the various courses the trainee experiences perhaps 20 or 30 such "calls," progressively covering the range from opening the initial contact to, most difficult of all for salesmen, "closing" the sale. At the same time they see more than 100 "calls" made by their fellow trainees. At the end of each "call" the instructor, together with the other trainees, reviews the "call," using what happened as the basis for a teaching session. The aim is to give the greatest possible range of sales experiences so that each can develop his *own* unique style; based on his own natural style and abilities. There is no attempt to teach any standard style; despite Buck Rodgers' emphasis in his book on the teaching of the "structured" sales call.

The belief in each developing his own style goes back to IBM's earliest days. T. J. Watson, speaking in 1917 to a New York audience, said: "When practising the art of selling use all your talents. Put everything you have into your efforts; above all put your personality into them. Never copy anybody. *Be yourself*" (Sobel op. cit.).

At the end of the review session the instructor rates the call, usually in the satisfactory range (from + to −) but occasionally good or weak. Only very rarely is it graded unsatisfactory. There is one further, IBM unique grade; UDH (unsatisfactory did harm). This admonishment is reserved for those trainees who breach IBM's sacrosanct rules of business conduct. The grades are summed over the course to give a final grade; and can accordingly terrorize poor students as they prepare to return to their branch!

This evaluation process reaches its peak in the sales school, which despite its title has nothing to do with learning, but is an extended exam. It is two weeks of evaluated calls and presentations on which the trainee has to obtain a satisfactory overall grade before he can pass-out (probably quite literally since the following sales school party often releases the tensions of many months; a very therapeutic, if unusually alcoholic, IBM device). Most trainees in fact pass; even I passed, and (as my instructors were only too willing to tell me) I am definitely not a natural salesman! Those few who do fail, however, face the ultimate ignominy of returning to the branch to try again (when they usually pass); no Japanese loss of face can match such an experience!

The Systems Engineers (SEs) who support the salesmen in the field, are not required to have the same degree of industry experience, and a number of them are recruited direct from university. They do, though, have to meet the same high intellectual standards. In general, they follow exactly the same training path as sales trainees, with the addition of some technical courses. They do not attend sales school, but instead have their own SE school; which, although more technically based, has an even more terrifying reputation than sales school.

Surely only IBM can afford to take in such high calibre, and highly paid, staff and then spend up to 18 months simply training them? The cost may be up to $100,000 per head. The end result, though, fully justifies the expense and effort; and represents the great strength of IBM.

Sales strategy

It is to IBM's great credit, and to its even greater profit, that it does not waste this reservoir of trained talent. The field force is given its head, with the very maximum of delegated responsibility. The salesman, once he has been given his set of accounts (or geographic/industry territory), is totally in charge. He alone coordinates all the IBM resources necessary to support existing, and win new, business. Typically the sales campaigns are extended, often taking many months. In this time he, and the SEs who support him, will get to know the customer's business in great depth; sometimes perhaps in greater depth than anyone on the customer's own staff. Again it is this knowledge, rather than any sales technique, that is the strength of the sales campaign.

The investment pays off, because IBM wins the largest share of new business, and virtually all of that from its own customer base. The individual amounts can reach into the millions. At the lowest end it is an Armonk/EHQ directive that even new business salesmen should not be allowed to waste time on accounts worth less than $40,000 (though in reality they sometimes are given dispensation, but not support, to go down to $20,000). It is clear why IBM is trying so strenuously to persuade agents to cover the mainframe business below this level.

Forecasting

The salesman may be autonomous in running his accounts, but he is very clearly accountable to his marketing manager (IBM's rather misleading title for a first level sales manager) and then to his branch manager. He has, at least once a year, to provide an account plan for each of his accounts. Then at monthly reporting sessions he has to provide his 30 day, 60 day and 90 day forecasts; and subsequently meet them. It is these forecasts, grossed up at each level to national (and beyond), that drive IBM in the short term. They are awaited each month just as eagerly by the general manager as by the branch manager.

It is reckoned by the *cognoscenti* that the branch manager is just about the best job in IBM. Each has his own small business; well hardly small, because its turnover will probably exceed $100 million per annum. The branch manager runs this as his personal fiefdom, with the absolute minimum of intervention from above; just so long as he continues to meet his targets. He manages between 50 and 100 of the most intellectually stimulating individuals you are ever likely to meet. It is a very nice life indeed for the few that reach it.

The branch is the building block of IBM (after the individual salesman). It is, in the very legitimate analogy of the army, the "line" unit (and "line" management is indeed the descriptive term used within IBM). Even the head office support departments tend to follow the army model; including the rotation of management between line and staff.

Motivation

The document that controls the salesman, and the field force in general, is the sales plan. At the beginning of every year its publication is avidly awaited, because it spells out exactly how the salesman will earn his living during the year. In the UK he may earn as little as 50 per cent of his income from the base salary, though more likely it will be 60 to 70 per cent; and in any case there could be guarantees that ensure he can rely on at least 70 per cent. As there is a 10 per cent uplift for moving from a steady staff income to the commission-based sales income, the actual maximum shortfall may be less than 20 per cent. The last time I went on quota, the IBM term for the commission system, I struck a deal whereby I was on a 90 per cent base salary and I still obtained the 10 per cent uplift; all the commission was pure profit. That was, though, an unusually generous deal, even for IBM!

This commission is paid on performance against quota. This quota is a set of targets usually measured in "points," an artificial measure applied worldwide (without distortions caused by currency fluctuations); originally one point equalled $1 rental income per month. The exact way the various targets are built up, to "incent" the salesmen to undertake the various actions that the country management—and ultimately Armonk—want, is a true work of art. It takes many man months of effort to produce the plan which in its simplest form runs into tens of pages. It is understandable, therefore, that the advice given to new salesmen by the "old hands" is to take it home and spend at least a week working out the most profitable use of their time over the next year.

The Hundred Per Cent Club

The real motivator, though, is the HPC (Hundred Per Cent) qualification. The targets for this might be different from those driving the quota system; but it is still the HPC which will win. It is worth relatively little, three days in a European resort for example, but the loss of face involved in not attending the "Club" is unthinkable. Back at the branch those failing drown their sorrows in their own (IBM unrecognized) Ninety-Nine Per Cent Club.

The HPC has been a matter of sales pride since T. J. Watson brought it with him from NCR. It is a matter of honour that each individual, and each Branch, should "make the Club." It is also a matter of honour that each branch manager should get the maximum number of his sales team into the Club; and this results in a brisk, but illicit, trading of points within the branch at year end. Indeed this is a key aspect of IBM's policy, for around three quarters of the sales force is expected to achieve at least 100 per cent performance (meaning that the "average" performance level is actually around 115 per cent). Other companies setting "realistic" targets are likely to see (by definition) only around half their salesmen achieving that magic 100 per cent. The result is that while up to three-quarters of IBM's salesmen are *winners*, in most other companies no more than half are; and in those (not infrequent) companies where the 100 per cent target is unduly optimistic, perhaps more than two-thirds of the sales force are *losers*. The use of such unrealistically high targets may allow the company to appear to offer very high "on-target" earnings, but this all too soon becomes obvious to the recipient, and the potential impact on morale and motivation (as well as losses of good salesmen) is obvious.

At the end of the day the lucky many, for usually at least three-quarters qualify, attend the Club. In Europe this is the "Convention." It is held in a suitable resort—Cannes is the favourite of most IBMers, but it can range from Rhodes to Berlin. The key requirement, which is difficult for most resorts to meet, is the ability to house more than 1,000 IBMers in bedrooms and the convention centre. This means that it is a rule that all non-managers have to share bedrooms. You are accordingly very fortunate if your roommate shares your lifestyle. My first club was in Berlin, where returning in the small hours, in the company of my roommate, we were disconcerted to hear an unholy racket emerging from the vicinity of our bedroom in the Kempinski hotel; evidently a party was under way, and our sleep was destined to be disturbed. This proved to be even more true than we expected, for the party was in our room! It was only closed down when the management objected to its participants roller skating nude up and down the corridors of the hotel!

Indeed it seems to be almost a matter of honour at European Clubs that salesmen, particularly those most recently qualified, should break as many of IBM's Business Conduct Guidelines in as short a space of time as possible. My most enduring memory of the Berlin Club is of the Kurfurstendam (the red light district) in the small hours of the morning filled with unsteadily weaving figures accosting every "lady" in sight; but to a man dressed in dark suits and white shirts!

The theory of the convention is rather different. It is intended to be an uplifting business meeting; at least that is what the tax authorities are encouraged to believe. Two half-days are, therefore, given over to business sessions with elaborate audio-visual presentations; often costing not far short of $100,000. As a result IBM is a pinnacle of the multi-media presentation, complete with orchestra, dancers and all the trimmings; though the one that had on-stage fireworks which burnt the set down and caused a major emergency is particularly well-regarded in the folklore! It brings in major outside speakers, Peter Ustinov is a favourite—to leaven the glowing descriptions of past achievements, and triumphs yet to come, by senior IBM executives. It is a very slick, professional event that may cost millions of dollars in total to mount and takes the efforts of most of the Communications Department (numbering some tens of IBM staff) for three months each year.

It is mainly an excuse for a beano, and a very enjoyable one at that; with lavish formal meals, crowned by the gala night which will feature at least one international star specially flown in for the occasion (ranging from Ella Fitzgerald to Elaine Page, depending on the organizers" taste).

The US HPC is rather different. It is a true recognition event, and follows that format strictly. The business sessions eschew visiting raconteurs and concentrate instead on the process of recognition. Thus for three hours at a stretch in the "main tent" (in fond memory of the 1940s heydays of the Club in "tent city" at Endicott) salesmen are personally "recognized" for every conceivable virtue and achievement. It starts with the "election" of the committee (by management) leading to that of the club president. At my first US Club this latter part of the action was signalled by the president elect being accompanied to the rostrum by a complete high school marching band. As everyone is "recognized" they *run* to the front, to the wild cheering of the members of their branch. Then the assembled masses sing the IBM songs, without any trace of embarrassment, and with great gusto.

To some of the few other Europeans who attended with me, this was embarrassing in the extreme. I didn't find it so: it was quite simply the public celebration of the US dream of salesmanship; and who would deny that hard-won pleasure? I actually preferred the US Clubs to their European counterparts; mainly because there was not the same frantic need for "enjoyment." Indeed the US Club is a much more sober event. The main drama at the first gala dinner I attended was the serving of the wine; it was the first time it had ever been served at a Club (and even then was strictly limited in quantity). Perhaps my preference is just due to the fact that I can recall fond memories without the accompanying memories of king-size hangovers!

Business Conduct Guidelines

The Club apart, the daily life of the field force is ruled by "Business Conduct Guidelines." This is a document which all IBMers in the field, and key personnel in staff, must read at least once a year (and have to sign to that effect). It lays down the philosophies that guide all the activities of IBM in the field. The even more detailed policies, to cover all eventualities from contact with competitors (don't) to receiving gifts from customers (don't), are spelled out in one of the sections of the multi-volume sales manual; the "General Information Section," which in printed form comes to more than 100 large pages of small print. The one formal reprimand I received while in IBM was for dispensing wine too liberally, above the carefully documented limit (which my assistant had not noticed), at one recognition event I ran!

Customer service

The behaviour of the IBM field force is, therefore, constrained by a set of principles which justifiably earn IBM one of its many nicknames: Snow White. Many of IBM's recruits expect this emphasis on ethical conduct to cramp their style. The reality is usually the opposite. Competitor's salesmen spend a great deal of their time trying to overcome their prospects'—usually fully justified—fear that they are being fed nothing more than a sales pitch. IBM salesmen, and in particular SEs (who I always held were IBM's most effective marketing force; simply because their customers trusted and respected them), start from the basis that their integrity is "guaranteed" by IBM's reputation. Quite simply this allows the sales force to spend all their time investigating their prospect's needs; the real hard selling.

This may be summed up by Frank Cary's reminiscence of his time as an IBM salesman: "What I liked was selling a product with high intellectual content. It was not a pitchman operation. It was very professional." (Fishman op. cit.)

The pay-off for the customer, which they fully recognize (in the oft reported quote intended to be derogatory, but actually rather flattering to IBM: "nobody ever got fired for choosing IBM"), is that they can rely on the integrity of IBM and of its staff. They may still have problems, there are cowboys in every company and IBM is no exception. The difference is that the customer can appeal over their heads, and senior management will ultimately live up to IBM's high principles. I have a number of times been involved in situations where such management have moaned and groaned and blustered (for they ideally would have wished to walk away from the problem), but after all the noise everybody involved knew that IBM's principles would triumph in the end. To all intents and purposes IBM is Snow White.

Indeed the real strength of IBM's sales operation, underneath all the superficialities, is an attitude of mind, a philosophy. It is enshrined in its second belief of "service to the customer." In the UK 1984 *Annual Review* (provided to all employees) it is explained as follows:

> In many offices in IBM you can see the slogan "remember the customer pays your salary." This is a constant reminder to everyone that their job is to meet the needs of the customer. Customer service is not only the responsibility of the salesman

> and customer engineer. It is also the job of the development engineer, the assembly line technician and the administrator.

It was summarized by Tom Watson Jr., in *A Business and its Beliefs* as: "We want to give the best customer service of any company in the world."

This was a philosophy embraced from the first day T. J. Watson arrived. His motto was "we sell and deliver service," and he believed that when a sale is made both sides come out ahead. It was a belief bolstered, until very recently, by IBM's method of doing business. Frank Cary stated: "If I was to select one single business practice that was most important to our success in the early days, it would be that we only leased equipment. This put a discipline on the business that was excellent. It motivated IBM people and it built a great relationship of trust between the customer and the company. The customer knew he had leverage."

In the days of the rental base the worst failure was the loss of an existing customer. Winners of new business were lionized. But the essence of the company was the growth of existing customer business. A loss of an existing customer had an immediate negative impact on sales (the rental was lost); hence the important measure, still applied, was *net* sales revenue increase. Worse, it lost the growth potential of that customer; worse still, it was a slur on IBM's competence, which would be gleefully seized upon by the winning competitor for his publicity. It is obvious why salesmen did not look forward to loss review meetings!

The impact is that the whole thrust of IBM's sales effort is to generate satisfied customers; the sale itself is only the first step. With such a philosophy any company will eventually win its customers' trust, and their business.

As already stated, it may be significant that IBM has experienced its first major problem just as it diluted its commitment to "Customer Service" in order to pursue the goal of "Lowest Cost Producer." Its problems with its dealers, where "Customer Service" is a joke (or at least dealer personnel think it is), even more graphically illustrate the dangers of abandoning this basic philosophy.

CHAPTER 10

Party Time!

Introduction

IBM's business has gradually evolved to the state where it is selling ever larger numbers of ever cheaper boxes. The only way that IBM could hope to handle the numbers of these new customers was by handing over the lower end of its business to "retailers."

It did this in the first instance almost by default, with the birth of the PC; and then, following the initial stupendous success of the PC, with great enthusiasm (as the answer to almost any problem). In the process it naively handed over reponsibility for its key end-users to a group of people who were often ill-equipped (certainly far worse equipped than IBM itself) to maintain IBM's normal high standards; and then it even stimulated pricecutting, which rapidly eroded any standards that *were* there. IBM is only now beginning to learn (and even then very slowly) from the mistakes it made then.

It is becoming more selective of the third parties to which it cedes its responsibility for end-users; and it is establishing a somewhat tighter degree of control over them. But it still does not fully understand, as would any more conventional marketer, the basic need to control the customer (the end-user) by conventional marketing techniques. Third parties are still, therefore, as much a threat as an opportunity; and indeed much of the blame for IBM's recent problems could be laid at their door.

This chapter could not have been written less than half a decade ago. Even at the end of the 1970s, IBM was still zealously guarding its sol to contact with its customer base. At that time even the suppliers of specialized applications software were viewed with suspicion as competitors. Towards the end of the decade, however, this attitude started to change, as GSD found that it couldn't make certain sales without this specialist software. Even more important it found that it was in need of the support of the personnel from software houses to help with its growing installation load. GSD thus found itself with the problem of how, within IBM's very strict rules on even-handedness, it could discreetly "recommend" such suitable software to customers.

The initial solution was that the salesman was allowed to provide a list of *all* the possible software houses; even those that would probably do a poor job. The prospect then had to rely on the salesman indicating, totally illicitly—by a twitch of the eye or a cough—which might be suitable! The need for such amateur dramatic skills in its sales force was progressively reduced, as IBM allowed smaller and smaller lists; until in the early 1980s it bowed to the inevitable and moved towards joint marketing. It set up an in-branch organization to handle SSOs (Systems Support Organizations).

IBM Office Products Division had already developed relations with some dealers who sold, reconditioned, the typewriters it took in part exchange. It still did not go as far, however, as allowing any of the many specialist typewriter dealers to sell new ones; that was the prerogative of the IBM salesmen patiently trudging from one office to the next.

PC dealers

The revolution in IBM's distribution channels, though, appeared with the PC. The *only* way the IBU, with no sales resources of its own, could sell the product was through dealers. It was fortunate that such a dealer network had already emerged to serve the growing market developed by Apple and the other infant micro manufacturers. One of the first of the dealers, the original Byte Shop (not to be confused with later stores using the same name), had already made its own contribution to the PC revolution, by buying the first 50 Apple IIs.

Perhaps the most important leader of this retail revolution was William H. Millard. In 1974 he launched a company, IMSAI, to build what was claimed to be the first truly integrated PCs; sold as kits to hobbyists and the rapidly growing numbers of retailers (through small ads in *Popular Electronics*). The computer, the IMSAI 8080, may not have made Millard's fortune, but his resulting experiences with the inexperienced and under-capitalized retailers did! In 1976 (at the same time as the Byte Shop was selling its first few Apples) he asked his sales director, Ed Faber (an ex-IBM manager), to start a new franchise operation, soon to become Computerland. Faber first designed a pilot store at Hayward, California, with the then revolutionary concept of providing a "full service" store offering under one roof all that the customer needed to support his PCs. He then moved very rapidly to set up the franchises. The first franchisee was in Morristown, New Jersey, and was rapidly followed by a chain across the USA. It set a pattern that still dominates PC retailing. By the time IBM arrived on the scene the network of branches, all run by franchisees, had grown to 190 in number. By the end of 1985, when Millard retired, there were some 800 branches (including some 200 outside the USA), and he had become another of the computer billionaires.

Thus, at the time the PC was launched there was already the basis of a retail network, which could be signed up immediately (and was); one that IBM made good use of. There were, of course, many other independent retailers, and many more sprang up to exploit the market tapped by the PC (and, of course, there were the inevitable competitors who copied Computerland; albeit on a smaller scale). PC retailing became one of the few explosive growth areas of business in the early 1980s.

Buoyed up by the success it had made distributing PCs via dealers, typewriter dealers were also introduced by IBM, as were a similar concept, VARs (value added resellers) for its languishing Series/1. This whole process was a revelation to IBM. Whilst not totally unplanned, the revolution soon overwhelmed what plans there were; no-one in 1980 would have ever thought in their wildest dreams (or nightmares) that up to one-third of IBM's total business might be handled by third parties in 1990 (the current publicly quoted IBM forecast). As a result of these revelations IBM indulged in its usual habit of setting up a number of task forces. The task force flavour of the month became "channels"; that is channels of distribution. No longer was IBM to be constrained by the limitations of its own sales forces; its future was also to be through third parties.

The "solution" of third parties came as an answer to a maiden's prayer. IBM had just realized that it was moving into the business of ever lower-priced boxes; selling in ever larger quantities. It had also just committed itself to the philosophy of being the world's lowest-cost producer. Although this was a philosophy largely aimed at manufacturing, justifying the massive investment in highly automated new plant, IBM was beginning to realize it should be paralleled by a similar commitment on the marketing front. This was a very difficult, if not impossible, objective within the parameters set by IBM's normal overheads. The target, that no IBM salesmen should ever visit a prospect that is worth less than $40,000 in business, would leave a great many accounts uncovered if it were not for the third parties.

Agents

Third parties, as evidenced by PC dealers, seemed to offer a very suitable alternative. So, following its new found enthusiasms and the recommendations of its task forces, IBM was now set on offering even its range of mainframes (at least the smaller ones, up to the smaller 4300s) by the same channels! It was understandably nervous, however, about allowing mainframe third parties the degree of freedom that PC dealers enjoyed; and it didn't, in any case, much relish the cost of supporting their relatively high margins. The apparent answer, identified by the task forces, was the use of agents. These would act on behalf of IBM, in exactly the same way as IBM's own salesmen and SEs. For a margin, or commission, they would sell and install; exactly according to IBM's rules. IBM would undertake all the other activities, and would accept all responsibility (unlike the dealers, where IBM accepted no responsibility for their actions).

IBM had already started some mainframe activity in the form of CMAs (complementary marketing agreements), whereby software houses with specific products (and skills) were funded by IBM to install the IBM products as well as their own. This was obviously attractive to the CMAs, who would have undertaken much of the effort anyway. It was not, though, a major marketing effort by IBM standards.

The die was thus cast for agents, but it took something like 18 months for IBM, with a number of task forces, to decide the details. It was obvious from the beginning that agents with specific products, the existing CMAs, would inevitably be included. The more debatable decision was that of territory agents; agents without specific products who would be given a geographical area (North Wales, for example) or an industry type, where IBM would not otherwise sell. In the end IBM *did* also include territory agents; though it proved more difficult to recruit these than the CMAs.

The second question revolved around *who* within IBM would manage the agents. Initially it was assumed that this would be by a staff function, located within BDD (Business Development Division), as too was PC Group at that time. Eventually, the somewhat surprising decision (at least to those in the team already set up in BDD) was taken to manage the agents out of the branches (specifically out of ISM; the small mainframes division).

The final decision was the level of discount (commission or margin). The original plan looked for only around eight per cent (compared with the 30 to 36 per cent for PC dealers); though this was eventually just about doubled (with what effect on IBM's profits it is difficult to quantify).

It is still early days, but the indications are that the agent programmes are not proving as much of a bonanza as those of the PC dealers; though this might be due to the less favourable business climate (the typewriter dealers set up at the same time have also had a less than dramatic degree of success). Since the beginning of the project there have always been those, though, who have held that *all* the business must go to the dealers, not agents; but time will tell (though there is already some evidence that the promoters of a totally dealer-based solution are now winning at least some of the arguments).

This has resulted in a three-level hierarchy of sales activities. At the top are the traditional IBM sales forces; selling in their inimitable style the larger mainframes to the larger accounts. In the middle come the newest addition; the agents selling low-end mainframes to smaller prospects (who might previously have been on IBM's calling list). At the lowest level are the dealers; selling, in particular, PCs to a myriad of end-users. The picture appears to be muddied by dealers being split into two tiers, with the upper tier limited in numbers (to perhaps 10 to 15 per cent of the total) providing a more sophisticated level of support on more complex machines that start to overlap the agent layer. Whatever the outcome of this latest change in strategy, the grand design appears to have a neat logic to it. It is, though, a significant departure from the style of selling IBM knows so well; which now only represents the top layer of the hierarchy. It is significant that Buck Rodgers devotes less than two pages of his book to the dealers (and doesn't even mention agents), despite his claim to have presented the original "scenario" for such new "channels of distribution." Armonk is nothing if not courageous in its moves. It almost seems to relish the new challenges. The jury is still out, however, on the verdict as to whether this new departure will be as all-conqueringly successful as all the others that have preceded it; and perhaps the key element, and the least predictable, is that of the dealers.

The retail picture

One rather peculiar factor common to the PC dealer networks worldwide is that they are almost exclusively the province of small businesses. The large chains, such as Computerland and its clones, are franchised; so that their 1,000 or more franchisees are each a small business; and, even so, the large chains have been struggling for survival. This has not been for want of ambition, or lack of expectation of profit, by the larger organizations. Even in the UK, which has some of the most sophisticated multiple retailers in the world, all their efforts have effectively come to nought. Entries from Tesco (one of the leading supermarket chains), W. H. Smith (the leading bookseller, stationer and supplier of low-price business equipment), together with Dixons and Currys (the two main domestic electrical and electronic goods retailers) have signally failed to make the expected inroads on the market; and even these companies have apparently had largely to abandon their more ambitious plans.

It is not clear why this should be. At least in the UK, multiples run in the high street by managers, have predominated in recent years. At the same time, in the computer industry it has most often been the giants, notably IBM, that have made the running. It seems most likely that, however low by most standards, the calibre of the individuals running the independent retailers is that much higher than for the multiples; where the intellectual calibre in the computer industry is generally high, that in management of high street multiples is not necessarily as high, and the multiples' existing staff were often uncritically drafted into these new ventures. Whatever its cause, the success of small business in this field should gladden the hearts of those "monetarist" priests still left influencing Western governments.

IBM has no direct control over such retailers; they are several thousand independent businesses, who simply stock IBM PC equipment along with that of other manufacturers. For obvious reasons, IBM cannot set or enforce any direct standards, such as setting retail prices. To achieve some limited degree of indirect control, therefore, IBM insisted on a *very* high standard for those items it *could* legitimately demand. Thus dealers were required to have a ground floor showroom with at least one demonstration model of each IBM product they are authorized to sell (where each product is authorized separately). The reason for this was not so much the belief in IBM that such facilities are essential, though the specifications are logically based on its own retail experience; which was in turn influenced most obviously by Computerland, as were most such retail stores. The real reason for these, and the other apparently unnecessarily onerous conditions, was probably that they were a device to raise the entry price to such a level that only companies of substance can afford to buy in to the game! This "cover charge" is of the order of $50,000 (but the true cost of setting up a new Computerland franchise, for example, is at least 10 times this); and certainly the most dubious operators have been held at bay. In Europe perhaps as few as 20 per cent of all PC retailers have qualified.

Unfortunately, as we will see later, this high entry price did not prove to be a successful filter for determining which dealers would best match IBM's, or the market's, real needs. Indeed its more arbitrary elements may actually have contributed to the subsequent problems. In particular, its emphasis on the "showroom" may have bred a generation of PC salesmen more closely related to those of the car showroom (and especially to those of the used-car showroom!) than to those of IBM's own professional sales force.

The high street retailer, based on the Computerland model, has been a strong force in the USA; probably accounting for the majority of sales. In Europe, and particularly in the UK, the picture is more complex. Due to the relatively late entry of the US chains such as Computerland (and its clones) the initial market was captured by software and systems houses; and these probably still have the major part of sales. The terminology is probably, however, now rather misleading, since a large proportion of these now offer services which are indistinguishable from the high street chains; only differing in their image (in particular, they are away from the prime high street sites). A few of them do however still offer, like the CMAs in the mainframe market, a degree of specialist (software) expertise, often relating to their own packages, which allows them to write and tailor special programs; and selling the PC itself has become a highly profitable sideline.

Discounting

There has, unfortunately, now developed another breed: the "box-shifters." These now tend to dominate the scene. These are the outlets, sometimes high street retailers or systems houses but mainly stores specializing in this form of business, which obtain their business by selling at a discount; with much of the flavour of the Eastern bazaar! The essence of this PC sales process has become the art of haggling; on the one front the customer holds out for the highest discount, and on the other the retailer pares his support to nothing and hopes (often foolishly) that he won't be forced into bankruptcy. It could not be further from IBM's usual style of sophisticated support for selling in depth. Yet it is possibly due in no small part to IBM's own (albeit unconscious) choosing. Compaq, for example, point out with great glee to dealers that their products are not as heavily discounted as those of IBM; and paradoxically Compaq has assumed, very profitably, much of the mantle discarded by IBM.

IBM's possible (if unthinking) involvement in this new price war is inevitably complex. In the first place, in the scramble to achieve the largest possible network of dealers, where sales were directly proportional to the size of the network, IBM occasionally allowed its standards to slip; some did not meet even the basic standards, let alone the very high standards IBM would really like to see. In fact I have visited some, fortunately relatively few, IBM authorized dealers whose style of business (and their premises. despite IBM's stringent specifications) were down-market of a junk shop. IBM may eventually regularize its network but in the meantime there are a number of such dealers constantly hovering on the brink of bankruptcy, desperate to keep their stock moving at almost any cost.

IBM's structure of price-breaks was the second incentive to discounting. When an order for 50 units was required, to achieve the magic 36 per cent margin, some dealers would sell the last few units at ludicrous discounts (even at a loss) to obtain the 36 per cent across *all* their purchases. IBM has now changed to larger "contract" periods but the effect is much the same. They thus hope to make the margin needed to stay in business on their "normal" sales, and don't notice when they cease to have such normal sales; and all sales are at the discount rate that almost inevitably leads to their bankruptcy. This process has now been accelerated by IBM's new found practice of promotional offers to clear its excess stocks at the end of a product life cycle. Again dealers are tempted to load in stock; where this may give an additional margin approaching 10 per cent it is difficult for any dealer to resist.

These pressures were first applied by IBM at a time when the market was in any case sensitive. It was the end of the PC product cycle, and buyers were nervously awaiting the launch of the PC2 (and accordingly were not willing to pay "premium" prices for the old line). The inevitable result was a discounting war for the larger buyers, business. Initially this development was welcomed at IBM; for lower prices (funded by the retailers, not by IBM) surely meant higher sales volumes. The fact that this price-cutting was alien to IBM's normal business practices was largely ignored. IBM also ignored the lessons learnt by many other companies selling quality products in other fields. Discounting not only slashes your profit margins, but also destroys your quality image: how often have you seen a cut-price offer on a Rolls Royce? As mentioned earlier it is now Compaq, without IBM's massive technical resources, which is increasingly seen (at least by the dealers) as the quality manufacturer!

Most likely IBM's, probably temporary, blindness in this area is a function of its history. It has become almost a tradition, for the larger mainframes which are its main business, that IBM milks the last ounce of profit out of the end of a dying product line. This is achieved by significantly reducing the prices in the last year or so of a product's life. The theory of this, which is borne out in practice, is that this tempts out all the buyers wavering over their decisions (plus some who decide they cannot pass up a bargain). In effect it is a sales "loader." The profit on the dying line (which has already more than recouped all its costs) is thus maximized, and the pipeline is cleared ready for the new product.

I suspect that the "stock pressure" applied by IBM to the PC during 1985 (offering special purchase discounts of up to 45 per cent) was a comparable technique. It was, however, applied to a new level of distribution, the PC dealers, who did not understand the subtleties of the process. As a result they, in effect, took the whole process too seriously, and magnified the impact far beyond what IBM would have normally expected. On the way they almost panicked, and destabilized the market, with unexpected and unwelcome effects even for IBM.

It takes a little time for a company as large as IBM to respond, however; particularly where its response could set new precedents. After all, the problem it was addressing was probably the result of a previous response. Armonk thinks long and hard before it commits itself. No Russian chess grandmaster ever pondered as deeply on the possible future moves and countermoves open to it. Thus the stock pressure was continued by IBM through into 1986, despite the fact that all its market research showed that support (which was widely sacrificed by dealers to allow for the discounting) was all important and price was secondary. It was despite the reports from the dealers that it was lack of support for end-users that was holding the market back; and that the bazaar-like atmosphere of haggling over prices did not inspire confidence. It was also despite IBM's historically successful policy of promoting the best *overall* deal, with support being the critical item justifying firm prices (but also being essential to ensure the customers' installations went well; a detail IBM tended to overlook in the case of the PC). It is possible that IBM PC management had earlier been seduced by the idea that it was its dealers who were subsidizing the prices, and consequently failed to notice the resulting impact on support.

This price-cutting has hurt IBM, since it stimulated the introduction of the cheap PC clones from the Far East, forcing IBM itself to cut prices and reduce its margins even more. This even caused John Akers publicly to speculate, in mid-1986, that IBM might possibly have to consider pulling out of the market if it in effect became a "commodity market"; an admission of the possibility of a defeat that would be very hard for IBM to accept (and would be very damaging to their customers as well; with the potentially calming influence of the only standard maker removed).

Solutions

In the USA, the first external move to bring dealers back into line with IBM's more usual philosophies of service and support was heralded by the freezing of the dealer network. No new dealerships were to be granted for a period; it was hinted that this was to be an extended period (perhaps a couple of years). This is an example of the blunt instrument approach which IBM uses so successfully to maintain internal discipline. Given the imminent announcement of the PC2, which would have tended to harden market prices, it was likely that IBM would reassert control (and at least stop the worst excesses of self-destructive discounting). In any case the initial move during 1985, of relocating PC in the Big Blue fold, promised a more traditional approach in future.

In the UK, and in Europe in general, the problem was more complex. Having seen the runaway success of the PC in the USA (but having been barred by limitations on manufacturing capacity from launching in Europe), EHQ was very enthusiastic to get started; and in its enthusiasm it probably negotiated an unnecessarily constricting deal with the EEC (at a time when IBM was still involved in the EEC investigation of its overall business). It accordingly gave guarantees of even-handedness in its treatment of dealers, which severely limits the control (or sanctions) it can now deploy. As one result, it cannot freeze the European network, as it might wish, but has to achieve the same result by stringently applying those rules it already has at its command.

Despite IBM's brave noises, it has not really imposed much discipline on its unruly rabble of dealers. To outsiders it has not even seemed to have much stomach for the battle. Where, if we are to believe DeLamarter's *Big Blue*, it has been ruthless in its pursuit of its competitors it has shirked the task of disciplining the puny (in IBM terms) dealers who are doing it (and IBM's customers) far more damage. My impression is that, for once, IBM's much vaunted sales machine is to blame. These "Dealer Account Managers" (DAM's) have the rather schizophrenic function of being both policemen (they have to monitor the behaviour and standards of their dealers) and salesmen (they are responsible for maximising IBM's short-term sales). As always, in IBM's operational units, the one prime thrust is for sales in the short term (since commission, and "Club" qualification) is dependent only on these. It is not surprising that the policeman's role has not been widely implemented, even though this is essential to IBM's long-term interests. Thus, the sales force make brave noises about discipline, and then get on with the real business of shifting more boxes; where the worst offenders (in terms of failure to meet IBM's standards) are typically the shifters of the most boxes (and, as a result, are most favoured, rather than disciplined, by their DAM's)!

On the one hand, IBM *has* successfully implemented a major new marketing structure which allows it to tap markets that were otherwise outside its grasp, and it has done this with a degree of success that has not been matched by any of its competitors; but as a result, it is faced with a major problem. This is the dilemma of how to integrate the activities of the two lower levels of the new hierarchy into its overall business. It is too early to say how agents will behave. It is clear, though, that PC dealers are not easily ensnared by IBM's culture and philosophies; though, as yet, IBM has not indicated that it wishes this. From the customer's point of view, however, IBM is just as much represented (albeit not legally) by its dealers (even the unauthorized ones!) as by its own sales forces. It will, accordingly, need to find some suitable device for imposing its ethics and philosophies on its unruly flock. What such a device might be is difficult to say; though a self-regulatory (and independent) body setting higher standards (with awards of rosettes, as per *Michelin Guide* for restaurants?) might not go amiss. What is likely is that, even though it has been unsuccessful to date,

Armonk will go on making the attempt to find a solution; and it is unusually successful in controlling the uncontrollable. I look forward with interest to developments; since it is not impossible that the mandarins in IBM may be able to add to their long list of organizational innovations one which resolves the perennial problem of controlling standards of service through third parties.

Since writing this paragraph at the beginning of 1986, it has become apparent that, as suggested earlier, IBM's chosen solution may well be a hierarchy of dealers (a pyramid structure). At the bottom will be the whole range of existing dealers selling the smaller, easily supported, boxes. In the middle will be a much smaller number (probably as few as 10 to 15 per cent) of specially selected dealers handling the more complex multi-user systems which require much higher levels of support. At the top will be a very few distributors, and dealers handling support for the most complex systems.

It is an attractive, and probably workable, solution to the problem. IBM will regain control of those areas (of more complex systems) which require the most careful support (and generate up to 70 per cent of the business). The existence of the hierarchy will also provide an incentive for good behaviour by the lowest level who will want to move to the more profitable higher level; though it might just as easily provoke a reaction at being barred from the business. For this approach to work, though, IBM will have to find the will to *make* it work. It will have to find a better device than its traditionally volume-oriented (DAM) sales force.

It was my original belief that many of the worst box-shifters would be forced out of business by the obsolescence of their relatively high stocks as new IBM products were launched. This was certainly the most direct measure available to IBM for cutting back on the numbers of dealers—where experience has shown that (in line with the 80:20 Rule) IBM really needs less than 20 per cent of its existing dealers (in the UK, for example, perhaps 50 outlets account for almost all of IBM's business, leaving 350 outlets as an on-going problem). Perversely, IBM actually set out to support those dealers that were in trouble (including, above all, the worst box-shifters who were so damaging to IBM's total business)! It granted lines of credit to many (if not all) on terms that make no commercial sense, and protected them from their own mistakes in terms of obsolescence. Again, I believe it was probably the culture of the "sales force" that forced these damaging concessions on IBM; for this strategy required very direct *positive* intervention by

IBM, not simply a negative reaction caused by the threat of any anti-trust actions.

The Painful Reality

While it initially appeared to herald a new dawn, the use of "third parties" has proven to be IBM's "Achilles Heel." These third parties have, by default, hi-jacked IBM's marketing strategy and its image—both to disastrous effect.

IBM has chosen, I believe wisely, to pursue (in technical terms) a policy of distributed processing (a policy started by Frank Cary nearly two decades ago). The ultimate outcome of such a policy is that an organisation will have many small computers communicating with each other through a complex of electronic links that owe nothing to the hierarchical structures (based on large centralised mainframes) of past decades. The essence of such computing will be networks, where all the computers (no matter how big or how small) will talk to each other as equals. The benefit of this will be that any user of any computer (typically in this scenario almost all users will have their own personal computer) will be able to access any piece of information (in theory from any connected network, anywhere in the world)—and all without having to know where the information is. He will just as easily be able to contact any other user, again anywhere, extending the ease of use of the telephone to computer data. It will revolutionise industry. Not just because, at last, it is a full blown implementation of what the "information revolution" should be about, but also (as discussed elsewhere in this book) because it will force dramatic changes in management style (and will outdate many conventional hierarchical management structures).

It is a noble aim and, potentially, a very profitable one if IBM gets it right. The complication is that it shifts control from the DP department, where IBM has traditionally been able to maintain a tight grasp of overall strategy, and diffuses it throughout the whole body of the corporation. Effective control will lie in the user departments and eventually with the users themselves. As usual, IBM has started to address this, probably successfully, by gaining control of the relevant standards. Its most recent bid, SAA, is an attempt (and one that I believe will succeed) to standardise *all* user application programs (or at least all the popular "packages" offered to the market) so that from the user's point of view they look, and work, in the same way. This is essential, in any case, if "peer to peer" communication between application programs is required.

This requirement is most obvious in the use of shared databases. The user of the PC will want to ask for data without having to know on which machine it is located. So, for example, the database programs on the PC need to work identically to those on the mainframes; and IBM has initially resolved this particular problem by specifying SQL (one of its strategic mainframe database languages) as one of the first SAA standards. In this process of standardisation there is a major secondary benefit: millions of users will generally have to learn just one "application program," where at present they have to learn (and relearn) each new package as they buy it (since each uses separate, often conflicting, styles of operation).

The major problem for IBM, caused by the failure of its "third party" policies, is that control of the new growth areas lies outside the data processing department; and control of the end-users (which will be critical if anyone is to control the networks) has been abdicated to the third parties, which is why this discussion is located in the present chapter. As described earlier, the use of third parties was forced on PC group by necessity: Don Estridge had no other means of selling his products. Further, the speed of recruitment of such dealers (to make the IBM PC Group a viable operation within the relatively short timescales it had available) precluded any real control over the inherent quality of the recruits.

It also precluded any of the extended training that was deemed essential for IBM's own front-line troops, its field force. Anyone who has been through IBM's "Dealer Authorisation Course" (as I have) will recognise how much of a sham this is. Designed for the key manager who will run each dealership, and will set the standards of that dealership and probably train its staff (if any training is done), this lasts just *one* week (where the IBM programmes for its own salespeople, let alone its managers, typically last in excess of a year). Inevitably, much of the week has to be given over to marketing pitches on IBM's range of products and services. There is some genuine teaching of skills (which is done well), but in the short time available it can only scratch the surface. But it is also an "Authorisation" course. This, in theory, means that the dealers attending have to *pass* the course; and no dealership is, again in theory, allowed to run without at least one such "Authorised Dealer." In practice every single member of the course that I attended was "passed," despite the fact that several very clearly, and publicly, failed to meet the standards (which were anyway not exactly overwhelming). IBM's standards for dealers start to be a sham at this very early stage.

All of this was understandable when Don Estridge was running a small new "Independent Business Unit."

The real problem only came when Armonk was seduced by the immediate success of the PC Group formula, and turned what was a relatively harmless device in a small subsidiary into a major plank of its long-term strategy—where it has now become IBM's most intransigent problem. For a critical few years, whilst the PC continued to be a rip-roaring success, Armonk fatally suspended its critical faculties. At that time it thought it had a major challenge on its hands, in terms of selling to millions of "customers" (as end-users). It, understandably, did not believe it alone had sufficient resource; and, more important, did not believe it could handle these contacts economically. At that time (influenced by John Opel's decision that IBM should become "the lowest cost producer") IBM management was all too aware of how much of its own costs were overheads. There was a commendable move to contract outside (where there would be no comparable overheads) everything that was not essential. It looked as if, unafflicted by IBM's overheads (or even by IBM's high salaries), dealers were the only solution to economically covering these "end-users." The calculations floating around IBM UK at that time compared the typical IBM salesman's cost (of around £60,000 per annum) with those projected for dealer staff (where the comparable salesman cost was estimated to be below £20,000 per annum, which was, as we will see later, a significant underestimate).

Unexplored Questions

Critically, there were several questions which IBM did not appear to explore (nor even, in my experience, recognise as issues) in its rushed "seduction" by the idea; it was the answer to a maiden's prayer—all of these analogies are particularly apposite, since IBM's problems with its dealers bear all the signs of a hastily arranged marriage that has gone sour (where neither side thinks it can afford to dissolve the marriage).

Logistics

The first major problem was that of logistics. In all its calculations IBM never asked where its dealers were going to obtain all the resources, in particular their expert personnel. Even within the UK the projections would have shown a need for tens of thousands of personnel to meet end-user needs. Yet in the UK at that time there were probably not many more than a thousand dealer sales and support staff in total (significantly less than IBM's own field force). A total that, perhaps surprisingly, has still not increased dramatically though there have been shifts between dealerships.

The result has been that the numbers of personnel have been much less than IBM would have used (and would have wanted used). Far worse is the fact that the calibre of personnel has been found wanting. To put it mildly, the standards of most dealer personnel are appalling. As a dealer myself, I interviewed dozens of aspiring candidates from other dealers, and I was shaken by the low overall standard (which, as far as I could establish, was representative of dealer staff as a whole). Their technical knowledge was almost non-existent (walk into any dealer and ask for a demonstration of any package, other than Lotus or Word Perfect, and see panic break out!), their business knowledge *was* non-existent (to the extent that most of them were afraid to approach anyone other than a member of a purchasing department, whom they surmised, usually correctly, was as ignorant as themselves), and their *only* sales technique was to offer higher discounts than anyone else.

If anything could be worse than the sales force, it was the standard of the sales management. Competent managers were almost impossible to find—to the extent that the most successful UK chain deliberately did without managers, letting its sales force follow their own initiative.

The standards of the whole industry are, justifiably, held in contempt by the rest of the selling profession and by the dealer sales staff themselves. It was not surprising that, for most of them, their ambition was not to become a sales manager in a dealership, but was to become a *real* salesperson with a mini-manufacturer!

Unfortunately, the "arrogance" of the IBM sales force apparently infected dealer staff, so that their sales force could not even see the need to change; they were proud of being "streetwise," and rapidly put down anyone who was foolish enough to question their standards. They were totally untrained, even in selling. On my authorisation course I listened fascinated while one dealer branch *manager* explained that it was not necessary to take notes in a call, because after a couple of minutes in the call he would know which product he was going to sell the prospect—the antithesis of professional selling. What *was* depressing was that this view was supported by many of the experienced salesmen present; and, even more surprising, was not even challenged by the IBM staff present! Dealer personnel will not become trained, because dealers believe they cannot afford such luxuries; and, in any case, the salespeople themselves do not see the need.

The culture that these dealer staff have inherited, or developed, is much more akin to that of the dirty tricks department of John Patterson's NCR; a madness which Thomas J. Watson put behind him, and he (and his sons) worked for almost three-quarters of a century to replace with the more civilised standards that IBM championed—before its adventure with dealers!

As a footnote to this madness, the costs of dealer selling were typically not even lower than IBM's own (the prime theoretical justification for their existence). As a result of the scarcity of dealer salespeople, no matter how abysmal their capabilities, they had to be paid far in excess of IBM's own sales force. The cost per head (including overheads, where those of dealers were inflated by some of the more arbitrary IBM requirements) was not too different between the two sales forces; and the "price performance" of the IBM sales force was dramatically better! It became obvious (though not to IBM) that dealers could not sell economically to prospects that IBM itself found uneconomic; and instead would be forced to sell to exactly the same customers as IBM, for the same financial reasons. This is exactly what has happened. Much of IBM's rationale for "third parties" has, correspondingly, disintegrated!

Loss of control

The second problem was that of motivation and control. IBM had traditionally exerted control by indirect means (as much of this book describes), but these devices (in particular the culture) were totally inapplicable to third parties. It was not obvious, therefore, how IBM intended to control its dealers. Most other manufacturers selling through third parties (classically the Fast Moving Consumer Goods—FMCG—companies selling through supermarkets) have actually distanced themselves from their outlets (in the case of a supermarket, for example, no-one thinks that Heinz has any degree of control over what happens to its products). The control (after some attempt to use contractual devices, which the courts would not allow) has been maintained via the consumer, the end-user, utilising all the techniques of "classical marketing." IBM, in its marketing naivety (as we will see in the next chapter) could not exert this sort of control. Worse still, its own "anarchical" organisation (even if it is a very controlled "anarchy," as the earlier chapter described) seemed almost to foster anarchy amongst its dealers. The result was a degree of *real* "anarchy" that can only be compared with that which infected those dealing in the post-war European black markets. It was totally alien to IBM's style, but IBM seemed almost unable to come to terms with this (perhaps this is one price to be paid for "control by culture").

This has undoubtedly damaged IBM in terms of market share; its usual subtle devices for containing competitors were unworkable without such control. But, far worse, it has undermined much of IBM's drive to expand the whole market (and that for mainframes too); and (where IBM was normally the main beneficiary of market expansion) this factor accounted for much of IBM's sluggish growth, which was at the heart of its "crisis" from 1985 on. IBM salesmen traditionally spent a large part of their time with customers seeking out new applications, and in the process driving the frontiers of computing ever forward. IBM's competitors, who usually launched more adventurous technical developments before IBM, may dispute this; but it is in the development of the *markets*, rather than that of products, that data processing moves forward; and IBM was the undisputed leader in this process. In the PC arena, however, there has been no equivalent process. PC dealer personnel are generally unsuited to exploring their customers' businesses to develop new applications, and are (perhaps as a result of an awareness of their own shortcomings) unwilling to divert their efforts into such luxuries. Indeed the dealers have acted as a very conservative force, preferring *not* to devote resources to leading edge developments; as IBM has found to its cost in trying to develop its key strategic offering of Token Ring. Instead, they would prefer to hold back development and concentrate on the basic mundane applications, which cost them little effort (and let them get on with the discount war, which they do understand). But this conservatism contributes nothing to the long-term development of computing or to IBM's long-term strategy (which is unfortunate, for a company—and its customers—so dependent on its dealers).

Dented image

The third casualty, which IBM did not appear to consider, was its image. Previously IBM had an image of infallibility ("no-one ever got fired for buying IBM"), combined with integrity (even its worst critics labelled IBM as Snow White). The dealers, though, developed almost exactly the opposite image. They were highly fallible (going spectacularly bust) and many were charlatans. To compound matters, IBM chose almost suicidally to closely identify itself with its dealers (where, as mentioned earlier, more experienced manufacturers maintain a suitable distance from their dealers). It stressed that it "authorised" them, it rushed to their defence when they were criticised (despite the generally indefensible nature of many of their operations), and built its advertising around them; and, of course, the dealers themselves heavily promoted their links with IBM. The result was that, to a considerable degree, IBM fused its public image (which was now largely based on the PC) with that of its dealers. IBM was then tarred, by perverse choice, with the far from savoury image of its "offspring."

At least in the short term, this had near disastrous results for IBM—even far from the PC arena. There *was* a honeymoon period (lasting until 1985), when the runaway success of the PC sales volumes concealed the underlying problems. But since that time, in the PC arena itself the "king" (IBM) has been seen to be wearing almost no "clothes." It has not been difficult for customers to determine that "clones" (much cheaper versions of IBM's PC that are "compatible"; that is, they run, with little or no problems, all the basic application packages that are the real source of the IBM PC's strength) were in reality just as good as IBM's offering, at least for the basic spreadsheet and word-processing work that most PC's are used for; and they were perhaps as little as a third of the IBM price! IBM did nothing to stop this. Indeed, once more, perversely, its promotions actually stressed price cutting and in the process legitimised the even cheaper "clones." All of a sudden it was no longer true that "no-one ever got fired for buying IBM." Instead, the new test of the macho buyers came to be just how low a price they could find, preferably still for IBM equipment but, increasingly, regardless of make (and the saying became "no-one gets fired for obtaining the lowest price"). The inevitable result has been that IBM has lost both share and image. It could no longer use its classical justification of "customer support" to underpin its PC products; everyone knew that customer support (from dealers) was effectively non-existent.

The final irony, in the PC market, is that most of these trials and tribulations have been endured by IBM for no offsetting benefit. The whole justification for dealers was to be that they would economically cover those prospects that IBM itself could not handle. But, in practice, most IBM dealers (after quickly realising how unproductive such customers would also be for them) did not even bother to deal with the smaller businesses that IBM saw them handling (in a war of massively reduced margins, they could not afford to provide the support such new users demanded); and, by default, much of this business went to IBM's competitors and allowed these to survive.

In practice, the dealers' main market has been precisely those "corporates" that IBM's own sales force targeted. What is more, to add insult to injury, the PC dealers did not even bother to call on the "departmental" users, but only called on the central buyers who would place large orders and who were IBM's own customers. Thus, the net effect was that IBM set up its own main competition, whose only tactic was to cut prices (with an identical product). IBM paid heavily, to lose business to itself.

Further, the support they were supposed to provide again had, in effect, to be arranged by IBM; though this time it was its customers who had to be persuaded to set up "Information Centres" and "Support Centres" to provide the missing resource for the end-users. In the absence of any significant support from dealers (or, for once, from IBM itself) these corporate customers *had* to put in place these programmes for self-support. Eventually, to IBM's even greater cost, they also became self-sufficient and could afford to shop around for the best deal, which was almost invariably a non-IBM machine.

Accordingly, the greatest (if not the most obvious) problem for IBM was probably that the contagion had spread to the large mainframes, which had long been the main generators of IBM's profits. Its large corporate customers had learnt (from their need to be self-sufficient on PCs) that they perhaps did not really need IBM's much vaunted "Customer Service"; and, in any case, IBM (following John Opel's plans to become the lowest cost producer) had visibly reduced its commitment to such service. They had also learnt, from the PC (and in particular from Compaq) that the best "compatibles" were not necessarily inferior to IBM machines; and sales of Amdahl (the premier large mainframe "compatible") soared. Finally, they had learnt that, despite its claims to the contrary, IBM *did* now offer discounts when pressurised. They had obtained discounts of up to 35 per cent (admittedly from IBM's dealers rather than direct, but under the new 1986 rules even these counted exactly as if they had come from IBM!) when they placed a large order. So they applied the same arm twisting when it came to ordering mainframes; and eventually IBM had to concede, allowing perhaps only 10 per cent or 20 per cent but that was straight out of profit. The PC "tail" was beginning to wag the Big Blue mainframe "dog" in a quite alarming way!

The loss of "general systems division"

Perhaps the most serious damage was not by commission (of its dealers) but by omission (of its agents). John Akers was probably close to the truth when he admitted in 1986 that PCs had become a commodity market. IBM has lost control, but as in any commodity market it can regain control relatively rapidly if it gets its total package right. The same is unfortunately not true of the layer above PCs. This was, for more than a decade, the province of GSD (General Systems Division). It was built on the sale of the small mainframes and minis that have been the heart of departmental systems in the larger corporations; whilst providing the total computing power for many medium-sized companies. Despite not making significant inroads into the scientific market that IBM had by default given to DEC in the late 1960s, GSD *had* been remarkably successful at winning the mid-range (departmental) business—growing to be, in its own right, the "second largest computer company in the world," approaching double the size of DEC.

This marketplace is also of great significance to the future of computing, because it represents the interface around which hinge IBM's ambitious plans for spreading networks throughout corporations. The departmental "node" is critical for the supplier who wants to manage the overall network; and, from a manufacturer's viewpoint, "ownership" of this node is fundamental to ownership of the complete network.

Once more seduced by its policy of becoming the "lowest cost producer," IBM was looking askance at the cost of covering the GSD accounts. Undoubtedly, GSD salesmen were less productive than those selling the larger mainframes in the "Data Processing Division"; though some of the more sophisticated analyses I undertook in IBM (which allocated overheads more realistically) showed that the difference might not have been quite as large as some managers thought. So, IBM again began to look at third parties. As explained earlier, in this case the chosen vehicle was agents, mainly because IBM now begrudged the margins it had to pay dealers, but also because it was beginning to see the need for a greater degree of control.

Again it appears that IBM forgot to ask at least some of the critical questions that should have been asked of its PC dealer policies, and overlooked a rather important additional one, which was simply "would there be enough agent resource put in to even replace that which GSD had previously supplied—let alone expand the business?" Despite the reservations of at least some of the task forces involved, IBM proceeded, once more, to put its faith (and its future) into the hands of such agents. It handed over to them the whole of the lower end of the GSD market.

Then, almost suicidally, it compounded the problem by reorganising its own sales force, which was supposed to be still protecting the larger GSD accounts. In the name of increased productivity, it effectively merged them with those sales teams selling the larger mainframes. In an IBM world where all operations are (deliberately, and usually productively) under-resourced this was a godsend to the embattled field management, who immediately redeployed the best salespeople (at least) onto the more important larger mainframes. The result was, as I predicted earlier in the book (in a section that was first drafted some three years ago, when IBM had just made this move), that the best resource was removed from "GSD"; avoiding this danger was one reason why, a decade or so earlier, Frank Cary had quite deliberately set it up as a separate division—though its accompanying use, as an anti-trust sacrifice, might have blinded Armonk to this (at a time when it was happily shedding all its anti-trust inhibitions).

Following these series of actions, IBM (by default) largely stopped active selling in the GSD marketplace. It was reportedly somewhat unsuccessful in recruiting large numbers of agents, and then even less successful in motivating them to go out and set the world on fire; inside IBM we had predicted that (because of the poor margins) these agents would do the minimum to keep IBM (barely) happy, but would mainly use the IBM authorisation to get their foot in prospects' doors to sell other (more profitable) lines. The indications are that this has, at least in part, happened. But the real problem has been the relative scarcity of such agents, and this has been compounded by the effective removal of IBM's own "GSD" resources. With no-one selling to the marketplace, then, it is hardly surprising that IBM's share slumped dramatically.

What *is* surprising was the pundits' explanation of the process. Almost as one, they decided that DEC's product range had suddenly become much more competitive than IBM's—a view that DEC, somewhat naively, also seemed to share. Clearly DEC was once more the beneficiary, but not as a result of anything that it did right. DEC's management admiring the "laurels" of their achievements would be wise to understand that these were the gift of

IBM's incompetence. Paradoxically it was the second major gift that IBM had made to DEC; and between them these two gifts accounted for the greatest part of DEC's business. DEC, too, could reasonably be counted an IBM creation (if hardly a deliberate one)!

IBM as its own worst enemy

Indeed, the recent history of IBM has been dominated by its own mistakes. It is difficult to think of a competitor who has positively challenged IBM. Instead, IBM has abdicated large parts of its business in favour of third parties: dealers and agents, both of whom have (after the initial heady days of the first introduction of the PC) signally failed to live up to IBM's normally high standards. The result has been a dilution of profit (it has to pay third parties' margins, representing a significant share of its profits), a loss of control (particularly in terms of creating the brave new future that IBM, and its customers, want), and a loss of confidence, which is debilitating to IBM as a whole.

IBM, as yet, shows no signs of being able to come to terms with its third party problems. It seems almost paralysed, like the victim supposedly hypnotised by the snake. Undoubtedly, there is a major problem, discussed in earlier chapters, of the IBM "culture" being able to come to terms with, and manipulate, the totally alien dealer culture (which may even be, like that of the Mafia, even stronger than that of IBM). IBM's responses have been more like those of a doting parent whose teenage child has just run amok and who hopes that doses of ever more "love" will cure everything. Sooner or later, though, IBM *will* realise its predicament, and it will respond; and it will find some means of disciplining its own dealer account management, so that they behave more as the policemen they are supposed to be. IBM is a very tough company that *is* willing to make tough decisions when it needs to. The worst offenders amongst its third parties (arguably most of them!), who have been so undermining IBM's position, may eventually find their days numbered. On the other hand it is just possible that IBM may never be able to come to terms with the issue. As we will see in the next chapter, IBM displays a peculiar blindness to some issues; in particular, it has an almost total blindness—which, against all the odds, has persisted for decades—to marketing. If it maintains a similar blindness to third parties, for as long, then it *will* have serious problems.

For the time being, though, despite the financial analysts misgivings (and despite the gloomy picture I have painted of the details of its third party operations), IBM remains an immensely strong company. It can afford to shed both its micro and its mini businesses and hardly notice. With $10 billion a year to invest, it can very rapidly change its own fortunes. In any case, there is no obvious competitor of any size (and it would need a giant to really compete with IBM) making a serious challenge to IBM. In the past decade it has very convincingly warded off major challenges from both AT&T and the whole Japanese computer industry; so it is difficult to see who else could succeed where these giants have failed.

In terms of the "model," though, the prime lesson to be observed from the sad story of IBM's third parties is in what IBM has done *wrong*. As you will have deduced, I believe that many of IBM's troubles can be traced back to its poor third party policies. Unusually for IBM (which is a company devoted to long-term planning) these largely emerged by accident; and it is not turning out to be a happy accident. Serendipity has a very valuable role to play in much company decision-making, but the IBM example shows what happens when this gets out of control.

One surprising aspect of the third party equation, though, is that IBM has so consistently failed to establish true communications links to its end-users, even though to a large extent it abdicated its responsibilities to dealers. It traditionally expected face to face contact with those it considered to be its customers, and in the PC area its dealers—the only group it was in such contact with—were thus considered its "customers"; and the sales campaign was largely limited to loading stock into these dealers. This leads on naturally to a discussion of IBM's marketing strategies, or possible lack of them, for end-users.

CHAPTER 11

End-User Marketing

Introduction

Despite the many utterances by commentators, the one thing IBM is not is a conventional marketing company.

In the larger mainframe computer market, where it has a face to face relationship, it *does* conduct near perfect marketing; establishing exact customer requirements and then creating individual "products" ideally to match these requirements.

Its weakness comes when it cannot talk face to face; when it has to market the PC through dealers. It simply has no experience of using the tools of the marketer. Surprisingly, its use of market research is very basic and unsophisticated, so that IBM's appreciation of the true needs of its end-users is much less sure than for larger mainframe customers. Its use of conventional market planning is also comparatively naive; and it has lost large segments of the PC market to much weaker companies with products better matched to market needs. Its use of advertising (handled, of course, by sophisticated agencies), however, has generally been sound (even if based on dubious marketing strategies); it has not been positively harmful and has even been creatively quite successful. In any case, the vast sums spent on it must be ultimately productive (where these will soon be large enough to dominate the media world-wide; that is, if IBM does not lose its nerve).

By default the PC has become the image of IBM, and the problems of deteriorating standards around this product (as dealers succumb to the price war) have begun to harm IBM more than it might have expected.

In the final analysis, though, IBM's dominance is so great that it probably does not need these sophisticated techniques that it still does not understand. Market segmentation and product positioning, for example, become academic when whatever IBM decides almost automatically defines the ideal market segment and product position. Other companies, on the other hand, are inevitably in much weaker positions and ignore the dictates of conventional marketing at their peril; in this case the model is *not* to be followed.

Finally, with all its lack of sophistication IBM's belief in customer service *will* eventually ensure that IBM conducts near perfect marketing, in any market—but to date dealers have failed to measure up to this standard in the PC market. The power of this belief (just so long as it really is fully implemented), even in the sophisticated field of marketing, should not be underestimated; and this part of the model *is* worth copying.

Customers as individuals

When I joined IBM, at the beginning of the 1970s, I had spent the previous decade working with some of the most sophisticated marketing companies in the UK. It came as something of a shock, therefore, to find that IBM seemed to have nothing even approximating to any of the marketing activities I had previously considered essential to the well-being of a modern company.

In many ways Buck Rodgers' book, *The IBM Way,* provides a fascinating insight into IBM's marketing. What is in the book is a very sound categorization of a range of *selling* techniques. What is *missing,* and by its very absence is particularly enlightening, is any significant reference to *marketing* in its modern sense. There are almost no references to key marketing activities; despite the subtitle, "Insights into the World's Most Successful Marketing Organization," and the fact that Buck was IBM's vice-president of marketing! The evidence is, amazingly, that Armonk has remarkably little appreciation of conventional marketing theory.

After spending some time in IBM it eventually dawned on me that in fact IBM had developed a near perfect marketing operation. The unit of this ideal marketing, however, was not the anonymous "average" consumer that I was used to in the consumer goods companies where I had previously worked. It was instead the very specific, identified, individual customer.

Thus there was no significant market research commissioned to discover general needs, because the needs of *each* customer were investigated by the field force (salesmen and SEs) in great depth—far more so than any market research could address, and of course quite specif ic to each unique customer. The overall IBM product strategy could be almost entirely technically based (a heresy to any committed marketing man!), because its job was only to provide a series of very generally applicable building blocks, from which the *field force* built ("configured" in the jargon) the unique end product that *exactly* matched the needs they had identified in the customer's business. Finally, there was no need for advertising or promotion, in the conventional sense, since the individual sales message was carried personally to the customer by the field force. It was indeed the perfect marketing medium; and one that IBM exploited superbly.

The IBM marketing staff institutions have been developed and refined to support this process. Thus there is great in-depth expertise to help the field force analyse the customer's needs and to answer them in ways few customers would have the expertise to aspire to. As part of this process the various elements of marketing staff also act as the key intermediaries, collating requirements and feeding these back to the laboratories (as "statements of opportunities"); so that the building blocks themselves are also optimized.

The extent and depth of this marketing staff expertise was shown by the exercise, described earlier, which I undertook as an attempt to institute a degree of control over their many diverse activities. My research turned up nearly 2,000 separate activities, covering in excess of 500 separate business areas! Despite all these activities, and all the great expertise behind them, the contact with the customers, including end-users, was still the exclusive province of the branches.

Mass marketing

Over recent years, even within Big Blue, there has been a move, of sorts, to what IBM calls "mass marketing." This is intended to make the salesmen more effective, and more efficient by running much of the prospecting, and end-user support from a special marketing unit within the branch; the "Customer Centre" (or "Customer Support Centre" depending on the local terminology). The techniques used, though, are still those of face to face selling; enhanced by mailings and seminars, to improve efficiency.

Less than half a decade ago this process probably addressed most of IBM's end-user base, as well as its more traditional DP departments. At that time teleprocessing, via terminals, had already arrived in many customers; but it was mainly limited to access by data entry personnel (usually for order processing). In most companies there were still only a few enquiry terminals, typically in a customer enquiries department. In that last half decade the picture has changed out of all recognition. IBM has long been promoting the idea that data processing should move into the provision of on-line management information systems (MIS). In the past five years this has started to happen on a large scale; and has been one of the factors that has fuelled the PC explosion.

Thus, for example, only five years ago IBM UK probably had less than 100,000 end-users, if data entry staff were ignored; and perhaps only 20,000 of these ever saw IBM face to face (even the most successful of IBM's "events" programmes covered less than 20,000 prospects every year). Now its end-user target "audience" may be as high as 10 million.

Investigating the market for Big Blue (not even PC Group), I eventually came to the conclusion that the most workable definition was simply *all* ABCl males (ABCl in UK market research covers all management, professionals and office workers; probably about half the male population). This was clearly beyond any of the normal Big Blue marketing activities.

In these five years, of course, the IBM PC has emerged, and with it have come extensive marketing programmes; and in particular advertising at the rate of many millions of pounds per annum. This has become, by default, the communications "vehicle" to all IBM end-users. Even those using "dumb" terminals, linked direct to their mainframe, obtain their information (and in particular their image) of IBM almost entirely in terms of the PC. Charlie Chaplin has very rapidly become one pervasive image of IBM.

It might be expected that, as a result, IBM would now be implementing all the sophisticated marketing techniques that any similar consumer durables company would consider. With numbers of PCs shipped running into millions every year, IBM is now in very much the same area as most car manufacturers and many domestic electrical goods suppliers. It is true that it is starting to learn these techniques. The process is, though, surprisingly slow by IBM's normally dynamic standards.

Dealer relations

IBM certainly recognizes its very new interface with its dealers. It is, after all, a face to face contact, and IBM feels comfortable with this since it is not too far removed from its traditional mainstay: face to face contact with its customer's DP departments. Big Blue has, in any case, tried (relatively unsuccessfully) to persuade its traditional DP department contacts to set up as "internal" dealers for their organizations. PC Group is centred in exactly the same (traditional) way on its relations with its dealers. Certainly these should be important to IBM, and it reacts well to such dealers' requirements, and drives them as hard and as effectively as it does all its normal customer contacts. This concentration is, though, in some ways at the expense of its contacts with the end-users beyond its dealers.

For what IBM has yet to do, consistently and deliberately, is to gain control of these end-users in the way that a conventional marketing oriented company would see as natural. The management of such companies spend much of their time making certain they persuade their end-user (archetypically the housewife) to make the buying decision that favours them. IBM is, of course, now spending considerable sums on advertising (in absolute terms that is; it still only represents around one per cent of PC overall revenue). Even this advertising, though, emphasizes the role of the dealer; almost as a token gift to keep IBM in such dealers' good books. Its competitors go even further, offering collaborative advertising with the dealers as an incentive to order.

IBM still undertakes surprisingly little market research. Indeed, like many companies, to a large extent it depends upon buying in the results of research that has been speculatively commissioned by specialist market research houses. Such research is almost inevitably rather basic in nature. Even this limited research seems to be largely ignored, in the face of direct feedback from dealers. This is not surprising where, in the UK for example, there were up to 40 high powered dealer account managers representing the dealer, against just one advertising professional; and, typically for IBM, in the 1986 cost-cutting exercises even that one expert was redeployed, to be more "productively" used as a Dealer Account Manager! The majority of personnel in the communications department (accurately named "dealer support") were involved in producing print material and supporting exhibitions; and, again, this department was decimated in the 1986 cost cutting. IBM UK no longer even appears at the (IBM) PC User Show; so that, by default, the image conveyed at that key exhibition is that the typical PC is a clone! At the 1987 show I counted just 6 IBM PCs out of several hundred—when this show was originally supposed to be dedicated to the IBM PC!

Overall marketing strategy, in any conventional sense, is fragmented and distributed throughout IBM. Its development is not heavily resourced or highly regarded; indeed it is often largely seen as a sub-set of corporate strategy handed down from Armonk. As a result most of the normal marketing decisions are not even considered. Product positioning, for example, is seen in purely technical terms, as is market fragmentation. In both these cases, though, the resulting limitations on IBM are minimal. Although IBM does not seem consciously to plan this, it behaves exactly as if its products were at the optimal market position and that any fragmentation was also optimal. In practice, for whatever reasons, these are the correct decisions. Due to its dominance, its overwhelming market and technological leadership, it automatically decides what are the optimum positions and fragmentation for the whole market! This position has now been institutionalized, by the fact that its main competition now comes from "compatible" machines. These depend for their compatibility upon IBM's positioning and fragmentation being the generally accepted "standard."

At least in this respect IBM succeeds, despite flouting conventional marketing theory. But it has to be argued that, at least in part, its success is made possible by the even greater failure of its competitors. It is arguable that IBM's positioning and fragmentation is actually less than optimal. Its competitors have, though, have split into two camps. One, the compatibles mentioned above, have used exactly the same parameters; and have almost inevitably been pale copies (only Compaq seems to have succeeded in carving itself a secure niche, but even this is dependent on IBM's "goodwill"). The other group, the non-compatibles (notably Apple), have chosen perversely to fight on product positioning that is clearly inferior to IBM's. IBM's loss then has not been in competitive position, but in terms of overall market size.

End-user needs

Where IBM *has,* I believe, suffered from its somewhat questionable understanding of marketing in the conventional sense, is in its approach to non-technical end-user needs. Its own market research clearly shows that support is the key requirement of every one of the different groupings of end-users. This need ranges from on-the-ground support by the local dealer, in language the customer can understand, through to the confidence that the equipment on offer will be capable of expansion to meet future needs. These are not just the fears of unsophisticated users, they represent well justified caveats about the whole PC industry. Anyone buying a PC commits himself not just to the cost of its purchase, but also to the subsequent cost of running it. This latter cost, the overhead of his staff involvement and (particularly) the potential negative impacts on the operation of his business, will far outweigh any hardware cost. It is indicative of the problems that such worries are now a major feature of PC customer attitudes, where Big Blue customers in comparison confidently look to the direct benefits in operational terms. The end result in the PC area is seen in press reports that claim that poor systems design is costing customers billions of pounds every year.

Against these requirements for support IBM has perversely chosen to distance itself from the end-users. Even those areas where it could have offered more direct influence—its software offerings and its own retail shops (which could have been run as advice centres, maybe avoiding the need for closure)—were given exclusively profit objectives; which inevitably drove them away from giving more general support (and in practice, the IBM shops gave less support than many dealers). IBM's main thrust has instead been to shift boxes. It has emphasized quantity rather than quality. Its activities in the price-cutting war, discussed in the previous chapter, have arguably destabilised the market. Possibly the greatest benefit that the PC originally conferred was a degree of stability. It was clearly setting a long-term standard in which end-users could have confidence. Part of that confidence has now been forfeited.

IBM has thus ignored, perhaps at its peril, the classic marketing rules for a market leader. It has debased its unique quality image, to the extent that it has now legitimized a horde of cheaper compatibles flooding out of the Far East, by emphasizing the traditional advantage of the smaller companies: price. Its lowest cost producer philosophy has not stood up, by itself, against the very low costs (albeit often matched by even lower quality standards) of the underdeveloped (and government subsidized) parts of the Far East. Again, it has reversed the rule that as the overwhelming brand leader it should concentrate on "above the line" expenditure, and has instead put most of its revenue into "below the line"; adopting the traditional promotional discounting more normally the preserve of the smaller brand, and in the process has destabilized the market!

IBM is yet to take seriously to "above the line" expenditure. On the other hand, even on a minute one per cent share of revenue it still dominates the PC advertising scene, and will increasingly dominate the total media scene; even one per cent, of the $30–50 billion IBM is projecting for revenue from the PC in the 1990s, will yield $300–500 million (making IBM one of the very biggest spenders). This one per cent compares, however, with the 10 per cent it can sometimes offer on below the line promotions.

The fact that IBM has yet to learn the most basic of marketing lessons was evidenced by the reported decision, in mid-1986, to respond to the problems of reduced margins on the PC by *freezing* advertising budgets; treating them as a simple *cost,* and not utilizing IBM's dominant position to wield them strategically to create a major product (image) advantage (as conventional marketing wisdom would suggest). The result is that IBM (still way ahead as market leader, even in the PC market) is being *outspent* on "above the line" advertising by some of its much smaller competitors; and, in the UK at least, one competitor (Amstrad) is outspending it by approaching a factor of 10:1, and is rapidly gaining share (though I believe it, like many other clone vendors, may face a questionable future).

However, this spend was already sufficiently large to have impact, provided the message is *not* positively harmful. IBM's innate conservatism in its public image has ensured that the message is not harmful. Indeed the Charlie Chaplin message has probably been a sound one, particularly in the USA, when combined with IBM's otherwise very staid image. It has provided a very good, and memorable, visual link to a product that is otherwise rather dull visually; and the fun element has helped demystify the feared technicalities. In any case the overall image has been assisted by its competitors, who have almost all made some ritual obeissance to IBM in their advertising; thus offering IBM invaluable further "testimonial" advertising! Paradoxically, for large parts of 1986 and 1987, when IBM itself chose (as a cost saving measure!) to carry out no large scale advertising, the *only* advertising for IBM was provided by such "testimonial advertising," provided for free by its competitors—which, perhaps fortunately for IBM, continued undiminished!

End-user education

What has been missing, though, has been the necessary end-user education to help expand the market. Given the chance IBM can succeed dramatically well in such a role. Its European EXHIBIT touring exhibition each week attracted around 20,000 members of the general public (mainly schoolchildren, who were the prime target for this public relations exercise). In just half-an-hour it conveyed a great deal of information about computing; using techniques and resources that left other exhibitions decades behind. Of course, being IBM, it cost nearly £250,000 per week to run, and at £10 per head that was perhaps expensive for schoolchildren (but would not be for end-users).

IBM, and the market it leads, have a peculiar blindness to their own jargon and technicalities that are irrelevant to end-users. I am as great an offender as most. This book is full of jargon; I can only excuse it by pleading, probably falsely, that it is included better to convey a flavour of IBM. The impact of this was brought home to me a decade ago. I was demonstrating the new S/32 computer, IBM's first user-friendly machine, to the staff of the London Business School. I was inordinately proud of the ease of use, for inexperienced users, and of the clear, jargon-free instructions shown on its very small display unit. My audience were much more critical about the "garbage" they saw on the screen. This was the control language instructions which flashed on to the screen between the user instructions. This jargon was incomprehensible to all but the most expert programmers, but I (and presumably the system developers) hadn't even noticed its flickering presence; we were blind to what the end-users saw.

The situation has improved somewhat in the decade since then, but in moments of panic the PC still reverts to an enigmatic "A" on an otherwise blank screen. The programs that drive it are gradually improving, but few of them avoid the use of (unnecessary) jargon and technicalities. It is thus thought necessary to attend at least a day's training for even the simplest of packages; and yet 90 per cent of users expect to pick it up as they go along, without the benefit of any training. Xerox, and later Apple, tried to make the user interface more friendly with the "mouse," but this is understandably disdained by most users; it may be visual but is clumsy and slow (and substitutes visual jargon for the verbal sort). IBM has the resource, and the market leadership, to address this problem properly, and will in turn benefit most from the market expansion that will result.

If IBM's claims for "Presentation Manager" (a variation on Microsoft's "Windows," which is in turn a derivative of the Apple/Xerox icon/mouse approach) on the PS/2 range are to be believed, it *will* address this problem. But I remain sceptical, as it is a problem that the whole industry has largely ignored for the best part of two decades; even icons (pretty though they are) can be as meaningless as the PC's "A" if they do not obviously help the user.

Future PC marketing

IBM could succeed in the PC market, and by extension also generate a successful image for Big Blue if its short-term marketing naivety can be rectified; IBM is normally a very fast learner. In particular its emphasis on below the line price-cutting will have to disappear, and it will need to handle its above the line activities in a manner that will benefit IBM most, by expanding the total market. PC marketing may currently be IBM's weakest link, but its weaknesses are not yet fatal, and Big Blue should continue to undertake its near perfect marketing to its own customers.

In any case its ability to determine the ideal product position simply by occupying it, gives it an almost invulnerable position. It scarcely needs to indulge in conventional marketing. You can be sure that IBM will learn *very* fast indeed when this skill becomes essential to its business. Until it does eventually get its PC marketing act totally together, it can probably rely on its competitors to do rather worse!

Underneath all the use, or non-use, of marketing techniques, IBM's greatest strength in its main marketplace is its second belief: "customer service." As long as it adheres to this, and it is in practice a belief that really is inviolable (though John Opel's "lowest cost producer" *has* gone a long way to undermine it), then IBM will quite naturally conduct a near perfect marketing operation. It doesn't need the armoury of sophisticated marketing techniques used by other companies. The one simple belief, if conscientiously implemented, is worth the knowledge of many tomes of marketing theory. The one gap which IBM still needs to fill comes about because it has not yet rigorously extended this principle to end-users. It is almost as if they are "out of sight, out of mind"; IBM does not yet seem to recognize them as full "customers" in its philosophical terminology (this privilege still seems to be reserved for face to face contact). Once it—inevitably—does recognize them, then the same belief will condition its mass marketing activities; with, I predict, interesting results!

CHAPTER 12

Personnel and Corporate Affairs

Introduction

It is within Personnel Department that, uniquely amongst Western companies, IBM's real strengths become apparent. For it is this department that is the guardian of the critical first belief: "respect for the individual."

The basic building-block of the philosophy is still the relationship between manager and individual; but this is strengthened and controlled by the formal institution of the appraisal and counselling (A&C) interview. Annually, the individual is made formally aware of just how his performance has been rated, and his objectives for the next year must be clearly spelled out and prioritized. Most important, the individual has to agree (and sign!) these statements; and, as the individual's salary depends on them, there is every incentive for him to insist on their accuracy (and the A&C is usually at least as stressful for the manager). Status, a problem bedevilling relations in many other companies, is minimized in IBM by being linked to a (confidential) abstract level, which is not necessarily directly linked to management position.

One of the key policies, if not even *the* foundation for IBM's success (as is often claimed for the Japanese corporations), is that of full employment. The corollary, as IBM changes rapidly, is that individuals must regularly retrain and change their careers, and Personnel Department is (at least nominally) also the guardian of their careers (and should ensure that they fulfill their potential). Equal opportunity and single status are also basic rights; though IBM (in common with the Japanese corporations) has large numbers of temporary and contract personnel, who are certainly treated as (unseen) second-class citizens.

Directly under Personnel Department's control are a number of key programmes ensuring that the overall policies are implemented. Two of these, the "speak-up" programme and the "open door," act as crucial safety valves, so that an individual always has an independent right of appeal. One, though, is the most powerful of IBM's personnel tools; the "opinion survey." Run every two years, this is a confidential (and anonymous) survey answered (voluntarily) by almost all IBMers. It gives a detailed insight into what they think of IBM and, most significant, how they rate their own managers. It is not an academic exercise, for every manager has to prepare an action plan to rectify the problems (and *agree* it with his subordinates). It is perhaps the easiest, and most powerful, device that can be immediately copied from IBM.

Three basic beliefs

This last chapter on the current anatomy of IBM, the last elements of the model, discusses one of its greatest strengths: its handling of people. IBM's Personnel Department is the guardian of the principles that are held near sacred and are, I believe, ultimately responsible for much of its success.

As a result, Personnel Department occupies a far stronger and more central role in senior management circles than in other Western companies. This is directly comparable once more with Japan, where the *senior* director is in charge of the personnel function.

These principles are largely the legacy of the Watsons, but they are just as zealously guarded by their bureaucratic successors. For example, they are clearly identified on the first page of Buck Rodgers' book, once more as the key to IBM's success.

Respect for the individual

The first, and most important, of IBM's three basic beliefs is respect for the individual. The IBM UK *Annual Review* 1984, for example, says that this: ". . . more than anything else accounts for our continuing success." This philosophy is a direct descendant of Tom Watson Jr.'s long campaign for the individual within IBM.

An IBM UK employee booklet (*Employment with IBM*) that describes its personnel principles, proudly bears on its cover a 1962 quote from Tom Watson Jr.: "I believe the real difference between success and failure in a corporation can very often be traced to the question of how well the organization brings out the great energies and talents of its people. I believe that if an organization is to meet the challenges of a changing world it must be prepared to change everything about itself except its basic beliefs." In most companies this would be public relations hype; in IBM it is at the root of its success.

In defining "respect for the individual," IBM in the same booklet underlines some common factors: ". . . drawing out the best of an individual's energies, talents, skills, creativity and adaptability; rewarding individuals for their achievements and contributions; creating opportunities for individuals to develop; ensuring that the individual's voice can be heard; protecting the rights and dignity of the individual; and providing a basic sense of security for the individual." These are objectives that might seem unduly idealistic to many managers. Yet at the core of each is not mere altruism but sound business logic. The list does not just encompass those terms that will reward the employees with a better job and greater fulfilment, but it also encompasses precisely those factors which result in a more productive work force; and this productivity leverage is demonstrated by IBM's enviable profit record.

Such public *beliefs* are predicted, by Theory Z, to be the first step in achieving the trust necessary for the type of success experienced by IBM. It is common for the senior executives of Japanese corporations to publish books detailing their philosophies. IBM is almost alone amongst Western companies in publishing its beliefs so widely—and, indeed, Tom Watson Jr. *did* produce a slim volume, *A Business and its Beliefs*, which is fascinating reading.

As the first-line troops implementing these policies, IBM relies on its managers; in particular it justifies the relatively high ratio on this basis (a ratio of around nine employees per manager overall; though there is some confusion, with Buck Rodgers for example quoting various levels between one to eight and one to twelve!).

This is comparable, once more, with the Japanese corporations. Ezra Vogel, in his book, *Japan as Number One* (1979; Harvard University Press), reported that the entire business and social structure of Japanese companies is built around the *Kacho*. This is the section head, typically running an eight to ten person group: "The essential building-block of the organization is the section. . . . The lowly section, within its sphere, does not await executive orders but takes the initiatives. . . . For this system to work effectively, leading section personnel need to know and identify with company purposes to a higher degree than persons in an American firm." This is also one of the elements (along with widespread use of task forces of a similar size) of the process described as "chunking" by Peters and Waterman, and stressed by them as a major contributor to effective management at the lower levels.

Appraisal and counselling interview

The key formal element in this relationship is the A&C (appraisal and counselling interview). At least once a year a manager *must* conduct a formal A&C with every one of his subordinates. The main drive of the A&C is to manage the individual's productivity, but the interview also reviews the employee's future career path and educational needs over the next year. It should be noted, however, that although these are side issues no manager is allowed to ignore them, since the welfare of their subordinates is their prime concern. A review of the employee's performance against the objectives set at the previous A&C is the major element of the interview. This is the reason why managers typically set aside half a day for each A&C and are, probably for the only time, strictly not to be interrupted during this meeting; the A&C is meant very clearly to be a sacrosanct rite of IBM.

The resulting rating of performance, against objectives, is graded from one down to five. It is unusual for an employee to be consistently rated a one performer. The system strongly suggests that such an employee should be considered for immediate promotion, and managers are loathe to make such a commitment as part of the A&C process. Most employees, therefore, fall into the range of two and three performers. Although a three performance should theoretically be the average (but of course, the average for *IBM*, which is very much higher than for most other companies), and as such applicable to most IBMers, many managers allow rather more leeway than the rules would suggest; and in practice the split in numbers may be nearly equal between two and three performers. In the 1980s IBM has, however, tried to implement this grading system more rigorously, discreetly chastising managers who are too generous.

Those very few employees who are seen to fail in their job are awarded a five performance, which is deemed unsatisfactory. There is an elaborate process, requiring the manager to set very clear short-term objectives, and to have at least two further A&Cs (with Personnel Department involvement) before the employee is finally dismissed (or "separated" in IBM jargon; the day you leave IBM was described by one alumni as "the loneliest day of your life"—the parallel with marriage and divorce is apposite). The complexity and difficulty of this process, combined with the rigorous selection procedures (and the many different jobs available to match individual's talents), ensures that remarkably few employees are actually dismissed. More likely the employee is moved to a suitable Siberia or penalty box; though senior management regularly issues instructions pleading that the nettle be grasped (where the issue is often evaded by a manager transferring the problem to someone else).

There are two main reasons why A&Cs often take an inordinately long time. The first is that the manager is required to obtain the employee's *agreement* (in the form of his signature on the elaborate document that details the matters discussed) to both the objectives for the next year and to the performance level recorded for the past year. Both, it will be apparent, are likely to be contentious. The second reason is that the employee is well aware that his next salary increase will be directly linked to his A&C performance rating. The negotiation, where most IBMers are natural negotiators, may thus be a long drawn-out process; and puts as much pressure on the manager as on the subordinate.

Most non-IBMers would probably view the A&C as a process to be feared, because it so very clearly is an evaluation, and what is more one that is formally documented. It may be seen to be redolent of Big Brother constantly watching the workers. The reality is that in *all* organizations management are constantly evaluating their subordinates; this is a basic and essential element of their job. Usually, though, this is a strictly informal and largely capricious process; based on "gut-feel" and favouritism as much as on performance. In IBM this process is recognized and codified. As a result the individual is, as far as is humanly possible, guaranteed a fair evaluation. No manager can give a grossly unfair assessment, since he *has* to obtain agreement from two other individuals, his own manager and the subordinate in question. Hence the A&C is a key discipline on management, and is the kingpin of the formal structure that ties the majority of IBM employees into the formal management and control structures.

I have dwelled upon the A&C process at some length, as I will on some of the other personnel processes, because (although it looks bureaucratic) it is at the core of the personal relationship between manager and managed. The employee knows exactly where he stands. He expects, and is guaranteed to get, fair treatment. He accordingly has confidence and that much more trust in IBM.

Salaries

The IBMers salary is governed by a rather complex set of calculations. The main bases are the performance rating, his "level" and his previous salary.

The level system

The level is a source of much mystery in IBM. In theory employees are not informed of their level; it is supposed to be a technicality normally linked to the position and not the person. In reality, of course, it is of very direct relevance and there must be very few IBMers who are not acutely aware of their own level, and of the levels of those around them. To complicate matters, for outsiders, the level is actually a two digit number, the first digit of which indicates the broad *type* of job (and in particular the type of remuneration). Thus salesmen (on quota, IBM's term for the commission system) are all in the 70s, where their comrades in staff (not on commission) are in the 50s; but as always IBM complicates matters by putting senior management in the 60s!

The all important second digit is a measure of the status regardless of job type. Taking the example of one area (that of marketing staff), the "professional" level (that is those who have moved on from the lowlier administrative levels) starts at 54 and rises to 56. The bottom level of professional management usually starts at 57. In theory professionals can reach level 57 and even aspire to level 58 without becoming managers. IBM likes to believe that it rewards each individual in full for his contribution, and management (even senior management) is just one skill amongst many. In reality, at least in the UK, IBM has taken a tougher line in recent years. There are indeed numbers of level 57 professionals around, but most of them date from the boom times of the 1970s; there have been very few created in the 1980s.

The typical marketing manager (IBM's title for a first level *sales* manager), running a team of five to 10 salesmen might expect to be at least on a level 57 (and probably would be on a level 58). The branch manager, reckoned to be the plum job in IBM, should merit at least a level 59.

This already complex picture is complicated even further by the fact that all the salary levels overlap quite considerably. Thus a high performing level 55 professional with a number of years behind him, may earn more than a level 57 manager.

The reason for describing the level system at some length is that it makes a major contribution to the flexibility of the work force, and to IBM's consequent ability to manage change. There is indeed a practical logic to the complexity; it is not simply bureaucracy gone mad. It means that levels can be compared across quite different areas of activity (and across countries). Thus the level 76 salesman can, allowing for the commission element, be directly compared with his level 56 opposite number in staff. Employees are, accordingly, willing to change to new jobs because the future is predictable. In part this is because they know that IBM's personnel policies, and in particular that of full employment, will protect them. Even so, the new job will be an unknown quantity; change in IBM runs at such a pace that there is no possibility of having standard jobs which are immediately understandable to employees.

The one known quantity, however, will be the level. Despite the fact that levels are not officially discussed, the first question an employee asks of a prospective new manager is: "What is the level?" The employee thus has a guarantee that at least the salary and status are what he requires; and in IBM the exact nature of any job is very much a function of what the individual makes of it. As a lubricant of change, therefore, the universal application of exactly comparable levels should not be underestimated.

At the same time, this determination of status by (secret; at least in theory) level fatally undermines the normal "hen-pecking" order. Even though most staff have a good idea of the levels of those other IBMers they deal with, there is always an element of uncertainty. This makes all status relationships somewhat equivocal, even those between managers and non-managers; for the professionals may actually have a higher status than the managers, which simply would not happen in most other companies. The end result is that most relationships (even manager to non-manager) are on a strictly equal to equal, peer to peer, basis. IBM is thus, by default, a truly egalitarian company; and this once more oils the wheels of its very unconventional, ever changing structures.

The conferring of status by these levels (even if officially they do not exist) has another benefit. It removes a substantial amount of the more destructive aspects of rivalry within the groups. Each person's status is determined independently, by the "neutral" levels system. There is, therefore, remarkably little of the jockeying for position that may be seen in other companies, where the hen-pecking order evolves dynamically as individuals win political battles over each other; in IBM there is usually little point in such counter-productive activities, since performance (usually based on teamwork) is the basis of the judgements that influence the system.

Despite the universality of levels, it can be seen that the salary structure in IBM is a minefield, to be negotiated with great care. If, as once happened to me, you bump up against the salary ceiling set by your level you might be lucky and be promoted. More likely you will be bought off by one of the range of special payments that IBM seems able to conjure out of thin air to mollify potential complainants.

The presence of this minefield may be one particular reason for IBM's unofficial, but well publicized, aversion to unions; and indeed it is difficult to see how any union could successfully negotiate its way through the complexities to agree wage rates (but perhaps that is one of the reasons for the complexities in the first place!).

Incentives

At least in theory, IBM believes that incentives are necessary to motivate its employees, as well as rewarding them for their contributions. The A&C process is supposedly the greatest incentive of all. The reality is that almost by definition IBMers are self-starters who generally have no need for such external, management-led stimuli to persuade them. There is little evidence that the various incentives have a direct effect; many members of staff work just as hard, without incentive, as their opposite numbers in the field. In addition, even some of the most productive members of the field are given "memorandum" (i.e., non-measurable) quotas, because their sales campaigns must extend beyond the one year that is IBM's only field time unit; and yet these non-incented salesmen still produce the results.

Incentives do, however, play an important series of indirect roles in IBM. The average IBMer is an achiever, indeed usually an over-achiever, who uses the measurement offered by the incentives to "pace" himself. Above all, the IBMer needs to achieve 100 per cent, for self-esteem rather than financial reward. This is why the Hundred Per Cent Club with relatively minor financial implications, is still the greatest influence on the field force. The incentives are also used by IBM to focus attention on key activities. Thus the sales plan, in theory a description of the incentives, becomes the key planning document in the field. Finally incentives are used to add a useful air of excitement and are accordingly used for dramatic effect; the HPC is pure theatre.

The above comments apply particularly well to the field force, but not to any great extent in the case of the great majority of IBMers. Apart from the A&C and its rating, the relatively few other incentives scattered around are invariably *post factum,* and they cannot be used to pace or direct efforts; though they may still be useful for building excitement and an *esprit de corps.* For most IBMers the A&C is thus the one key process.

Full employment

Personnel Department itself is the guardian of a number of philosophies and processes that even more clearly distinguish IBM from other companies. The first, and absolutely fundamental, of these is the commitment to full employment. The relevant UK booklet (*Employment in IBM*) says: "Full employment is a commitment on the part of IBM to maintain, through every reasonable and practical effort, continuous employment for regular employees who perform satisfactorily." IBM would like to think that its employees will have a job for life, but it is very careful to make certain that it does not put that in writing; ASTMS (the UK management and staff union) at one stage challenged the apparently quite specific wording of this promise, only to be told that it was an "intention" and as such was not necessarily legally binding!

IBM does, though, protect employment of its work force, and does not go out of its way to decry the widespread belief (even reported by Buck Rodgers) that it has not made any of its work force redundant in more than half a century (in reality there have been a few exceptions, but the record shows that in these cases IBM effectively had no alternative and was very generous indeed in its treatment of the "victims"). Certainly its employees believe that there is true security of employment. In the UK opinion survey more than 90 per cent of employees state that they are satisfied that they will be able to work for IBM as long as they perform satisfactorily.

Employment security is not, however, the same as job security. Jobs are constantly disappearing in IBM, and their holders are moved on, retrained, to new positions. Due to the general feeling of job security, and the guarantees offered by the levels system, this is not normally seen by employees to be a problem; and many IBMers, myself included, looked forward to the interest in learning a new job and new skills. These changes do have the effect of producing a non-specialized career path for many IBMers, which is unusual in Western companies, but is almost standard in Japanese companies. However, when you have just uprooted your family for the third time in four years, as some of my colleagues experienced, you do begin to have some doubts!

From IBM's point of view employment security is a basic moral commitment. In addition, though, it has the very real advantage that the IBM work force is uniquely flexible; and accepts, or at least tolerates, "I've Been Moved." The most obvious comparison is with the larger Japanese corporations who have, since the 1950s, also offered a "job for life"; and have been similarly rewarded by loyalty coupled with flexibility on the part of their work forces.

It is difficult, however, for most firms even to consider the apparently absurd extravagance of full employment, when they are subject to cyclical booms and recessions. On the other hand the IBM, and Japanese, experience says that it is a form of investment that shows a return far in advance of most others. In any case IBM typically staffs for the recession, low end of the cycle and draws on the loyalty of its staff to cope with the extra work generated by the booms; and such is their calibre that they do. It has to be admitted, though, that IBM has long had the luxury of almost constant growth which can be used to balance out any short-term miscalculations; and the philosophy might be more difficult to apply in a static company (but then a static company would not be looking for the sort of adventure that the IBM approach offers).

This employment security—a very unusual policy for a Western company—is probably the most important link between IBM and the major Japanese companies (where it has been standard since being "imported" by MITI in the 1950s, though it still does not extend to the lower two-thirds of Japanese business). It is also the key element that William G. Ouchi identifies as the basis for *trust*; which in turn is said to be the main driving force of the "Japanese miracle," and also of IBM's comparable success.

Career opportunities

Beyond the basic feeling of security, though, IBMers are offered the prospect of personal development. This may not be to management for, as in all companies, there are usually bound to be more Indians than chiefs. But the IBMer can still expect to be trained and educated to fulfill a considerable amount of his personal potential, and a great deal more than would be developed in another company. He will, in any case, have the opportunity to graduate to ever more senior levels of the professional staff; and such senior professional staff, even though not managers, are given high status in IBM. He should have an interesting job or, more accurately, series of jobs. At its most basic this involved IBM in implementing one of the first job enrichment programmes in its plants, switching from the monotony of impersonal assembly lines (which are now, in IBM, largely the province of the robot) to small groups. Following the report of this in Peter F. Drucker's *The Practice of Management* the Japanese also adopted this approach, which is now said to be one of their particular strengths.

At its most exotic, an IBMer, such as myself, who is strong-willed enough (or probably more accurately, bloody-minded enough) can demand his choice of interesting jobs (though usually at the price of forfeiting management progression). In my 15 years I had eight different jobs, in at least four totally distinct disciplines. Thus, while I spent about a third of this time in sales and marketing activities, which had been my bread and butter for 10 years before joining IBM, I spent a further third as a lecturer, teaching computing skills and sales techniques at one extreme and business management (in conjunction with the staff of the London Business School) at the other. In the remaining third I became one of the world's leading experts in the new, and very esoteric, medical discipline of Apheresis; at the same time in effect running my own small business within IBM. It was a fascinating 15 year voyage of discovery, and one that I was allowed to choose for myself. A number of times I was pressurized by senior management to take other jobs, but when I resisted I was allowed to follow my own choice.

Again, this long-term personal development process across functions within the same company, as opposed to the more usual Western practice of across companies within the one functional specialization, is directly comparable with the deliberately slow evaluation and promotion process adopted within the larger Japanese companies.

For many IBMers, though, the most tempting prospect is a move into management, and this is made more likely by the fact that *all* (with virtually no exceptions) promotions to management, and within management, are from *within* IBM. It is only where very exotic skills are required, which cannot be met from within IBM, that it goes outside. This is a commendable practice, once again shared with the Japanese, in terms of employee motivation and natural justice; but it does occasionally result in some symptoms of "in-breeding."

Single Status

In recent years, though, the enviable employment security has been bought, at least in part, at the expense of creating first- and second-class citizens. This may come as something of a surprise to IBM since it is inordinately proud of being a single status company; and ascribes at least some of its success to this factor, as do Japanese companies. Every permanent employee is entitled to the same conditions. Thus everyone, from chief executive to cleaner, eats in the same restaurant (as compared with one UK subsidiary of a multinational, where I worked in the 1960s, which had six carefully graded levels of restaurant and canteen for a mere 600 employees!). In IBM no-one even has the status accorded by a reserved parking space (which ensures that there are usually plenty of spaces provided; no-one seriously wants to face the possible ire of a director with nowhere to park!). Since 1959 when Tom Watson Jr. put all IBM employees on salary, single status has been a philosophy taken very seriously throughout IBM, and one that genuinely works in practice as well as theory.

It goes without saying that IBM is an equal opportunity employer, though it was only with Tom Watson Jr. that this was first implemented; prior to that IBM had followed a typical white Anglo-Saxon Protestant approach (the Watsons were Methodists). IBM is now dedicated to equal opportunity, though it refuses to implement reverse discrimination. I was present a few years back at a quarterly meeting of the 50 or so top UK managers when the agenda ambitiously called for them to review the problems of sex discrimination. Their agonizing went on for nearly an hour, the consensus being that IBM did not really have a significant problem (though it was clear from the nature of some of the comments that a few of those present, as in any company, had some serious reservations; not to say prejudice). It was finally agreed that progress *must* be by merit alone. The cult of the meritocracy is basic in IBM, and will outweigh any more tender moralities.

It should be noted that equal opportunity is *not* a feature of Japanese companies. Their women employees are frequently treated as second-class citizens (as are those who are not of pure Japanese stock). They are often employed as temporaries; to be laid off before any men, even if they have been with the organization for 20 years. Not all Japanese lessons are so admirable in Western eyes! Theory Z predicts that organizations such as IBM should (as an extension of their innate xenophobia) also be somewhat racist and sexist; one prediction that IBM generally disproves.

Temporaries

The discrepancy which allows first- and second-class citizens, despite IBM's brave claims to single status, is that between regular (ie permanent or established) and temporary employees. In the UK, for example, perhaps a third of the total work force are either temporary, hired for 10 months and then fired (or "released" in the suitably inoffensive IBM jargon), or contract labour (supplied as part of contract catering for example). Where its employment practices for regular staff are exemplary, its use of this other category of labour is far less commendable; indeed IBM would seem to have a complete blind spot about them. They are effectively "non-beings." They are hired from agencies which are generally chosen on the basis of the lowest bid; cheap labour, with all its implications. IBM is lucky, though, that its reputation still attracts a high level of candidates; probably in the mistaken hope that such temporary employment is the route to a permanent job. In practice very few temps *are* allowed to make the transition.

They are offered none of the rights and privileges accorded to other IBM employees, and indeed IBM's approach is probably most accurately described as turning a blind eye to them; it apparently does not even want to admit they exist, perhaps because its personnel policies simply could not cope with a problem on this scale, if acknowledged. In fairness to IBM it has to be conceded that the theory, at least, is that IBM is currently in the process of moving to a new computer based structure, where significantly less administration and secretarial staff will be needed. The temporary staff are needed only in the short term; true temporaries. It is also fair to say that the temps receive better treatment from IBM, and from IBMers, than they would with other companies. But even so it is still hard to equate the feelings of a tearful temp on her last day with IBM, being released after 10 months as part of the IBM family, with IBM's genuine commitment to respect for the individual.

This is though an anomaly, hopefully over a relatively short term (though it has already existed for half a decade), which highlights just how fair and equitable is IBM's treatment of its regular employees.

Cynics might claim that this use of temporaries was an introduction of the policy that is widespread in Japan; where a significant proportion of the work force (usually women, as mentioned earlier) are temporaries, to be laid off instead of the permanent work force (usually men). Similarly IBM's increased use of contractors and suppliers might also be seen to parallel the (perhaps rather morally questionable) use made by the top Japanese corporations of the smaller companies that comprise the remaining 65 per cent of the economy. These small suppliers are again regularly "laid off" by the corporations in order that their own permanent work forces can remain unaffected; a job for life is only offered to the chosen few in the larger Japanese corporations (and is in effect subsidized by the less fortunate two-thirds in the smaller companies). The parallel is there, but I believe that in IBM's case this usually *is* an anomaly, not a deliberate policy as it is in Japan.

Communication channels

Speak-up

For the regular employees there are a number of communications channels, under the guardianship of Personnel Department, which are intended to guarantee that the theory is borne out in practice. Of these the most frequently used by individuals is the speak-up process. Surveys in the UK show that at some time or another one-third of IBMers use this process; and the running rate in the UK is around 1,000 per annum. Under it an employee can complain anonymously and have this complaint addressed by the highest level of management necessary to answer the problem; with a guideline of a reply in no more than 10 days. The evidence is that, because of its anonymity (which is guaranteed by being handled by a special speak-up coordinator within Personnel Department), this process is respected by employees and management alike.

Open-door

In theory the other main communication channel for individuals, the open-door process, should carry more clout. Under it an employee can "open-door" up his management ladder (in theory as far as Armonk) until he receives a satisfactory answer. Again, according to surveys (in the USA in this case) about one-third of personnel use this process, about nine per cent each year. Most problems are resolved fairly low on the management ladder, but a quarter go as far as divisional management; and two per cent go as far as Armonk. The process is taken very seriously by Armonk. Thus Tom Watson Jr. supported its continuation, on the grounds that: "it acts as a deterrent to the possible abuse of managerial power," although even he conceded: "from time to time we have had second thoughts on this practice" (article by ILT Caddick in IBM's magazine *Management Topics,* January 1985). Frank Cary later again (in the IBM booklet, *Employment with IBM—*

Principles at Work) supported it with the view that it is: "my assurance—and yours—that IBM can be flexible and big enough to cope with error."

The open-door process is, however, less highly regarded than the speak-up process by all concerned, probably because in this case anonymity is lost. Employees often feel that using it will damage their career. In fact most such appeals are lost (despite the clear conviction by the employee that some wrong definitely has taken place). On the other side of the table the managers involved report, according to the UK opinion survey, that they also see it as a threat.

Bridge interview

Such communications processes are, though, largely peripheral. They are safety valves to let the employee vent his feelings rather than a genuine means of change, To supplement them, at the end of the 1970s IBM instituted a programme with rather more teeth. This was the "bridge interview"; referred to as the "executive interview" in the USA. Under this scheme each employee had an obligatory interview, at least once a year, with his manager's manager. This was more effective simply because it did not require the employee to take the initiative and thus possibly label himself as a trouble maker. It certainly was an excellent incentive to management to take their subordinates views seriously, for they knew that these might otherwise surface in this bridge interview. This programme has, however, been quietly dropped in recent years (though Buck Rodgers still dutifully records its existence in his book); possibly management found it too onerous. This is a pity since it was becoming one of IBM's braver, and most effective, personnel devices.

Opinion survey

The one communications process that *does* have significant, and long lasting, impact is the opinion survey. The process is very simple. Every two years IBM conducts an opinion survey amongst its employees. The survey is once more guaranteed to be anonymous; even to the extent that no results are reported for groups of less than 10 employees (since it might otherwise be possible to deduce individual's answers). It is a mark of the trust that its employees have in IBM that, despite the fact that confidentiality is in the hands of an internal IBM department, the very great majority, of the order of 90 per cent, complete the survey; honestly and critically.

The survey is lengthy, it typically takes an hour to complete, and is thorough as well as wide ranging. Its questions strike right to the heart of how IBM manages both its employees and its business. The key questions relate to the employee's view of how IBM affects them; their conditions of employment (ranging from the perpetually vexed question of salary through to the more parochial details of their physical environment). In addition, though, it also asks questions, at some length, about how the employee views IBM's management of its operations. Finally, and most daringly of all, it asks employees to evaluate their manager!

Where possible the questions remain the same from survey to survey, so that trends can be seen as they emerge. In particular, results on the key questions are combined to derive a "morale index." The results of the survey are eagerly awaited by all IBMers, not least those at the higher levels. For IBM takes the results very seriously indeed. Only a serious failure to meet his quota target is worse for a manager than a vote of no confidence by his subordinates. At times, when a poor quota performance is matched by a slump in morale, such as happened in 1976 to GSD in the UK, even the divisional manager may feel uneasy for a while.

A network of senior managers is set up throughout IBM, specifically to monitor the results presentations and the subsequent action plans. For the climax of the process is not publication of a sanitized report. It is, instead, a series of departmental meetings (of *all* departments throughout IBM) at which each manager has to present the results relating not just to the whole of IBM but also to his specific group. It must surely be the most difficult moment in a manager's life when he has to face his department and tell them that they have just given him the thumbs down! What is worse is that he next has to agree with his subordinates an action plan to resolve all the problems that they have reported; this action plan is then registered by the senior manager handling that part of IBM's opinion survey.

The opinion survey, together with the associated action plans, is first of all a discipline on management. It is a very cogent reason why they should look after their employees, if they are not otherwise to pay the price in a maximum of two years' time. It is fair to say though that the impact of this discipline is most obvious in the few weeks immediately prior to the survey, when managers suddenly seem much more approachable!

The programme really does have teeth, which is its great strength. For example, Buck Rodgers reported that: "At one time the marketing reps' opinion of a particular division's management had dropped significantly. The complaints were justified. We gave the division president 90 days to get things turned around, or he would be replaced. We had to replace him."

At the level of senior management, either in the countries or at Armonk, the top level results are avidly seized upon as a very good barometer of opinion inside IBM. Employee morale has been a key measure of IBM performance since the time of the Watsons.

The opinion survey is a device that could be very profitably adopted by other companies. Indeed its use is almost a prerequisite for all the other actions I would recommend; since it alone, in my experience, will truly show how effectively these other policies are being implemented. It is the one device in IBM that guarantees that senior management can never become divorced from the realities. It may give them some nasty shocks—even IBM at times receives such shocks despite its enviable record—but *not* to know the bad news, to be able to rectify the problems, is far worse.

For example, a recent international survey of employee attitudes, carried out by the Chicago based consultancy International Survey Research (ISR), showed some very surprising results in terms of Japanese workers' morale. Fewer than half (47 per cent) of Japanese workers would recommend their company as a good place to work; and indeed Japan comes bottom or next to bottom in nine of the 14 categories reported on. Two key examples are:

Per cent of employees giving a favourable response to:

	company management %	pay %
West Germany	64	55
Britain	59	50
United States	55	53
Japan	43	36
Italy	42	37

The Japanese have a long history of being hypercritical in such surveys, but the trend in the results has been downwards in recent years. It somewhat deflates the much vaunted employment relations in Japan; though it should be noted that these have only ever been the prerogative of the large corporations, employing perhaps less than a third of the total work force.

By whatever means, IBM *does* have an enviable and fully justified reputation for the most enlightened personnel policies. This is no short-term fad; such policies have been at the core of IBM's business since Thomas J. Watson first joined it in 1914. As such there is a great element of morality behind their implementation; it is the only way IBM would now want to do business. At the same time, it is eminently profitable, for it has resulted in a work force of very high intellectual calibre which is superbly motivated, and this is central to IBM's extraordinary success.

Possibly uniquely amongst Western businesses, IBM has achieved many of the positive employee relationships that are seen to be so important to the success of the Japanese business style. This is less surprising when it is realised that in the 1950s the Japanese copied at least some of these from the leading US companies, and most probably from IBM itself.

IBM has, most importantly, persuaded its employees that they have the security of a job for life. Unlike the Japanese, though, it now does this without paternalism. It does not get involved in the private lives of its employees. It might once have done so but Tom Watson Jr. put an end to such intrusions. For there are some significant hidden problems associated with the paternalistic approach earlier adopted by IBM; and which is still at the heart of the Japanese management style.

The problems are hidden not just to the outside world but also to the participants; for the culture is typically blind to any of the flaws. Indeed, such strong cultures share the feature of any strong belief or religion that they are almost impervious to outside values, to the extent that they will deny to themselves even the possibility of any fallibility. John Akers may not claim any degree of papal infallibility, but IBMers do assume such infallibility for the IBM way of life. This blindness is perhaps seen most clearly in the modern IBM in terms of its quite untypical treatment of its second-class citizens, described earlier in this chapter. Its apparently uncaring attitude is, I believe, better described as *unthinking*; the culture ensures that its adherents are not even exposed to such an unpalatable thought.

Possibly the best review of the hidden problems of the pure paternalistic culture is that in Rodney Clark's description of his pseudonymous Japanese company, Marumaru; in the book *The*

Japanese Company (1979, Yale University Press). Even the now sacrosanct lifetime employment is shown by him to be a strictly limited concept—with many exceptions—to which the culture remains steadfastly oblivious. He does, though, come to the important conclusion that the strength of the system is not in the reality but in the *perception* of the participants: quite simply, if the employees *believe* that there is lifetime employment then they will make the commitment to their employer that is so typical of the Japanese work force (even where the reality shows significant exceptions to this philosophy, it still cannot destroy the commitment).

The modern IBM has, as a result of Watson Jr.'s reforms, avoided the worst of the Japanese problems highlighted by Clark; but even in IBM, albeit to a limited extent, most of them are still present under the surface, still unnoticed by the culture. One of the differences that distinguishes the modern IBM is that it has been able to go beyond the crudest level of "holistic" relationships that are central to Japanese organization, and are its strength. Something of this ilk was clearly an important part of the earlier IBM culture under T. J. Watson. His son, though, moved IBM on to the next level; successfully achieving the same results without having to pay the full price of corporate paternalism. In modern times IBM deliberately shuns anything that might be considered unwonted contact with employees' private lives. Even "family dinners," which used to be regular events, are relatively rare; indeed I have only attended two in 15 years. IBM now appears to lean over backwards to avoid any such contact. Indeed, relatively few IBMers have *any* contact with other IBMers outside of work. In any case, this is usually difficult where there is a relatively wide dispersion of IBMers, who because of their typical history of moves tend to commute from further away than do employees in other companies. The culture may be strong, but it now ceases as soon as an IBMer returns to the bosom of his family.

Public relations

Personnel Department also "hosts" those functions that interface, as a corporate identity, with the "non-commercial" outside world. Elsewhere it might be called, in general terms, public relations, but in IBM it is referred to as "corporate affairs"; perhaps a particularly apposite title for what is often a love/hate relationship. It does, however, cover a much greater scope than simple press relations.

Certainly there is a press relations department, which is infamous with the press. The press in general believe that its function is the exact reverse of the normal exuberant PR wish to feed information galore. It is believed that instead, its prime objective is to stop any press reports ever getting out. Almost all the predecessors of this book have commented at some length on the lack of assistance, if not even obstruction, from IBM; though the authors of books emerging since the beginning of the 1980s seem to have experienced a slight thaw in relations. There is a deal of truth in their views. As one of the few individuals actually allowed to be an official IBM spokesman (all others, be they employees or management, are specifically instructed to make no comment to the press) I was very aware that I was always accompanied by at least one "minder" from Press Relations. I never actually found this constricting, and I suspect other IBM spokesmen also found it no problem. But I was aware of a very defensive attitude by the PR professionals. This is perhaps understandable where there is a body of journalists, at least in the computer press, which digs very hard and long to unearth the "dirt" on IBM. There is relatively little mileage, or at least column inches, to be made from reporting that Snow White is still a virgin; and there is a consequent tendency to chronicle even the most minor of peccadilloes to titillate readers. Despite the real persecution to which IBM Press Relations is subjected, I still agree with the other commentators that IBM is unduly defensive. It has a very good story to tell and, as I hope this book shows, there is much for others to learn from its expertise—from the model.

Public responsibility

Within Corporate Affairs, IBM also makes its charitable donations to the community. Some of these are simple monetary amounts. In the UK, for example, IBM is one of the largest charitable donors, indeed it is number three in the corporate lists; and worldwide it gave $145 million to charity in 1984. One large part of this goes to the arts, which (being perennially underfunded) welcome it with open arms. One is conscious though that this is also an area of high profile with IBM's customer management; and one is particularly aware of the receptions and events around these donations, which are well attended by customers. I myself have so "entertained" key customers, and have found it an excellent way of doing business without any possible opprobrium that might otherwise result from such lavish entertainment.

The other major beneficiary of monetary donations, educational institutions, is openly admitted by IBM to be the subject of an investment in the future. By influencing schoolchildren and students, it believes it can enhance the long-term future of the computer industry in general, and of IBM in particular.

Perhaps the most positive contribution, however, has been the secondment of staff to support community ventures. A typical example was that IBM was one of the founders, in 1981, of the UK "Business in the Community" programme to help new businesses; and subsequently supported more than 20 of the 120 Enterprise Agencies in the UK. It was not a massive programme, there were just 100 secondees in the first 10 years (to 1982), but the evidence is that within its limits it was very successful; a theme I will return to in the next chapter.

IBM is not a charitable trust, however, and like many other companies its specifically charitable actions are a very small proportion of its overall business. Its main contribution to the community is, therefore, of an ethical nature. It is, as a key element of its main business strategy, committed to being a good "corporate citizen." It does not like being the "ogre," misunderstood by the community in general, and by government in particular. One result of this has been the emergence of a key group in Corporate Affairs whose one job is to persuade the UK government of IBM's claims to be regarded as the ideal corporate citizen. The short-term aim was articulated to me by the key manager as being to "reach a position where government ministers were on first-name terms with the board [of IBM]." This position was finally reached in 1984 after a decade's hard work. Perhaps coincidentally, IBM's share of government business also increased; though it is fair to record that this was most probably due to the fact that only IBM could supply the very large mainframes then required (but the group in Corporate Affairs discreetly claimed some influence in moderating the overt nationalism, not to say jingoism, which had previously attended such buying decisions).

It is too easy to read unduly cynical motives into IBM's relations with the community, and particularly with government. It is also too easy to assume that in the furtherance of its interests IBM would covertly indulge in some of the underhand tricks that have been employed by other companies. I can only say that in the dealings with government that I was involved in, I never felt any pressure from IBM to do more than tell the exact truth; indeed, if there was any pressure at all, it was designed to ensure that I did not "gild the lily" and exaggerate IBM's good points.

IBM has taken its corporate responsibilities to the community very seriously, perhaps uniquely so, for a long time. In the McKinsey Lectures in 1962 Tom Watson Jr. spelled out the philosophy that had been initiated by his father: "Bigness itself is a relatively new phenomenon in our society. Even if nothing else had changed" the vast concentrations of power in our society would demand that businessmen reconsider their responsibilities for the broader public welfare. I believe we're going to have to ask ourselves a little more seriously if what we are planning to do in our business is as good for the employees as it is for the stockholders—and as good for the country as it is for both these groups.

"Business is subject not only to existing law—but to the tolerance of the public. Lawful or not, if business does things which the public regards as wrong and abusive, that public has the power to demand new laws with which business will have to comply."

This has since been codified to the extent that, for example, the IBM UK 1984 *Annual Review* (sent to all its employees) specifically talks of ". . . our responsibilities to our stakeholders who all benefit from our achievements:

- the shareholders (stockholders)
- the employees
- the customers
- the suppliers
- and the community at large."

In association with this are described: ". . . our basic beliefs which have stood us in such good stead for many years, and which, more than anything else, account for our continuing success:

- respect for the individual
- service to the customer
- and the pursuit of excellence as a way of life."

There can be few companies that will put such "stakeholders" as customers and suppliers on an almost equal footing with the stockholders and employees; let alone include the community at large in the same category. But IBM as an entity, and its employees as a group, genuinely want to make the most positive contribution to the community; and such is the level of success in its main business that it can actually afford the luxury of indulging resources and time in community affairs.

I was always aware, while involved with Biomedical Group, that the interest of senior management (in Europe and in Armonk, as well as in the UK) was not limited to the profit figures. There was an underlying feeling that it was a project peculiarly in line with IBM's commitment to the community. Saving lives—and Biomedical Group's activities may well ultimately result in the saving of many thousands of lives—had a very real place in IBM's accounting. Indeed, in proposing the discontinuation of that group, the one fact I had to prove was that other companies were then in a position to follow through the various developments that had been started; it was clear that IBM would not have left the market if it had not had guarantees that the patients and medicine would not suffer. While it was in business the exploits of the group were followed with interest, and something approaching pride, by a great many IBMers. John Kennedy's plea, in his 1961 Inaugural Address: "Ask not what your country can do for you: ask what you can do for your country," sums up much of the IBM approach.

SECTION 3

The Lessons to be Learnt

CHAPTER 13

The Japanese Lesson

Introduction

This final chapter contains what I believe are the main lessons to be learnt from IBM. They are also the major lessons to be drawn from the Japanese corporations (the first part of the chapter is an explanation of the links; and, in particular, IBM's likely role as one of the original models for the "Japanese miracle").

The lessons are about management style. They comprise the "Philosophies I." The first set, of 10, of these closely approximates to those described by William G. Ouchi in his *Theory Z*. They are essential to creating the partnership between employer and employee (based on a feeling of mutual trust), which is so characteristic of IBM and the Japanese corporations. Their basis is strong *beliefs*, and the most fundamental of these is full employment. Thereafter the essence of the style is involvement of the individual in the future of the organization; enriching his job and effectively giving him the right to personal development within a strong corporate culture.

The second set, again 10 in number, of "Philosophies I" is however described for the first time. It is the management style uniquely developed by IBM to counter its increasingly bureaucratic tendencies. It is based on an emphasis on individualism (utilizing very capable and well-trained individuals), indeed on encouraged dissent. It supports the individuals by a remarkably strong communications network (increasingly computer based). The essence is the development of the autonomous teams or cells (and most basically the individuals) that are the building-blocks of the newly emerging cellular organic organizational structures (which are steadily replacing the traditional functional organization).

This second set of philosophies counters the problems, typically those of credibility (eventually found in almost any paternalistic bureaucracy), now being experienced even by some of the most dynamic of Japanese corporations. It also removes many of the cultural barriers that prevent Western companies, steeped in a tradition of individualism, from adopting the most beneficial elements of Theory Z.

I little thought when I started the research for this book that I would be referring so extensively to Japan as well as IBM. My intention was to promote the "gospel" of IBM; quite simply because in my experience it held a number of *unique* lessons, which had resulted in it being so dramatically successful.

IBM and Japanese management

This chapter, then, was to be the key to my task. It was to draw out the most important lessons for business management. This, in fact, remains the case. The only diversion is that occasioned by the intrusion of the Japanese, for not all the lessons are, in the event, unique to IBM. As will emerge, the lessons of IBM are perhaps just as important in helping understand what makes the Japanese corporations so successful.

As part of the research I naturally looked for other groups of companies that had been as successful as IBM. The most obvious comparison was with the Japanese corporations, for only they had consistently matched IBM's growth rate; but my first instinct was to dismiss them as not being relevant to Western culture, as have many other observers before me. For it is a widely reported fact that their success is a result of their unique national culture, which is not transportable to the West; a great many firms have tried to copy their success, but have ultimately not been able to penetrate the mysteries of the culture.

For example, one spin-off from the McKinsey work was a book, *The Art of Japanese Management* by Pascale and Athos. But surprisingly, despite its shared origins (for William G. Ouchi also worked with the McKinsey team), this did *not* report the same lessons as Ouchi. Indeed it concentrated on the, by now traditional, view that uniquely Japanese qualities, largely resulting from Zen (particularly "ambiguity" and "interdependence"), were the key elements of the Japanese miracle. It also rather idiosyncratically ascribed much of the modern philosophy to Kanosuke Matsushita (whose company they investigated in some depth). Their view can perhaps be summarized as a belief that the key philosophies can be traced back to his influence, from as early as 1918 when he started Matsushita. They even recorded that T. J. Watson visited Matsushita in the 1930s, claiming that he "presumably was influenced by what he saw there"; in fact, the IBM evidence is very clear that he had *already* been building the basis of his own philosophies for more than a decade, where it was to be another two decades before they were to be adopted—I believe copied from IBM and not the other way around—by the modern Japanese corporations.

This attribution of the modern Japanese practices to Kanosuke Matsushita, even where many Japanese authorities also credit him with a very influential role in the development of their industry, does not I feel satisfactorily explain why these practices were not widely adopted by other Japanese companies until the 1960s, more than four decades later (surely a remarkably slow process for a nation that thrives on plagiarism!), and then were so rapidly implemented.

It should be noted that, in any case, there are a great many factors that differentiate the Japanese corporations from their Western counterparts, almost any one of which might be the source of their success. Rodney Clark, in *The Japanese Company,* lists more than 20 major differences, and links a number of these: ". . . the fact that [Japanese] firms are so often part of one industry makes market share a natural measure of success and an obvious management goal. To the extent that managers are not aiming primarily for profit, something that benefits only one group of people, but growth of sales, which benefits everyone, management becomes not coercion but leadership. The distinction between managers and workers may be insignificant. . . . The company can be a community in which everyone has interests in common. . . . Similarly there is an association between a firm's dependence on bank and trade credit, and the development of hierarchical relations between companies. . . . Again, all these features are consistent with the predominance of enterprise unions."

On the other hand "functional" explanations and more "culturally based" theories are not mutually exclusive: I would suggest that they are often *complementary*. For example, the views of Abbeglen and Stalk (in *Kaisha, The Japanese Corporation*), commenting on the very aggressive competitiveness of the Japanese corporations, offer a useful balance to the more esoteric cultural ideas. According to them: "The competitive fundamentals chosen by the successful kaisha (corporations) include:

–a growth bias
–a preoccupation with actions of competitors
–the creation and ruthless exploitation of competitive advantage
–the choice of corporate financial and personnel policies that are economically consistent with all of the preceding."

Indeed these are phenomena shared, at least in part, by IBM. It too is aggressively competitive; though this is certainly *not* its prime characteristic as it is with the Japanese (otherwise IBM could not have survived the various anti-trust actions relatively unscathed). Most important, though, is that IBM shares the dependence on growth, and has been masterly at maintaining such growth by moving from one market to another as they developed. It should be emphasized that such functional theories of management are not supplanted by the theories of management style put forward in this book. Style is important, but it is clearly an adjunct to the basic essentials; the theories of which are best to be found in the classical management text books.

On the other hand I believe Abbeglen and Stalk are equally at fault in claiming the *exclusive* explanation for these functional factors (as stated in the subtitle of their book: "How Marketing, Money and Manpower Strategy, Not Management Style, Made the Japanese World Pace Setters"). Aggressive competition alone is not enough. The fourth set of factors listed above (in particular personnel policies) must have the strength to serve that competitiveness. Abbeglen and Stalk still do, despite their protestations to the contrary, recognize the cultural elements. For example they report: "A phrase much used in Japan is nihonteki keiei, or Japanese style management, referring to what the Japanese see as considerable differences between Japanese management methods and those commonly used in the West. The differences cited are usually those having to do with personnel policies. . . ."

Misconceptions

Fortunately, despite the large number of possible factors and the many conflicting theories, I still went ahead with my research. For what I found was, at least in some respects, almost the complete reverse of the traditional thinking. A number of the most deeply held beliefs about Japanese corporations were revealed to be probably an even greater collection of bunkum than were those about IBM, which I had first set out to debunk.

The route to this revelation was in the first instance via a number of incomplete reports (including those alluded to in the McKinsey-based work of Peters and Waterman) that suggested that some of the key management practices in Japan were very similar to those that I had observed in IBM. Obviously the parallels interested me, since they might provide independent corroboration for the success of these.

One of the best summaries of these Japanese practices is contained in William G. Ouchi's book, *Theory Z.* Most interestingly, in this book he also identified IBM as one of his key Theory Z companies that, almost alone in Western culture, follow patterns similar to the Japanese companies. Indeed he credited IBM with the initial revelation that led to his theory. He described a meeting where he presented his interim results to a group of IBM executives. One of the IBM vice-presidents spoke up: "Do you realize that this form you have been describing as Japanese is exactly what IBM is? Let me point out that IBM has developed this form in its own way—we have not copied the Japanese!" Although Ouchi went on to say: "this man's reaction was an opinion with which other IBM employees might strongly disagree," and thus effectively dismissed the range of other lessons he might have gone on to learn from IBM itself, he did then (stimulated by this incident) go on to develop his cross-cultural Theory Z. One interesting implication is that neither he, nor the IBM executives, apparently appreciated that the similarities had probably come about precisely because the Japanese had, in one way or another, copied IBM!

Even when I discovered (after completing the initial draft of this book) that Ouchi too had found the source of his inspiration in IBM, I still did not begin to appreciate the links to the Japanese experience. That final enlightenment came, in fact, with my discovery of *MITI and the Japanese Miracle,* by Chalmers Johnson (1982, Stanford University Press). He ascribes their miracle to the actions of MITI, the Japanese Ministry of International Trade and Industry. This is a view that, as you will appreciate from the earlier sections, I would fully support. MITI's control of the large Japanese corporations, using "administrative guidance" (backed by government organized cartels) to integrate national activities, has been as successful as it has been different from the Western (by comparison) *laissez-faire*.

Buried in this book, however, were some references that suggested a possible explanation of how the revered Japanese management practices came about. Johnson identifies one key development as that of the creation of the Industrial Rationalization Council (Sangyo Gorika Shingikai) in 1949 under the auspices of the newly formed MITI. This, in the form of 45 committees and 81 subcommittees, was the main means of liaison between the government and the business community. He goes on to say: "... perhaps the council's least known but later most applauded activities were in the areas of reform of management, the institutionalization of the lifetime employment system, and the raising of the productivity of the Japanese industrial worker."

He also referred to the comments of Noda Nobuo (in *How Japan Absorbed American Management Methods* (Asian Productivity Organization, Manila, 1970), a former Mitsubishi executive and chairman of the Council's Management Committee. These were to the effect that he had always contended that the committee got its ideas for quality control and the measurement of productivity from the USA.

Johnson also goes on to explain how: "... excited by the American concept of 'scientific management' the Industrial Rationalization Council churned out publications and sponsored speakers, leading during the mid-1950s to what was called the 'business administration boom' (keiei bumu) and to *making bestsellers of books such as Peter F. Drucker's 'The Practice of Management'* (published in 1954 and translated into Japanese in 1956)." The italics are mine!

This reference to Drucker's book is, for me, the crucial link. For on looking to my own copy (which was my "bible" in the 1960s; as it was many other manager's), I was fascinated to rediscover that the book contains a section (Chapter 19) which is nothing more than a eulogy to IBM's working practices (specifically lifetime employment, job enrichment and the precursors of quality circles) which also turn out to be those, in this combination, of modern Japan.

The timescales are supported by a number of writers, including Abbeglen and Stalk (though they draw rather different conclusions, somewhat similar to those of Kenichi Ohmae): "The system of organization and personnel relations of the kaisha is not an old system in its present integrated form. Essentially a product of the elements of earlier systems and the conditions prevailing after World War II, it dates from around 1950. . . ." Paradoxically it is arguable that Abbeglen's own "discovery" (reported in his *The Japanese Factory*, published in 1958—four years after the first publication of Drucker's book) of the importance of the Japanese belief in lifetime employment was a key catalyst in the consolidation of this philosophy.

The "Japanese miracle": a Western model?

If these various reports are correct, and it is admittedly difficult to establish a definite basis for such facts in a society that tends to lock up its key secrets, then I believe a possible scenario might have been as follows. In the mid-1950s MITI was just getting into its stride and was stimulating very rapid growth—the average investment rate was better than 25 per cent between 1956 and 1961, and this was when the foundations of the "Japanese miracle" were laid. At that time it had a work force desperately seeking a better life. The late 1940s and early 1950s had been times of terrible hardship imposed by SCAP (Supreme Commander for Allied Powers, the occupying administration), particularly at the time of the "Dodge Line" (Joseph M. Dodge, the US ambassador, imposed a savagely deflationary policy). One result was that there was little job security, and considerable unemployment; MITI had seen its own numbers cut from 13,822 in 1949 to 3,257 in 1952.

MITI contained the cream of Japanese intellectuals, and they saw it as their personal duty to reinvigorate the economy. To this end they adopted a very successful strategy of copying from elsewhere. This has been most obvious in their copies of technology, and to a lesser extent lifestyle, from the USA. But it also, in the mid-1950s, extended to copying management techniques, where Japan previously had no body of theory. MITI's great success, on all these fronts, was its selectivity; it only copied the very best and most suitable.

MITI, as a great bureaucracy (for Japan far more than other non-Communist countries is run by bureaucracies), would soon have identified with IBM's structures and beliefs. What is more, the core of the belief (as reported by Drucker), that of lifetime employment (bolstered by job enrichment) would have been particularly attractive to them in terms of solving their worker unrest, and would have reminded them of the "permanent employment" which was a much respected, if not widely copied, feature of the pre-war zaibatsus (the conglomerate precursors of the modern Japanese corporations). These factors, in any case, had (at least according to Drucker, their mentor) already been responsible for the success of one of the great American business giants.

It probably was a heady brew for MITI. The trail of evidence is there. More important, though, is the fact that these key IBM policies, in combination, are now (three decades later) central to modern Japanese management practices; where they did not exist prior to that date (apart from the permanent employment mentioned above—and even this had largely fallen victim to the post-war financial stringencies), and indeed were (at least in combination) largely alien to the then current practices. The new practices were probably so readily and rapidly accepted precisely because they held resonances for existing Japanese national culture. Lifetime employment, as the most obvious example, was in many respects a quite natural extension of the zaibatsus' permanent employment; and even if (as the statistics suggest) its true pre-war implementation was much less widespread than has been popularly reported, it was a practice widely respected and even envied (albeit in retrospect) by the Japanese work force (very few of whom had, however, been exposed to it in practice). The implementation was, though, complex and took on further elements of that culture; and it is these later additions, almost of a decorative nature, which often make the processes impenetrable to Western viewpoints. But the skeleton underneath is still recognizably IBM; and it is an interesting point that the culture of IBM itself is often described as impenetrable.

The reason for the extended historical introduction to this chapter is that it is important to understand that IBM has a wider importance, in that (despite the view of Pascale and Athos that the very reverse was the case!) IBM was quite probably also a key model (at least in terms of the combination of these critical factors) for the Japanese corporations; even if it was only the Western model that gave them the confidence to reintroduce some of their earlier practices, where the then current belief of the Japanese business experts—particularly of those scholars in the industrial relations field—was that such practices could be attributed simply to the *backwardness* or *immaturity* of Japan's capitalist development. In the final analysis it is not essential to prove that IBM *was* the model for the Japanese corporations; though that adds a certain historical interest. Its real importance (as stressed by Ouchi) is that it follows the same management philosophies and techniques that have made the Japanese so successful. A study of how IBM operates its philosophies will, therefore, also derive the lessons that so many have tried to deduce from the Japanese; and these lessons are "written" in a cultural context which is more understandable (and is not confused by irrelevant Zen accretions). In addition, its practices as developed by Tom Watson Jr. (after the time that MITI probably made the Japanese copy), go *beyond* the Japanese examples to begin to form the "cultures" needed to handle the cellular organic organization structures increasingly demanded by the information revolution.

These lessons are in the direct line of theory which moved from a Theory X approach to that of Theory Y (led by Douglas McGregor). The next step, if we exclude the McKinsey-based work of Peters and Waterman which in part parallels these developments, was that of the much less well-known Theory Z, of William G. Ouchi. There was no reference to his ideas by Peters and Waterman (despite the fact that he contributed to the earlier stages of their own work), and Abbeglen and Stalk dismissed his theory by the criticism: "The explicit quantification of the relationships between cause (management style) and effect (high productivity) are generally sidestepped"; a rather gratuitous dismissal when much of their own detailed evidence supports his views. Ouchi took the Theory Y philosophy (that employees were fundamentally hard working, responsible and need only to be supported and encouraged) one stage further; to a state where the onus was on the employer to build a relationship of trust with the employees, leading to a "partnership."

It should be recorded, however, that at least some of the views expressed by Peters and Waterman, in their book *In Search of Excellence* (most specifically their four "Soft Ss," shared values/skills/staff/style—where they are less constrained by their general concentration on the functional aspects of management), parallel those of Theory Z (not surprisingly in view of the fact that Ouchi worked with the McKinsey team during the early stages of their investigation) and also parallel IBM's actual practices. As such they complement the views expressed here. In general, though, they tend to be rather more intimately linked to the earlier functional (or rational) approaches; despite the avowed intention of moving away from these. Theory Z, in my view, offers greater clarity and a more coherent basis (albeit somewhat more simplistically, and less popularly presented) for the next step.

The conclusion I eventually drew is that the lessons to be learnt from IBM may be that much more valuable; since they encompass much of Theory Z (which is, in any case, a brave attempt to encapsulate the Japanese miracle) but go rather further, and are in the more digestible Western idiom.

Philosophies I

The IBM lessons fall fairly naturally into two parts. The first is, indeed, that relating to those beliefs which build trust. This is comparable in many respects with Theory Z; and I would suggest that Ouchi's book can be profitably read as a complement. It is also, historically, broadly the legacy of Thomas J. Watson (and being fully developed in the 1950s when MITI imported it, *is* the part of the IBM story so successfully copied by the Japanese).

Under this category I broadly include 10 "philosophies":

Strong beliefs (leading to objectives set in terms of philosophies);
Shared ethical values;
Full employment policies (lifetime employment);
Job enrichment;
Personal incentives;
Non-specialised career development;
Personal (consensual) involvement, in decision making;
Implicit (value) control, rather than explicit (figure) control;
Development of a strong culture;
Holistic approach to employees.

If the first category has already been described, albeit in slightly different terms, I am not aware that the second category detailed below has been explored to any great extent; though once again Peters and Waterman hint at some aspects of it. This is the anarchy of individualism that IBM has promoted as an antidote to its emerging bureaucratic tendencies and to the paternalism that most probably accompanies the first category. It was no accident that in its early days IBM was clearly a paternalistic organization. Nor is it a purely national phenomenon where Japanese corporations expect their employees to subjugate their own personalities to the needs of the group. The holistic aspect of Theory Z works powerfully in *both* directions. IBM's antidote to these tendencies was, historically, led by Tom Watson Jr. and his successors; and was *after*

MITI's promotion of IBM's virtues (and is accordingly *not* incorporated in modern Japanese practices). As far as I am aware this category is unique to IBM, and it is what makes IBM such a valuable model, particularly for Western managers, and particularly in the context of the developing cellular organic organizational structures. Under this category I would include a further 10 "advanced Philosophies":

Strong (published) beliefs in individualism (respect for the individual);
Personnel processes, to guarantee the working of these beliefs;
Single status, across the company;
Recruitment, of the highest calibre individuals;
Extended training, particularly for top management (institutionalized nepotism);
Maximal delegation, to the lowest possible levels;
Planned constraints, on first-line management;
Encouragement of dissent ("wild ducks");
Development of horizontal communications;
Institutionalization of change.

I believe that the two categories complement each other, and in fact both will *need* to be combined to produce the successful, well rounded, corporation of the twenty-first century; the first (Theory Z) category alone could probably now no longer survive in the more sophisticated (and individualistic) Western culture. I would, however, hesitate to describe any of the observations as a theory, because that would endow them with too rigid a code. It would also give them undue significance. There are a great many factors that management must be aware of in running its day to day operations. Charles B. Handy identifies more than 60 variables in the area of organization alone, and there can be no panaceas universally applicable to all situations in all companies. Industry is already too burdened down with such theories. Indeed, even the often excellent work of Peters and Waterman seems to me at times to be unduly distorted by the need to produce an easily *memorable* (rather than applicable perhaps?) set of theories. This leads to at least one rather jarring note, where "people" (as a key element of their theories; and one with which I would wholeheartedly agree) have to be forced into the remarkably unsuitable description of "staff" (which actually undermines the principles they wish to communicate, at least according to its conventional meaning; which as a result they have to redefine at some length). This somewhat cavalier manipulation of the English language is simply to allow "Seven Ss" to be used.

Instead I have grouped the factors together under the very general (and I hope suitably neutral) title of "Philosophies I." If that still seems too pretentious may I offer in defence the observation that "shorthand" labels are inevitably given to any "technical" concept that is being discussed, even (perhaps particularly) in business management theory; and if I do not suggest a title then someone else will, and in the process will probably add a degree of weightiness that is unjustified.

I would particularly stress that these "Philosophies I" in the main relate to only one aspect of management theory, that of management style. Complementary to them, and indeed basic essentials for the profitable and effective management of any business or organization, are the many "functional" aspects of management theory. This book makes no claim to give detailed guidance, for example, on such matters as marketing or production theory. For these basics the reader must search out the more classical management texts; and once more I would suggest that a sound starting point is the work of Peter Drucker.

"Philosophies I" is the chosen descriptor because the key elements are *beliefs*. They are not hard and fast mathematical rules. They simply represent viewpoints, the management style, which a company may adopt to confront the world at large. To quote Tom Watson Jr.: "I firmly believe that any organization, in order to survive and achieve success, must have a sound set of beliefs on which it premises all its policies and actions." The "I" is simply a recognition that the model is IBM; my contribution has simply been to interpret that model. The original itself is the best touchstone of any further interpretation. This is the main reason that this book covers such a wide spectrum, certainly more than is necessary as a context for the most basic understanding of the philosophies; it is an attempt to provide a "reference" book based largely on examples (and the whole of IBM is rather more than the sum of the parts). Apart from Ouchi's *Theory Z*, two further books can usefully be read as complementary in this context. Nancy Foy's *IBM World* gives a somewhat more detailed account (albeit from 1973) of some of the areas I cover only briefly. As a definitive account of the beliefs (up to 1963), Tom Watson Jr.'s own book, *A Business and its Beliefs,* cannot be bettered. Unfortunately both are out of print, but they are well worth the effort if you can persuade your library to track them down for you.

At the same time Rodney Clark's book *The Japanese Company,* which is a very thorough case study of a modern Japanese corporation, provides a useful comparison to the model of IBM; and also highlights some of the hidden problems that are inherent in the first (Theory Z) leg of "Philosophies I." These problems were also present in the earlier history of IBM; and, though they have been ameliorated by the second leg of "Philosophies I," they can still lurk below the surface. It is as well to recognize them; for not all of them can be simply summed up as the problems of bureaucracy.

At this stage it should be added that, although most of my comments have been directed at the company level, a number of the "Philosophies I" can also be applied at the divisional, or even departmental, level. Clearly, the impact of overall company policies and actions can easily upset the best departmental implementation; and departmental solutions must be correspondingly fragile where they fly in the face of a hostile company environment. Yet they can still make some (albeit possibly small) positive contribution even then; and they can certainly create a more rewarding local environment for any manager to work in.

The backing to the various philosophies can be found in the earlier chapters (particularly Chapters 6 and 11). The rest of this chapter, though, abstracts what I believe is most critical about these key factors, as IBM approaches them. Thus, I expand the first 10 philosophies, those most clearly corresponding to Theory Z.

Strong beliefs

Tom Watson Jr.'s statement, quoted earlier in this chapter, suggests just how important beliefs are to IBM. Indeed the one common factor that holds IBM together in a very rapidly changing world is not its technology, but its unique ethics and culture.

It cannot be stressed too strongly just how important are the beliefs as the main driving force of IBM, as they will be for other companies seeking to emulate its particular style of management. They are not optional, or philosophical bunkum (as most observers have previously concluded). As Peters and Waterman also stress (using the different terminology of "shared values" or "superordinate goals") they are the essential prerequisite to, and mainspring driving, the whole business. Without them the whole structure of "Philosophies I" would collapse.

Just how important are such strong beliefs is evidenced by some aspects of IBM's recent problems. IBM has never abandoned its three main beliefs, or philosophies. On the other hand, its second philosophy, of "Customer Service," has, as we've seen, been seriously undermined by the conflicting (but supposedly lesser) "objective" that John Opel introduced in the late 1970s: that of being the "lowest cost producer." Through the 1980s, IBM became steadily obsessed with this lesser objective, which was, by implication, almost diametrically opposed to the second philosophy—though IBM management chose not to see any contradictions. This dilution of a major belief weakened IBM in a number of ways. Amongst its own employees, in general, it produced an undesirable element of confusion. Amongst its management, particularly amongst its planners, it allowed a degree of schizophrenia which justified some adventures that would never have been contemplated previously. This process was exacerbated by the ending of the anti-trust actions by both the US government and the EEC—decisions which DeLamarter (in *Big Blue*) thought would be prejudicial to IBM's competitors, but which, paradoxically, turned out to be most harmful to IBM itself! The less responsible managers within IBM took this as a signal to bend, and then break, many of IBM's "Business Conduct Guidelines." With its weakened beliefs, IBM found this difficult to resist; and, for one obvious example, discounting (often selectively) began to be considered (to ultimately erode IBM's profits, as well as its image).

The most glaring example of this weakening of the "Customer Service" belief, though, lay in IBM's handling of its "third parties." As I have stressed, in earlier chapters, IBM's greatest marketing strength was in its commitment to "Customer Service." This one belief, by itself, compensated for almost all of IBM's obvious shortcomings in the area of marketing. It was almost inevitable that IBM would have some problems with its third parties, for other reasons, but if it had only implemented its philosophy of "Customer Service" most of these problems would probably have remained minor. As it turned out, in this arena, IBM's contradictory policies clashed; and "lowest cost" won the day. IBM turned a blind eye to the activities of its *authorised* dealers. It never challenged what they were doing, often in its name, to its previously successful policy of "Customer Service." Even when it became obvious to everyone else that IBM dealers were giving poor service, IBM still couldn't react. If the antics had been observed in one of its own salesmen he would have been instantly dismissed; despite

IBM's personnel policies, such a flagrant breach of IBM's cherished beliefs would have been intolerable. But, when seen in its dealers, IBM was unable to react. There are other reasons which may go some way to explain this surprising paralysis (the juxtaposition of alien cultures for example), but I believe the main reason was the weakening of IBM's beliefs; and, at least in this case, the contradictory objective (of "lowest cost") was allowed to justify inaction; on failings that the Watson family would have seen as inexcusable, if not heresy!

Clearly it is not possible for any manager of an individual department to enshrine a set of beliefs as powerful as IBM's; and as beliefs are the bedrock of "Philosophies I" it is just as clear that such departmental solutions can only offer a poor second best to a company-wide commitment. In the absence of such a company-wide implementation, however, departmental solutions should not be despaired of. In fact such solutions frequently emerge spontaneously. These unofficial versions are most often based on beliefs of the type encapsulated in IBM's third belief, "the pursuit of excellence." They are most probably tied to a functional manifestation. The department, if it has any spirit at all, will sincerely believe that it is good, indeed best, at doing its own thing; though what that thing *is* may surprise the company planners (and the most powerful implementation is often seen in the vigorous application of bureaucratic, near veto powers by staff departments).

It is, thus, near essential that a departmental manager at least understands what are the *real* beliefs that motivate his department; for only then can he start to use and manipulate them to optimize the performance of his team.

The problem, of course, is that such beliefs may well be implicit, unspoken; and the manager may be so deeply enmeshed in them that he cannot distinguish them from the more general business principles. But a manager of sensitivity *should* be able to detect them; if only he takes time to stand back and dispassionately analyse what his subordinates hold most dearly (and probably what causes the most friction in disputes with other departments).

Full employment policies

The *prime* belief was seen by Tom Watson Jr. to hinge on "the IBM policy on job security." This is central not just to IBM's beliefs, but also to Theory Z and to the policies of the Japanese corporations; though it should be noted that lifetime employment is a feature only offered by the larger Japanese corporations (employing only 35 per cent of the work force)—and Rodney Clark suggests that even then it is often less of a commitment than the observers (and the employees) believe.

A policy of full employment (or even a general belief by the employees that such a policy of lifetime employment exists) is the major prerequisite for building trust with employees. The evidence shows that a lifetime job is reciprocated, by employees considering all their actions in terms of what is best for the whole organization; where in most Western companies they desperately protect their own little empires, often against the interests of the whole, due to the constant fear of redundancy hanging over them. This is one reason why employee relations are often better in a boom; even though that is when, with some scarcity value, employees should be taking a tougher line.

I personally first came across the benefits of job security, as directly applicable to the effective running of a company's operations, early in my career; when I was a brand manager at Gallahers (a leading UK tobacco manufacturer, now part of American Tobacco). The Belfast factory, with which I worked closely, had a justifiable reputation for very poor labour relations (and indeed even suffered the indignity of a strike, something almost unknown in Gallahers). My own experience was that the work force was uncooperative, surly and generally gloomy. There was much discussion of unfair treatment, stretching back nearly 50 years (when most of the workers hadn't even been born!). It was just the sort of work force one dreads inheriting. Yet less than a year later I had, unwittingly, changed the whole picture. Then the labour relations were about the best in Gallahers; they were the most productive, cheery and confident workers that you could wish for! The reason for the dramatic change turned out to be quite simple.

When I arrived sales of pipe tobacco, which is what the factory produced, were steadily and relentlessly declining; and the main talk of the work force revolved around predicting just when they would be made redundant. A year later I had turned the main brand, "Condor," around and sales were *growing* at a steady 10 per cent per annum. Suddenly the work force had a future! It was a simple solution to an apparently intractable problem.

The security of full employment is not just reflected in greater flexibility (for which the Japanese workers are renowned, but are at least matched by the IBM work force); it is also reflected in an infectious feeling of optimism. Indeed according to Tom Watson

Jr.: "... the importance we attach to job security is one of the principal reasons why people like to work for IBM."

As important to IBM is respect for the individual. Again according to Tom Watson Jr.: "... it [is] equally important that the company respect the dignity of its employees." Most companies would consider such a philosophy as esoteric in the extreme, and largely irrelevant to business needs; but it is an essential ingredient necessary to make Theory Y work (at least at the Theory Z level; though Ouchi does not document it).

Full employment may still seem to be an idealistic luxury for many companies, constantly riding the roller-coaster from boom to bust and back again. IBM, though, has a particularly effective solution to this. It largely resources, in manpower terms, to meet the troughs. The peaks are met by its employees working that much harder; sometimes very much harder (a key measure in the opinion survey is the hours worked). This may appear a naive approach, but such is the relationship of trust that it works! It has the added advantage that employees are rarely underemployed; and in my experience the employees most ready to complain about working conditions (and, most paradoxically, about "overwork") are precisely those who have time to spend on such things—IBMers simply do not have tirne to waste on such unproductive discussions.

The Japanese rely more on their ability to lay off the many temporary workers, and (perhaps even more important) to pass the problem on to their suppliers. This "industrial dualism," where the very large numbers of small companies and their workers suffer markedly worse terms than do the favoured large corporations (who are typically their customers), is a feature of Japan which is not widely appreciated in the West (where it is only the large corporations that are in evidence).

The individual departmental manager clearly cannot guarantee full employment; indeed his own tenure, as much as his subordinates', is usually at the whim of more senior management. He can, though, at least build a degree of trust with his team (that *his* decisions will not be arbitrary, and that their jobs will not be gratuitously at risk from him); and, as is recognized by most workers, the person most likely to threaten their employment is their immediate manager.

A subsidiary device employed by IBM, and (as mentioned earlier) to a much greater extent by the Japanese corporations, is the use of temporary staff and contractors. These are laid off first in any recession, leaving the permanent staff still in employment. It is a cynical approach which might seem to be against the tenor of the other beliefs, but it works (even in IBM); since the very strong culture blinds its participants to such unpalatable facts.

But in any case, IBM will always cut other costs before people costs. IBMers may have to work, temporarily, in marginally less congenial surroundings but their salaries will be protected. In the extreme, Hewlett-Packard (another Theory Z company identified by Ouchi, as well as being one of Peters' and Waterman's favourite examples) recently asked all employees to take salary cuts rather than create any redundancies. This was accepted by the staff. It may have been uncomfortable, but it maintained the security of full employment.

The reverse process can, unfortunately, be undertaken even faster. At the beginning of the 1970s Unilever had many of the trappings of a Theory Z company. It then fell to the siren calls of the government for greater productivity, and started to lay off workers. There is no evidence that this resulted in any increase in productivity, but it is clear that almost by the stroke of a pen it lost its (very valuable) status as a Theory Z company; regrettably any such lapse can destroy the relationship of trust which has taken decades to build.

The second basic belief reported by Tom Watson Jr. was that: ". . . we want to give the best customer service of any company in the world." As this is not a personnel management issue, Ouchi does not refer to this. It is, however, an important part of IBM's overall beliefs. In fact it does have a personnel dimension, because pride in one's job is an important motivator; if any of the "intrinsic" theories (in Charles B. Handy's terminology) of motivation, such as Theory Y, are to be believed. As reported by Peters and Waterman, it is also a key factor shared by all the successful companies in their investigations for McKinsey & Co.

This is, however, the only reference I am going to make to marketing in this chapter. This is not the sort of strategy that marketing theorists (such as Philip Kotler) might look for; and is perhaps unexpected of a company that is apparently so marketing oriented, and from an author whose career has largely been in marketing! Yet it turns out to be an immensely strong strategy; just as long as all those involved follow it (and of course in IBM they do). It is so strong because it does not just focus the sales and marketing activity of the company on the customer needs (which is the essence of good marketing), but it focuses *all* company activities on this most important requirement. Many companies, immersed in the great sophistications of marketing theory, forget this simple fact of life; highlighted in IBM by a recent poster campaign that quite simply stated "the customer pays your salary!"

Indeed IBM is only weak, in marketing terms, when this philosophy is not carried through by its third parties: the dealers in particular. Its weakness in this area should not be underestimated, though, by any company using IBM as a model. It may eventually be IBM's undoing, and it certainly would be for a lesser company.

Perhaps one reason Ouchi overlooks any reference to anything resembling customer service is that, surprisingly, this does not appear to feature significantly in Japanese philosophies. Thus, Kenichi Ohmae, for example, defines Japanese corporate strategy in a way that seems slightly strange to Western (marketing indoctrinated) ears: "What business strategy is all about—what distinguishes it from all other kinds of business planning—is, in a word, *competitive* advantage. Without competitors there would be no need for strategy, for the sole purpose of strategic planning is to enable the company to gain, as efficiently as possible, a sustainable edge over its competitors." This aggressive competitiveness is also the main factor to which Abbeglen and Stalk ascribe the Japanese corporations" success. Such single-minded concentration on competitive advantage (copying and improving; as all its corporate victims would instantly recognize) provides a clear edge in the "battle" (as the Japanese appear to see it) for markets. It does, incidentally, leave them rather vulnerable when they have won; for then there is no longer anyone to copy!

As a slight digression from my main theme, Abbeglen and Stalk provide a very succinct guide for companies that may be threatened by Japanese incursions: ". . . increased competition in Western markets from the Japanese can be expected when:

> The product is produced in large volumes
>
> Japanese demand for the product is stagnant and declining
>
> The Japanese have a factor cost advantage
>
> The Japanese have a labour productivity advantage."

The third basic IBM belief (again unreported by Ouchi) is, to quote Tom Watson Jr. once more: ". . . the force that makes the other two effective. We believe that an organization should pursue all tasks with the idea that they can be accomplished in a superior fashion." This "pursuit of excellence" resulted in: ". . . what might best be called a *tone*. It was a blend of optimism, enthusiasm, excitement and pace." A work force infected with such a tone sometimes can work miracles (certainly "Japanese miracles"). As explained earlier, in one shape or other this is probably the belief most commonly shared by members of organizations across the whole spectrum of business activity.

Implicit control

Although IBM has very clearly annunciated objectives in terms of numeric targets, the Stratplan is the key strategic control document; its main controls on the day to day business are as much by the beliefs (Ouchi refers to this as "implicit controls"). The main motivation for individuals, often largely unrecognized, is the set of beliefs that add up to the overall IBM culture. Thus even when cost savings programmes produce economies that really hurt, the main complaint (genuinely held) is usually that these are impacting IBM's efficiency and service to the customer; the impact on employees is rarely discussed.

It is too easy for any company to concentrate on maximizing its performance in terms of financial measurements—often because these are the easiest to see—without appreciating the wider impact on less tangible (and sometimes more important) investments in work force loyalty. No doubt Unilever was motivated by such a commendable desire to optimize its financial performance, but the true price was very heavy indeed; and apparently took a number of years to recover from.

It is perhaps significant that the Japanese have a reputation for being poor accountants. In addition they do not even have a business school to teach the orthodoxies of management. In Western terms their financial control procedures are often a disaster; and yet as their results will demonstrate their effective control is second to none. As Abbeglen and Stalk report: "Few Japanese companies employ the elaborate capital budgeting processes widely practised in the West. Indeed, few Japanese companies have the massive organizational apparatus called 'Finance' which is characteristic of Western companies." This is perhaps even clearer in the lack of an obvious organizational structure. Kenichi Ohmae, for example, says: "Most Japanese corporations lack even a reasonable approximation of an organization chart. Honda, with $5 billion in annual turnover, is obviously quite a flexible, strategy-oriented company, capable of making prompt and far-reaching decisions. Yet nobody knows how it is organized, except that it employs project teams very frequently. . . . From the Western corporate point of view, such an arrangement would be confusing and unworkable. Yet most Japanese corporations can react to a changing environment much more readily than their Western counterparts." Abbeglen and Stalk also report: ". . . the kaisha seem not as prone to vertical organizational structures as their Western competitors."

IBM does have a published organizational structure, but due to the frequent changes it is often unclear what the titles mean; and departmental briefs may be accordingly flexible (helping IBM to change as rapidly as the Japanese). Of course IBM, like Honda, has its task forces.

This indeed parallels Kenichi Ohmae's comment that: "Japanese organizations, in which each position is loosely defined and each manager's area slightly overlaps others, are typically much better placed to identify interface issues, and act accordingly without major reorganization."

Here the departmental manager has the great advantage that almost all his contacts with his team revolve around implicit instructions. The use of direct (financial) measurements represents a very small part of such a manager's activities (though paradoxically it does preoccupy a great deal of the management literature he is exhorted to read). Perhaps, however, such a manager should from time to time review his "communications" to check that the implicit messages are the correct ones; where the most often delivered (unconscious) implicit message is, "don't bring me any bad news."

Again there is a caution to be derived from IBM's recent difficulties. Implicit controls (no matter how trendy they may have become) do not mean that the planning process should be abandoned or even weakened. One of IBM's great strengths, over the years, was the effort it put into long-term planning. The difficulties experienced with "third parties" can be seen to be, at least in part, a result of it abandoning its normal careful, indeed conservative, planning processes—to be seduced by a "happy accident."

Michael Porter, as a professor on sabbatical from the Harvard Business School, incisively summed up many of the dangers of "culture" based solutions in an article in "The Economist" (May 20, 1987). His theme was that "Corporate culture . . . popularised in part by the runaway success of 'In Search of Excellence' . . . Companies lavished attention on the 'soft' side of management. . . . It had suddenly become embarrassing to talk about strategic planning." His own position was clear: "there are no substitutes for strategic thinking." It is a view that I would wholeheartedly support. "Philosophies I" are, as I have stressed, complementary to the more conventional aspects of running a business; they can never substitute for these, as IBM found with its relatively unplanned adventure with "third parties."

Personal incentives

It is my belief that most IBMers require no incentives to persuade them to excel; the belief in the pursuit of excellence is too well engrained in the culture. In a similar fashion it is difficult to believe that the Japanese need direct incentives to persuade them to work. Yet incentives do appear to have a central role to play in both cultures.

It is true that in IBM they offer one antidote to the bureaucracy, by very clearly setting the priorities. It is only too easy for any bureaucracy to set its own rather different objectives; but the incentives are an ever-present reminder as to what makes the business really run. This may be one reason why franchises are now becoming so successful; their "managers," as owners, have the most direct of incentives.

Certainly the incentive programme is important in Japanese companies. Their annual bonuses, earned as a group rather than as individuals, often come to the equivalent of five to six months' pay. As an additional benefit the presence of such high levels of bonuses, at least in Japan, allows the corporations to absorb short-term downturns in the market. Wage costs are automatically reduced by the lost bonuses, without any need for salary levels to be reduced.

Within IBM great care is taken to ensure that the implementation of incentives is fair, not arbitrary. The heart of this process is the A&C (appraisal and counselling) where the individual *agrees* with his manager what his objectives will be. It is a demonstrably fair and open process that demystifies many of the negative aspects of incentives.

Although it is still not clear why such incentives are so central to the culture, perhaps, as they are directly related to the business process (to which the culture has unequivocally committed itself), they form a highly visible, unifying set of values which aids the building of a common identity. Within IBM, and the Japanese companies as well, the rituals that define the group culture are most often related to such incentives; reaching their peak within IBM in the theatrical drama of the Hundred Per Cent Club.

Non-specialized career development

As described by Ouchi, this is a philosophy that allows the employee to develop and change jobs (and even specialties), within a company. The Western alternative has him staying within his specialty and changing companies; retaining a job security which is based on his specialty, since this is just as applicable in other companies. This ensures him against redundancy from a company (an endemic problem in the West) but does not protect him against the redundancy of his specialization; hence the conservatism, if not Luddism, of many Western (craft unionized) worker groups. The Japanese need have no conservative ties to outdated specialties since their security in the company is not at risk. This is reflected in the practice of unions, in Japan, being related to individual corporations (and across all crafts within them), where the Western alternative is unions organized by craft (across a number, typically all, companies). This is held by many observers to be a major contributor to Japanese productivity, and certainly the many inter (craft) union demarcation disputes add nothing to Western productivity.

In a similar environment, IBM builds career paths which allow individuals to develop, probably within a broad specialization (such as manufacturing or marketing; though switches across even these boundaries are possible) but ranging quite freely within these.

The changes have the added virtue of allowing individuals to build contacts across the organization; and accelerates the formation of a sound horizontal communications network. Indeed, it is probably the main (and possibly the only) basis for the all important horizontal communications of the Japanese corporations.

In IBM these changes are deliberately planned to develop the individual; to offer him more satisfying work, and IBM a more productive employee. They are often used to provide interest where an employee cannot be rewarded with promotion; and so can take some of the pressures out of the rat race.

Job enrichment

This leads naturally to the concept of which IBM was one of the pioneers; and which featured in Drucker's very influential *Practice of Management*. There is already much literature on the subject, so I will be brief. IBM now expects (to the extent that it does not publicize the fact) all its staff to "grow" their own jobs. It is quite natural for an IBMer to add functions to his job specification; often without even discussing it with his manager (but simply as a result of the job needing to be done). There is less of the territorial imperative which makes demarcation disputes so bitter elsewhere.

For the departmental manager there is, though, an imperative (spelled out in the A&C if nowhere else) that he has to provide his subordinates with satisfying roles in the organization. The result is that job enrichment in IBM is no longer the parcel of gimmicks it often is in other companies, but is once more an engrained (if unspoken) philosophy. The best people to advise on job enrichment are those whose jobs you want to enrich; and this is responsible for a great deal of the success of quality circles.

In my own case, for example, at each of the job changes I made within IBM, I was fully consulted as to what *my* future needs were; and jobs were sought to meet those needs. The choice was very clearly mine, and on two occasions I resisted very strong pressure from senior management to take jobs they thought more suitable (and in both cases, I have to report, time proved their judgement correct; but the right even to make your own *mistakes* is entrenched in IBM!). The extreme of this process, in which surely only IBM would indulge, was that I arrived in one job to find that I had no manager to report to; so IBM allowed *me* to choose my own manager (who, incidentally, was the best I ever worked for within IBM).

The most important equivalent element of the Japanese corporations is perhaps that contained within the "section." As described by Ezra F. Vogel in *Japan as Number One*: "The essential building block of the organization is the section. A section might have eight or ten people, including the section chief. Within the section there is not as sharp a division of labour as in an American company. To some extent, each person in the same section shares the same overall responsibility and can substitute for another when necessary. . . . Within the general work of the section, one's assignment to a task at a given time is affected by one's general abilities, skills and aptitudes more than by one's title within the section. The section is, in a sense, an organic unit composed to match a variety of talents rather than a team with clearly distinct, independent role assignments."

Personal involvement in decision-making

Within IBM there is no formal process that requires consensual decision-making. As with most Western companies the decision is apparently the manager's hierarchical prerogative. In practice, though, a great many of the more important decisions are, as in many other Western companies, taken in committee; certainly at the departmental level. The style of these meetings *is* different in IBM, and *can* be described as consensual. It is thus the style of meetings that to a large extent determines the degree of involvement. Of course the attendance at these meetings delineates the range of personnel involved, and it is significant that IBM meetings tend to be more open than most to a very wide range of attendees. Usually everyone involved in the implementation, not just the managers responsible, will enter the meeting circuit before irreversible decisions are taken. Thus, although some part of the formality of the Japanese consensus decision (the ringi system) may be absent in IBM, an *informal* consensus is observed.

Implicit in this informal process is, as identified by Ouchi, an emphasis on interpersonal skills. IBM trains almost all its personnel (no matter how lowly) in interpersonal skills. At the higher levels, of course, most of the management have been through the best sales force in the world; so that interpersonal skills are raised to an art form. It is a training that pays dividends, particularly in the meeting environment; for a connoisseur of meetings (which I have become over the years in IBM), such meetings are a joy to behold.

Arguably IBM should stand for "I'm Busy in a Meeting"; for they take up a disproportionate part of the time of key personnel. But in many ways they are the powerhouse of IBM, where much of the action (not just talk) really is, and they work; they work very well!

Peters and Waterman in this case take a rather different line, stressing "entrepreneurship" ("small is beautiful"). Although this has been a popular concept in recent years, and IBM has itself attempted to encourage "intrapreneurs" (most obviously in the establishment of the Independent Business Units), there is little evidence that this has ever become an important element of IBM's operations.

Development of a strong culture

The almost inevitable outcome of the "tone" of excitement, that Tom Watson Jr. talked about, is the development of a strong culture. It is, indeed, the strength of the culture that most distinguishes IBM and the Japanese corporations (to the extent that many of the features, originally imported from the USA, are now mistaken for a part of Japanese national culture).

Once more the work of Peters and Waterman showed a similar

level of importance ascribed to the culture in each of the successful US companies they studied. Even in the early days of CTR (pre-IBM), T. J. Watson put a great deal of effort into developing the culture. Much of this effort went into theatrical activities (largely because he couldn't afford anything more tangible); and this still remains in the form of the Hundred Per Cent Club. It was clearly targeted at developing a shared identity; and it worked.

It would be naive for a company to think of going out and buying a culture off the shelf; that is simply not how it works. The problems of conflicting cultures, that have apparently bedevilled the interface between IBM and its dealers, illustrate how difficult positive use of cultural factors can be. Neither IBM or its dealers have really been able to come to terms with each other's cultures, a problem which might have been exacerbated by the fact (discussed earlier) that PC Group—the guardians of this interface—subscribed to yet another subculture! A really powerful culture will not be an import, it will be a natural outgrowth of how people feel about the company. Only if the employees feel that they want to "belong" to the company will they consider it worthwhile committing themselves to a shared group identity. The essential prerequisite is, once more, the trust built on the basis of full employment and company beliefs. If the beliefs are rich and strong (and genuinely strongly held by top management) it is more likely that the resulting culture will be rich and strong; as is IBM's. A company will have made the grade when its employees naturally refer to themselves (and think of themselves) as "nationals" of that company. The term "IBMer" is normal, and meaningful, in IBM. It simply states a fact about individuals that they believe is as descriptive of them as their nationality; and that is a very unusual degree of personal commitment.

Once more, within limits, a departmental culture can be built to compensate for a missing (or unacceptable) company culture. This is most obviously seen in those departments where the loyalty is to the manager rather than to the company. This is, of course, a potential threat to the company; for such a manager is in the position to take a complete team with him when he moves (a phenomenon that I, and most managers, have observed happening—at least to some degree—a number of times).

This development of departmental cultures is evident in most companies. It can be seen in the different languages that are used to keep strangers at bay—especially in the frequent use of acronyms which are meaningless to the outside world. It is, at least in part, often at the root of interdepartmental rivalries. These are usually seen, with some justification, as debilitating; but properly channelled could represent a source of strength (and management could profitably seek the cultural source of each department's strength to try to integrate it into the company culture). IBM is just as prone as any other company to departmental cultures; one of the first tasks in moving to any new department is to learn the special language and procedures that it cherishes—where these are directly comparable with tribal rituals and taboos. The significant difference in IBM is that the company-wide culture *always* takes precedence over the departmental; where the reverse is more normally true.

Holistic approach to employees

One definitive aspect of the development of the common culture may be an involvement in the whole lifestyle of employees. This certainly happened in the early days of IBM, when paternalism (in the best sense) reigned supreme. In recent years, though, IBM has carefully "backed off" to a more modern relationship (which goes to some lengths *not* to intrude in the private lives of its employees). The compromise works because it is still based on the *philosophy* of trying to understand exactly what are the employee's "whole" needs. It is an attitude of mind which is set by putting the needs of employees highest in the list of the company's priorities. The stockholders of IBM have always had to accept that they come behind its employees in its list of priorities; yet one more feature that it shares with the Japanese corporations.

Again, such a holistic approach can work within a department as much as within a company. Indeed, it is much easier to operate at this level. Tom Watson Jr. claimed that he had always tried to keep IBM like a small company (a claim that was not even true of IBM in its earliest days; but a philosophy that favoured more personal contact with employees). A departmental manager has the opportunity to take a personal interest in all his employees. There *are* managers who do not practise a philosophy of holistic relations and who are still respected by their teams (for dynamism and enthusiasm, and sheer competence, go a long way in leading any team), but my observation is that most good managers (as rated by their subordinates) that I have observed have been very much involved in addressing the personal aspirations of all their team members.

As explained earlier, the whole thrust of the first category of philosophies is to create the partnership between employer and employee; and between departmental manager and his team members. The first step is for the employer to create a feeling of trust (based on its beliefs; particularly that of full employment) and only then can all the other contributors to a shared culture be profitably introduced. As emphasized by Ouchi these are very subtle processes, which cannot (as yet) be subject to any rule book. All that can be said is that a genuine commitment to the philosophies should by itself encourage the development of the desired cultural phenomena. The effect is more akin to a religious commitment than to scientific management; but it is no less powerful as a result.

Advanced philosophies

The second category is rather more sophisticated, and even more subtle. In addition to making the first category culturally acceptable to Western society (which has moved away from an acceptance of paternalism in the raw), this category is needed to counter the predations of the fully fledged bureaucracy which infects many modern corporations.

The essence of them is the creation of the environment in which the cell-like structures of cellular organic organization (which is a developing feature of the information revolution) can flourish. This encourages the autonomy of these small structures (at the most basic level that of the individual; hence the importance of individualism). At the same time it sustains the structures, particularly in terms of information flow.

To a degree it also reflects a change in society, identified in the Taylor Nelson Report for the UK National Economic Development Office (as yet unpublished). This describes three stages of human development: the agricultural era, producing "sustenance-driven values"; the industrial era with "outer-directed values"; and the post-industrial era of "inner-directed values." In the UK 36 per cent of the population already come into the latter category (compared with 47 per cent in Holland and 34 per cent in Sweden; but, interestingly, only 19 per cent in the USA and a mere 10 per cent in Japan). Economic growth is no longer the priority for this group; the quality of life is. Networks of small overlapping cells will dominate the structures of their society. Individual freedom and responsibility will be paramount. The conclusion of the social scientists involved was that these "new people" will bring a much faster pace of change; and will develop the use of information technology three to five times as fast as the industrial era workers.

These are, I believe, the individuals who will most successfully implement "Philosophies I" in general, and the second category (of "Advanced Philosophies") in particular; Most of these philosophies are, necessarily, only capable of implementation at company level. The departmental manager will not have the luxury of even a partial implementation; but he will be very directly affected by their impact (so he still has every incentive to understand what lies behind these emerging practices).

Strong beliefs in individualism

Once more the foundation is the development of strong beliefs, in this case in terms of the need for individualism as a fundamental aspect of the business. Such beliefs must be *very* firmly held by the people who matter most in this context: the board of management. This commitment must be made obvious—public—to those who matter most in the more general context: all the employees. Certainly Tom Watson Jr. spent a fair proportion of his time preaching the virtues of individualism, the "wild duck" story, to his flock. In the process he was almost totally misunderstood and dismissed by the outside world; which mattered little, since the important audience was within IBM (and that *did* listen).

The requirement is in the first instance to understand how the organization can be fragmented (on a matrix in which the horizontal links are stronger than the vertical; the exact reverse of the normal) to produce self-sufficient cells, which can integrate independently; to run operations in a completely flexible, dynamically changing manner (to meet changed conditions). The departmental manager, as much as senior management, will be impacted by direct exposure to the cells for which he is responsible. The commitment has, then, to be published and publicized. IBM has issued a number of such documents, ranging from Tom Watson Jr.'s own book through to a range of reports for its employees. The work force has to be *convinced* that the company really believes in individualism.

Personnel processes to guarantee individualism

These beliefs need to be backed up by personnel procedures which guarantee the position of the individual. In IBM a number of these already existed from T. J. Watson's time. The speak-up process, which allows individuals to complain anonymously, is perhaps the most widely used. Although the open door is held in less high esteem, it is still a communication channel of final resort; and it does impose important disciplines on management.

The key process, though, is the more recently developed biannual opinion survey. This reports how well the programmes are progressing. It is the most potent constraint on management at all levels, and it most *clearly* demonstrates to employees the sincerity of intentions. Arranging to conduct an opinion survey is so simple as to be almost trivial. The hard part is the implementation; for the management *must* take the results seriously (and act, publicly, to address any problems). Even so I would recommend it as the most important, and immediate, first step for any company; even the discipline of addressing the results is by itself a major step in the right direction.

The critical requirement is a recognition that the organization needs to put real "teeth" into its personnel processes. This implies an upgrading of the Personnel Department from its more usual lowly position. Most important, though, it requires senior management to decide exactly how they can *guarantee* that all employees have the necessary (confidential) access to that senior management in order to highlight any breaches of the basic beliefs.

Single status

A further prerequisite for a successful corporate pursuit of individualism is a clear policy of single status; otherwise individualism just becomes another description of the various classes of citizenship. IBM's position, both in theory and in practice, is unequivocally in support of single status (though it doesn't go as far as the Japanese practice of all staff wearing identical uniforms).

Single status also allows links to be generated quite naturally between different levels of the organizational matrix. In IBM it is quite natural for a fairly junior member of staff to talk as an equal with a senior manager; where his expertise justifies it. This is a rather different approach from that of the Japanese, where strict deference to seniority is observed; and is circumvented only by the practice of having the most junior participant prepare the recommendation—so that his contribution, and inventiveness, cannot be ignored.

In IBM the functioning of single status is significantly enhanced by the policy of divorcing status (represented by the level system) from its more usual links to management position (which in turn usually means that status, the hen-pecking order, is very visible and often intrusive). In IBM the essentially confidential nature of the system reduces the worst excesses of the status battles that bedevil so many other companies.

Recruitment of the highest calibre individuals

I believe that this, perhaps above all the other factors, is probably the key to IBM's strength; as it is for any company. It is well nigh impossible to fail if you have a collection of such high calibre individuals as IBM has invested in. Although it may seem self-evident, the fact is that most companies have become acclimatized to accepting second best. It might be argued that not all companies can attract the cream, but in practice there is a considerable element of matching talents to jobs; the cream a company is looking for may not be the same cream that IBM is monopolizing. The job for any employer is to select and develop these talents.

Of course it is much easier to recruit if you already have the philosophies in place. The IBM experience shows that employees are attracted by them (particularly job interest and security), frequently as much as by the financial arguments normally considered paramount; though IBM does, in any case, pay at least an attractive "market rate" (but for better than average talent; so it usually still gets a bargain).

As much as anything it is the sheer high calibre of the individual employees that underwrites the "Philosophies." These employees simply would not accept anything less, and would rapidly vote with their feet if any of the principles were endangered; IBM is well aware of this, a factor which helps keep it on the straight and narrow.

An "anarchy," which in some respects is what IBM has now become, places a great deal of responsibility on the individual. The calibre of the individual is thus a basic factor in determining exactly how successful the overall anarchy will be.

Extended training

Training and retraining is something that consumes a large amount of IBM resource (perhaps well in excess of five per cent of its manpower resource). But the result is that change can be endemic without causing chaos. It is a prerequisite for the first category (Theory Z) philosophies, but IBM goes far beyond this and commits significant resources to ensure the *personal* development of each individual; which is quite understandable when the importance of the performance (and capability) of *each* individual is appreciated, in the context of the overall anarchy. A crucial element of the A&C process is planning each individual's personal development in general, and training in particular; resulting in a specific, documented plan for the next year.

Such training, and in particular retraining, is often neglected by companies. It may be seen as a luxury; where key staff are needed to fight today's "fires." This overlooks the fact that its existing staff are usually a company's greatest investment; and development of this resource to fulfill its long-term potential is a very sensible, and highly profitable, investment. It is not something that can, however, be run as a low priority sideline. This is one lesson to be learned from IBM's mistakes, as well as its successes. As mentioned earlier, one of the problems IBM has experienced with "third parties" has been the lack of any significant numbers of acceptable calibre personnel in its dealers. This was compounded by a signal failure by these dealers (or by IBM, which could insist on higher standards) to undertake any meaningful training of their staffs. Many of IBM's recent problems with its end-users are occasioned by the fact that even its senior dealer personnel are worse trained than the most junior admin clerk within IBM!

Education in IBM is staffed by some of its best people, and it is resourced accordingly. My budget for business training alone approached £250,000 a year to be spent outside IBM (say £500,000 for the two-year programme overall). But the GSD sales force (200 of whom went through the programme) is now responsible for bringing in revenue worth up to *£1* billion per annum; so even to recover the cost in the first year the productivity increase needed to be only 0.1 per cent!

Etched in stone at the entrance to IBM's education centre in Endicott, New York, are the words: "There is no saturation point in education." IBM means this: it spent $600 million backing this belief in 1984 alone.

A specialized form of training (officially titled the "Executive Resources Programme") which applies to only a very few individuals, but is very important to IBM's success, is that given to the top management high-flyers (on their way to Armonk). I have described this as institutionalized nepotism since it duplicates the process that happened to the two Watson heirs, and thus represented the positive side of nepotism. The candidates are identified very early, when they are relatively junior managers (typically when they have reached branch manager level; that is, second level management). They are then *very* carefully groomed for stardom; a process that may take more than a decade. In this time they are inserted into a series of jobs that expand their skills and knowledge. At the same time, though, they are protected against the risks of management failure (their "guardian angel" will soon pull them out of any tricky situations). This avoids the major problem with conventional management progression, that of the "multiple filter"; where a senior manager is required to be successful at *each* level before he is promoted to the next (so that a top level manager has to combine *all* the talents of the jobs below him—in practice his least well-developed talents are precisely those needed for his ultimate position!). IBM senior management do *not* have to succeed at all levels, so that the emphasis can be put on succeeding at the one level that matters; which seems to me to put the priorities in the right order. Whatever the theoretical merits, the practical merit is that Armonk's managers are immensely capable and confident. Such is their personal command, and security, that there is no challenge to their authority; and they can get on with running IBM as it should be run (rather than indulging in the prolonged political battles that enliven the top management suites of so many other companies).

Maximal delegation

All the management textbooks stress delegation; but in IBM it is not just theory, it is an unavoidable fact of life. In part it is forced by the pressure of work (another advantage of deliberately under-resourcing manpower). In part it is encouraged by loading managers with communication work (they are best seen as providing *support* to their subordinates). In part it is enshrined in various documented procedures. In the main, though, it is a result of filling the lowest levels with high calibre personnel who very vocally demand delegation rather than have it thrust upon them.

This is often, for the departmental manager, a difficult step. My advice has always been to try and imagine the conventional management structure turned upside down. In this view the manager is a resource to be used to support his subordinates. The question he then needs to ask is not (as usual) what they can do for him, but what he can do for them to make them more effective.

The Japanese system approaches the problem from a different direction, by having recommendations drafted by the most junior staff; thus ensuring they are actively involved in any planning process. At the same time, though, the Japanese "section" does assume significant delegated powers. These are described by Ezra F. Vogel as: "The lowly section, within its sphere, does not await executive orders but takes initiatives. It identifies problems, gathers information, consults with relevant parts of the company, calls issues to the attention of higher officials and draws up documents. . . . Good decisions emerge not from brilliant presentations of alternatives but from section people discussing all aspects of the questions over and over with all the most knowledgeable people. . . . Section people take great pride in their work because of their initiatives and because they have a chance to develop their leadership and carry great weight within the company on matters relating to their sphere. Consequently, the morale of young workers in their thirties tends to be very high." This description would also be almost as applicable to the "teams" within IBM.

Planned constraints on management

It sometimes seems as if IBM deliberately sets out to cripple its first-line managers; producing a job that is recognized to be the toughest in IBM. It forces them to delegate, by the measures listed above. Then it sucks them into never-ending cycles of meetings, which means that they cannot be a constant presence in their department; again forcing delegation.

For the lowest ranks of management even status is no refuge, for the level system, which operates independently of management responsibility, ensures that few junior managers can "pull rank."

In any case the system proceeds systematically to undermine their hierarchical position with the personnel processes of the A & C (where they have to obtain agreement from their subordinates), backed up by the speak-up and open-door programmes to handle complaints. Most insidious of all is the opinion survey, whose "rating" many managers dread.

One can almost pity the management under this kind of pressure. But it does ensure that they tend to run close-knit teams rather than hierarchical empires. It allows the individuals at the lowest levels to maximize their contributions, and managers to get on with the real job—of managing. Most important of all, it clearly works; IBM doesn't have any problems persuading its people to take on the onerous role of junior manager!

Again the departmental manager has the advantage. He is in direct control of his team. He does not have to resort to structural subterfuges. He does, though, have to ensure that his managers/team members work smoothly together to maximize their contributions (and their individual sense of achievement and fulfilment).

Encouragement of dissent

Tom Watson's support of "anarchy" reached its peak in the encouragement of dissent. There are many deliberately planned opportunities for this to occur in IBM. Important decisions often require a sign off process that rivals the Japanese ringi system. It may appear bureaucratic but it ensures that all the functions, and people, involved are actually required to sign their *commitment* to the decision. The numbers of signatures may be as high as 20 or 30 (somewhat lower, though, than the 50+ in the typical ringi approval). The pay-off for IBM (and the Japanese) is that, while negotiations may be more extended, the implementation is much smoother and faster; simply because every person involved has already agreed his personal commitment.

In this process it is possible for anyone to disagree, even the most junior; as a very junior member of IBM I did once stop a major project, albeit very temporarily, by being the only one to disagree (when the whole negotiating process had to start over again). Even the language in IBM encourages dissent. You do not have to disagree (a very negative sounding approach), instead you can merely non-concur (a much more positive activity)! Indeed the *right* of non-concurrence is formally enshrined in IBM's procedures. It may sound trivial but it really does contribute to a climate where the participants can speak their mind, without being accused of the sin of being "negative"; and, of course, is most productive *within* the department.

Of course the real encouragement for dissent was in the philosophy of the "wild duck," which has now entered the culture; guaranteeing its continued implementation (though it has to be admitted that Buck Rodgers gives it just one throwaway mention in his book).

In the Japanese system, where interdependence, as opposed to the Western ideal of independence, is highly valued (and change is achieved gradually—a favourite saying from the Tao being: "It is well to persist like water," slowly wearing away the rock), overt dissent is clearly not encouraged. Instead there is an acceptance of ambiguity (there are reportedly 19 different ways of saying "no" in Japanese, and in Zen the concept of "empty" is replaced by "full of nothing"), which in effect allows a similar degree of freedom in action for individuals and sections (the shopfloor groups).

I would inject one note of caution at this juncture. The last three philosophies, all of which are designed to maximize individual responsibility, are powerful devices when working with an integrated structure that has the culture capable of containing them. There is, however, a danger that if these approaches are allowed to "leak out" to organizations that are not integrated with the main body, or do not have the strong culture (or subscribe to an inappropriate culture), then genuine anarchy may ensue—at least at the interface. This is one of the lessons to be learnt from IBM's troubles with its dealers. Acceptance of dissent, within IBM, has been translated by these "aliens" into a licence for true anarchy, which is undermining IBM's business.

Horizontal communications

The effect of all the above "anarchic" institutions is to thrust most of the work down to the lowest level, and then allow the (very high calibre) staff at that level to get on with it relatively unsupervised, despite IBM's high management ratio. To match this with the requisite information provision and coordination, however, requires a horizontal communications network of great sophistication and subtlety. The normal vertically-oriented structure simply could not cope.

To date in IBM this has largely been cultural. The culture encourages contacts across departmental boundaries (indeed it barely recognizes any boundaries), and the grapevine is sophisticated in the extreme. As a result the individuals have a very good, but largely informal, perspective of what is happening throughout IBM. This network of contacts is encouraged by the non-specialized career paths, and frequent moves, which ensure that individuals normally already have excellent contacts in a number of other departments (the Japanese career process produces the same invaluable benefit). This process is also enhanced in IBM by the regular mixing of personnel on the various training courses. It reaches its peak, in particular, in the use of task forces (recruited from a range of different departments) to focus on the key issues. These teams have access to a very wide range of IBM experience and skills.

Some of the Japanese corporations have adopted a different approach. Under the guidance of Kenichi Ohmae (the head of McKinsey's Japanese subsidiary) they have developed the concept of "samurais." To quote him: "The answer I came up with involved the formation within the corporation of a group of young 'samurais' who would play a dual role. On the one hand they would function as real strategists, giving free rein to their imagination and entrepreneurial flair in order to come up with bold and innovative strategies. On the other they would serve as staff analysts, testing out, digesting and assigning priorities to the ideas and providing staff assistance to line managers in implementing the approved strategies. This 'samurai' concept has since been adopted in several Japanese firms with great success."

He goes on to say: "Such a solution would not fit the circumstances of the typical American and European company." There is no direct parallel in IBM, but there is a related approach. Those high-flyers on the extended management training (executive resources) programme (particularly those on their way to the dizzy heights of Armonk) spend a critical part of their time as AAs (administrative assistants) to senior management. As with the samurais, these AAs are partly used (as their title suggests) to provide staff assistance to their management. But at the same time they do contribute to the development of strategy; which does to a limited extent parallel the samurai concept, and also adds considerably to the amount of experience they have had when they eventually take on a more direct responsibility for strategy.

The meeting is the cornerstone of IBM's activities. Members of staff may spend between a quarter and a half of their time in face to face meetings, with a large part of this comprising formal meetings (with up to 20 participants). This is a lower rate than that of IBM management, but may be higher than in most other organizations. Such meetings are usually well run (a really poorly run meeting is such a rarity that news of it travels fast on the grapevine). The participants are specially trained in communications skills. Ouchi stresses the need for interpersonal skills training as part of Theory Z; and IBM already trains all its personnel to a high standard, and some (in the key market areas) to a superb standard, which rubs off on everyone else; the presentation is often the standard by which individuals are, perhaps unfairly, judged. The effective use of visual aids, usually overhead projected foils is excellent and meetings are normally well (but informally) chaired; and are generally enjoyable to the participants, an important secondary factor where they are so prevalent.

In addition to these cultural factors, though, IBM is now implementing horizontal communications physically. All IBMers have their own telephone and unrestricted access to any other IBMer anywhere in the world (even to executive management who usually answer their own phones!). A typical IBM office, therefore, will probably reveal up to half of the individuals who are not at meetings on the phone at any one time; horizontal communications is the basis of IBM's work.

This voice network is now being complemented by a data network. Already nearly all IBMers have access to a shared terminal, and within the next two to three years most of them will have their own dedicated terminal on their desk (a seemingly unnecessary luxury, but in practice a near essential if you are to encourage the maximal use of horizontal communications as a natural part of all activities). Like the telephone, this terminal will connect to any other IBMer anywhere in the world. It also provides instant, and invaluable, access to departmental and company databases. But its key role in IBM (unlike that, as yet, in many other companies) is as a horizontal communications device. It cuts down the amount of telephone traffic (and the very frustrating queuing, where the target is very likely already on the phone to someone else) and at the same time it documents the "conversations" so that there can be no confusion. What is more, it propagates information; it is just as easy to copy all the people involved (instantaneously) as it is to contact one.

The use of the network reflects, at a higher level, the results of the experiments undertaken by the Robotics Institute at Carnegie-Mellon University, reported by S. Kiesler. According to these, data networks encourage more people to get involved in decision making, and managers using computers to "mediate" were more efficient because they used fewer words. But they still made unconventional decisions; indeed Kiesler found less inhibition in computer mediated groups. Users were far more ready to indulge in outspoken criticism (described as "flaming"). These experiments highlighted the long term social and organizational effects of such networks; in particular they appear to help overcome the alienation of office working. She also noted (in an article in *Computing*, B. Felmay, 1986) that: ". . . computer mediated communications can break down hierarchical and departmental barriers, standard operating procedures and organizational norms." These are benefits that IBM already enjoys.

As so many organizations are about to introduce data networks on the large scale, the first requirement is, accordingly, that they understand the social and organizational implications as well as the purely technical. The second, and most important, is that they appreciate that this new technology offers the opportunity to move more rapidly (more rapidly than the 10- to 15-year timescale otherwise involved) to a Theory Z company, and then (quite probably simultaneously) to use most of the "Philosophies I." It is a unique opportunity which should not be overlooked in the excitement of the technical challenges.

Institutionalization of change

This was Frank Cary's great contribution. It is simple to implement, but dangerous if the groundwork (in essence most of the other "Philosophies I") has not been soundly based. Quite simply it requires that the whole organization is changed, from top to bottom, no less frequently (at least in the case of IBM) than every two years. Although Armonk would argue otherwise, I believe that the form of the new organization is almost incidental; though *some* care is needed. (John Akers' decision to reintegrate the rump of "General Systems Division" into the large mainframe sales force turned out to have near disastrous implications for sales of IBM's mid-range systems.) The IBM organizational matrix is already a jelly-like amoeba that almost instantly adapts to new patterns, matching the structure to the real needs of the business. A rigid, hierarchical organization would, however, be destroyed by the stresses this sort of change would induce.

Such change does have the great virtue of breaking down any bureaucratic tendencies. It shakes up the whole structure, takes out logjams (and those managers who have reached their Peter Principle level of incompetence) and allows a new organization to emerge which best matches the new needs. It is the ultimate lubricant in "anarchic" social engineering (and is a process few companies other than IBM could yet handle).

Despite the deliberate implementation of the policy, and its clear benefits to the business, Armonk now appears to be somewhat sensitive about its personnel implications. Buck Rodgers takes almost a page in his book to explain that it is not really true (at least in the most literal sense requiring house moves by families); he is clearly very sensitive to the "I've been moved" joke!

Regular reorganization is also one element of the "breaking old habits" pillar underpinning successful companies, suggested by Peters and Waterman (the other two pillars, incidentally, being "stability" and "entrepreneurship"). In addition it is (in relation to a growth culture) heavily stressed by Abbeglen and Stalk: "The competitive behaviour of kaisha has been shaped by a key factor in the Japanese environment; the historically unprecedented rate of growth and change in the Japanese economy. The requirement to keep pace with change—in a context of intense domestic competition—has been a principal driving force behind corporate strategies."

Growth (and the resulting change) has long been an *essential* part of IBM's business practices; as it has been of the Japanese corporations. Growth has allowed IBM to escape from problems that would have crippled other companies. Abbeglen and Stalk, commenting on the Japanese corporations, state that: "If the kaisha are to escape their troubles they must grow out of them and moreover bring about that growth through internal resources and internal development. . . . The cost of failure is high." These comments could just as well apply to IBM, and should be borne in mind when following the IBM model.

The second leg of "Philosophies I" thus takes the process of management into new regions, and is particularly relevant to the environment creating, and in turn being created by, the information revolution. It has the added virtue, for Western companies, that it simultaneously makes the first leg (Theory Z) more palatable to their more individualistic cultures.

Amitai Etzioni of Columbia University, asserts that a holistic based network comprises an effective means of control, but one that is incompatible with modern industrial specialization; that is, with normal Western business practices. "Philosophies I" allows this incompatibility to be overcome.

Trade unions

I have not mentioned the role of trade unions, quite simply because they are virtually non-existent in IBM; with "Philosophies I" their role is so diminished as to be negligible. It must be recognized, however, that most companies will have to take them into account. Ouchi, quite correctly, gives high priority to their involvement.

"Philosophies I" should be the ideal solution for unions if they are truly concerned to further their members' interests. On the other hand, it has to be realistically assumed that they will be suspicious of such overtures. In addition, their role will change (and may appear to decrease). No longer can they negotiate blanket wages (the ultimate virility test for a trade union negotiator); for it is likely, under the complexity of "Philosophies I," that there will be no such thing as a standard wage. Instead they will have a particularly valuable role as the independent guarantors of the individual's rights. Even though employees generally trust IBM, there is a detectable degree of diffidence about using some of the personnel processes. Even in IBM, therefore, it is arguable that the independence of a union view would better guarantee these (which would be as much in IBM's interest as that of the individual); this is particularly true of the open-door process, which can often be somewhat suspiciously viewed as management ganging up on the lone individual making the complaint.

Unions thus have an important, and very positive, role to play in improving their members' futures. My own contacts with shop stewards prior to IBM indicate that this is an opportunity that they will relish. In my experience they far more often bent my ear about the poor business decisions I was making (and were often more perceptive, and certainly less blinkered, than my management team who were usually too immersed in the problems) than they ever did about their members' working conditions. The one limitation is that imposed by the narrow viewpoints forced on craft unions (and this may be one reason why IBM is so nervous of any union presence). It is the breakdown of these, by the emergence of company unions ("enterprise unions"), that is one great strength of the Japanese system. The challenge, thus, is still for unions to tap their members' goodwill, and harness it to the development of "Philosophies I."

Organizational structure

I have concentrated on the philosophical aspects because these, I believe, represent the driving forces which will shape successful companies through the turn of the century. There is, though, an organizational aspect which parallels these.

The pyramid

In a somewhat simplistic sense, apart from small entrepreneurial companies, Theory X is by definition based on a hierarchy (with a unidirectional flow of instructions from the top down). Indeed the pyramid (a hierarchy) is what most of the population would immediately think of when asked what a management structure looks like (and, at least on paper, that is exactly what even IBM looks like to the outside world). Charles B. Handy describes it as "functional" organization, and chooses the Greek temple (with its columns) as the visual analogy; but the principle is the same.

This is moderated somewhat in Theory Y, where there is a two-way flow (management starts to listen to its workers). Typically, though, even with Theory Y the emphasis is on the efficient flow of instructions from the top to the bottom of the pyramid (these instructions, it is now recognized, need to be persuasive rather than coercive).

Neither theory, however, seeks to topple the pyramid. This is unfortunate, for although the pyramidal hierarchy was developed as the correct solution to controlling the physical work in the dark satanic mills of the Industrial Revolution (where the previous anarchic rural organization could not match the pace of the machines), civilization has now moved on, and its organizational requirements have correspondingly changed. I would suggest that it is now suitably symbolic that the pyramid has stood for more than four millennia as the syrnbol of formalized death!

The matrix

Although it might be difficult to conceive of a society more ritualized than the Japanese, I believe that Theory Z is broadly paralleled by an organizational structure that has a matrix form; though in this case with the horizontal contacts being informal, rather than the formalized contradictions of personnel reporting to more than one superior demanded by some matrix theories. Communications are channelled horizontally as well as vertically. Even in somewhat limited form this is already a great strength of the Japanese corporations, who often profess no formal structure at all. It was certainly a great strength of IBM in its earlier days, where the horizontal communications network often outweighed the vertical one.

Apart from J. K. Galbraith's direct references, this perhaps most closely approximates to the systems structure described by Peter Drucker. Charles B. Handy, along with other commentators, believes that such non-functional forms of organization may be inherently unstable: "But although beloved of many theorists and idealists' task cultures appear to be extremely difficult to manage well, particularly when surrounded by other cultures. Perhaps it is that organizations have more experience with management of steady-state activities, perhaps that, when it comes down to hard reality, people are more role-oriented, more fond of the steady-state than they are prepared to admit (*Understanding Oganizations*, 1976, Penguin Books)." I believe IBM shows that such forms of organization are now generally applicable, as Peter Drucker suggests.

The cellular organic structure

The second leg that completes "Philosophies I" has, however, taken such task based organization one step further; to what I will call cellular organic.

Superficially this looks rather like its predecessors, the matrix and team organizations. But under the surface it is even rather different to the systems structure (a combination of team and simulated decentralization) that Peter Drucker identifies as being the present embodiment of the large transnational company.

The most important difference is that it is constantly changing. The cells grow, change their function, develop links to other cells, and die; in a manner that can best be described as organic. The cells, which may be individuals but are usually small groups (the "teams" of team organization), have their own self-defined identity. This is clearly influenced by outside events as the superior organization (for example, Armonk) reallocates roles or even splits groups; but the final shape of the cell (its detailed role and relationships) is determined by the cell (the group or team) itself.

Its links to other cells are directly analogous to the nervous system of the living body. They may appear random (and in the cellular organic structure often change over time). They retrieve and disseminate the information that is now almost the sole business function of the cell. Which "neurons" are activated (and hence which "contacts" are used to provide the information) is under the control of the cell itself and is (again the analogy of the nervous system holds up) richly complex.

Finally the key instructions that control the workings of the cell, that program its activities, are *not* typically received directly from outside. They are contained in the equivalent of a living cell's DNA. In the cellular organic structure the behaviour of the cell is above all determined by the "culture" (derived from the beliefs and philosophies). I have frequently referred to the "anarchy" within IBM, but this should not be taken too literally. It is the "anarchy" of the growing, living cell (in the biological analogy the original "pluripotential" cell is shaped by its DNA to become the differentiated cell with a specific role).

In IBM, though, all cells always remain, at least partially, "pluripotential." They can change, without outside instructions, to respond to changes in the external or internal environment. This is most noticeable in the biannual reorganizations, when the cellular structure adapts to its new role in a matter of a few weeks (or even days); so that the change often goes unnoticed by the outside world.

More subtly, though, the culture (the "DNA") programs the cell to optimize its performance. By default, within the welter of changes, IBM cannot say exactly what the cell's detailed role is (titles in IBM are often so strange as to appear to be in a foreign language; and are usually no clear guide to a group's role), but it simply requires the group to seek out and fill that optimal role closest to their "brief."

This is also the type of structure forecast by the Taylor Nelson Report; specifically it reports that networks of small overlapping cells will dominate the structure of society.

It offers the prospect of a very different shape to working lives within the next few decades. I suspect the "electronic cottage," with the information worker hunched over his terminal in his dream house in the woods, will not be typical; for much of the communication within (and without) the cell is still best carried out face to face (typically in meetings). It does, though, indicate that those dark satanic office blocks may soon become as obsolete as the mills of yesteryear.

Conclusion

"Philosophies I" is firmly based on the Theory Z approach to business management, but it develops far beyond this to the individualistic, anarchic and cell-like structures which will probably become the shape of society in the next century. In keeping with this "anarchy," though, it is ill-definable; it has no hard-edged theories, but only philosophies and beliefs that guide the individuals as they work out their own dynamically changing compact with the world around them. The role of business management will be to provide the framework and resources, the culture medium, for these amoeba-like colonies to grow and change; leading to a more organically structured society.

Paradoxically, if the Taylor Nelson Report is correct, the Japanese (who took to Theory Z so successfully, if unknowingly) are the least likely to be able to take advantage of "Philosophies I";

though one should never underestimate the ability of MITI to change Japanese corporate life!

One thing that *is* virtually certain is that IBM, despite its current problems, will continue to develop, to change and to be ever more successful. It is a growing, dynamic model, not a static one (it has clearly changed considerably since the Japanese first made their photographic copy of it in the 1950s). It fully warrants continuing interest from academics and businessmen alike.

I will end with the quote from Tom Watson Jr., which for me encapsulates much of what is IBM: "I firmly believe that any organization, in order to survive and achieve success, must have a sound set of beliefs on which it premises all its policies and actions."

APPENDIX A

The Sources of IBM's Financial Strengths

As William G. Ouchi observes, it is the beliefs (the implicit rather than explicit controls) which are the key to Theory Z companies such as IBM. This book has, therefore, concentrated on these. For the sake of completeness, though, this appendix reviews some of the financial statistics; up to 1986, and (after 1973) based on the figures recorded in IBM's Annual Reports.

The first, and most obvious, are the sales (revenue) and profit (earnings) figures. In Table 1 I have annotated the historical figures with the key events.

Year	Revenue ($ million)	Per cent Change	Earnings ($ million)	Per cent Change	Earnings /Revenue	Key events
1914	4.20		0.49		7.6%	T. J. Watson joins CTR
1917	8.30		1.60		4.2%	
1919	13.00		2.10		5.2%	Expansion programme begun
1920	16.00	23.1%	1.90	−9.5%	7.4%	
1921	10.60	−33.8%	1.00	−47.4%	9.6%	Retrenchment; loans needed
1922	10.70	0.9%	1.40	40.0%	13.1%	
1928	19.70		5.30		26.9%	
1929	19.40	−1.5%	6.60	24.5%	34.0%	
1930	20.30	4.6%	7.30	10.6%	36.0%	Automatic Scale bought
1931	20.30	0.0%	7.40	1.4%	36.5%	
1932	18.40	−9.4%	6.70	−9.5%	36.4%	405 alphabetic tabulator
1933	17.60	−4.3%	5.70	−14.9%	32.4%	Dayton Scale sold
1934	20.90	18.8%	6.60	15.8%	31.6%	
1935	21.90	4.8%	7.10	7.6%	32.4%	Social Security contract won
1936	26.30	20.1%	7.60	7.0%	28.9%	First Anti-Trust suit lost
1937	31.90	21.3%	8.10	6.6%	25.4%	TJW Jr. joins IBM
1938	34.70	8.8%	8.70	7.4%	25.1%	
1939	39.50	13.8%	9.10	4.6%	23.0%	
1940	46.30	17.2%	9.40	3.3%	20.3%	
1941	62.90	35.9%	9.80	4.3%	15.6%	Wartime profits tax starts
1942	90.70	44.2%	8.70	−11.2%	9.6%	
1943	134.90	48.7%	9.20	5.7%	6.8%	IBM Mark I "computer"
1944	143.30	6.2%	9.70	5.4%	6.8%	
1945	141.70	−1.1%	10.90	12.4%	7.7%	ENIAC computer (non-IBM)
1946	119.40	−15.7%	18.80	72.5%	15.7%	600 electronic calculator

Table 1: Sales and profit earnings 1914–86

Year	Revenue ($ million)	Per cent Change	Earnings ($ million)	Per cent Change	Earnings /Revenue	Key events
1947	144.50	21.0%	23.60	25.5%	16.3%	UNIVAC started in development
1948	162.00	12.1%	28.10	19.1%	17.3%	
1949	183.50	13.3%	33.30	18.5%	18.1%	701 computer development starts; World Trade formed
1950	214.90	17.1%	33.30	0.0%	15.5%	Remington Rand buy UNIVAC
1951	266.80	24.2%	27.90	−16.2%	10.5%	Crash 702 programme started
1952	333.70	25.1%	29.90	7.2%	9.0%	TJW Jr. made president Anti-Trust action starts
1953	410.00	22.9%	34.10	14.0%	8.3%	
1954	461.40	12.5%	46.50	36.4%	10.1%	702 computer sales begin
1955	563.50	22.1%	55.90	20.2%	9.9%	702 deliveries begin STRETCH programme starts
1956	734.30	30.3%	68.80	23.1%	9.4%	Anti-Trust action conceded TJW Jr. takes over
1957	1000.40	36.2%	89.30	29.8%	8.9%	Control Data corporation formed
1958	1171.80	17.1%	126.20	41.3%	10.8%	Sales of 7000 series start
1959	1309.80	11.8%	145.60	15.4%	11.1%	1401 & 1620 sales start
1960	1436.10	9.6%	168.20	15.5%	11.7%	
1961	1694.30	18.0%	207.20	23.2%	12.2%	CDC 3600 announced S/360 development starts
1962	1925.20	13.6%	241.40	16.5%	12.5%	
1963	2059.60	7.0%	290.50	20.3%	14.1%	Honeywell H-200 sales start
1964	2306.00	12.0%	307.00	5.7%	13.3%	S/360 announced
1965	2487.30	7.9%	333.00	8.5%	13.4%	S/360 deliveries begin DEC PDP/8s shipped LEASCO formed
1969	7196.00		934.00		13.0%	S/3 announced Anti-Trust suit started
1970	7498.00	4.2%	1017.00	8.9%	13.6%	S/370 announced
1971	8273.00	10.3%	1078.00	6.0%	13.0%	T. V. Learson becomes chief executive
1972	8933.00	8.0%	1279.00	18.6%	14.3%	Virtual-storage announced
1973	10993.00	23.1%	1575.00	23.1%	14.3%	CDC suit settled; Frank Cary made chief executive
1974	12675.00	15.3%	1838.00	16.7%	14.5%	GSD formed worldwide SNA announced
1975	14437.00	13.9%	1990.00	8.3%	13.8%	General Business Group formed
1976	16304.00	12.9%	2398.00	20.5%	14.7%	Apple corporation formed
1977	18133.00	11.2%	2719.00	13.4%	15.0%	3033 announced
1978	21076.00	16.2%	3111.00	14.4%	14.8%	
1979	22863.00	8.5%	3011.00	−3.2%	13.2%	$1 billion borrowing on Wall Street; 4300 announced
1980	26213.00	14.7%	3562.00	18.3%	13.6%	
1981	29070.00	10.9%	3308.00	−7.1%	11.4%	John Opel becomes chief executive; IBM PC announced
1982	34364.00	18.2%	4409.00	33.3%	12.8%	Anti-trust suit dropped Regrouped to ISAM/ISM

Table 1 *cont.*

Year	Revenue ($ million)	Per cent Change	Earnings ($ million)	Per cent Change	Earnings /Revenue	Key events
1983	40180.00	16.9%	5485.00	24.4%	13.7%	IBM PC announced in WT
1984	45937.00	14.3%	6582.00	20.0%	14.3%	John Akers made chief executive
1985	50056.00	9.0%	6555.00	−0.4%	13.1%	Regionalisation
1986	51250.00	2.4%	4789.00	−26.9%	9.3%	

Table 1 *cont.*

As with any company's results, the figures are complex and often confusing. A few key trends can possibly be discerned though. It is clear that there have been a number of high growth periods. The first of these started in the late 1930s and continued through World War II. Its beginnings were reportedly due to the requirements of the US government's social security programme, but the real growth resulted from the logistical demands of the war effort. Although sales slipped back somewhat after the war, the growth did still continue at a reasonable rate through the early 1950s. It hit a sustained high growth rate again after the mid-1950s when Tom Watson Jr.'s first computers came on-stream, and again in the 1960s when the S/360 was shipped. Since that last burst the growth has been relatively slower; but on a much higher base, and still at a rate that would be the envy of other companies.

In more recent years a slightly more subtle process, but with essentially the same origins, has been noticeable. There is a peak of revenue following the first deliveries of new ranges—which gradually tails off until there is a lull following announcement of the next range—and when this is delivered revenues pick up again. Sales (orders) would show an even more cyclical nature. To a certain extent the overall effect is "smoothed" by announcements in the different sectors of the market being staggered; but even so they tend to clump together over a two- to three-year period to produce a mini boom and bust cycle every half decade or so. This process was compounded in 1985, as it was in 1979, by a business downturn in the overall market, resulting in particularly poor results (though even then a 9 per cent increase in revenue was recorded). Had this recent dip stopped there, it could still have been seen as part of IBM's cyclical pattern. But the dip continued, and indeed worsened, with only 2.4 per cent growth in 1986 (an uncharacteristically slow growth pattern that continued into 1987)—constituting IBM's worst period of sales growth since the 1930s. On the other hand it was still growth; and it is not clear yet if it represents, as some financial analysts predict, a more permanent change in IBM's growth patterns.

In terms of profit the early years showed a remarkably healthy rate (the humble punched card was very profitable), only to be drastically reduced by the excess profits tax of wartime. Thereafter profits have returned to a very healthy level, by most companies' standards (though at half the rate of the pre-war years). In recent years the profit cycle lags two to three years behind the revenue cycle, as might be expected; the first deliveries consume a great deal of resource. It is the later deliveries, towards the end of the cycle (when most of the costs have already been recovered), that are most profitable; hence IBM's careful balancing act, delaying the end of each range just as long as it can. Again, a market downturn (such as in 1979 and 1985) can compound this process to produce particularly bad results; the 1985 figure of -0.4 per cent may not look particularly bad, but IBM had to work very hard indeed (and bring forward some future business) to achieve even that result. Again, the results worsened in 1986; with earnings (profits) down by 27 per cent—by far the worst performance since the 1920s. The indications, in this case, are that IBM's profitability *may* now be suffering a longer term decline. Though, once more, the product cycle clouds the issues.

If we look at the latest results in slightly more detail (see Table 2), it is clear that in recent years there has been a significant swing to outright sales; where rental business in 1985 only accounted for eight per cent of the total (see Table 3); IBM ceased reporting rental sales in 1986. This is one reason that IBM's latest results are depressed, in comparison with those of the early 1980s. From 1982 to 1984 IBM switched large numbers of customers from rented to

Year	77 on 76	78 on 77	79 on 78	80 on 79	81 on 80	82 on 81	83 on 82	84 on 83	85 on 84	86 on 85
Gross Income from:										
Sales	19%	23%	8%	15%	18%	30%	38%	28%	16%	−0%
Services				33%	20%	21%	19%	25%	20%	
Rentals				8%	−0%	3%	−17%	−29%	−37%	
Service/Rental	7%	12%	9%							
Maintenance									16%	21%
Program Products									30%	32%
Rentals & Other									−30%	−25%
Total	11%	16%	8%	15%	11%	18%	17%	14%	9%	2%
Earnings (NBT)	13%	14%	−4%	6%	2%	37%	21%	17%	0%	−28%
Assets	7%	9%	18%	9%	11%	10%	15%	14%	23%	10%

Table 2: Per cent changes 1977–86

purchased equipment. This represented a one-time windfall (since, in effect, IBM swapped a typical three years rental, in the future, for an outright sale, at the time). The price would have to be paid later, and is being paid now. This is also seen later in the reduction in funds flow from sale of rented machines. The effect of this windfall, though, was a significant boom in profits. This rosy picture may have fooled outside observers, but Armonk, as astute as ever, uses future projections which discount this short-term effect.

If we examine the figures in more detail, in terms of the splits between the various categories (see Table 3), perhaps the most obvious feature is the increase in cost of sales at the beginning of the 1980s, so that the cost of outright sales is now nearly half as much again (47 per cent versus 32 per cent) than it was a decade ago. IBM may have the objective of being the lowest-cost producer, but so far the price reductions have had to outstrip the cost savings, at the expense of the NBT (profit) line. In the early 1980s the reduction in gross margins was offset by the relative reduction in the sales and (particularly) administration overheads; though the proportion of these rose again in 1985 (as the reduced sales growth failed to compensate for the inherent growth in these costs).

With the static sales in 1986, the proportion rose, significantly, to 30 per cent (reflecting IBM's inherent inability to hold down these overheads); though 1987 saw considerable redeployment of staff to more directly productive areas as one attempt to counter the problem, it will be interesting to see if this tactical manoeuvre to stem the long-term trend succeeds. R & D has remained at its traditional level (the slight increase to 10 per cent in 1986 just reflecting how bad IBM's sales results really were).

Interestingly, both Maintenance and Program Products, which were the only significant growth areas of IBM's business (and which IBM now splits out separately; the annual report has to contain *some* good news!), show steadily increasing profitability.

Perhaps the worst result, from IBM's point of view, is that shown by the earnings ratios. The 1986 figures for both earnings as a percentage of sales and as a percentage return on assets were reduced by nearly a half as compared with those of a decade previously (though it should be noted that earnings were still nearly three times as great, taken in absolute rather than relative terms)—another reason for IBM now being under the scrutiny of the financial analysts.

For the sake of completeness the basic figures are shown in Tables 4 and 5. These show, for example, that although the pro-

Year	1973	1974	1975	1976	1977	1978	1979	1980	1981	1982	1983	1984	1985	1986
Per cent Sales Split:														
Sales	31%	34%	31%	37%	39%	42%	41%	42%	44%	49%	58%	65%	69%	67%
Services/Rentals	69%	66%	69%	63%	61%	58%	59%	58%	56%	51%	42%	35%	31%	33%
Services							15%	17%	18%	19%	19%	21%	23%	
Rentals							44%	41%	37%	32%	23%	14%	8%	
Maintenance												11%	12%	14%
Program Products												7%	8%	11%
Rentals & Other												17%	11%	8%
Costs as a Per cent of Sales:														
Cost of Sales														
Sales	37%	33%	36%	33%	32%	32%	34%	38%	41%	40%	42%	42%	43%	47%
Services/Rental	39%	40%	38%	37%	37%	38%	38%	39%	41%	40%	39%	40%	40%	38%
Services							50%	49%	48%	47%	46%	45%	41%	
Rental							35%	35%	38%	36%	34%	33%	37%	
Maintenance												43%	42%	41%
Program Products												36%	29%	28%
Rentals & Other												40%	45%	48%
Others														
Selling/A&G/R&D	37%	38%	39%	39%	40%	39%	40%	39%	38%	36%	35%	34%	35%	40%
Selling/A&G										27%	26%	25%	26%	30%
R&D										9%	9%	9%	9%	10%
Interest	1%	1%	0%	0%	0%	0%	1%	1%	1%	1%	1%	1%	1%	1%
Earnings (NBT) Ratios:														
%Income	27%	27%	26%	28%	28%	28%	24%	22%	21%	24%	25%	25%	23%	16%
% Assets			97%	25%	27%	28%	23%	22%	20%	25%	27%	27%	22%	15%

Table 3: Per cent sales split, costs as per cent of sales, earning ratios 1973-86

Year	1973	1974	1975	1976	1977	1978	1979	1980	1981	1982	1983	1984	1985	1986
Gross Income														
Sales	3372	4282	4545	5959	7090	8755	9473	10919	12901	16815	23274	29753	34404	34404
Services							3321	4425	5330	6428	7676	9605	11536	
Rentals							10069	10869	10839	11121	9230	6579	4116	
Service/Rental	7621	8393	9891	10345	11043	12321	13390							
Maintenance												5266	6103	7413
Program Products												3197	4165	5514
Rentals & Other												7721	5384	4047
Total	10993	12675	14437	16304	18133	21076	22863	26213	29070	34364	40180	45937	50056	51250
Other Income	270	341	361	494	475	412	449	430	368	328	741	800	832	1005
Costs														
Sales	1242	1427	1631	1960	2256	2838	3267	4197	5321	6682	9748	12374	14911	16197
Services							1655	2181	2543	3047	3506	4347	4689	
Rentals							3491	3771	4152	3959	3141	2198	1503	
Services/Rental	2952	3327	3718	3866	4042	4646	5146							
Maintenance												2289	2561	3032
Program Products												1166	1194	1519
Rentals & Other												3090	2437	1958
Selling/A&G										9286	10614	11587	13000	15464
R&D										3042	3582	4200	4723	5221
Selling/A&G/R&D	4025	4759	5665	6409	7177	8151	9205	10324	11027					
Interest	97	69	63	45	40	55	140	273	407	454	390	408	443	475
Earnings (NBT)	2946	3435	3721	4519	5092	5798	5553	5897	5988	8222	9940	11623	11619	8389
Tax	1371	1597	1731	2121	2373	2687	2542	2335	2680	3813	4455	5041	5064	3600
Net Earnings	1575	1838	1990	2398	2719	3111	3011	3562	3308	4409	5485	6582	6555	4789

Table 4: Gross income 1973–86

Year	74 on 73	75 on 74	76 on 75	77 on 76	78 on 77	79 on 78	80 on 79	81 on 80	82 on 81	83 on 82	84 on 83	85 on 84	86 on 85
Gross Income													
Sales	27%	6%	31%	19%	23%	8%	15%	18%	30%	38%	28%	16%	0%
Services							33%	20%	21%	19%	25%	20%	
Rentals							8%	−0%	3%	−17%	−29%	−37%	
Service/Rental	10%	18%	5%	7%	12%	9%							
Maintenance												16%	21%
Program Products												30%	32%
Rentals & Other												−30%	−25%
Total	15%	14%	13%	11%	16%	8%	15%	11%	18%	17%	14%	9%	2%
Other Income	26%	6%	37%	−4%	−13%	9%	−4%	−14%	−11%	126%	8%	4%	21%
Costs													
Sales	15%	14%	20%	15%	26%	15%	28%	27%	26%	46%	27%	21%	9%
Services							32%	17%	20%	15%	24%	8%	
Rentals							8%	10%	−5%	−21%	−30%	−32%	
Services/Rentals	13%	12%	4%	5%	15%	11%							
Maintenance												12%	18%
Program Products												2%	27%
Rentals & Other												−21%	−20%
Selling/A&G										14%	9%	12%	19%
R & D										18%	17%	12%	11%
Selling/A&G/R&D	18%	19%	13%	12%	14%	13%	12%	7%					
Interest	−29%	−9%	−29%	−11%	38%	155%	95%	49%	12%	−14%	5%	9%	7%
Earnings (NBT)	17%	8%	21%	13%	14%	−4%	6%	2%	37%	21%	17%	0%	−28%
Tax	16%	8%	23%	12%	13%	−5%	−8%	15%	42%	17%	13%	0%	−29%
Net Earnings	17%	8%	21%	13%	14%	−3%	18%	−7%	33%	24%	20%	−0%	−27%

Table 5: Income costs and earnings per cent changes 1973–86

portion of administration costs has fallen, its absolute value has risen (but, at least until 1985, had been constrained well below the overall increase in sales).

If we look at the split between Domestic and World Trade (see Table 6), in the mid-1970s this showed a slow growth in World Trade share. This trend was dramatically reversed in the 1980s; not, though, as a result of a physical shift in business (though the PC did lag by 18 months in World Trade) but simply as a result of the disproportionate strength of the dollar. With the dollar falling in value the trend was reversed in 1985. It is clear, however, from these results that the major set-back in 1986 was largely restricted to IBM's home market (the US). As a result, the share of business provided by World Trade rose significantly, once more to (just) outstrip the US.

Table 6 also shows the doubling of sales per employee over the seven-year period; one reason why IBM is so profitable. In this case the World Trade figures kept pace with Domestic, even despite the strength of the dollar; and, with the dollar weakening, 1985 saw World Trade outstripping Domestic; in 1987 its performance was nearly 50 per cent better than the US.

Inspection of the balance sheet (Tables 7 and 8) shows just how strong IBM is. It has current (i.e., largely "liquid") assets of $28 billion! Even the net current figure (after deducting current liabilities) still exceeds $15 billion; and even when inventories are removed (leaving almost "cash in hand") the figure is almost $7 billion. The most obvious changes are those revolving around the switch from the rental base. Not unexpectedly the asset value of the rental assets has dropped by more than two-thirds since 1980.

Year	1977	1978	1979	1980	1981	1982	1983	1984	1985	1986
% of Total										
Sales US	50%	48%	46%	47%	52%	55%	58%	60%	57%	49%
Sales EMEA	35%	37%	39%	38%	32%	30%	28%	26%	28%	33%
Sales AFE	15%	15%	15%	15%	16%	15%	14%	14%	15%	17%
Assets US	53%	49%	51%	51%	54%	58%	62%	66%	61%	54%
Assets EMEA	35%	38%	37%	36%	32%	28%	27%	23%	27%	33%
Assets AFE	14%	15%	14%	15%	16%	15%	14%	13%	14%	15%
Per Employee	$'000	$'000	$'000	$'000	$'000	$'000	$'000	$'000	$'000	$'000
Sales Total	58.5	64.7	67.8	76.8	81.9	94.2	108.7	116.3	123.4	127.0
Sales US	52.8	55.5	55.8	64.0	73.5	88.8	105.8	114.6	117.7	106.9
Sales WT	65.4	76.4	83.4	93.8	93.3	101.9	112.3	119.0	131.9	155.7

Table 6: Split between Domestic and World Trade 1977-86

	1976	1977	1978	1979	1980	1981	1982	1983	1984	1985	1986
Assets											
Current Assets											
Cash	209	252	274	298	281	454	405	616	600	896	755
Mktbl Securities	5948	5155	3757	3473	1831	1575	2895	4920	3762	4726	6502
Notes/Acc Receivable	2626	3104	4134	4671	4562	4382	4976	5577	7393	9757	9971
Other A/R					315	410	457	645	718	809	854
Inventories	770	994	1561	1842	2293	2805	3492	4381	6598	8579	8039
Prepaid Expenses	368	568	594	566	643	677	789	1191	1304	1303	1628
Total	9921	10073	10320	10850	9925	10303	13014	17330	20375	26070	27749
Rental MC					15352	17241	16527	9201	6375	4637	
Depreciation					6969	7651	7410	4335	3425	2804	
Plant/Property					11018	12895	14240	19986	23048	29846	
Depreciation					4384	5207	5794	8710	9635	11999	
Rental MC/Property	15677	17071	19175	22744						34483	38121
Depreciation	8714	9181	9873	10551						14803	16853
Investments	840	1016	1148	1486	1761	2005	1964	3989	6070	6884	8797
Total Assets	17723	18978	20771	24530	26703	29586	32541	37461	42808	52634	57814
Current Liabilities											
Taxes	1384	1466	1460	1718	2369	2412	2854	3220	2668	3089	2583
Loans Payable	116	172	241	933	591	773	529	532	834	1293	1410
Accounts Payable	2583	3147	3607	3795	721	872	983	1253	1618	1823	1970
Compensation/Benefits	553	808	1072	1395	1404	1556	1959	2105	2223	2460	3001
Deferred Income					305	389	402	382	340	391	414
Other					1136	1318	1482	1670	1957	2377	3365
Total	4636	5593	6380	7841	6526	7320	8209	9162	9640	11433	12743
Long-Term Debt	275	256	286	1589	2099	2669	2851	2674	3269	3955	4169
Other					1443	1184	1198	1475	1353	1606	2004
Deferred Taxes	63	88	110	139	182	252	323	931	2057	3650	4524
Equity											
Stock	4032	3961	3942	3974	3992	4389	5008	5800	5998	6267	6321
Retained Earnings	8737	8678	9575	11012	12491	13772	16259	19489	23486	27234	27834
Translation							−1307	−2070	−2948	−1466	307
Less Treasury stock	20	21	24	25	30	0	0	0	47	45	88
(Current Assets- Liabilities)	5285	4480	3940	3009	3399	2983	4805	8168	10735	14637	15006
(-Inventory)	4515	3486	2379	1167	1106	178	1313	3787	4137	6058	6967

Table 7: Balance sheet 1976-86

YEAR	77 on 76	78 on 77	79 on 78	80 on 79	81 on 80	82 on 81	83 on 82	84 on 83	85 on 84	86 on85
Assets										
Current Assets										
Cash	21%	9%	9%	−6%	62%	−11%	52%	−3%	49%	−16%
Mktbl Securities	−13%	−27%	−8%	−47%	−14%	84%	70%	−24%	26%	38%
Notes/Acc Receivable	18%	33%	13%	−2%	−4%	14%	12%	33%	32%	2%
Other A/R										
Inventories	29%	57%	18%	24%	22%	24%	25%	51%	30%	−6%
Prepaid Expenses	54%	5%	−5%	14%	5%	17%	51%	9%	0%	25%
Total	2%	2%	5%	−9%	4%	26%	33%	18%	28%	6%
Rental MC					12%	−4%	−44%	−31%	−27%	
Depreciation					10%	−3%	−41%	−21%	−18%	
Plant/Property					17%	10%	40%	15%	29%	
Depreciation					19%	11%	50%	11%	25%	
Rental MC/Property	9%	12%	19%							11%
Depreciation	5%	8%	7%							14%
Investments	21%	13%	29%	19%	14%	−2%	103%	52%	13%	28%
Total Assets	7%	9%	18%	9%	11%	10%	15%	14%	23%	10%
Current Liabilities										
Taxes	6%	−0%	18%	38%	2%	18%	13%	−17%	16%	−16%
Loans Payable	48%	40%	287%	−37%	31%	−32%	1%	57%	55%	9%
Accounts Payable	22%	15%	5%	−81%	21%	13%	27%	29%	13%	8%
Compensation/Benefits	46%	33%	30%	1%	11%	26%	7%	6%	11%	22%
Deferred Income						28%	3%	−5%	−11%	15%
Other						16%	12%	13%	17%	21%
Total	21%	14%	23%	−17%	12%	12%	12%	5%	19%	11%
Long-Term Debt	−7%	12%	456%	32%	27%	7%	−6%	22%	21%	5%
Other						−18%	1%	23%	−8%	19%
Deferred Taxes	40%	25%	26%	31%	38%	28%	188%	121%	77%	24%
Equity										
Stock	−2%	−0%	1%	0%	10%	14%	16%	3%	4%	1%
Retained Earnings	−1%	10%	15%	13%	10%	18%	20%	21%	16%	2%

Table 8: Balance sheet per cent changes 1976–86

Against this decline has been the steady rise in total inventories (to a level of $8 billion, but still less than two months).

The biggest increase though has been in plant and property, in line with IBM's massive investment in the new automated plants necessary to meet its objective of being the lowest-cost producer. Indeed IBM overall spent a total of more than $60 billion (including depreciation) on plant and property in the six years to 1985 (and in the same time also invested $20 billion in R & D). IBM itself made more modest claims; claiming that it spent more than $20 billion on *additional* plant and property over the five years to 1985. This process started in 1979, and it is clear that in the short term it was funded by the issue of long-term debt; indeed if the net current figures (without inventory) are further reduced by the long-term debt there was a shift of two and a half billion dollars in 1979 (a situation that worsened through to 1981). Since 1982, however, the position has been strengthening (though of course in some respects at the expense of depleting the rental base). Even though IBM effectively reversed this process in 1986, by reducing its level of investment by $2 billion, it is still making substantial investments in this area; though any change in policy will take some time to work through—where commissioning plants can take a number of years.

The apparent 1979 reduction in accounts payable was a bookkeeping feature, as the figures were split in later years to other categories. The recent increase in deferred taxes similarly represents changed bases, partly due to tax benefits derived from the acquisition of Rolm.

Overall then, despite all the reported problems, the balance sheet still shows a remarkably successful company that is in a position to switch vast sums of money into new directions at very short notice (indeed the purchase of stakes in a number of other companies, including Rolm, shows in the "Investments" line but otherwise barely makes a blip on the overall curves!).

The pattern of funds flow is confirmed by IBM's own analyses (Table 9). These too show the growing liquidity (and reduction in the use of long-term debt), and the switch from funding rental machines to plant and property; as well as the recent investments in acquisitions. It does also show that IBM can still generate an "investment" flow in excess of $10 billion, even in a bad year! This by itself gives IBM an impressive degree of invulnerability. It is reinforced by IBM's ability to react to events, at least at the finan-

	1979	1980	1981	1982	1983	1984	1985	1986
	$ millions	*$ millions*	*$ millions*	*$ millions*	*$ millions*	*$ millions*	*$ millions*	*$ millions*
Funds (Cash & Security)								
as at 1 January	4030	3771	2112	2029	3300	5536	4362	5622
Sources:								
Net Earnings	3011	3562	3308	4409	5485	6582	6555	4789
Depreciation (expense)	1970	2362	2899	3143	3362	2987	2894	
Depreciation						3215	3051	3316
NBV rental m/c sold	779	1009	1255	1642	2108	1483	867	647
Amortizd Prog Prods				249	311	486	425	672
Other (deferred Tax)	353	90	−189	84	749	1004	1880	1257
Total	6113	7023	7273	9527	12015	12542	12621	10681
Depreciation (capital)	351	397	430	419	265	228	157	
Total	6464	7420	7703	9946	12280	12770	12778	10681
Uses:								
Inv in Rental m/c	4212	4334	4610	3293	1412	858	313	
Inv Plant & Property	1779	2258	2235	3392	3518	4615	6117	
Inv Plant/Prop/Rent						5473	6430	4620
Inv Prog Prod				468	588	803	785	907
Investments & Assets	338	275	244	−320	1887	1764	454	454
Working Capital	343	310	−151	370	855	4043	3101	−1149
Total	6672	7177	6938	7203	8260	12083	10770	6056
Translation Effects				30	−147	−324	677	842
Net Provided by Ops	−208	243	765	2773	3873	363	2685	5467
Provided Externally:								
Net Long-Term Debt	1304	510	570	182	−177	595	686	214
Net Loans Payable	691	−342	182	−244	3	302	459	117
Total	1995	168	752	−62	−174	897	1145	331
from Employee Plans	−38	−62	423	613	788	73	133	23
Capital Stock Retired								1488
Total	5779	4120	4052	5353	7787	6869	8325	9955
Less Cash Dividend:	2008	2008	2023	2053	2251	2507	2703	2698
Funds (Cash & Security)	3771	2112	2029	3300	5536	4362	5622	7257

Table 9: Funds flow 1979–86

cial level. In 1986 its use of funds within the business was reduced by $6 billion (almost a 60 per cent reduction). No financial analyst can afford to write of a company with such a tight control on its assets.

APPENDIX B

What Should a Customer Expect?

The history of computing has moved from its origins in scientific number crunching, through commercial data storage and retrieval, to the current terminal networks. In the near future it will truly move into an era of distributed data processing, with each individual having his own personal computer and access via a network to vast databases of information. More important, based on IBM's own experience, he will have access to a horizontal communications network that will revolutionize the structure and operations of business. To power this the indications are that IBM will at long last implement major elements of its Future Series, bringing in a genuine further generation of computers (the first since the S/360) as well as integrating its product line (again for the first time since the early days of the S/360).

In such a rapidly changing world the customer needs to plan carefully; and to consider the degree of long-term supplier (manufacturer or dealer) support, rather than short-term discounts. There is sound commonsense behind the much maligned comment that "Nobody ever got fired for buying IBM."

This appendix also tries to draw some lessons from IBM. In this case there is rather more about how one can profitably deal *with* IBM, but (as with the earlier chapters) there is also extensive use of IBM itself as a model; indeed largely as the "ideal" model, to see what might reasonably be achieved in practice. The possible futures of computing (or data processing or information technology; depending on how wide you draw the boundaries) will be considered. I am aware, though, that the population at large is fascinated by the much narrower question of the technology and I will accordingly attempt to offer a mix of the two; the broader perspective to educate and the technology to "entertain!"

I will therefore start from the position that information handling is now becoming the predominant activity of mankind in developed Western cultures. This parallels the development of society from the nomadic hunters to agrarian society, and thence through the Industrial Revolution to industrial society; until we are now moving into the post-industrial information society. The impact of these "revolutions" is recorded most graphically in the changes in employment patterns. Thus in the UK in 1983, barely two centuries after the start of the Industrial Revolution, only 1.7 per cent of the working population was employed in agriculture. Less than one-fiftieth of the workers were able to feed the rest of society, and to a level far beyond that achieved before the Industrial Revolution (for the impact was as much on agriculture as on industry).

The trends emerging in the post-industrial society (less than half a century into the information revolution; perhaps only two decades if you date it from the launch of the S/360) may be seen in the figure for total employment in manufacturing and construction which, again in 1983 in the UK, was only 34 per cent (a drop of one-fifth from only eight years previously, 42 per cent in 1975). Even these "industrial" employment figures include large numbers of people involved in information handling (albeit on pieces of paper). What is apparent is that already no more than one-third of the work force are needed to produce all the population's physical wants; and there is no reason why the figure should not ultimately drop to match that in agriculture. The *majority* of the work force is already employed in handling information; and the proportion is growing rapidly.

It is not misleading as a result to talk about an information revolution comparable with the Industrial Revolution. The true picture of the typical worker is no longer someone standing by a lathe, it is someone sitting at a desk! It is misleading, though, to talk about this "revolution" just in terms of technology. The Industrial Revolution was as much about organizational changes; though perhaps only Marx really saw this clearly at the time (and his conclusions are still very debatable!). The information revolution will be even more one based on organizational changes; and perhaps IBM's own approach is indicative of one possible future.

The handling of information thus already represents the greatest part of mankind's activities (at least in the developed countries), and almost *all* of this data handling is potentially capable of being carried out by some form of computerized systems. The resulting structural unemployment, the direct result of de-industrialization, is not without its pain; the long-term future may be rosy, but that will be little comfort to those thrown out of work. The boundaries have to be drawn very wide indeed in the long term. It is clear, therefore, why business is becoming increasingly preoccupied with information technology; it probably is already a major factor affecting profitability in many companies, and perhaps even survival in some.

What have the trends been within data processing, towards these growing needs? During the earliest days of computing—in general terms the 1950s—the emphasis was almost entirely on number-crunching: scientific computing. The CPU, the central processing unit, developed in the late 1940s was all important; really only requiring a printer as a peripheral. In the 1960s the data processing world expanded to encompass the accounting functions of business. This was still a figure-oriented operation, but requiring some "word" handling and most important, needing large amounts of on-line data storage, with the advent of tape and, in particular, disk technology (but still run in "batches," typically with punched card input). In the 1970s the main development was real-time computing, with increasing numbers of users linked directly to the machine via terminals. This was still largely accounting based, but it now started to provide database enquiry functions for a few privileged managers. At the same time the development of the micro-processor led to the personal computer. More importantly, in the short term it stimulated the introduction of word processing; and words rather than numbers began to be the staple diet of computers.

The 1980s have seen the wide scale introduction of DDP (distributed data processing) allowing more and more staff to use computers in their work; whether it is word processing or (accounting) number crunching. As yet, though, the full power of the computing capacity available has not been tapped. The end-users have recognized the potential, probably better than the DP experts, but their usage has inevitably been limited by the lack of suitable application software. A great deal of the usage is still related to the, by now, traditional computerized accounting functions. The databases, even if they are made available to end-users (and this is usually not the case), largely relate to this accounting information. The two main developments which have been occasioned by the advent of the PC are the more widespread use of word processing by general staff (who are not secretaries) and the emergence of the spreadsheet as a powerful numeric management tool.

The impact of word processing, even when implemented on a

department wide basis (often now grandly described as "office automation") has so far been largely limited to giving end-users the ability to produce their existing documents rather faster, and without the usual complications of using the typing pool or shared secretaries. Its main impact has yet to come; of which more later.

The spreadsheet, though, has already had significant impact. Visicalc is normally said to have been the first contender, but in practice IBM had offered similar programs since the early 1970s; but on mainframes only. The breakthrough achieved by Visicalc was to put the principle to work on PCs, and thus make it easily available to *any* manager. The almost revolutionary impact of such spreadsheets is the "what if" facility. Once a set of figures are entered—and in any case use of the spreadsheet is the easiest way of preparing any figures (particularly budgets)—it is particularly easy to change the factors to see what is the impact of alternative strategies. Previously the work involved in considering alternatives was so extensive that there was an almost universal tendency to avoid the problem. With a spreadsheet the only work is typically two or three minutes changing the key figures and then waiting (again only for two or three minutes) while the computer does all the hard work of carrying out the perhaps many thousands of calculations involved.

Although the use of spreadsheets only takes a few hours of computing time (and users then look around for a more regular use for their new toy!), it should have a disproportionate impact. It should lead to rather more innovative, as well as better thought out, management strategies and tactics. The use of "what if" should become a natural extension of the management process; certainly the success of Armonk has been in no small measure due to its constant evaluation, and reevaluation, of *all* the alternatives. Paradoxically, the use of spreadsheets is probably less widespread in IBM than in some other companies; perhaps because its usual, mainframe, solution (ADRS) is rather clumsy.

This brings me to IBM, for IBM is a very good model of the next stage of development. IBM is, in one way at least, rather different from most other companies. Its own implementation of DDP is very heavily centralized on massive mainframes; the typical IBM internal processor is a 3080 or 3090 water-cooled mainframe, as far removed from a PC as you can get. IBM is, in fact, approaching this next stage of development from the opposite direction to almost everyone else. It is committed to a massive programme of installing PCs, to allow the maximum benefits of DDP to reach the end-users; and also to offload some of the computing power loads imposed on the central mainframes.

Having highlighted this one difference, the model of IBM could be applicable to most other sophisticated companies. Almost certainly IBM's original intention in building its massive networks was to tap the potential offered by large databases. As a result the IBM networks have on-line not just statistical data (indeed this is the one component that, typically, has restricted access), but vast amounts of "printed" data (IBM is the world's second largest publisher, only surpassed by the US government!). Undoubtedly access to this information does have a value, and is very productive. For example IBMers now do not have to move from their desks to review all IBM's publications on a given subject, or any of a product's characteristics, or any of IBM's multifarious "business practices."

Having been given the access to these networks, though, the real benefit and use has emerged elsewhere. It is quite simply that offered by communications. Word processing capability, to take up a theme from earlier, is a critical element of this; but IBM's own implementation of this now goes far beyond the narrow confines of conventional office automation. As we have seen, horizontal communications are the essence of IBM: the main activity of staff is communications, frequently in meetings but most often on the telephone, and to date, only rarely on paper. The advent of widespread access to networks has, however, revolutionized the "paper" element, albeit in the "paperless office" (the "paper" is now electronic). The networks have made it remarkably easy to communicate with others. A message can be keyed into a terminal almost as fast as the idea comes to the end-user. It can then be transmitted to the "target" virtually instantaneously (and if he isn't at his desk it will wait patiently until he next uses his terminal, when it is immediately available, unlike any other form of communication). Furthermore, it as easy to send the message to a hundred people as to one; so information propagation is encouraged.

The indication, from the IBM model, is therefore that this horizontal communication process is the essence of the next stage of development (or "generation"). Its effect should not be underestimated; even in IBM, where horizontal communication is a way of life, the impact has been dramatic. In other companies it may well be close to revolutionary.

The data processing implications are equally massive. The basic requirement is that almost every individual has his own terminal (now most likely in the form of a PC). The benefits are, however, very sensitive to the proportion of users. Quite simply, if the "message" can only be transmitted to a small proportion of the "targets" the user will probably not bother, but will continue to use conventional means. If, however, most of the targets can be reached via the system then it *will* be used; and typically those *not* on the system may be ignored, resulting in pressure to get them on the network (thus escalating demand for the system). At this point, the first stages have to be an act of faith; but it will not be long, in my estimation, before such data networks become a basic administrative tool of business. This will be in much the same way that a telephone is now considered to be an essential adjunct to every desk; the principle is identical. Indeed the analogy of the telephone is the one which best illustrates the likely impact, the type of use and also the organizational implications. Can you imagine how a modern office could work without universal access to the telephone? The same question will be equally applicable, in less than a decade, to the then ubiquitous PC or terminal.

The saving grace of this process, which could otherwise require a horrendous level of investment in a very short space of time, is that for the critical point to be passed, not all individuals need have their own terminal; perhaps a ratio of one terminal shared between two or three individuals will suffice—at least in the first instance but it should be recognized that there will be heavy pressure from staff rapidly to extend the provision to one per person. The second moderating factor is that the process can be implemented (in stages) by groups, for individuals usually communicate most within their own group, typically within a department (and certainly within a building/establishment). The benefits are thus still obtained when nearly all the members of the *group* (which can be quite small) have the facility. Again, though, it has to be recognized that there will be pressure from other groups excluded from this benefit. The costs can, however, be contained.

Even so the cost implications are not trivial. Providing the PCs for a typical 500-person office building might cost around £5,000 each (with the necessary network adapters). If each were shared by three people this would still add up to a total cost for terminals of around £1 million. To this has to be added the cost of cabling (at perhaps £150,000) and training (at two days, say £200 per person; another £100,000). The total cost of the investment within the building (excluding the TP connections to the mainframes) is thus likely to be in excess of £1 million.

The next bad news is that one of the reasons for IBM's very keen interest is that it has estimated that the amount of computing power needed centrally to support these local networks will be *twice* as great as that required locally (costing say another £1 million; since central processing power may cost less than half the cost per mip that distributed power costs). The total cost may, therefore, be in excess of £2 million! The direct cost to IBM of bringing 11,000 managers, professionals and secretaries in the UK on to its own internal "NOSS" (PROFS based) implementation is estimated to be around £70 million (even though it doesn't have to pay the full price for its own products) spread over five years.

The good news is that, offset against these costs, should be at least the 7 per cent increase in productivity that IBM has reported is the target for its own implementation. The actual IBM performances reported to date reflect the "threshold" effect. At a site where only 65 per cent of the users had over six months' use, the productivity gains were only 3.6 per cent. On the other hand at one where 98 per cent of users had more than six months, use, the figure had risen to 8.7 per cent (with an estimated eventual potential of around 20 per cent). Assuming the total cost per head (including overheads) of an office worker is (even in the relatively low paid UK) around £20,000 per annum the productivity benefits could amount to some £700,000 per annum, recovering the cost in less than three years on direct savings alone (and this is the payback period forecast for IBM's own NOSS project). Remembering that IBM is already a remarkably productive company, it would seem likely that other companies should better this improvement. Clearly the pay-back period will also be significantly less in countries where workers are higher paid; so that it seems very likely that few companies will be able to resist the pressures to install such extensive networks. In any case the additional, intangible benefits of horizontal communications will inexorably drive the whole process forward.

On the other hand the trade-off between benefits and costs will vary from company to company; so the first step for any organization should be to study in depth exactly what are its needs.

The key lesson from the IBM experience, though, is that it is the complexity of the centralized network that is the easiest to underestimate. Thus the user demands, where most individuals will now come to depend on their terminals as much as they previously did on pencil and paper, are heavy. It is easy to find another pencil, but impossible to find another terminal if the network is down (a not uncommon occurrence in the early days of IBM's experiment). This means that in practice at least 95 per cent availability is needed if efficiency is not to be seriously impacted (and probably closer to 99 per cent it morale is not to deteriorate). Equally a sub-second response time is necessary on a terminal based system. The worst temptation for all DP departments is to bend to pressure from those still in the queue to bring them on to the system early, by pushing the number of users close to the critical limit; just below where the system falls over. Of course the inevitable result forced on any system by the random statistical fluctuations in load, is that the critical point is then sometimes exceeded; and the system falls on its face with monotonous regularity (and the overhead of recovering just adds to the load!). The moral is that the load must always be kept below the design limit, no matter *what* the pressures from management and users. Realism is the most valuable quality in any network installation project.

In terms of reliability, IBX eventually found it was necessary to double up on all the critical hardware (having *two* 3725 network controllers in each building for example). More important, the number of possible network paths had to be increased *tenfold,* from around 500 covering the total UK, to nearly 5,000.

The above figures, however, relate to a terminal based network driven by mainframes, with largely hierarchical links; requiring that much heavier use of data communications on the network. Where PCs are supported on local area networks, which in turn link into the mainframes only to access the large central databases and to pass data to other local area networks, the problem may well be more manageable (at least in terms of computer power; IBM has two 3090 water-cooled processors just to control the network). Clearly the problems of downtime are also much reduced where each individual can still continue to work on his own PC, with a sub-second response guaranteed for most of the time. Even so, the complexity of the problem (particularly in terms of network design and software) should not be underestimated; nor should the impact on the loadings where some PC users may well decide to download whole files rather than just screenfuls of data (thus undoing all the savings in data flow).

In terms of the hardware and software needed to meet this complexity, only IBM as yet can begin to measure up to the problem. Its architecture (SNA), is as yet the only one that can cope with the scale of the interconnections; and even then the UK network implementation forced SNA to a new (order of magnitude greater) level of complexity. Needless to say this caused major problems and delays, as almost inevitably does the first introduction of any new software. At least in this case the bugs were ironed out within IBM and not, as usual, by the first customers! It is difficult to see how the competitive OSI standard, or any other, could begin to match this; particularly as the IBM UK experience showed that the requirements to be met in fact changed into a rapidly moving target!

Even IBM has a long way to go in terms of completing its next generation of network offerings. Clearly there are gaps in the hardware and software that will be needed to support the new local area networks (particularly the "token ring" protocol which is the strategic offering). Although one of IBM's failures in terms of sales, the RISC (Reduced Instruction Set Computer) machine, the 6150 or PC RT, announced at the beginning of 1986 may give some hints of what is to come. Ostensibly offered as a stand alone CAD (computer aided design) system it has a number of key features which are largely unnecessary as a stand alone machine, but which would be very valuable indeed as a component in a network. In particular it has a 40 bit addressing capability (compared with 31-bit for MVS/XA, IBM's flagship operating system). This means that it potentially can handle very complex communications. In this vein it also reportedly supports virtual machine (as well as virtual memory) and a sophisticated relational database; all while running under its own (AIX) version of UNIX (which thus looks set to be the main standard at the interface between local area networks and the mainframes). Although the 9370 (launched later than the 6150), which is reportedly the major offering as the "interface machine," once more looks (at least superficially, from its specification) as if it is based on 360 architecture, it is interesting that the new PS/2 personal computer range was announced with the avowed intention of offering AIX on its larger machines—again implying that at least one interface may yet lurch in the direction of UNIX. IBM appears to be mildly schizophrenic on this subject. Clearly the gaps in the market could be filled with some very adventurous machines.

The picture I have described represents IBM as it now is, and hence probably hints at what the rest of the market may look like in half a decade or so. Are there any other signs that might show where developments may lead? Such predictions are a very risky business; though they are, of course, the essence of Armonk's planning processes. For example if we, with much less sophisticated information sources, look back a decade we return to the punched card, batch-processing era; and which of us (as opposed to Frank Cary then at Armonk) would then have predicted the latest developments!

In the broadest sense, though, it seems possibly most likely that the key developments will be of the communications process. This view is reinforced by IBM's determined investment in satellite communications (via MCI) and telephone systems (via Rolm). All that I have described so far limits communications and documents to mere variations on the inter-office memo that has long been the staple diet of office paperwork. There is clearly nothing revolutionary in the content; even if there is in the technology of transmission.

In real life conversations, paper plays but a small part. It does, of course, have one crucial role; it often gives the definitive statement of the ideas involved (particularly where electronic communications are involved). The conversation, though, involves a large amount of voice content (conveying information by tone as much as by words) as well as non-verbal visual content (diagrams, for example, as well as gestures and body language which convey the visual equivalent of tone).

Paradoxically at present it is the cheaper home computers that address these additional communications channels, with their games making maximum use of visual (non-verbal) and sound channels. The new display standards of the PS/2 are much better but still do not match those of some home computers. Although these home computers may set some presentation standards for future achievement in office systems, they do not, however, provide any answer to future developments. The key will be the provision of systems that make it easy for users to put into (as well as take out of) electronic form their normal communications processes (which are far removed from games). The "painting" functions offered by some systems (with their "mouse") offer some possible options, but are limited in scope and do not match normal "conversational" usage; so that they are borderline in business PC terms.

IBM has already made a number of false starts. It announced a voice based message "distribution" (ADS, based on the Series/l) which was quite well received by those few who used it (there was a queue to use it within IBM, where use was rationed). It was, however, only a rather more sophisticated version of an answering machine, and was not integrated with other communications. In the visual field, IBM pinned its hopes on the Scanmaster device, which was designed to read and transmit for storage on disk, whole page images (which could then be called up at will on a suitable terminal, a 3279 for example). Unfortunately the scanning process produced around half a megabyte of information from each A4 page. The hope was that software would be able to compress this by a ratio of 20:1 (most pages are largely "empty space"). The result should have been perhaps as few as 25,000 bytes of data (still considerably more than the 5,000 to 10,000 bytes it might contain when in word form). In practice the algorithm apparently was nowhere as efficient as was hoped for, and this resulted in an unacceptable overhead in terms of massive amounts of disk storage. The system was discreetly de-emphasized. IBM in its internal NOSS system has resorted to teams of data entry staff (typists!) to enter all correspondence originating from the outside world (and in inconveniently non-electronic form) into the system so that it too can then be manipulated, transmitted and archived electronically.

IBM of course has, in its labs, very sophisticated technology under development. At Yorktown Heights it already has a system that converts spoken to printed words (only awaiting suitable computing power to drive its very heavy processing demands). The UK Scientific Centre has, in turn, been working on leading edge image processing (and as a fascinating, but I suspect largely irrelevant, sideline has even looked at simulated feel; using a variation on glove boxes). The answer does not lie in the individual technologies though, but in how they are put together as a package.

Just how open IBM itself is keeping its options is shown by the various standards it is working to. SAA (Systems Application Architecture) has hogged the headlines recently, and standardisation of application programs is essential if computers are to be able to successfully exchange data on a "peer to peer" basis; and it is also needed to make the use of such computers by millions of untrained users less traumatic. But apart from SNA, perhaps the two key elements are DIA (document interchange architecture) and DCA (document content architecture); both of which complement SNA, but are of more recent origin. They in effect describe how data should be organized and handled. Interestingly, both of them make provision for both images and voice as well as more conventional data. These too are seen merely as "documents" with somewhat different attributes (which means that, potentially, they can be fully integrated with the other media to provide the total "conversation" package). When conversations between two or more end-users thus have a multi-media approach, business communications may move into a new dimension; if not to a new artform! In terms of networks the open ended commitment is shown by the IBM cabling standards. These are significantly over-engineered for conventional data handling, and are indeed quite capable of distributing video level information. The message is that users should keep their own options as open as IBM is; once more the safest route is to follow the IBM standards closely. It is unlikely that IBM will actually implement all the potential offerings implied (its touchstone is commercial viability, not technical merit), but it wili implement a good number of them.

That communications will be at the heart of future systems is already clear. At the same time, it is also inevitable that the networks will be expected to provide an increasing amount of support for the end-user. The current trendy technology is AI (artificial intelligence), which is supposed to turn the computer into a professional adviser; a philosophy that the Japanese, in particular, are developing. In the shorter term the most useful aids will probably be less dramatic. In most areas AI will initially only lead to ways of helping to develop the ideas, to be communicated by the network, more easily and logically. In the specific area of running the network itself, however, IBM has already developed AI to take over some of the role of running the equipment (from the present human operators).

Parallel with this, the availability of information should expand geometrically. There is no reason, for example, why a manager considering a strategic decision should not have instantaneous access to a great proportion of the most relevant information contained in the whole library of management textbooks. With word search facilities (such as IBM's STAIRS) the relevant paragraphs can already be found in a matter of seconds; this is certainly the user-preferred means of addressing the databases on the IBM internal networks. Again flexibility in design is probably the best advice, if networks are not to be soon locked into obsolete structures.

In terms of computer technology it is clear that the emphasis too will be on communication and distributed processing. This philosophy may even apply to the central processors themselves. The various functions currently handled, in broad terms, by the single ALU (arithmetic logic unit in the older terminology) could well be split up into separate elements, each of which would be handled by a RISC machine specifically optimized for that function. Thus image processing could be very well handled by an array processor (as could mass data retrieval), where logic could be better handled by pipeline processing. In effect the whole CPU would become a parallel processor, but with the parallel elements being very different; not the large number of similar elements currently proposed, outside IBM, for such parallel processing. The traditional sequential (Von Neumann) processing may thus, at long last, be superseded. In this context, it is particularly interesting to note that one really new feature of the PS/2 range, the "micro-channel," has this capability. Although it has already been demonstrated, by IBM, running distributed processors, the commentators do not yet appear to have grasped the significance of this!

These "distributed" or parallel processors may well be linked by optical links; though the true optical computer is still some way over the horizon.

The technology of these CPUs requires no great steps forward; the concept has already been around for over a decade (it was very likely a central feature of the abandoned Future Series, and was implicit in parts of the S/38 architecture even when launched!). But the operating system complexities will be horrendous. On the other hand this distributed approach will allow optimized dedicated processors (following conventional 360 architecture) to run the existing MVS/XA based software (and the additional addressing structure of this begins to make sense), while other new processors will be able to concentrate on the next generation operating system that IBM has been looking to introduce since the Future Series. Thus IBM will finally be able to break with the 360 based architecture (which was revolutionary in its day, but is now constricting). The massive investments by the customer base will be protected, and yet the doors will be opened for a quantum leap into the future.

IBM has already pushed the development of magnetic media—largely hard disks—close to their theoretical limits (their tolerances even now are within that of the wavelength of light!). Yet it does not, as yet, appear to be overinterested in optical (laser) disk technology which would seem to be the most obvious answer to mass archiving. Such storage of vast amounts of data becomes a necessity where images become a major part of the data. As one very specialized example of the scale of the problem, a typical X-ray (traditionally recorded on photographic film, but increasingly handled by electronic image intensifiers; and even now often in digital form) will generate 4,000,000 characters (four megabytes) of information. A normal district hospital may well generate up to 200,000 such X-rays a year; and these may need to be held (for quasi-legal reasons) for up to 25 years. The result is perhaps a database of some 20,000 gigabytes (that is 20,000,000,000,000 characters) for *each* such hospital!

As this X-ray example illustrates, though, much of this image data does not need to be "rewriteable"; once recorded it remains unchanged thereafter. Such technology is already available and offered, for example by Phillips who are perhaps the current leading exponents of laser technology; with whom IBM did have a joint venture, somewhat surprisingly since discontinued. Indeed, at long last, IBM itself is now offering WORM (Write Once Read Many times) optical disks on the PS/2 range. What is not yet reliably available is rewriteable laser disk equipment; which would be able to handle the requirements of the very volatile, rapidly changing data stored by normal commercial processing; and it is this that IBM appears to be waiting for. In the case of the large mainframes, the problem is not easy, for such a medium must be stable (storing information without degradation) for decades.

Another reason for IBM's apparent tardiness may, once more, be the software. For it will be difficult enough keeping track of the vast amounts of information without the additional (and very considerable) complexity of setting up linkages to point to the most recent piece of some changing, volatile information if this is held on write-once-only media. The problem increases by several orders of magnitude where the database starts to be distributed (which is a trend implied by networking). Perhaps the first element of information you want will be held in London, but the next may just as easily be in Los Angeles. Hence, once more, software is the critical part of any new developments (as it always has been; despite the proud claims of the plug compatible *hardware* vendors).

In fact, true distributed storage and processing will be key to the next generation. It is already implicit in the most open-ended of IBM's standards, its wiring specifications. The nodes on this are clearly where it is expected that distributed computing power will be located. At its simplest level, the specification for the wiring closet (which is the hub of the departmental systems) leaves a great deal of air space; which must surely be filled by computing power of one sort or another (the departmental file server for example; perhaps based on the type of RISC architecture built into the PC

RT). It is almost inevitable that the outside links to this will be by optical (fibre optics) means, since Conventional electrical cabling would not be able to handle the projected loads.

What is not yet clear is whether there is another level of node, say a larger local database for a location, before the largest nodes (comparable with the traditional computer rooms that are the province of the DP department). Whatever the answer, it can be seen that the control of the network is the most complex task of all; and it is here that IBM's UK experience is such a valuable guide to possible future directions.

This naturally leads on to the new building block of the DP system; the individual workstation (where in the past the central computer has been the prime focus of attention). It is already clear, from the short history of the PC, that it is the "intelligence" contained in this that will drive the whole system; and the raw power being deployed is even now awe inspiring. The larger models of the PS/2 range, based on the 386 processor, are already as powerful as a medium range mainframe; and far more powerful than the top end of the 360 range! Thus the hardware is there, but, as always, it is the software that is eagerly awaited. The indications are that the kernel of this interface between the end-user micro and the mainframes will revolve around UNIX or something similar. The all important, user friendly, outer shell (the only part seen by the user) will, though, be what makes the system work; and will surely be developed far beyond the current rather crude offerings (and will probably be proprietary, and not transportable, against all the forecast of the experts; perhaps IBM's AIX is one forerunner of this).

It is similarly difficult to believe that the one crude display unit per desk (if you are one of the lucky few) is the definitive method of presenting the increasingly large and complex sets of data to the user. On the other hand, the technology built into the conventional CRT (display monitor) is difficult to beat. It is cheap, flexible and can offer very high resolution; so it is likely to stay as the main display element for the foreseeable future. The "flat screen" technologies (usually plasma or electroluminescent devices, since the LCD displays are very difficult to read) are much easier to put where the user can "handle" them (they can be built into the surface of the desk for example, allowing the user to manipulate the pieces of data much as he would paper). Perhaps the compromise will be such flat displays for "handling" the data as the "conversation" is built up, with CRTs to show the assembled package.

One, perhaps unexpected, impact of the new work practices will be changes in the *physical* environment. Despite all that has been said to the contrary, networks actually require significantly *larger* buildings for the same number of office workers; though they will of course be much more productive than a similar number of conventional office workers. For a start the size of IBM's professional (i.e., staff) workstation (i.e., desk) has already been expanded by 30 per cent, where IBM was previously not ungenerous, simply to allow for the electronic equipment to fit on the desk. The preferred workstation is now "L" shaped, comprising a desk (2.25 m by 0.75 m) with a "return" top (usually a cupboard, 1 m by 0.5 m); where the PC sits in the corner of the "L" (with a printer typically on the return). In addition the various local machine rooms (excluding the large mainframe facilities—water cooled machine rooms need special facilities which can't be easily slotted into office buildings), TP equipment rooms and printer areas can eat up another 15 per cent.

The environment in the work area also has to change. Not least is the problem of cabling, for the IBM standard calls for not less than 1.3 data lines to each desk. Each cable, which is a version of twinax and significantly thicker than ordinary coaxial cable, has to be pulled the whole length of the office from the riser (in the quaintly named—to UK ears—WC; wiring closet, not water closet!). On a typical 10,000 sq ft floor of an office building this means a bundle of 70 to 100 such cables. Few buildings can cope with cabling to this level, so major conversions are necessary (IBM typically uses false ceiling space, or in some cases space frames suspended from the ceiling; a solution that works well). At the workstation more electrical sockets have to be provided (an extra power drain which may mean regrading the whole building supply), screens have to be provided to minimize noise transmission (from the printers in particular) and lighting has to be modified so that it does not cause glare on the VDUs. Another surprising outcome is that the horizontal communications so generated actually require more face to face meetings; with a resulting need for more meeting rooms and informal meeting spaces. In the case of IBM this adds a further 10 per cent to the space needs.

The outcome is that installation of networks requires a significant amount of architectural design and construction work; something that may not be appreciated.

This, though, is only a modification of the existing desk layout. It does not allow for the development of the true electronic workstation, whatever that might be. As suggested earlier it may be difficult to predict just how exotic this may eventually turn out to be, but perhaps the money-dealing rooms of the banks (currently costing between £30,000 and £50,000 per workstation) can hint at some of the potential complexity.

The biggest problem for the traditional DP department will be controlling their end-users. In practice with the spread of PCs such control has already been lost; a fact that research shows DP managers worry about (though on balance they recognize the benefits of faster, easier installation which removes a load from their departmental resources). With the advent of networks, even local area networks, some degree of control will return; but so will many of the problems. No longer will the individual be stand alone, with no impact on other users. With network access the same individual will be able to bring the whole system down; at the same time as making unrealistic demands for support!

Clearly it is impossible for the usual DP department to even consider "policing" literally hundreds or thousands of end-users. The answer must in the first instance be to set rigorous standards, much as IBM does for the industry, for all users to follow. It also demands the establishment of a structure of local coordinators, trainers and service personnel. Each such system needs to be designed separately, and needs even then to be kept as flexible as possible; it's all too easy to set standards that are easy to control, but so constricting that they dissipate all the benefits.

One of the solutions is to draw on the resources of the main supplier. Inevitably most of these systems will be supplied by IBM, which fortunately has just about the largest body of very high calibre support personnel in the world. The objective of the customer should therefore be to tap this resource and redirect as much of it as possible for his own use. The naive user (and in particular his purchasing department) may devote his attention to obtaining the cheapest bargain; maybe saving up to 10 per cent overall (though more on individual components) by selecting lower specification products. The wise customer will devote his time to building the relationship with IBM, to divert the resources which are unavailable elsewhere. A discount can be recouped in a matter of months if the system works well; on the other hand if the system works poorly, as is likely with an under-specified system, there will be no productivity gains (and probably a negative impact on efficiency).

The best way to suck in IBM resource is to make friends of the IBM team. Nothing makes an IBM salesman a hero back at the branch more than to have a friendly and cooperative customer (IBM often feels embattled and in need of friends; and certainly in need of friendly "reference" accounts). My advice is to make the IBM salesman part of your team, and flatter him by treating him as if he is working for your company; and he will be! It is worthwhile, however, maintaining some contacts with IBM's main competitors; making sure that IBM is discreetly aware of this. After friendship, nothing keeps IBM on its toes better than a little competition; and it also impresses your own senior management, who were probably getting worried about your undue bias towards IBM!

Use of third parties is much more problematic. It is, though, inevitable because even with IBM's help no company will be able to field sufficient resources to install all the boxes needed, or to train all the personnel. With the current chaotic state of the dealer network this clearly poses problems. The first advice again is *not* to follow the route of choosing the biggest discounts; for it is this very route that has recently brought dealers into some disrepute.

The trick is once more to demand free support instead of discounts. If the dealer staff are of high calibre (and it is essential that they are; and that you check that they are!), their time is worth far more than any discount; and if they are not of high calibre—and unfortunately many of them can be of remarkably low calibre—then you would be very unwise to use such a dealer! Have a clear idea of what you want, a well thought out specification; and suggest to users that they do the same. Then check out the dealers you are considering, using all the sources of information that you can find. Check their other customers" opinions (but beware the tame reference account who will only tell you about the good times), attend their training courses, interview *all* the staff who will be working on your business (not just the front men), and above all understand how they propose to solve your problems (in detail), and do not be put off by their jargon; if they cannot explain their ideas in *your* language then there is a good chance they will not be able to implement them in your organization (this is particularly true where it is end-user managers who are taking the decisions). The ultimate reality, though, is that you are probably unlikely to find all (or indeed any) of the support resources you will need from IBM's third parties; despite the attractive theory, most such dealers actually make their money by cutting their costs to the bone, and hence avoid providing support at any cost (apart from maintenance, which is a very profitable business for them). You will need, therefore, to be prepared to develop your own internal support; and here you should seek advice from IBM (or other major suppliers) as to how you should develop and control this expertise.

All of the above comments apply to the larger organizations. Smaller organizations are even more vulnerable to the predations of the more unscrupulous dealers. The advice is much the same. Undertake the same investigations; common-sense goes a very long way (too much technical knowledge often only gets in the way of sensible solutions), and *you* should understand your own business needs. Do not be put off by the jargon; again I repeat, if they cannot explain their solution in your language then they probably won't be able to implement it. Above all do not be seduced by the discounts. Insist instead on support; your need for such support is even greater.

Above all follow the old, but wise, IBM motto and THINK for yourself.

APPENDIX C

Political Lessons?

This appendix contains those lessons which are more specific to individuals involved in government and politics. Although perhaps its most productive lessons are to be learnt by businessmen and managers, IBM is also the archetypal multinational which holds many lessons for the politician and political scientist. Most important of all in this context, it is (like many government machines) a large bureaucracy; but it, perhaps uniquely, has managed to *control* the worst excesses of its bureaucracy and indeed turn it into a flexible and creative management tool (and these are lessons that may be invaluable to other, less well controlled bureaucracies).

IBM itself does not overtly involve itself in politics. The Watsons may have supported the Democrats for many years; most notably Roosevelt and Kennedy (though also, quirkily, the Republican Eisenhower!). More recently the Carter administration recruited six IBM senior management into its ranks. Such actions, though, were very clearly undertaken by individuals. They were definitely not a reflection of any corporate thrust. IBM remains, determinedly, a political eunuch, and would not dream of undertaking subversive adventures of the kind reportedly once indulged in by ITT and Lockheed. IBM knows its place, and it is definitely not in the public arena.

Although the Realists (using the terminology of international politics) of the right do not admit to multinational corporations (MNCs, such as IBM) having any significant place in politics, the Pluralists, generally of the centre and representing the current consensus of political opinion in much of the West, do take MNCs seriously. Indeed, MNCs are seen by them to be one of the major interstate non-governmental actors; seen by some such Pluralists as on a par with governments. Such "demotion" of government is a view which would not find favour with IBM, which would always wish to *defer* to government. It may talk with them, and may even enter into "partnership" agreements, but the evidence is that it genuinely sees itself as the junior partner (even with smaller countries—whose GNP may well be less than IBM's revenue!).

Pluralists also recognize a degree of tension, if not conflict, between MNCs and the host governments where their subsidiaries operate. This is seen as inevitable where MNCs are bound to see nation states as obstacles in the path of their goal of global development; and where states, on the other hand, may see themselves threatened by loss of control (particularly over economic policies). Put at its most contradictory, George Bull has said the transnational corporation: ". . . is a modern concept evolved to meet the requirements of the modern age," while the nation state: ". . . is still rooted in archaic concepts, unsympathetic to the needs of our complex world" (R. J. Barnet and R. E. Mueller, *Global Research: The Power of Multinational Corporations,* 1974, Simon & Schuster). Samuel P. Huntington, though, saw their role as complementary not duplicative, and hence not in direct conflict: "It is conflict not between likes but between unlikes, each of which has its own primary set of functions to perform. . . . For the immediate future a central focus of world politics will be on the coexistence of and interaction between transnational organizations and the nation-state" ("Transnational Organisations in World Politics," *World Politics* XXV, April 1973). I believe that this latter view is the one that Armonk might subscribe to, and certainly one that the facts would generally support.

Even those Pluralists who would see conflict inherent in the relationship, would expect both sides to court each other assiduously, since the mutual benefits (which are not zero-sum) are believed to be too great to ignore. In Pluralist theory this courtship revolves around the right of access, whereby the state in effect gives an MNC a licence to operate; in return for negotiated, usually informal, controls.

Classically, Pluralists would expect the negotiations to be about control. In return for being granted access to the market of that country, the MNC is expected to cede some degree of control (and the penetration of Europe by Japanese corporations, establishing local plants, has clearly involved such negotiation). In practice the evidence suggests, however, that such a dialogue does *not* take place in the case of IBM. Typically it already has access, having operated in most nations for a number of decades; and would claim to be a good national of each of these countries. More important, it will not concede any degree of control which might impact its autonomy. This was best exemplified when IBM shut down its Indian subsidiary rather than follow that country's policy of requiring a majority shareholding to be held by Indian nationals. It is fair to say that this did not cost IBM a great deal, for India was and still is a small market for computers (despite its vast population). It is questionable whether IBM would so readily walk away from any of its five major overseas markets. Negotiation does take place, but IBM's bargaining counter is employment (and to a lesser extent, exports); usually in terms of the location of a new plant. The government's opposing counter is its purchasing power. The relation is thus arguably much closer to that between customer and supplier than that between actors on the international political scene, expected by Pluralists.

Although the MNCs, in particular IBM, would argue that they do not intend, and in practice do not have, any wide influence on political matters (a view that would be strongly held by IBM management), it is seen by Pluralists that they may have considerable autonomy, at the expense of national governments, in pursuit of their own special interests. This is especially true of IBM. In its particular field of computing it has a greater degree of autonomy than many national governments; even, it turns out, than the otherwise all-powerful Japanese government that has mounted a, so far, unsuccessful frontal attack on IBM. It, by itself, sets the international standards; and in the process is (perhaps unwittingly) able to dictate to national governments how effective their own, lesser, national computing policies will be.

Pluralists have highlighted the fact that the US government uses its legal control over its own MNCs, including IBM, to compel them, albeit very much against their will in some cases, to be its agents. The evidence of this is particularly damning in terms of the friction generated by the US government's insistence on controlling the technology licences offered by its MNCs, even in their overseas operations. In particular, the requirement for IBM's UK customers to sign licence agreements which effectively subjected them to US government instructions, was taken by the UK government to be an affront to national integrity. In this case IBM fought as hard as the UK government to avoid what it considered to be unwarranted intrusion on its autonomy; but ultimately to no avail, as US law prevailed.

Overall then, Pluralists see MNCs as largely neutral, with any disadvantages balanced by benefits; and essentially independent actors with an important, but not dominant, role complementing that of government. IBM sees itself in very much the same light, and strives to be a good corporate citizen wherever it operates. Peter Drucker, on behalf of management rather than political theory, summarizes this by his view that the MNCs' objective of profit maximization is also best for national growth; a view that IBM would probably support (even though its own objectives are more complex).

Structuralists, the Marxists/Leninists of the left, would go much further in emphasizing the central role of the MNC. The simple nation-state based, two-class, system of Marx was eventually developed by Lenin into monopoly capitalism, which recognized the international dimension. Most of the modern theories derived from these foundations revolve around the concept of the centre (the developed world and primarily the USA) versus, and dominating, the periphery (the Third World); with a relationship of unequal exchange in favour of the centre. Indeed it is argued that this international development is essential to the maintenance of capitalism if it is not to collapse under the joint problems of underconsumption and polarization of society. The chosen agents for promoting capitalism on the international scale are now the MNCs, according to the almost unanimous reports of Structuralists.

The resulting division of labour, according to the Chandler–Redlich scheme, leaves only the operational management scattered through the periphery, with coordination concentrated in a limited number of national and regional centres, but with strategic control reserved for the international centre (typically in the USA, Europe or Japan). This structure, as predicted by the Structuralists, is, at least on the surface, very true of IBM. Its various country organizations *are* largely limited to operational management. The regional centres, notably in Paris, *are* mainly involved with coordination. This leaves Armonk at the centre to exercise strategic control; which it clearly does to some effect. The implicit Structuralist criticism of this arrangement, which is essential to a complex operation such as IBM's (where plans must be integrated globally), is that the centre at Armonk uses its power for its own selfish purposes. This may be true of more conventional capitalist organizations, but in the case of IBM (and to a lesser extent other MNCs) the "self" is a complex organism. In particular the most important element is the work force. As a result the strategies Armonk implements are primarily designed to enhance the well-being of its employees. Indeed the influence of the work force goes much deeper in the case of IBM. The reason for this is the great strength of the culture. Much as Armonk uses this as a control on its distant outposts, it is in turn a constraint (and indeed a control) on what Armonk itself plans. The resulting strategies are, therefore, an amalgam of the views and wishes of its work force—worldwide. The focal point may lie at Armonk, but it can be argued that the pressures on it are truly transnational.

Perhaps the major Marxist/Structuralist criticism laid against the MNCs is their manipulation of inter-nation prices to extract the most advantageous profit patterns and this, coupled with the taxes paid at the centre (both on the company and on its highest paid employees), results in (again using Galtung's terminology) exploitation of the periphery by the centre. This particular criticism may be true of some MNCs, and indeed the Grand Duchy of Luxembourg has long depended on income from such organizations seeking a tax haven. IBM, though, has a strict policy of *not* manipulating inter-company prices to obtain the best tax advantages. It follows strict protocols for all such pricing; and no deviation is normally allowed. In particular, shipments out of the USA (which in the theory would be the main device for covertly transferring profits) are strictly controlled. These do have a high mark-up (as would be predicted by the Structuralists; in order to return untaxed profits), but as far as I could ascertain the best explanation is that this is a "penalty" cost to force World Trade to manufacture to meet all its own needs. Certainly the trade between the two halves of IBM is negligible (contrary to the predictions of this part of the theory). IBM has no need of such subterfuge. The income it derives from transferred profits and royalties is quite sufficient and (wisely) it does not wish to invite the long-term wrath of governments merely to improve short-term results.

Again there is an implicit criticism. This is that the MNCs extract profit from the Third World and return it to the centre; thus exacerbating the existing inequalities. This may well have been historically true of the predecessors of the MNCs, the international trading companies who for several centuries simultaneously stripped the Third World of its natural resources (to feed the factories of the Industrial Revolution) and used their populations as captive markets for these factories' products. Paradoxically, since 1945 the importance of these companies has rapidly waned, largely as a result of the break up of the European empires, at the same time as the MNCs have emerged. The Structuralists ignore the main feature of these new MNCs, that their trade is largely between the countries of the *developed* world; this typically represents around two-thirds of their total marketplace, and in the case of IBM the proportion is very much higher. Thus the argument that the MNCs are agents of capitalist exploitation of the Third World is essentially misleading. It hides the more important fact that the MNC's largely ignore the Third World, because their markets are too small and their business potential is unprofitable, The Third World is thus deprived of an important part of the infra-structure that is now provided by the MNCs in general, and IBM in particular, in the developed world.

As with most political issues the complexity is best addressed by using the two perspectives (Pluralism and Structuralism, since the realists make no claim to relevant views) to illuminate separate facets. Thus the Structuralists' emphasis on the key role of the ideology does provide some insight. The concept of capitalism, in the form of free enterprise, is a "natural" (Structuralists would claim insidious) component of Western culture; its existence is taken for granted, and as such its effects are allowed to go unnoticed. Peter Drucker, for example, provides a prime model of an author who is writing "pure" management texts with the commendable aim of teaching managers to do their job better; and yet all his work presupposes the continued existence of capitalism, and becomes unconscious propaganda for it. In general though, the more complex picture offered by the Pluralists, with the MNC being one of the more important actors on the international scene (on a par with the nation states), provides the richest of pickings; and best matches the evidence on the ground.

These brief references to the alternative political perspectives may seem somewhat irrelevant to some managers in MNCs. But the interaction of MNCs with the rest of the community, a broadly political activity, takes a not insubstantial part of their company's time and resources; even if this is not always very obvious to more junior management. Thomas Watson Jr. was well aware of this, and about one-third of his McKinsey lecture was given over to the relationship between the company and the state. Even the criticisms of the Structuralists, however improbable in the light of the actual IBM experience, should be of interest to MNC management; since these are often the basis for much of the vehement criticism such MNCs meet in their "overseas" operations (and not infrequently some of the criticism is justified; reinforcing the prejudices of their opponents).

The following discussion is largely based on a Pluralist perspective.

It is evident that IBM is, at the very least by default, a major actor on the international scene. The standards it sets, unilaterally, shape the future of data processing; and thus the very nature of the information revolution that is taking place on a global scale. Even if this basic role were to be ignored, IBM still is a major contributor to that ephemeral proposition, "business confidence." It is arguable that IBM's dominance has by now become so complete that the unfortunate coincidence of the end of a number of its product cycles (when IBM's presence in the market traditionally reaches a low ebb, as the last ounce of profit is wrung out of the dying products) in 1985, destabilized the whole of the DP marketplace, and to a lesser extent the overall business climate. As another example of its influence, in the mid-1970s when the breakdown of the Bretton Woods agreements had resulted in the development of the international currency markets, IBM used its then vast liquid assets to make large profits by gambling on the world's currency markets. Although these activities were perfectly legitimate it may thus, at least indirectly, have been one of the "Gnomes of Zurich" that contributed to the downfall of the pound sterling during the period! IBM has thus to be taken very seriously as a major actor on the international scene.

DeLamarter, in *Big Blue: IBM's Uses and Abuses of Power*, catalogues a long list of problems that IBM has caused, mainly for its competitors. To a degree I sympathise with him, because IBM's monolithic position makes it very difficult for anyone else to compete. As DeLamarter states: "IBM's success is the result of a sophisticated strategy for exploiting its substantial power—power that its competition cannot match. As a result of its power, IBM's competitors cannot win. If they ever get close, IBM changes the rules in its own favor."

I believe, however, that he somewhat overstates his case when he says: ". . . the implications of IBM's monopolistic hold on the basic equipment of the information revolution are frightening . . . it alone . . . will have the power to decide which information technology companies will succeed and which will fail. . . . It is perilous to trust a single company with such power."

His book does not set out to offer a balanced picture. It is clearly an extension of the prosecution's case that was developed when he was on the US government anti-trust team investigating IBM. This is a pity. But it means that I must, as you might expect, disagree with him *fundamentally* when he says: "IBM has very little to teach. . . . IBM's power has less to do with twenty-first century work ethic . . . than it does with crafty but hitherto unrecognised violation of the very spirit, if not always the letter, of anti-trust law." After all, my own book is quintessentially about the lessons to be learnt from IBM. Unlike DeLamarter's book, though, it is not primarily (or even to any great extent) about how governments might set out to control IBM.

A great deal of DeLamarter's book concerns IBM's pricing policies. His analysis is interesting and (if you ignore the overt bias) illuminating in terms of just how large companies go about making such decisions. For example, I would agree with him that: "It priced products selectively so that profits were maximised in secure market sectors and were virtually ignored in more competitive arenas." And that: "IBM's true craft is its ability to segment its product line and selectively set prices at levels precisely calculated to maintain control over the value customers perceive. . . ." Though, unlike him, I would not claim this was IBM's only craft. More important, I would disagree with him when he ascribes sinister motives to IBM in all its pricing decisions. I was involved in some of them, and saw no evidence of anything sinister (and I was not completely naive in such matters; in the UK I had, in a previous company, helped organise a form of cartel—before, I hasten to add, this became illegal!). IBM is undoubtedly a very competitive company, and that extends to pricing; though not to predatory pricing which is DeLamarter's claim (which was, however, not proved in the 13 years of the case). Its main (pricing) concern, as is that of any company operating in the private sector of a capitalist economy, is to maximise its profit where it can. This almost inevitably means that its margins will be higher where it has weak competition. I believe that this is, however, an economic reality (and sound commercial management) rather than a sinister manipulation of its customer base for unfair competitive ends.

Perhaps the most conclusive evidence in support of IBM comes from its recent poor performance. DeLamarter makes much of IBM's monopolistic control of profits, and highlights the almost obscene growth of these over the early 1980s. Unfortunately, for his thesis, IBM's performance over the two years since his book was published (and since IBM was released from anti-trust threats) has been abysmal, which is hardly in line with his theory of IBM's monopolistic capabilities. He would now be skating on fairly thin ice in saying: "We have seen that for three generations of computer systems the market has not responded as the competitive economic model would predict. IBM's abnormally high profits have not attracted the added competition one would expect."

I do believe, however, that he is right in bringing to our attention how important IBM has become to modern society, where he says: "IBM's size and the importance of its markets for the security and vitality of our nation, if not the western world in general, demand that it be scrutinized from a different perspective than soda pop and razors are. That perspective should be informed by a concern for what is best for society as a whole rather than by a concern for what is good for IBM."

I also sympathise with his statement: "IBM is in fact a major problem for practically every country in which it does business, even in the United States. By maintaining everywhere a self-perpetuating, lopsided market structure in which it towers over all competitors, IBM has amassed entirely too much power to be considered 'good' for any nation as a whole." Though I am not certain that I agree with it, since I believe it overstates IBM's real threat.

Once more, though, I disagree fundamentally with his projections that see IBM building alliances to take over large sections of industry. I do not think that any government (no matter how weak its anti-trust law, which is one of DeLamarter's complaints) would allow this. More important, I believe that IBM (along with many other large companies in a similar position) has demonstrated a remarkably poor track record of such diversifications (which is how it would describe these processes).

But because of its size, and the importance of its products, it is important to many governments. So, who then is to control, or at least direct, its burgeoning power, along with that of the other MNCs? For some time I felt that perhaps the United Nations Commission on the Transnationals might successfully take on this role, but unfortunately it apparently has yet to develop sufficient teeth. On the other hand those supranational bodies with real teeth, such as the EEC, have so far shown partial, and indeed partisan, interests which colour their judgements too much to allow them to be sound. Control to be truly beneficial to the community should not simply be a form of shackling in order merely to emasculate. It should be a *positive* contribution, which directs the available resources (including those of the MNC) into the areas most fruitful for the community at large.

It is fair to ask if such an agency could control IBM, or at least direct its course to the most beneficial directions. It seems clear that control is, at least for the present, out of the question. IBM is already too deeply enmeshed in the business operations of *all* the developed countries. Any crude attempts at surgery would surely result in a very severe illness for some of the patients. It is, in any case, clear that such control is not achievable within the political constraints of the Western nations. Both the US government and the EEC, arguably the two most powerful actors in the Western world, spent the best part of a decade trying to obtain some form of armlock on IBM (using their most powerful weapon of anti-trust legislation) only, in the end, to have to concede defeat. It is unrealistic, therefore, to expect any such action to be more successful in future; though this is not to say that the threat of some such action should not be employed as the stick to accompany any carrots offered.

DeLamarter would really like to make changes by drastic action: ". . . only by changing the structure of the computer industry, by rearranging its productive capacities and corporate entities, can IBM's power be reduced and competitive vigor restored." But even he now believes that the anti-trust route is unworkable. His suggestion is to create an "Institute for IBM Documentation to collect further data on the company." In essence it would bring IBM's internal decisions (together with their outcomes) into the public domain, though I suspect his own motives might be described (at least by IBM) as "sinister," where he suggests that "The Institute could also help private litigants in their efforts to sue IBM for redress of its actions against them."

Regrettably, I do not believe that such an institute is feasible. It represents too overt an action for any government to contemplate, and is clearly directed against just one company (whose actions have, at least in theory, already been cleared by the legal system). But I think that a constant, on-going, interest (publicly expressed) by the various administrations (particularly the US government and the EEC) might help keep IBM in line. This might stop short of anti-trust action (but only just; the threat to IBM has always been more powerful than the reality).

As you will have appreciated, I believe (some, possibly including DeLamarter, would say perversely) that the threat of anti-trust, keeping IBM "squeeky" clean, was actually a source of great strength to the company. I believe its poor performance since scrutiny was removed evidences that. If such "supervision" was reimposed (remembering that there is no longer the Watson family to internally stiffen IBM's moral backbone) I believe that this would strengthen IBM again; something I suspect DeLamarter is not looking for.

But the ultimate threat posed by IBM is not its sinister plans to take over the world. It is, instead, the much more real danger (which, indeed, we are currently seeing) that it will fail; and one of the key driving forces of the Information Revolution will be debilitated, which would be bad news for all of industry. It is IBM's possible failure that is the threat, not its success.

In terms of the more specific issue of IBM's control of DP standards, an alternative approach has been that of setting internationally agreed standards. Regrettably this too seems doomed to failure; as is shown by the continuing saga of OSI, the proposed standard for data communications; which is struggling—so far rather unsuccessfully—to displace IBM's *de facto* standard, SNA. Any international standards body is almost bound to be excluded from knowing what is already in IBM's laboratories, and in Armonk's long-term strategies; and these, not the wishes of the international experts, are the facts which *will* determine the emerging standards.

DeLamarter also makes much of IBM's changes of "interface" specification as a competitive device. It is probably true that IBM does use its control of the interfaces to discomfort its OEM "plug compatible" competitors (those who produce what are in effect carbon copies of IBM's products). As DeLamarter gleefully recalls, this was perhaps most blatant in the introduction of the IFA (the Integrated File Adapter) on the 370's, as a device to make life difficult for Memorex and Telex. At the time, within IBM, the joke going the rounds was that the whole central processor was designed to fall over if (as the OEM's wanted) the IFA was removed!

It is also clear, from what IBM has said, that the "micro-channel" on the PS/2 range is, at least in part, an attempt to make the PC interface proprietary; though, unlike many commentators, I believe that there is much more to the "micro-channel" than being a simple competitive spoiler.

Again, though, DeLamarter overstates his case. He appears to believe that almost *all* IBM interfaces have been made incompatible for sinister, competitive reasons. This is simply not true. There *is* considerable incompatibility, which IBM would dearly love to overcome; since it hinders its own business; and its long infatuation with FS (Future Series), which I still believe will one day see the light of day, is partly prompted by a desire to overcome such incompatibilities.

Some of the incompatibilities arise simply because of the enormous range of products that IBM covers; no other manufacturer has a range that is a quarter the size. The problems caused by this were evident from the very start of the 360 range, when the prime operating system (OS) was found to be too large to fit the smaller machines, and another operating system (DOS) had to be rapidly unearthed. Incidentally, DeLamarter is (surprisingly) wrong in saying that DOS was a cut down version of OS. If it had been, IBM would have been delighted, as it would not have been seriously incompatible; but it was a totally different, and largely incompatible, product.

Some of the worst incompatibilities are seen in the mid-range machines that were the province of GSD. In this case I know, for a fact, that these too were largely the result of operating system sizes. There *was* a whole range of smaller systems planned (including one to replace the "stop-gap" S/34), which would have used the S/38 operating system. But, once more, the operating system was too large and the incompatible S/36 (based on the stop-gap S/34) had to be launched instead.

Another reason for incompatibilities is that different products are developed in different laboratories, which simply refuse to follow the same standards as other laboratories. The PC 3270, for example, was a totally different (incompatible) animal to the ordinary PC because, even though it was based on the PC, it was developed in a DP Division laboratory. As a result, despite DP division's somewhat arrogant aspirations, it fell by the wayside.

Sometimes the incompatibility is forced by the marketplace. The biggest operating system divide is between MVS (IBM's chosen flagship) and VM (which has been, perversely perhaps, chosen by much of the marketplace).

IBM's intentions are not sinister. But the interface problems that DeLamarter describes do exist and cause problems for everyone (not just IBM's competitors—indeed the worst sufferer is IBM itself). As mentioned earlier, IBM's own solution to this is to set its own *de facto* standards. In the process, by default, it consolidates its hold on the marketplace. It *has* shown a surprising degree of willingness to participate in making genuinely international standards, but a number of the international standard bodies have seen fit to reject these overtures; I believe foolishly so, since they probably represent the best route for those bodies to influence the real, as opposed to theoretical, standards.

Returning to the general question of IBM's relations with government, any attempt to control IBM centrally makes the assumption that Armonk *itself* is truly in control. This is, as discussed earlier, a questionable assumption since Armonk's control is limited to the relatively small increments it can persuade the culture to accept. The built-in inertia is immense. It is, for Armonk, a cross between riding the tiger and tobogganing down the Cresta Run. It is exhilarating, but the degree of control is marginal. Any degree of government control would be even less predictable.

If control is out of the question, can direction be employed? The answer to this is, I believe, just as positive a "yes" as it is "no" to outright control.

Armonk already has a deep respect for governments of all complexions. In part this is just good sense. A government *can* cause serious inconvenience for IBM, and there is no point in courting its displeasure unnecessarily. The evidence though is that such respect goes much deeper. As described a number of times earlier, the very foundations of IBM are represented by its ethical commitment to "integrity"; indeed, these beliefs are perhaps now IBM's most important commercial asset. Its genuine commitment to the community in general, and to government in particular, is a natural outgrowth of these ethical principles. The popular culture within IBM simply would not accept any values which were damaging to the community. The desire to be a good corporate citizen is not just a public relations exercise by IBM, it is an expression of a basic belief held by the individuals throughout IBM just as much as by the executives at Armonk.

It should be in everyone's interest to persuade other MNCs to adopt positive codes of ethics, perhaps similar to those which IBM so profitably follows, as a *fundamental* element of their business operations. The long-term result should be as genuine a commitment to good corporate citizenship as is IBM's.

There is another powerful motive which will force IBM's concurrence with government's wishes, and that is enlightened self-interest. IBM, along with other MNCs, needs stability (particularly in the international economic scene; as will be discussed later) as a prerequisite to its complex planning processes. Destabilization to any degree may hurt it less than it does smaller companies, but it hurts all the same; and IBM is accordingly highly motivated to participate in any programmes which might reduce the instability.

Direction is thus something which most MNCs in general and IBM in particular, might even welcome; if it was not partisan, but was a genuine attempt to stabilize the future of the world economy. Unfortunately, to date, those (generally of the right) who might be most sympathetic to IBM's business needs do not believe in such intervention, and those who are willing to commit government to such direct tactics (generally of the left) have largely adopted a partisan, antipathetic, approach. What is needed for success is a consensual bipartisan approach by government, without the usual overt political content.

In the absence of a suitable supranational body it is difficult to see how this process could start. Perhaps the initiative could come from the MNCs themselves, and perhaps from IBM. They would certainly stand to gain from the creation of a forum where they would contribute, as equal partners, to the process of managing the world economy. They cannot, however, undertake this process alone. If nothing else the threat of anti-trust legislation makes any extensive contacts between MNCs a very risky activity. What is needed, perhaps, is a suitable "sponsor." In the case of the government bureaucracies, which are usually similarly debarred from direct contact, this facility is already offered under a number of suitable pretexts by various supranational institutions. Regrettably there are very few, if any, similar occasions for the MNCs to get together.

It is notable that one feature of the corporations in Japan is that, although the competition between them is savage, they are very willing to meet regularly to decide what is best for the industry (and market) they share. This is possible in Japan where anti-trust measures are only marginal, and in practice MITI actively encouraged the type of oligopolistic "cooperation" which would be viewed as a flagrant breach of anti-trust regulations in most other countries.

If we look at the possibilities available at the national level, it seems that to date the most predictable reaction of most governments to IBM has been to confront the "problem," as they see it, by bolstering national suppliers. Unfortunately this has usually been to the great disadvantage of all involved. The national competitor to IBM has ultimately been incapacitated. "Featherbedding" is not the best stimulant to high growth. The strategic direction chosen usually pushes the company in the wrong direction, since the business available from a government to subsidize their protégé is mainly in the mainstream IBM business; where the most sensible place for such a competitor should be in carving a specialist niche well away from head-on confrontation with IBM. Almost as inevitably, this forces the supplier to look for suitable technology elsewhere. As the only real alternative is Japan this provides a "Trojan Horse" for the penetration of that industry by an alternative that is scarcely better than IBM; rebadging Japanese equipment as that of the national supplier is now almost routine. Finally, government involvement leads to the introduction of the government bureaucracy (to look after their investment); an overhead which few companies can afford.

On the other side of the balance the nation saddles itself, and often its industry, with second-best solutions; all whilst tenderly destroying its computer industry and squandering vast sums. Needless to say, I fear such policies are almost bound to be counterproductive. Much better would be to stimulate these national companies to find suitable niches *outside* IBM's mainline business; and use IBM productively for the work it does best.

It is my belief, as suggested earlier, that IBM would positively welcome contacts with most national governments. After all, it spent a decade in the UK painstakingly building a limited relationship; surely an indication of a very positive desire to cooperate. Indeed, is it not a criticism of government that such effort on the part of IBM should be needed? The dialogue should be just as important to both sides, but this is not to say that government should be IBM's poodle. The evidence suggests that IBM respects strong government and will react most positively to hard bargaining, just so long as the discussions are positive.

If, then, there *can* be some synergy where government collaborates with IBM, what outcome can reasonably be expected? In reality it can probably expect IBM local management (with the support of Armonk) to commit to their part in any reasonable national plan. There may even be the possibility of attracting some extra IBM investment; though no government should expect too much of such investment (since the indications are that it will not create large numbers of jobs, and the net benefit to the balance of payments will not necessarily be large). There will be some net benefit though; even if the Pluralists' bargaining for access turns out to be a rather empty gesture.

This then leaves the area of good corporate citizenship as possibly the most fruitful for development by government. Where, to date, most governments have treated IBM as an adversary, they have been most aware of its weaknesses. As an ally they might look more positively to its undoubted strengths; which could be used for the benefit of the community at large. In turn IBM, somewhat embattled, has so far been strictly limited in what it could offer.

As stressed earlier, IBM's most valuable resource is its people. At the same time, probably the greatest harm it (unintentionally) does any nation is to lock up such people resource and remove it from the pool available to the rest of that nation. A government might therefore be well advised to persuade IBM to unlock some of this resource, to be used for the national good. It might not be too difficult to persuade IBM, for there are also advantages from its point of view. In the first place, even the temporary release of such personnel would clearly demonstrate its commitment to being a good corporate citizen. At the same time, such community work could be a major contribution to IBM's personnel development programmes. In the process, and not least, it would assist IBM's management of internal change; the destabilizing effect on the bureaucracy of regular exposure to the outside world would be a useful degree of stimulation. The other main argument is that IBM already has some potential locked up that it would itself wish to use more productively, but which it cannot currently tap. These personnel are the senior staff, typically over the age of 45, who are not following the management trail and who are consequently in danger of becoming stale; IBM is very much a culture of youth, and it sometimes becomes difficult to cope with this at the "male menopause." IBM certainly needs a proportion of such individuals, for they are central to its horizontal communications and controls and procedures. The IBM system, though, now generates too many of these individuals. In past years, attrition caused by recruitment to the rest of the computer industry thinned out the ranks; but since the recession began at the end of the 1970s this no longer happens to the same degree. Having too many of these individuals is an embarrassment to IBM, since (in line with its full employment policy) it has to create suitable jobs for them; and this can lead to the worst excesses described by Parkinson's Law. At the same time it dilutes the job interest and fulfilment for these senior individuals. On the other side of the fence, the individuals themselves are locked in by the security offered by IBM; at the age of 45 they realistically have no option to do otherwise.

Some 30 years after the start of the "Japanese miracle," the Japanese corporations are starting to run into the same problem. In their case it is the managers in their 40s and early 50s who do not make the grade. Unlike IBM, the over 55s are not a problem since the retirement age is 55, despite the longevity of the Japanese and their lack of a Western style pensions structure (a not inconsiderable reason why they save so hard during their working lives). When growth was faster, the corporations could afford these "failed" 40- and 50-year-olds. These lost souls were called the madogiwazoku or "the window-gazing tribe" because they literally had nothing else to do. Now with increasing economic pressures, the corporations are employing head-hunters to find jobs for them outside. Perhaps governments in the West could offer to head-hunt some IBMers.

IBM has already released small numbers of these personnel for community work and the evidence is that this has been successful; particularly in the case of small business agencies. Their depth of experience and sheer intellectual calibre, make them worth their weight in gold to most other organizations. As part of the process they, as individuals, broaden their horizons and become even more valuable to IBM when they return. At the same time they operate as remarkably cost-effective ambassadors for IBM, and unofficial salesmen for its products.

All of these are very cogent reasons why IBM UK, for example, might be persuaded to release in excess of a thousand such individuals at any one time. This may appear a small number, but their calibre is such that they might well be managing directors in smaller companies (and indeed are paid as such) and their impact on the chosen areas would be out of all proportion to their numbers.

Such programmes might make some contribution to countering the problems of MNC élites in the developed world, but they do not address any of the deprivation of MNC infra-structure experienced by the Third World. Only if MNCs could be persuaded that it were in their own interest to develop the Third World (and indeed in their own interest they *are* constantly seeking new developing markets), sufficient resources to support more rapid modernization could easily be made available; and perhaps far more effectively than by any of the existing aid agencies.

In summary then, some of the main political lessons that can be learnt from IBM are on the one hand the essentially negative lesson that it is probably at best likely to be a considerable waste of time, and ultimately counter-productive, to attempt to control IBM directly. The positive lessons, on the other hand, include the suggestion that IBM's ethics can be used as an example for other MNCs to follow. It is further suggested that a forum needs to be created where governments and MNCs might regularly meet to start to plan the future of the world economy. Finally IBM's good corporate citizenship should be tapped, particularly in terms of releasing its "surplus" high calibre personnel.

I have deliberately excluded from the discussion so far the subject of bureaucracies. This is, I believe, the area of political theory (and practice) where study of IBM can make the greatest contribution. Once more, therefore, I will set the perspective.

A bureaucracy is now an inevitable part of government. Its exponential growth has come about because of the range of matters for which governments increasingly hold themselves responsible. There is now barely any matter in which governments can avoid taking an interest; even liberal, anti-pluralist, right-wing governments are forced into these activities, despite their strident protestations. I believe the problem is best summed up by Anthony King's comment (in *Why is Britain becoming Harder to Govern?* 1979, BBC Publications): "Once upon a time, then, man looked to God to order the world. Then he looked to the market. Now he looks to Government."

Returning to our political perspectives, bureaucratic behaviour is primarily a feature of Pluralist models. It is not generally referred to by either the Realists or the Structuralists (though Lenin believed, probably mistakenly, that it would have a central role in transferring revolutionary politics to the plane of organization!).

The most positive views of bureaucracy were those of Max Weber, which held sway until the 1960s. They saw the bureaucracies as a positive and essential element of coping with the inevitable new complexities of modern government. Based on a well-ordered, stable system of exhaustive rules, a hierarchical organization was supposed to manage primarily through the medium of documentation. The bureaucracy was assumed to be an analytic or rational actor, dedicated to the common good. It is fair to say that this was based on the experiences of Prussia some 75 years ago; where the largest organizations employed only a few hundred, and where kinship relations were strong. In this turn-of-the-century environment, Weber wanted to counter the real evils of nepotism by using standardized working practices.

Unfortunately, the academics enticed into the new frontier bureaucracies in the 1960s found that the reality was often very different. From this disenchantment emerged two models of bureaucracy which, often in amalgamated form, are now favoured by by many Pluralists. The first of these concentrates on bureaucratic behaviour, where the first instinct of such a bureaucracy is seen to be survival. This imposes a superordinate goal to which the ostensible function of the bureaucracy is harnessed, justifying its self-fulfilling and self-perpetuating role. To enable the overwhelming complexities to be coped with, the decision-makers are conditioned to respond only to certain kinds of stimuli, related to a limited number of variables that they have prejudged to be most important. Indeed one bureaucracy's frame of reference may be totally incompatible with another (and a rational decision in one may appear foolish in another).

The other model, as described by I. M. Destler, describes bureaucratic politics; the process of bargaining between and within government bureaucracies. It is accepted that the views of different bureaucracies, conditioned by their different frames of reference, are likely to conflict, and this has to be contained. The process is handled within government by having issues formally channelled by the established rules of the game. But at the same time there is widespread use of the media—now often by the ubiquitous leak—to generate support with the electorate as a whole (by presenting that part of the bureaucracy as alone working in the national interest). There is, of course, the possibility that the final result of this "competition" could still be the selection of the right policies, determined on a free market basis (analogous with Adam Smith's "invisible hand"). Most Pluralists would, however, agree with Destler that the end result is more likely to be an irrational compromise biased against change, resulting in unresponsive and inappropriate behaviour by the bureaucracy; and it was indeed such behaviour by the CIA bureaucracy in Vietnam that led to the development of the model.

It is against this recent pessimism that I believe the success of IBM in controlling its own bureaucracy is an important antidote. The IBM bureaucracy is comparable in most respects with a government bureaucracy. Its numbers, at around 400,000, are similar; and the function of most of those numbers—pushing paper—is identical. That Armonk considers that it runs a bureaucracy has been clear since Frank Cary took over the reins and stated: "Some aspects of bureaucracy are terrible, but some are essential." (Fishman op. cit.) It is certainly my experience, particularly that with Biomedical Group, that IBM is a bureaucracy. My estimation, then, that any new IBM venture needed rapidly to achieve a revenue in excess of $100 million was based on the need to cover the bureaucratic overhead (a fixed cost directly attributable to the existence of the bureaucracy).

The important difference, though, is that in IBM the bureaucracy actually works; indeed it is supremely successful, totally against the predictions of the pessimists. This is despite the fact that it only meets one of Weber's three rules for an ideal bureaucracy. It *does* depend on a well-ordered, stable system of exhaustive rules; the massive tome that is the "General Information Section" of the sales manual confirms that fact. On the other hand although IBM is, on paper, hierarchically organized the practice is very different. Again the theory of control by documentation may appear to be true, at least in an electronic form, but the reality is that control is by very different means (ranging from headcount to culture). The question that has to be asked is how has IBM managed to make the bureaucracy work, where conventional management wisdom now recommends the break up of any organization into autonomous operating units with no more than 5,000 individuals (a process that even IBM may be adopting, to add to its armoury of techniques, in its latest regionalization moves).

The first indication comes from the days of Tom Watson Jr. Since his time, IBM may have become a bureaucracy but it is, due to his determination, one based on individualism. His "wild duck" speeches may have been dismissed by the pundits, but they eventually had the impact he wanted. The first antidote to the worst excesses of bureaucracy, therefore, is a clear belief, publicly promoted by the head(s) of that bureaucracy, that its strength lies at the individual level; and not in the paperwork beloved of Weber.

To complement this view IBM also has a battery of personnel policies that are grouped under the very relevant theme, "respect for the individual." Of these perhaps the opinion survey, with its status-undermining feedback session, is the most powerful antidote to an overweening hierarchy. It should be noted that IBM still ascribes its success to its beliefs.

This leads on to the second antidote, which is the general application of objective measurements of performance, particularly in the A&C process, and the establishment of incentives for achievement. I stated earlier that I believed such incentives had little impact on motivation, in terms of achievement. They do, on the other hand, provide a constant reminder of the importance of performance, and are a very useful antidote to the natural tendency to drift towards more bureaucratic priorities.

The third antidote is encouragement of a horizontal communications network. At its simplest level this is encouragement of the grapevine that already exists in most organizations; though the sophisticated IBM version takes time to develop. At a more formal level the provision of horizontal data (and voice) communications networks, freely available to all members of the bureaucracy, probably now offers the best opportunity to stimulate the development of such horizontal communications.

The fourth antidote is the development of powerful, but inevitably rather crude, non-financial control devices. The UK civil service is already adept at using at least one ultimate weapon favoured by IBM; that of control by conviction and commitment. This technique is simply, but quite deliberately, to put in place numbers of barriers or hurdles that must be crossed before a positive decision can be obtained; so that only those who have the very necessary conviction that the decision is absolutely essential, and the degree of commitment to devote their time to its pursuit, will break through. It is a very effective device for screening out the trivial.

IBM's main sledge-hammers of control revolve around absolutely rigid control of headcount, space and capital. It is argued by IBM that control of only these three will still largely control total costs, since most running costs are a direct function of these basics. In particular it simply is not possible to generate costs if there is no headcount to spend them, and in any case that headcount cannot be recruited if space is rationed. There is no reason why the civil service (administration) bureaucracies should not follow suit. They are controls that are easy to implement; there can be little sophisticated argument about grey areas. Yet they are very direct and very powerful in their impact and even avoid the black hole of most financial controls, which is creative accounting.

The fifth antidote might lie in manipulation of the culture. In my experience the civil service already has a commitment to the pursuit of excellence which is probably as strong as that demonstrated within IBM. The problem is the precise definition of what is excellent. The high point of creativity, within the civil service, is reportedly the minute. The laurels go to that civil servant who can produce the most erudite, and in particular literate, minute. There are even civil servants who, while encapsulating all the salient facts on the two sides of one piece of paper, can still embed a number of jokes, so that the minister does not get bored with his reading! The problem is that its content, and in particular the recommended action, is often seen as less important than the style. This is perhaps understandable where the ultimate decision will in any case be taken on political grounds; the content is thus largely ephemeral, but the style lingers on. The task, the fifth antidote, is to redirect the culture of the civil servants, and of their political masters, to pursue a different, more productive excellence.

The sixth and final antidote, and possibly the most important, is the institutionalization of change. Thus Frank Cary said: "We changed the organization every couple of years—changed the approval procedures and so forth. If you leave the structure in place you endanger it. We don't change the organization just to be doing it—we change because the problems change and we need different leverage." (Fishman op. cit.) Regular change in IBM jolts the bureaucracy out of any ruts into which it might be settling. It allows the relatively painless removal of any managers who have obviously reached their (Peter Principle) level of incompetence. At the same time it allows individuals to build the contacts that are the basis of the horizontal communications. The denizens of the higher levels of the government bureaucracy may claim that change is endemic, as the political complexion of succeeding governments changes, but the very reverse is probably true. The changes forced through by politicians are typically superficial (even though they may have a great symbolic message for the electorate); often changes in title only. What is more the desire for change, on "unworthy" political grounds, is strenuously resisted by the civil service; to the extent that avoidance of change, to provide the community with an essential degree of continuity, has become the highest motive in the bureaucracy. It is arguable, therefore, that what is needed is the longer-term stability of a political consensus, which might allow (with some inspired leadership) the civil service the opportunity to create its own organization for change (instead of its current immovable structure).

In summary then, the antidotes to bureaucracy consist of some of the guides to sound management which were developed in Chapter 13. These start from a basis of beliefs that encourage individualism, and incent individual performance. These individuals need to be linked by a powerful horizontal communications network, as opposed to a hierarchical structure, and the culture will need to be redirected to a more productive view of excellence. The controls applied will need to be similarly powerful, if crude; and above all change will need to be institutionalized, to lubricate the wheels of progress.

Throughout this appendix I have described bureaucracies as if they were the prerogative of government. In practice, all large organizations are afflicted by the disease; as was IBM, which found it could not avoid such a fate and, typically, turned it to its advantage. The above antidotes are very relevant, therefore, to most commercial organizations; perhaps only the smallest, with under 1,000 employees, can justifiably consider themselves exempted. The problem is even greater in the commercial sector, simply because it goes unrecognized.

When we move to the field of economics we find that, with the notable exception of J. K. Galbraith, the study and theory of large corporations have been relatively neglected. The theory of the firm and of the market were enshrined by Alfred Marshall and the nineteenth century neo-classical economists, who tried to turn Adam Smith's brilliant concepts into a more scientific, mathematical form; in the curves of supply and demand. The body of this theory was, for simplicity, built on the assumption of perfect competition between large numbers of small firms.

The reality, certainly in recent years, has been very different. Large corporations have come to take ever larger shares of the economy. Thus S. Aaronovitch and M. C. Sawyer showed that the 100 largest firms in 1968 accounted for 42 per cent of the net output of the UK economy. About the same time H. R. J. Larner, in the 1966 *American Economic Review,* showed that 84.5 per cent of the largest 200 corporations had no groups of stockholders owning as much as 10 per cent of the stock.

The difficulty that neo-classical micro-economics has in dealing with these large corporations (where, due to their domination of the market, true competition can no longer be said to hold—there is, in the terms of the economists, an oligopoly) is described by K. Lancaster (*Introduction to Modern Micro-Economics,* 1969, Rand McNally): "There is no general theory of oligopoly, only models of specific oligopolistic situations that provide signposts as to types of possible behaviour." Indeed the various graphical treatments, led by the "kinked oligopoly curve," shed remarkably little light on the real-life market influence of the large corporations; and have long since been discarded (except from the undergraduate textbooks!).

This leaves the explanation of this grey area of economics largely in the hands of behavioural and organizational theories. One of the most important conclusions was that of H. A. Simon. He suggested that the conventional theories of maximization (most conventionally in the form of profit maximization) could be replaced by organizational goals of "satisficing"; where the goal set is to obtain a certain minimum (safe) performance. This is seen to be more realistic because the true maximizing path may be difficult and costly to identify. Despite its enviable profit record, this would certainly appear to be true of IBM; its prime objective is long-term survival, and its growth objectives are required to be safely achievable before being maximal.

The most important body of theory, though, has come from J. K. Galbraith. He distinguished between that part of the economy comprising a few hundred technically dynamic, massively capitalized and highly organized firms (of which IBM is one of the best examples), which he called the "planning system," and that remaining part containing the large number of smaller, more traditional firms, which he referred to as the "market system." He developed Simons's theory, arguing that profit maximization was not essential where the corporations were not necessarily subordinate. This is certainly true of IBM. Even the Watson family only held three per cent of the stock; their control was by personal influence not by financial means. Equally IBM has been almost completely independent of outside financing for 60 years. The 360 range was the last major project where IBM had significant recourse to Wall Street; more recently the only impact of the massive investment in new plants and acquisitions was a $2.5 billion rise in long-term debt (a matter of financial convenience rather than necessity, where the internal investment flow was $10 billion per annum!). Virtually all IBM's massive investments are generated by internal cashflows. It is thus subject to no higher authority, other than government. Its management decisions, taken in Armonk, are invulnerable to outside criticism; which is not to say, though, that Armonk is totally insensitive to such criticism. Its position in relation to the financial markets is summed up by the fact that of its annual available funds flow, barely 20 per cent is returned to the investors in dividends, where nearly 80 per cent is ploughed back in investment; scarcely what neo-classical economists would expect of a stable, mature company.

The result for Galbraith is that in the planning system the entrepreneur, or owner manager, has been replaced by management in the decision-making function; which is certainly true of IBM, as evidenced by the complexities of the process described earlier in this book. He goes further, however, to identify not just the senior management but all the people participating in this process; and groups them together as the "technostructure." This extended technostructure may certainly be observed at work in IBM. In part it is informal, where the culture includes almost everyone in the ultimate decision-making. More formally it is seen in the extended sign-off processes, requiring key decisions to be agreed by a significant number of managers (in a manner very similar to the Japanese ringi system). Galbraith posits that this extended technostructure has goals which are organizational rather than financial. In particular he stresses that these goals will probably have a social purpose; so that the largest possible number of staff can identify with them. Once again this is very true of IBM. Its beliefs (enshrined in the three main beliefs of "respect for the individual," "service to the customer" and "the pursuit of excellence as a way of life") take precedence over its goals ("to grow with the industry," "to exhibit product leadership," "to be most efficient in everything we do" and "to sustain our profitability"), at least according to the IBM UK *Annual Review* in 1984.

Galbraith in any case stresses the achievement of growth (which implies expansion of the technostructure and advancement of its members) as the main operational goal, after that of survival; and it can be clearly seen that the first IBM goal refers to just such growth (and the other three goals are designed to bolster it). IBM is addicted to growth, and it is debatable if it could now survive without such growth. Galbraith's main thesis, though, is that the technostructure aims to gain control over its environment so that its survival cannot be endangered by unforeseen external factors. At one end this requires control of costs, and IBM's third goal of efficiency (spelled out as being the lowest-cost producer) echoes this. At the other, more controversial extreme, Galbraith expects that the technostructure will attempt to control the markets it trades in. This is discreetly contained in IBM's first goal; since "growth with the industry" (and indeed ahead of the industry if its more ambitious plans are realized) presumes IBM's dominant position in these markets will be at least maintained.

The aspect of control that most offends the neo-classical economists is that over price; since the price mechanism is central to their theories of economics, and it, to a large extent by itself, links consumers to producers. But no longer, if Galbraith is right, will price be set by the consumer in the market, with price-driven supply and demand balancing each other. Rather the price is determined by the producer, and is just one of the factors he manipulates to direct resources where he chooses. Once more this is true of IBM, where price is set bureaucratically (albeit with some estimation of impact on sales levels) at the centre. No-one, not even country management, may unilaterally change prices.

In *The Price System* (1964, Prentice Hall) R. Dorfman suggested brand names as a key feature of market control; in essence the task of the marketing man is to establish (via a unique brand identity) a quasi-monopoly (or at least imperfect competition) for the producer. Indeed in the computer marketplace the IBM brand has a uniquely strong image. It covers the complete package, including support (and integrity), as well as the specific product. It is encapsulated in the industry saying: "No-one ever got fired for buying IBM." This gives it immense power in the marketplace. In recent years IBM has taken control of its marketplace far beyond that of most other corporations. It has managed to become the *de facto* setter of global computing standards. Its products are, by definition, at the ideal product position; leaving others to follow as closely as they can.

Galbraith in his later work, particularly in *Economics and the Public Purpose,* goes much further. The conventional marketing wisdom, to which I largely subscribe, suggests that the prime use of market research is to establish what are the consumer's true needs; which the producer will then aim to match as closely as he can. This generally makes good sense since the producer with the product closest to the consumer needs usually wins by far the largest market share (as even IBM found when Compaq produced a better portable PC, and IBM's own version became a poor also-ran). It would be wasteful of any producer to adopt any other strategy (unless the cost of meeting consumer needs was disproportionate; which would be unusual). IBM is probably so successful precisely because its field force take this market research to the ultimate extreme in almost exactly matching *individual* customer needs. Where, with the PC, it has to match average needs, it has shown it is just as vulnerable as lesser companies. In addition to the Portable PC, the PC Junior was also a clear failure, even though it too was only marginally less well-matched to consumer needs than its competition; and despite the enormous resources of IBM, that Galbraith would have predicted should have won the day. On this score, therefore, at least some of Galbraith's later theories are not substantiated by IBM practice. On all other fronts, though, the main body of his work is supported by the facts of IBM.

Unfortunately, the popular (albeit usually misunderstood) message being promoted by Galbraith was eclipsed by the rise of Milton Friedman's monetarism. It was the simplistic message of this, first dramatically propounded in his 1967 presidential address to the American Economic Association, that destroyed the previous almost universal acceptance of Keynesianism and has preoccupied many governments for the decade since. At its most basic, it is a feature of such monetarism that these governments now believe that their only influence over the economy is through control of the money supply. No longer do they worry about aggregate demand, as required by Keynes, let alone do they consider the nuances of Galbraith's theories. But money supply is clearly *not* an ingredient that can be used to control IBM, or most other corporations, since it is largely independent of the money markets; generating its own funds internally from cashflow. There is unfortunately a heavier price to pay, in that monetarism precludes planning on the larger scale. In the face of this new international disbelief, the control of aggregate demand, using government spending to stimulate growth by the "Keynes Multiplier," is no longer an option open to governments.

There may however be a glimmer of hope coming out of the later developments of monetarism; from some of the attempts to explain its more obvious failures in practice. One of these derives from a theoretical explanation of why government cannot exert any positive control. It quite simply says that all government actions will be immediately discounted by market reactions, as those in the market forecast the outcome of government policy and then discount their own actions to compensate for this. This is the theory of "rational expectations," which was in turn a development of Milton Friedman's theory of "adaptive expectations" (combined with reference to the theory of "perfect markets"). In essence this observed that expectations were not just based on historical data, but took into account rational expectations of what might happen in the future. The definitive example was the increase in prices caused by the 1973 OPEC oil price increase. Under adaptive expectations this would only gradually be absorbed, where under rational expectations it would be included immediately as a known fact, regardless of historical inflation; and of course, this was the case.

The further key observation by supporters of rational expectations is that the participants are fully aware of the model. Accordingly, when a government changes one or more of the variables (by increasing money supply, for example), the participants (who are the corporations and large trade unions, well informed by the media) will *immediately* discount its effects.

It would seem possible to extend the theory of rational expectations beyond its current position to explain some of the other phenomena. As presently expounded, for example by David K. H. Begg, the theory posits that the participants are rationally aware of a model of the process and will immediately compensate for any manipulation of the related variables by government intervention. Although this theory has been largely built around prices, related to money supply, by implication it extends into other areas and covers other variables. The basic assumption, however, is that underneath all the expectations about the variables there is a hard "physical" model (for example, monetarism) on which these all hang. Because of the fluctuations imposed by the posturings of the participants there is, unfortunately, little measurable evidence, in the form of definitive correlations, to support one or other of the models against any other. Despite this it appears to be generally agreed that the participants will base their rational expectations on a widely accepted "true" model.

The, true, model in reality would reflect, using the example of the Phillips "J" curve which was central to Milton Friedman's dismissal of Keynesian economics, the movements of wage inflation against unemployment. It does this by giving a physical aggregate to the many individual movements in prices and employment. At the cellular level though each of these movements results from a single decision. These are *not,* in generally oligopolistic markets (such as those where the large corporations dominate), impartially imposed by market clearing (that is, by the laws of supply and demand). Rather they are the result of management deciding, on the basis of the best information available to them, the most suitable prices or manning levels. Most suitable here may be decided by that management on a quasi-market clearing profit basis (as the neo-classical economists would suggest) or on a structural, organizational basis (as predicted by Galbraith); the mechanism of each decision does not necessarily affect the model, since on average it too is decided by the currently favoured management practices, which are in turn again a function of the total information available to that manager.

What this does mean, however, is that the physical model in aggregate reflects socially determined decisions. Unlike the physical sciences there is no genuine physical connection between the variables. The mediator between the physical inputs is a social process and it is this that the physical model aims to represent. But the major input to this social process is the information flow within the society of participants. It is already acknowledged that rational expectations of those involved will require communication of the physical model, so that the participants are fully informed of this. It is but a short step to the hypothesis that the physical model itself is only a formalization of the agreed views of the participants as to what they might reasonably expect, or wish, the relationships to be.

This extension of the theory, to what I will call "rational modelling," implies that, subject to relatively wide limits (imposed by genuine physical resources bottlenecks rather than money based limitations) the effective structure of the model *itself* may be determined by the consensus views of the participants. Monetarism or Keynesianism will work equally as well as each other, only depending on which the participants agree to choose as the true model.

Thus, for example, over a relatively long period, a specific model may work quite acceptably (as for example did Keynesianism for nearly four decades) by tacit agreement of the participants; only to be replaced later by a different model (such as monetarism) that too may in due course work well, as it obtains the tacit agreement of an increasing number of the participants. The model here becomes a generalized framework of agreement defining how the participants expect to do business.

A further outcome of this observation is that in times of change, between models—when a model is breaking down, perhaps due to its inability to handle a change in the gross physical variables or more likely due to a new social view of the process, such as the onset of monetarism in a society moving to the right—there may be considerable instability due to dissonance between competing models. This model dissonance may, as in the late 1970s, escalate into a crisis of the economic system; until there is once more widespread commitment to the new model. This is directly comparable with the "paradigm shift" described by Thomas Kuhn, in *The Structure of Scientific Revolutions.*

This then returns us full circle to Galbraith: "The emancipation of belief is the most formidable of the tasks of reform." (*Economics and the Public Purpose,* 1974, André Deutsch) He goes on to say, though, that: "The belief to be contested is that the purposes of the Planning System are those of the individual. The power of the Planning System depends on instilling the belief that any public or private action that serves its purposes serves also the purposes of the public at large." Galbraith's answer would thus be to mobilize public opinion, "the emancipation of belief," to pressurize government into taking a stand against the planning system.

My own view, based on IBM's relations with government and its good corporate citizen philosophies, is that the *opposite* process might be most fruitfully employed. The corporation might more easily be persuaded, on its own account, to match its actions to the public purpose. IBM, in the first instance, genuinely believes that its actions are *already* in the public interest; and there is no evidence that overall they are not. This belief is contained within IBM's general set of beliefs and ethics, and cannot be abrogated by IBM without destroying its own culture. What is perhaps at issue is *what* is in the the best interests of the public at large. Undoubtedly IBM has its own biased view; though this will be the view of the total culture, and the many thousands of employees that this comprises, rather than of a few managers contained in its élite. Equally, though, any politically based government is likely to have an even more unbalanced view. What is necessary is a dialogue to establish what might be a reasonable consensual combination of these views. I believe that IBM (and its culture), as well as most other similar corporations, would find no difficulty in entering into such a dialogue; and in fact as good corporate citizens would probably welcome it with open arms. Underneath their very thick skins most MNCs really want to be loved!

There is an even more powerful motivation for the corporations in general, and IBM in particular, to start the dialogue. Galbraith, correctly at least as far as IBM is concerned, identifies a strong drive by corporations for stability. IBM puts substantial resources into planning, and making massive investments, up to a decade ahead. It needs stability best to reap the rewards of this foresight. However, the experience of IBM in the UK strongly suggests that, at present, accurate forecasts can be made no more than 13 months ahead, following the 13-month cyclical indicators. These incorporate Financial Surplus, FT 500 Share Index, Three-Month Interest, Total Dwellings Started, and CBI (Confederation of British Industry) Business Confidence. The last item (containing the results of a survey of business) is by far the most important. In effect this says that what businessmen think is what (at least in 13 months' time) determines the direction of the economy.

The option that may thus be available is that the corporations could be persuaded, very much in their own interest, to participate fully with government in creating a truly viable national (or preferably international) plan. Where this would differ from previous inconclusive experiments is that the new theories behind rational modelling should ensure that, as these corporations represent more than half the economy, their combined (consensually agreed) predictions *will* become self-fulfilling; their decisions by themselves will effectively determine the "model." Stability would thus be guaranteed by the corporations own plans, in concert with government. It is a theme that deserves to be explored. A mathematical version of rational modelling should show that there is a break point (typically around 50 per cent in terms of dissonance versus legitimacy in the eyes of the actors involved) above which point there rapidly comes almost universal acceptance of the model. With active involvement of the corporations, it is likely that any agreed course of action—a model—will already have received this critical level of support; and the model will automatically be a stable model; exactly what is required by the corporations for their planning.

In fact not all the previous experiments have been inconclusive.

Returning to my sub-theme of comparison with the Japanese experiences, surprisingly rational modelling can also find support from this direction. The Japanese miracle has, I believe correctly, often been laid at the door of the Japanese Ministry of International Trade and Industry. The actions of MITI, particularly over the critical period from its inception in 1949 to 1975 when its power was somewhat diluted, exactly parallel the very direct involvement of government with large corporations that would be required to make the rational modelling approach work; though MITI did have the extra leverage of its control of import licences to bring its recalcitrant charges into line. MITI's involvement was, of course, not as a result of its acceptance of this theory (nearly four decades in advance of it being propounded!). It was largely fortuitous, being a compound of the legacy of the (then barred) pre-war Zaibatsu system (large firms grouped around a large holding company or bank; and in turn exerting bilateral monopolies on their many hundreds of small suppliers) with the immediately post-war US-imposed administrative reforms. Whatever the cause, the result was a policy described by Chalmers Johnson as "plan rational" (to distinguish from most other Western government's policies which he calls "market rational," and communist policies which he calls "ideology rational"). The Japanese government did not own the corporations, but it effectively did *control* them; allowing a nationally planned set of policies to be developed and, most important, implemented.

The "miracle" that resulted from this symbiosis of government and corporation is, I believe, transportable from Japan to Western societies. All that is needed, in the first instance, is the belief and confidence to start the dialogue; and to agree a suitable rational model. With one of the most sophisticated planning systems in the world, IBM has much to give to the process and even more to gain from it; as do all the MNCs and almost all governments.

Bibliography

There is a vast library of books on the general subject of management. It would be invidious to select even the few dozens whose contents I suspect have indirectly contributed to the contents of this book. Consequently, I detail below only those books that I believe might be most directly relevant.

IBM history

DeLamarter, R.T. *Big Blue: IBM's Use and Misuse of Power* Dodd, Mead, 1986

Fishman, K.D. *The Computer Establishment* Harper & Row, 1981

Foy, N. The *IBM World* Eyre Methuen, 1974

Graham, T.; Robins-Belden, H. *The Lengthening Shadow* Little Brown, 1962

Larsen, J.K.; Rogers, E.M. *Silicon Valley Fever* George Allen & Unwin, 1985

Rodgers, B.; Shock, R.L. *The IBM Way* Harper & Row, 1986

Rodgers, W. *Think* Stein and Day, 1969

Sobel, R. *IBM: Colossus in Transition* Truman Talley Books, 1981

Watson, J. Jr. *A Business and its Beliefs* McGraw Hill, 1963

Business/management theory

Drucker, P.F. *The Practice of Management* Harper & Row, 1955

Drucker, P.F. *Managing for Results* Harper & Row, 1964

Drucker, P.F. *Innovation and Entrepreneurship* Harper & Row, 1985

Handy, C.B. *Understanding Organizations* Facts on File, 1976

Kotler, P. *Marketing Management* Prentice Hall International, 1976

McGregor, D. *The Human Side of Enterprise* McGraw Hill, 1960

Peters, T.J.; Waterman, R.H. *In Search of Excellence* Harper & Row, 1982

Japanese management theory

Abbeglen, J.C.; Stalk, G. Jr. *Kaisha, The Japanese Corporation* Basic Books, 1985

Clark, R. *The Japanese Company* Yale University Press, 1979

Johnson, C. *Miti and the Japanese Miracle* Stanford University Press, 1982

Ohmae, K. *The Mind of the Strategist* McGraw Hill, 1982

Ouchi, W.G. *Theory Z* Addison Wesley Publishing Company, 1981

Pascale, R.T.; Athos A.G. *The Art of Japanese Management* Simon & Schuster, 1981

Vogel, E. *Japan as Number One* Harvard University Press, 1982

Index